CONVEYANCING 2016

CONVEYANCING 2016

Kenneth G C Reid WS

Professor of Scots Law in the University of Edinburgh

and

George L Gretton WS

Lord President Reid Professor of Law Emeritus in the University of Edinburgh

with a contribution by Alan Barr of the University of Edinburgh
and Brodies LLP

Avizandum Publishing Ltd
Edinburgh
2017

Published by
Avizandum Publishing Ltd
25 Candlemaker Row
Edinburgh EH1 2QG

First published 2017

ISBN 978-1-904968-81-8

British Library Cataloguing in Publication Data
A catalogue record for this book is available from the British Library.

Typeset by Waverley Typesetters, Warham, Norfolk
Printed and bound by Bell & Bain Ltd, Glasgow

CONTENTS

PART III: OTHER MATERIAL

PART IV: COMMENTARY

PART V: TABLES

PREFACE

This is the eighteenth annual update of new developments in the law of conveyancing. As in previous years, it is divided into five parts. There is, first, a brief description of all cases which have been reported, or appeared on the websites of the Scottish Courts (www.scotcourts.gov.uk) or of the Lands Tribunal for Scotland (www.lands-tribunal-scotland.org.uk/records.html), or have otherwise come to our attention since *Conveyancing 2015*. The next two parts summarise, respectively, statutory developments during 2016 and other material of interest to conveyancers. The fourth part is a detailed commentary on selected issues arising from the first three parts. Finally, in part V, there are three tables. A cumulative table of decisions, usually by the Lands Tribunal, on the variation or discharge of title conditions covers all decisions since the revised jurisdiction in part 9 of the Title Conditions (Scotland) Act 2003 came into effect. Next is a cumulative table of appeals, designed to facilitate moving from one annual volume to the next. Finally, there is a table of cases digested in earlier volumes but reported, either for the first time or in an additional series, in 2016. This is for the convenience of future reference.

We do not seek to cover agricultural holdings, crofting, public sector tenancies (except the right-to-buy legislation), compulsory purchase or planning law. Otherwise our coverage is intended to be complete. It has been possible to include a small number of cases from England.

We gratefully acknowledge help received from Alan Barr, Ian Bowie, Charles Keegan, Rebecca MacLeod, Colin Miller, Roddy Paisley, Elspeth Reid, Andrew Steven and Neil Tainsh.

Kenneth G C Reid
George L Gretton
14 March 2017

TABLE OF STATUTES

TABLE OF ORDERS

TABLE OF CASES

PART I

CASES

CASES

MISSIVES OF SALE

(1) SDG Tulloch Homes Ltd v European Development Company (Hotels) Ltd and Carlton Rock Ltd
[2016] CSOH 36, 2016 GWD 8-151

SDG Tulloch Homes Ltd concluded missives to sell property at Glebe Street, Inverness to European Development Company (Hotels) Ltd, at a price of £2.9 million. This sale fell through. The seller then concluded missives to sell the property to Carlton Rock Ltd at a price of £1.5 million. This sale also fell through. The seller then concluded missives to sell the property to Tulloch Homes Ltd, a company in the same group, for £800,000. This sale proceeded to settlement.

SDG Tulloch Homes Ltd then raised the present action against the first two companies. It concluded for (i) damages of £1.6 million against the first defender and (ii) damages of £805,000 against the first and second defenders, jointly and severally.

In a challenge as to competency, it was **held** that, as the losses averred were not attributable to a single wrong caused by both defenders, it was not competent to sue them jointly. The Lord Ordinary (Lord Tyre) went on to offer some *obiter* views on various points of relevancy that had been argued before him.

The main issue of relevancy concerned the second of the two failed sales. The sale was subject to a suspensive condition that the buyer must apply for and receive detailed planning permission by 8 February 2014. In the event that the condition was not fulfilled, either party was free to 'resile from the bargain'. The buyer applied for planning permission but then withdrew the application shortly before the planning meeting which was scheduled for 21 January 2014. The seller argued that either (i) the condition must be deemed to have been purified because the failure to obtain planning permission was due to the buyer's withdrawal, or, in the alternative, (ii) that by withdrawing the application, the buyer was in breach of an implied term of the contract. But these two arguments, the buyer responded, were mutually exclusive. They were based, respectively, on speeches by Lord Watson and Lord Blackburn in *Mackay v Dick & Stevenson* (1881) 8 R (HL) 37. As the former had been criticised by later writers, it was the latter which should be applied; but this required the seller to show that such an implied term was needed in order to give the contract business efficacy. Lord Tyre's view was that the *ratio* of *Mackay v Dick & Stevenson* was in line with Lord

3

Watson's speech, which in turn was based on a rule of the civil law. Nonetheless, he would have allowed proof of all the averments, including an averment by the buyer that there had been a significant risk that planning permission would have been refused.

Another issue in relation to the second sale was whether damages should be measured by (a) the difference between the contract price and the resale price (which the defenders averred to be artificially low) or by (b) the difference between the contract price and the market value of the property. Lord Tyre thought that market value was the correct measure, but that the resale price would often be an accurate guide as to what that value was.

Finally, and in relation to the first of the failed sales, the first defender argued that, before reselling, the seller should have given the first defender a fresh opportunity to buy the property at the original price; the first defender was now in funds and would have wished to buy. Lord Tyre thought that there was no sound basis in law for this argument.

(2) Reilly v Brodie
[2016] SC EDIN 36, 2016 GWD 15-280

The pursuer averred that he had sold a fishery business, and in particular the lease of the business premises, to the defender, and sued for implement of the contract. The defender argued that no contract had ever been concluded. **Held:** Action dismissed. The agreement between the parties had not been reduced to formal writing. Furthermore, the pursuer was not entitled to payment of the price until delivery of an assignation of the lease, which had not taken place. See **Commentary** p 156.

(3) Landvest PCC Ltd v Cushley
[2016] CSOH 109, 2016 GWD 24-442

The defenders, the trustees of the Roman Catholic Archdiocese of St Andrews and Edinburgh, were in negotiations with the pursuer for many months for the sale for development of St Joseph's School, Tranent, East Lothian. Draft heads of terms were circulated in various versions by agents acting for the defenders. Eventually and, to the pursuer, unexpectedly, the defenders sold the school to someone else. The present action was brought for damages for breach of a promise to sell to the pursuer.

The promise was said to be contained within the final heads of terms that were circulated. This contained, in clause 11, an undertaking that: 'The vendor agrees to provide an exclusivity period to the purchaser until 31st July 2015 in order to execute a contract and conclude of missives.' There were a number of reasons, said the pursuer, to regard this as a binding promise, including: (i) its apparently clear terms; (ii) the fact that, unlike on all previous occasions, the heads of agreement were signed and no longer marked 'draft'; and (iii) the consideration that for clause 11 to have any commercial value, it had to take effect before the missives which would follow on from the other heads of terms.

Following a proof, the Lord Ordinary (Lord Bannatyne) was not persuaded. It was wrong to consider clause 11 in isolation from the rest of the heads of terms. These included a clause which indicated that the terms were still subject to approval by the decision-making organs of both parties: 'We trust that the above proposal meets with your approval and look forward to receiving confirmation of such in order that we can seek the relevant internal approvals from the vendor.' Such approvals had not been obtained. Finally, even if commercial sense was on the side of the pursuer's interpretation – which was far from clear – it had been emphasised in the Supreme Court decision of *Arnold v Britton* [2015] UKSC 36, [2015] AC 1619 (*Conveyancing 2015* Case (50)) that a court should be slow to reject the natural meaning of a provision simply because it appears to be an imprudent term for one of the parties to have agreed. The defenders were assoilzied.

(4) Kennedy v Dickie & More Holdings Ltd
[2016] CSIH 37, 2016 GWD 18-325

A development company, Dickie & Moore Holdings Ltd ('DMH'), concluded missives to buy 6.293 hectares of land at Doonholm, Alloway, Ayrshire with a view to building houses on it if planning consent could be obtained. Later DMH withdrew from the missives owing to financial difficulties, but continued to pursue a planning application in the hope that funders or other developers might show interest. Keen to recover the cost of the expenditure involved, DMH then entered into a minute of agreement with the sellers in the following terms:

> [I]t has been agreed between the parties that in the event of the Sellers concluding unconditional ... missives with a third party for the sale of the said subjects ... during the shorter of the period when the Planning Consent obtained or to be obtained by DMH for the development of the said subjects remains extant and the period of five years from the date of these presents, as the case shall be, the Sellers will reimburse DMH the full amount of the said professional fees together with any further professional fees (up to a maximum of £10,000) incurred by DMH in obtaining such Planning Consent.

In the event, no planning consent was obtained.

When the site was sold on to Miller Homes Ltd within the five-year period, DMH sought reimbursement of its costs. A dispute then arose as to the meaning of the minute of agreement. For the sellers it was argued (i) that the resale must occur within the *shorter* of two periods, ie the duration of the planning consent and five years, and (ii) that, as no planning consent had been obtained, the duration of the planning consent was zero. Therefore resale had not occurred within the stipulated period. For DMH it was argued that planning consent and the five-year period were alternatives so that, if the first period did not apply, then matters were governed by the second.

At first instance the Lord Ordinary found for DMH: see [2015] CSOH 103, 2015 GWD 25-436 (*Conveyancing 2015* Case (3)). On appeal, an Extra Division has now found for the sellers. As with the previous case, there was some reliance on the more literal approach to interpretation advocated in *Arnold v Britton* [2015] UKSC 36, [2015] AC 1619 (*Conveyancing 2015* Case (50)). But the court was also alive to the commercial background to the minute of agreement. Lord Malcolm summarised his approach as follows (para 23):

> The starting point is the wording used in the agreement when read in its context. If the words can be given a sensible meaning, which is free from ambiguity, and reflects the commercial sense which the parties are expected to possess, then, absent some compelling countervailing factor, that meaning should be employed to resolve the dispute.

Lady Clark of Calton thought that if the minute of agreement was 'properly construed', then there was no 'lack of clarity in the wording'. She continued (para 20):

> I consider that this is an agreement whereby the respondents agreed that they will continue to seek planning consent and that in the limited circumstances set out in the minute of agreement, may become entitled to payment of professional fees already incurred prior to the minute of agreement. I do not consider that the parties agreed to a situation whereby the respondents could do and achieve nothing in respect of planning consent but provided that there was a sale within five years of the date of the minute of agreement, the respondents would be entitled to payment of the professional fees already incurred.

The Lord Ordinary had thought that, if it had been intended that payment was due only in the event that planning consent was obtained, it would have been easy to say so expressly. Lord Malcolm, reading the agreement as suggesting a need for planning consent, thought that matters were the other way around, ie that 'if DMH wanted reimbursement whatever happened in relation to their planning application, in my view they would have required to insist on an additional term to that effect' (para 30).

(5) Kenwright v Stewart Milne Group Ltd
[2016] CSIH 45, 2016 GWD 20-351

This was a fact-specific case about the interpretation of an indemnity letter granted by developers to the owner of fields in respect of which a purchase option applied. The letter covered obligations due by the owner in respect of an agreement under s 75 of the Town and Country Planning (Scotland) Act 1997 entered into in association with a grant of planning permission. One obligation under the agreement was to convey an area of land to the Council. The developers accepted that they were liable to the owner for the costs of the conveyancing. What was in dispute was whether the indemnity letter extended to the value of the land which was to be conveyed (which was said to be £292,800). At first instance it was held that it did not: see [2015] CSOH 86, 2015 GWD 22-389 (*Conveyancing 2015* Case (11)). On appeal the First Division has now taken the opposite view.

TENEMENTS

(6) Waelde v Ulloa
[2016] SC EDIN 30, 2016 GWD 11-221

The pursuer was the owner of the upper flat in a converted house. The defender was the owner of the middle flat. At issue was whether the defender was liable to contribute to the cost of repairing (i) a skylight and (ii) felt and flashing next to a velux window. In terms of the split-off writs, which dated from the 1950s, the roof was common property, and the maintenance of the roof was a shared responsibility. **Held** that: (i) while the skylight was not part of the roof and so did not fall under the maintenance burden, it had acceded to the roof, was therefore common property, and so fell to be maintained as 'scheme property' under r 4 of the Tenement Management Scheme; (ii) the fact that the felt and flashing had been added after the burden was created did not prevent the burden from regulating their maintenance. See **Commentary** p 169.

(7) Humphreys v Crabbe
[2016] CSIH 82, 2016 GWD 35-634

The owner of the lower flat in a two-flat tenement refused to agree to the erection of scaffolding for repairs to the roof unless the owner of the upper flat agreed to meet the whole cost of the repairs. The maintenance burden in the title provided for equality of contribution. In an application to the sheriff by the owner of the upper flat under s 6 of the Tenements (Scotland) Act 2004, the sheriff ordered that access for scaffolding should be allowed, and declared that liability for the roof repair should then be on a 50:50 basis. The owner of the lower flat appealed to the Inner House but without success. See **Commentary** p 172.

SERVITUDES

(8) ASA International Ltd v Kashmiri Properties (Ireland) Ltd
[2016] CSIH 70, 2016 GWD 27-493

In 1994 a company which owned office premises at numbers 6 and 7 Coates Crescent, Edinburgh sold number 6. No access servitudes were included in the disposition. At the time of the sale it was normal for those working in number 6 to take access over the car-park at the rear of number 7 in order to reach a public lane which in turn allowed access to William Street. The use of this shortcut continued after 1994 but was challenged by the owner of number 7 in 2010. The owner of number 6 raised an action of declarator of the existence of a servitude of pedestrian access over the rear car-park at number 7. The argument was that the servitude had been created by implication in the 1994 disposition.

After proof, the argument was rejected by the sheriff and absolvitor pronounced, and it has now been rejected again, on appeal, by an Extra Division of the Court of Session. There were already two uncontested means of access to and from number 6, one at the front, to Coates Crescent, and the other at the rear, to the lane. It was true that the latter was awkward to use as it involved going through a garage in which a car was often parked. In this respect the shortcut through number 7 was much to be preferred. But a servitude could only be implied where the right was reasonably necessary for the comfortable enjoyment of the property, and the facts fell well short of meeting that standard. See **Commentary** p 133.

(9) Wall v Kerr
30 July 2015, Airdrie Sheriff Court

In 1948 James Gardner acquired a farm extending to 186.77 acres and known as Blacktongue Farm, Greengairs, Lanarkshire. Many years later he disponed a plot from the farm to a son, John Gardner, and to his wife, Marion. The original plan was to build a workshop for a welding business on the plot, but subsequently it was also agreed to build a house for John and Marion to live in. Both were built before the plot was disponed, in July 1978. The house was known as Blackton House.

The plot was situated on a private road known as Blacktongue Farm Road. There were public roads at either end, namely Loanhead Road and Greengairs Road. To reach Greengairs Road from the plot it was necessary to pass through the farm, and hence the stretch of Blacktongue Farm Road which belonged to the disponer, James Gardner. Nonetheless, the disposition did not grant a servitude of way over this stretch of road. To reach Loanhead Road from the plot it was necessary to travel along Blacktongue Farm Road in the opposite direction. In the 1978 disposition James Gardner *had* granted a servitude over that part of the road 'in so far as I have right thereto'. In fact he had no right thereto, and it proved necessary for John and Marion Gardner to obtain a separate deed of servitude from the person who had the right.

The son, John Gardner, died in 1985. John's widow remarried and disponed the property to her new husband, Eric Wall, and herself in 1988. At around the same time, the father, James Gardner, disponed the farm to eight of his relatives. In 2003 the farmhouse, but not the rest of the farm, was disponed by the eight relatives to a Mr and Mrs Miller who, in 2011, disponed it to James Kerr and Kelly Kavanagh. The present litigation was between the Walls (the pursuers) and Kerr/Kavanagh (the defenders). The parties were in dispute as to whether the pursuers had a servitude right of way (including a right of way for vehicles) over the section of Blacktongue Farm Road, leading to Greengairs Road, which ran past the farmhouse and belonged to the defenders.

The split-off disposition of 1978, as we have seen, was silent on the subject. But the pursuers argued that a servitude had been created (i) by implication in the disposition, or (ii) by positive prescription.

The difficulty with (i) was that a right of access already existed from Blackton House, albeit in the opposite direction. Often the existence of one means of access is fatal to the creation of another access by implied servitude: see eg the previous case (which, however, was decided after the present case). After a proof, however, the sheriff (Petra M Collins) decided that the necessary servitude could indeed be implied, for the following reasons. (a) Loanhead Road (to which the undisputed access led) was not safe for pedestrian use. (b) Loanhead Road was not as safe as Greengairs Road for vehicular use. (c) The access to Greengairs Road was used by heavy vehicles going to and from the workshop. (d) 'It can readily be inferred that James Gardner Senior, who was happy that his son and family were living nearby, would not want the family, and in particular his grandchildren, to be placed in danger by using an unsafe route to conduct their daily life' (para 34). In short, while there was an existing means of access, this was unsatisfactory and could not be regarded as equivalent to the means of access which the alleged servitude would provide. The use of that access 'was much more than a matter of mere convenience' for the pursuers. Hence it satisfied the test in *Cochrane v Ewart* (1861) 4 Macq 117 of being reasonably necessary for the comfortable enjoyment of the property.

It was true that the 1978 disposition contained a servitude over the other part of the road, which might be taken to argue against implying a servitude over the road to Greengairs Road. But this was simply James Gardner's way of providing for the heavy traffic from the workshop – and in any case (as mentioned above) it was ineffective.

The sheriff was therefore satisfied that a servitude had been created by implication in the disposition of 1978.

That decision having been reached, it was unnecessary to decide the second point, namely whether a servitude had been created by prescription. But the sheriff indicated that, had she taken a different view of (i), she would have taken a positive view of (ii). All the evidence was consistent with the use of the road as of right for a period of 20 years. The quality and the frequency of use indicated that the use was as of right. It was true that, at one stage, a gate was placed across the road which was locked at night, but the pursuers were provided with a key.

In argument, the defenders had made something of the fact that, for the initial period, the road had been owned by a family member (ie the father/father-in-law of the original disponees), which suggested an informal licence rather than possession by right. An example (not mentioned in the judgment) is *Greig v Middleton* 2009 GWD 22-365 (*Conveyancing 2009* Case (20)). But the point was not referred to in the sheriff's reasoning.

It may be added that the defenders in the present action were also the defenders – but successful defenders this time – in another litigation in Airdrie Sheriff Court with other members of the Gardner family and in respect of a servitude right of access over the same stretch of road. The decision was handed down three days earlier, on 27 July 2015: see *Gardner v Kerr* 27 July 2015, Airdrie Sh Ct (*Conveyancing 2015* Case (14)).

(10) Straub v Hamilton
15 September 2015, Lanark Sheriff Court

This was a fact-specific case in which the pursuer sought declarator that she had a servitude of drainage over fields and a road belonging to a neighbouring farm, at Blackwoodyett, Lesmahagow, Lanarkshire. The titles were silent, and so the case was based on prescription.

The dispute focused on a pipe which had been laid only in 2011. The pursuer argued that the pipe replaced a previous pipe which had been used for drainage since the properties, now belonging to the pursuer and the defender, were split in 1985. The defender said that there was no previous pipe and that drainage was previously by a different route. It appears that the defender was seeking £30,000 for the grant of a servitude to cover the new pipe.

The evidence was patchy, especially in the absence of extensive (and expensive) excavation of the drainage system. The sheriff preferred the pursuer's evidence to the defender's, and granted decree.

(11) Scobie Farms v Greenyards Garden Centre Ltd
[2016] CSOH 75, 2016 GWD 17-307

A servitude of access was granted in a disposition on the basis that it would come into effect only if the grantee were to be refused planning permission for construction of a roadway. In the event, planning permission was refused but the application had been made by a different company (Watermation). In an action of declarator of servitude, the pursuer's case was that Watermation had acted as its agent. At debate, the defender disputed the relevancy of the pursuer's pleadings. A proof before answer was allowed.

(12) Johnson, Thomas and Thomas v Smith
[2016] SC GLA50, 2016 GWD 25-456

This was an action of declarator in respect of a servitude of parking said to have been constituted by prescription. In a debate on the relevancy it was argued for the defender (i) that a free-standing right of parking was not among the servitudes recognised in Scots law, and (ii) that, in any event, the unlimited right to park claimed in the present case was repugnant with the defender's ownership and hence incapable of being a servitude. Both arguments were rejected, and a proof before answer was allowed. See **Commentary** p 141.

WAYLEAVES

(13) William Tracey Ltd v SP Transmission plc
[2016] CSOH 14, 2016 SLT 678

This is the first of two separate but related cases concerning a site at 49 Burnbrae Road, Linwood, Paisley which was used by the pursuer as a recycling facility. The site was bisected by an overhead electricity cable operated by the defender. The presence of the line and an associated tower had a significantly adverse effect on the pursuer's use of the site. The cable had been put in place when the site was under previous ownership, and with the consent of the then owner, who granted the required wayleave. But that wayleave had come to an end automatically when the site changed hands in 1996. The pursuer had been in occupation of the site since 1997, first as a tenant and later as an owner.

Schedule 4 of the Electricity Act 1989 contains provisions for cases where an existing wayleave comes to an end. In terms of para 8, the owner or occupier can give the licence-holder (in this case the defender) a notice requiring that the cable be removed. The licence-holder then has three months during which it must either apply to the Scottish Ministers for the grant of a wayleave, under para 6 of sch 4, or remove the cable. If a wayleave is granted, the owner can apply for compensation under para 7 of sch 4.

These provisions presuppose that disgruntled owners will make haste to serve a para 8 notice. The pursuer, however, had done no such thing. For years it had put up with the cable. And even after a notice was finally served, on 8 December 2010, it was not until 13 August 2014 that the Scottish Ministers granted the necessary wayleave to the defender, with the result that compensation became due under para 7. But what of compensation for the period before 13 August 2014? The pursuer had suffered significant losses due to the cable's presence, which it calculated as amounting to more than £6 million for the period from 1997 to 2014. In the present action, it sought to recover this amount.

Schedule 4 did not confer a right to compensation, because the statutory regime offers compensation only in respect of the grant of a wayleave by the Scottish Ministers. The pursuer's case was therefore based on the common law. The argument was straightforward. (i) From 1997 until the grant of the wayleave in 2014, the defender had no right to make use of the pursuer's land. (ii) Having the electricity cable in place was thus the delict of encroachment. (iii) The defender was liable for any loss suffered thereby by the pursuer.

In response the defender, while not disputing the pursuer's account of the common law of encroachment, argued that sch 4 provided a complete regime for the parties' rights and liabilities. No sums were due under the common law because the common law had been superseded by the Act.

The Lord Ordinary (Lord Brodie) agreed with the defender. Schedule 4 provided 'a comprehensive solution to the problem of a line having been installed by virtue of a consent which thereafter comes to an end' (para 31). Its provisions could have been activated by the pursuer, by service of a notice, much earlier than turned out to be the case. That was the pursuer's choice. This view was reinforced by looking at things from the perspective of wrong. Once the notice was served, the defender was entirely within its rights, under para 8, to keep the cable in place, so long as it made an application to the Scottish Ministers for a wayleave. There was no delict here. That had already been determined by Lord Glennie in *Patersons of Greenoakhill Ltd v S P Transmission Ltd* [2009] CSOH 155, 2010 SLT 115 (*Conveyancing 2009* Case (24)), a decision upheld by the Inner House on 13 January 2011 (unreported). Furthermore, the Lord Ordinary continued (para 32):

> if no delict is committed by a licence holder which maintains an electric line in position after being given notice to remove it (provided it responds to the notice by applying to the Scottish Ministers) can it be said that a delict is committed where no notice has been given? It would seem curious if the answer were yes. That would mean

that for as long as the landowner did not ask for a line to be removed its presence would be unlawful, whereas as soon as he did ask for it to be removed its presence would become lawful. I doubt if that was the intention of Parliament.

There were also policy considerations (para 25):

There is much that is unsatisfactory in the result contended for by the pursuer. Where, as here, the landowner refuses to grant a wayleave and does nothing more, it involves imposing delictual liability on a licence holder which is doing no more than carrying out its statutory obligations by keeping in place equipment necessary for the continuing public supply of electricity. It is a liability that may arise without the knowledge of the licence holder and, at least in circumstances where the continued installation of an electrical line is necessary for 'an efficient, co-ordinated and economical system of electricity distribution' (see 1989 Act s 9), it is a liability that the licence holder may be unable to avoid.

The action was dismissed.

(14) William Tracey Ltd v The Scottish Ministers
[2016] CSOH 131, 2016 SLT 1049

This case follows on from the previous one. A wayleave having been granted by the Scottish Ministers on 13 August 2014 under sch 4 para 6 of the Electricity Act 1989, the petitioner claimed for compensation under para 7. Paragraph 7(1) provides that:

Where a wayleave is granted to a licence holder under paragraph 6 above –
(a) the occupier of the land; and
(b) where the occupier is not also the owner of the land, the owner,
may recover from the licence holder compensation in respect of the grant.

As the wayleave granted was prospective only, it might be supposed that compensation could be awarded only in respect of the period after 13 August 2014. But the petitioner also sought compensation for the period before, beginning with the service of the para 8 notice on SP Transmission Ltd on 8 December 2010. This statutory claim followed on from the failure of the petitioner's common-law claim in the previous case.

Unsurprisingly, the Lord Ordinary (Lord Glennie) was not persuaded by the claim. The wording of para 7 was clear and unambiguous. It offered compensation for the grant of a wayleave, not for the period preceding the grant.

(15) British Waterways Board v Arjo Wiggins Ltd
12 May 2016, Fort William Sheriff Court

The pursuer owns the Caledonian Canal. In 1968 the defender (formerly called Wiggins Teape & Co Ltd) entered into a wayleave agreement with the pursuer so as to allow it to construct a mains water pipe under the Canal at Corpach, in order to supply the defender's paper mill at Annat. For this there was to be annual payment, adjusted with inflation, and currently amounting to a little over £6,000. The wayleave agreement was to run until 2099.

Arjo Wiggins sold the timber mill to BSW Timber Ltd. Clause 10.2 provided that:

> The Seller warrants that neither they nor the Wayleave Granters are in breach of their obligations under the Wayleave Agreements, no claims against the Seller or the Wayleave Granters are outstanding and the Seller shall relieve the Purchaser of any such claims against the Seller under the wayleave agreement arising prior to the date of settlement, the Seller will continue to comply with its obligations under the Wayleave Agreement until the date of settlement.

From the closing words of this clause it might be assumed that, if Arjo Wiggins was to be liable for the obligations under the wayleave agreement until the date of settlement, liability thereafter would pass to BSW Timber. And certainly it is hard to see the commercial sense in Arjo Wiggins retaining liability for annual payments until the end of the century when it had disposed of the mill. Be that as it may, when the assignation of the wayleave agreement came to be drawn up and signed, it made no reference to obligations.

The issue to be determined was who, after the sale and assignation, had liability to make the annual payments under the wayleave agreement. Had liability passed to BSW Timber or did it remain with Arjo Wiggins?

After considering the generous amounts of authority provided by both counsel, the sheriff (Richard A Davidson) accepted the argument advanced by counsel for BSW Timber. Only rights can be assigned, not obligations. While obligations can be transferred ('delegated' in the technical sense of that term, from the Latin, *delegatio*), this requires the consent of the creditor. Leases are subject to a special rule of implied delegation, so that an assignee, having acquired the benefit of the lease, is also subject to the obligation to pay the rent. But wayleaves are not leases, nor are they even real rights. In general there is a presumption against delegation. There was nothing in the present case to disturb that presumption. 'There was', concluded the sheriff, 'nothing in the missives, the wayleave agreement or its assignation from which it could be inferred that there was an intention to transfer the liability to pay for the wayleave agreement from the defenders to the third party irrespective of what the parties may have meant to do.' Liability for payment thus remained with Arjo Wiggins Ltd.

We add a postscript about canals. The Transport Act 1962 vested most canals in the pursuer. (Previously they had been vested in the British Transport Commission under the Transport Act 1947.) Under the British Waterways Board (Transfer of Functions) Order 2012, SI 2012/1659, the pursuer's canals in England and Wales were transferred to the Canal & River Trust. But for Scotland nothing changed. Thus the British Waterways Board now operates solely in Scotland. Today it calls itself 'Scottish Canals' but that is just a trading name, its legal name remaining unchanged. Its head office, once in Watford, is now in Glasgow. It is not to be confused with the Scottish Waterways Trust, the Scottish successor to the Waterways Trust, a UK body that no longer exists south of the border, having been merged with the Canal & River Trust. The Scottish Waterways Trust is separate from Scottish Canals, though it appears that they work closely together.

REAL BURDENS

(16) Thomson's Exx
2016 GWD 27-494, Lands Tr

This was an application for a ruling as to the enforceability of real burdens. The background was as follows. In the late 1950s an area of ground was divided into five plots. One was retained. The other four were feued subject to burdens which were virtually identical. Among the burdens were an obligation to build a house, and a restriction against further building. The houses were duly built. No provision was made in the deeds as to right to enforce the burdens.

The applicant, who owned one of the plots, wished to build a second house, which would be contrary to the burdens. The superior's enforcement rights had, of course, been lost with the abolition of the feudal system. The question to be determined by the Lands Tribunal was whether the owners of any of the other plots had enforcement rights by virtue of ss 52 or 53 of the Title Conditions (Scotland) Act 2003.

The Tribunal **held** that s 53 (but not s 52) applied. See **Commentary** p 120.

EXECUTION OF DEEDS

(17) Khosrowpour v Mackay
[2016] CSIH 50, 2016 GWD 21-366

The pursuer's case was that, in 1989, he had lent his mother-in-law, Ann Bowden Mackay, £8,000 to buy her council house at 7 Partick Bridge Street, Glasgow, on the basis that she would bequeath the house to him in her will. Such a will, the pursuer averred, had indeed been drawn up and signed but was now lost. When Mrs Mackay died in 2012 it was found that she had made a subsequent will, in 2003, leaving the sale proceeds of the house to her children. By this time the pursuer was no longer married to Mrs Mackay's daughter. The present action, one of damages for breach of contract, was raised against Mrs Mackay's executor.

An initial obstacle was that the alleged agreement had not been reduced to writing. As the Lord Ordinary (Lord Turnbull) held, the arrangement was properly classified as a contract relating to heritage and not merely as a contract of an innominate kind, so that, under the law in force in 1989 (ie prior to the Requirements of Writing (Scotland) Act 1995), it needed writing for its constitution. Cases vouching for this proposition were *Fisher v Fisher* 1952 SC 437 and *McEleveen v McQuillan's Exr* 1997 SLT (Sh Ct) 46. The pursuer, however, pled *rei interventus* and in particular the fact that Mrs Mackay had made a will in the pursuer's favour. The Lord Ordinary allowed a proof before answer: see [2014] CSOH 175, 2015 GWD 1-8 (*Conveyancing 2014* Case (17)).

The defender appealed. In the Inner House the arguments resolved into two main points. First, as the appropriate form of personal bar was homologation rather than *rei interventus*, it was essential that the person said to be barred (ie Mrs Mackay) knew, at the time of the actings relied on (ie the making of the first will), that she had the power to resile from the (alleged) agreement with the pursuer due to its failure to comply with the rules as to formality. Normally the onus of proof would be on the person seeking to establish homologation. In those circumstances, therefore, the pursuer had to aver, and thereafter to prove, either (i) that Mrs Mackay had full knowledge of the right to resile, or (ii) that facts and circumstances existed which had the effect of putting the onus of proof on the defender (on the basis, perhaps, that 'competent persons are expected to know about and look out for their own interests, otherwise they must accept the consequences': para 19). The pursuer had failed to do either.

Secondly, the pursuer's case appeared to be contradicted by the existence of a standard security over the house which had been granted by Mrs Mackay to the pursuer in 1991 for all sums due and to become due. This made no mention of an obligation to bequeath the house to the pursuer.

The reclaiming motion was allowed and the action was dismissed.

(18) DWS v RMS
[2016] SC GRE 47, 2016 GWD 22-402

Among the juridical acts that must be in formal writing is 'a contract or unilateral obligation for the creation, transfer, variation or extinction of a real right in land': see s 1(2)(a)(i) of the Requirements of Writing (Scotland) Act 1995. It is because of this provision that missives of sale must be in formal writing. But how wide is the category of contracts to which the provision applies? Does it still apply where the obligation to transfer a real right in land is only one of the terms, and perhaps not even the main term? The answer, one would suppose, would be yes. But that was not the view taken in the current case.

The case concerned an alleged agreement to compromise a divorce action. A principal term provided for the future disposal of heritable property held in joint names by the parties. Certain properties were to be disponed by the wife to the husband, and, once the husband's 'release from the mortgage' was obtained, the matrimonial home was to be disponed by the husband to the wife.

Compromise agreements are, by their nature, often informal, and this was no exception. The alleged agreement was said to have been formed by a letter from the husband's solicitor which 'offer' was then 'accepted' by an oral communication by the wife's solicitor.

For no doubt good reasons, courts have tended to be indulgent in respect of such informality. In an earlier case much relied on in this one, *McFarlane v McFarlane* [2007] CSOH 75, Lord Menzies had gone so far as to say (at para 41) that:

> Actions which are pending in Scottish Courts are settled routinely by the most informal methods. Frequently actions in this court involving large sums of money (and often involving heritable property) are settled by means of verbal agreement

between counsel or between solicitors, or by means of an informal exchange of correspondence. Sometimes the agreement is thereafter set out in more or less formal terms, in a minute of agreement or a joint minute, but this is far from being the universal practice. There is no requirement in our law for a particular formality or method of concluding a contract for the compromise of a court action.

The compromise agreement in *McFarlane* also involved the transfer of heritable property, but it had been conceded by counsel (see para 34) that the Requirements of Writing Act did not apply. That stance was presumably approved of by Lord Menzies, because he said that (para 42):

> [I]t is important to bear in mind that what is being considered in the present case is not a contract for the transfer of title to heritable property, nor for the transmission of any real right; this is a contract for the compromise of a court action, conferring only personal rights.

This *obiter dictum* is perhaps rather loosely expressed. It lays itself open to the interpretation that the final, and indisputably accurate, words – that the compromise agreement was one 'conferring only personal rights' – were being contrasted with 'a contract for the transfer of title to heritable property' and that, therefore, the latter type of contract conferred real rights. It seems unlikely that this is what Lord Menzies meant. After all, it is trite law that contracts, by themselves, confer no more than personal rights, even if the personal right in question is one to acquire a future real right. (As the *Codex* of Justinian puts it at 2, 3, 20: *traditionibus et usucapionibus dominia rerum, non nudis pactis, transferuntur.*) But the sheriff in *DWS v RMS* (W M D Mercer) appears to have read the *dictum* of Lord Menzies in this way.

In *DWS v RMS*, unlike in *McFarlane*, the question of whether formal writing was needed for the compromise agreement was one of the matters in dispute. On the basis of *McFarlane*, the sheriff concluded that formal writing was not required (para 29):

> A compromise agreement, if proved, confers only personal rights. It is therefore not a contract for the transfer of a real right in land. Evidence of alleged written offer and oral acceptance is admissible.

The reasoning is mistaken. It does not follow from the (undoubted) fact that a compromise agreement 'confers only personal rights' that it is 'not a contact for the transfer of a real right in land'. Contracts for the transfer of real rights in land are, likewise, contracts which confer only personal rights.

As it happens, the reasoning did not affect the result. Following a proof, it was held that the parties had failed to agree all the necessary terms. There was no compromise agreement between the parties.

For careful analysis of and criticism of the decision, see Craig Anderson, 'Compromise agreements and heritable property' 2016 SLT (News) 169.

STATUTORY NOTICES

(19) Ewing v Inverclyde Council
[2016] SC GRE 65, 2016 Hous LR 121

As part of a regeneration plan, Inverclyde Council proposed to demolish five blocks of flats within the Clune Park area of Port Glasgow. In June 2014 the Council served demolition orders in respect of a substantial number of the properties. No fewer than 270 summary applications to revoke these orders were then served by the owners of the affected properties of which applications more than 230 remained alive. The present case concerned six such orders. A similar application in respect of another property in the same area had failed in 2014: see *McWatters v Inverclyde Council* 2014 SLT (Sh Ct) 155 (*Conveyancing 2014* Case (19)).

The demolition orders were issued under s 115 of the Housing (Scotland) Act 1987. This empowers councils to make an order where (i) the house does not meet the tolerable standard and (ii) the house ought to be demolished. The definition of 'tolerable standard' can be found in s 86(1) of the 1987 Act (as amended). Among the factors that must be satisfied in order to reach that standard, the very first is that the house is structurally stable. In assessing this and other factors, s 86(1A) requires that 'regard shall be had to any guidance issued by the Scottish Ministers'. Guidance was issued in 2009.

The appeals against the demolition order were made under s 129 of the 1987 Act. This has been taken to allow the court to consider anew whether the statutory basis for making the order existed – as opposed merely to deciding whether the council had no reasonable grounds for coming to its decision (para 24). A proof was heard, with expert witnesses giving evidence on both sides.

There was a dispute as to what was meant by structural instability. Following the Guidance issued by Scottish Ministers the sheriff (Derek J Hamilton) held that, not only must there be signs of recent or fresh movement, but the movement must indicate that the house may be at risk from either partial or total collapse (para 181):

> What requires to be considered when looking at the structural stability of a house are the structural elements, and that clearly includes the roof, gables and elevations. Those structural elements (the roof in this case) should not exhibit signs of fresh movement which may indicate a risk of partial or total collapse. That does not mean that every movement of a structural element renders a building structurally unstable. Buildings, and that includes their structural elements, are designed to move. It is only where the movement might indicate there is a risk of partial or total collapse that there is an issue. So, in considering structural stability, it is only when the structural elements exhibit certain signs of movement, ie ones that may indicate partial or total collapse, that there is an issue.

Furthermore, it was the collapse of the house that was at issue and not merely the collapse of an individual structural part.

The Council's case was that the buildings were structurally unstable due to movement in the roof caused by corrosion expansion of embedded steel and also – but this was a post-notice argument – by debonding of the concrete in the roofs. On these matters, the sheriff preferred the evidence of the pursuers' expert witnesses, and held that the Council's case had not been made out. Furthermore, the Council's expert conceded that the buildings would be safe for five to ten years (paras 229–30):

> He accepted however they were not currently failing. He considered the buildings to be safe for between five and ten years. It has not been proved that there is any current movement in the main structural elements of the buildings. It has not been proved that the structural elements are liable to partial or total collapse. Importantly, it has not been proved that the properties are at risk from partial or total collapse. ... If a building is deemed to be safe for the next five to ten years, it clearly is not liable to partial or total collapse.

The sheriff was also critical of the Council's actions, or inactions, prior to issuing the notices (para 219). There had been no proper investigation of the condition of the properties. The Council's surveyor had not been inside any of the six properties in question, and was not aware of the purpose of his limited inspection or of the extent of his instructions. In summary (para 222):

> I am satisfied there was no proper basis for the defender's decision to serve demolition orders in respect of the appeal properties. The properties were not adequately inspected; the expert evidence relied upon was based on a false assumption as to the roof structure; there was speculation as to the extent of corrosion expansion in the roof slabs; there was no evidence of corrosion expansion of the embedded steel ribs; the cause of movement of the walls and gables had not been established; and there was inadequate investigation of any current movement in the buildings.

The demolition orders would therefore be quashed. But, warned the sheriff (para 234), this should not 'be taken as a declaration of structural stability for any of the appeal properties'.

(20) Priya Properties Ltd v Inverclyde Council
[2016] SC GRE 81, 2016 GWD 40-718

This case follows on from the previous one. The reasons for quashing the demolition orders in relation to the six properties featured there had obvious implications for the 230 or so appeals in respect of other properties in the Clune Park area of Port Glasgow. An immediate consequence had been the (necessary) quashing of demolition orders in respect of other houses in the same buildings as the six original properties. The present hearing was in respect of four further properties. Following the decision in the previous case, the appellants enrolled a motion for an order quashing the demolition orders without the need to hear evidence. This was opposed by the Council on two grounds. In the first place, in the period since the original decision the Council had carried out a series of further inspections as to the stability of houses within the estate. The evidence thus obtained required to be tested in a proof. In the second place, there were live issues concerning *other* aspects of the tolerable standard in respect of the four houses (structural stability being only one of a number of factors set out in s 86(1) of the Housing (Scotland) Act 1987 for the purposes of defining the tolerable standard). These too required proof.

The sheriff (Derek J Hamilton), who had also presided over the previous case, rejected these arguments and quashed the demolition orders. In summary proceedings, it was 'not appropriate or just to delay matters to enable [the Council] to make further enquiry in an effort to secure evidence to support its conclusion' (para 51). Furthermore, neither defence was strong.

In regard to the first defence, the further inspections carried out by the Council had only included one of the four properties with which this present appeal was concerned, and no clear evidence was being offered even in respect of that property. This was one of the key problems identified in respect of the Council's conduct in the previous case. '[I]t is simply not appropriate to inspect a limited number of properties and then make sweeping generalised comments concerning the structural stability of other properties that have not been inspected' (para 48). Although the Council had served several hundred demolition orders, the court had to consider each individual order. The Council had not paid proper regard to individual properties (para 52):

> It simply cannot be the case that the Defender can inspect a property in one area of the estate and use the evidence from that inspection to serve a demolition order on an entirely separate property in another area of the estate. That is so, particularly where the report which the Defender relies upon acknowledges that the construction of the properties vary, the levels of corrosion vary, and the condition of the slabs vary.

The Council's second defence was no stronger (para 45):

> It has to be recognised that the demolition orders were served on the basis that the properties were structurally unstable and therefore below tolerable standard. There was further specification as to what was causing the structural instability. I accept that even if I had found that the basis upon which the demolition orders were served was incorrect, if there was evidence now before me that the properties were now structurally unstable, then in considering the matter *de novo*, I would be bound not to quash the demolition orders. I do not accept however that I am bound, in considering the matter *de novo*, to consider all aspects of the tolerable standard as detailed in section 86 of the Act. When a demolition order is served a proprietor is entitled to fair notice as to the basis on which it is served. If a proprietor proves that the reasons given for serving a demolition order do not render the property below tolerable standard, he does not need, before the demolition order is quashed, to thereafter satisfy the court that the property meets the tolerable standard in every other aspect of section 86. If it were otherwise it would mean that a local authority could serve a demolition order on a property without having a proper basis for doing so, and even once that had been shown, the onus would still be on the proprietor to show the property met the tolerable standard in respect of every other aspect of section 86.

COMPETITION OF TITLE

(21) Gallacher's Exx v Nelson
[2016] CSOH 35, 2016 GWD 9-174

This is the first of three cases involving challenges to gratuitous dispositions granted by elderly persons.

In this case Mary Gallacher, at the age of 92, granted a disposition of her house (24 Eaglesham Road, Clarkston, Renfrewshire) in favour of the defender, who was a nephew and who was closely involved with Miss Gallacher and also with his mother, who was Miss Gallacher's sister. The disposition was challenged by a niece from the other side of the family who had not seen Miss Gallacher since 2001. The two sides of the family were not on good terms. The disposition was signed and recorded in July 2007. Miss Gallacher died on 31 March 2011 having lived in residential care since April 2008.

Two grounds for reduction were advanced: (i) that Miss Gallacher lacked the capacity to grant the disposition, or (ii) that the disposition was vitiated by facility and circumvention.

Following a proof, the Lord Ordinary (Lord Clarke) was satisfied, on a balance of probabilities, in respect of (i). While the defender and his family presented a 'rosy picture' of Miss Gallacher's state of health, and said that she was 'as normal as she always had been' (paras 37 and 78), the reality was that, by 2007, she was suffering from advanced dementia. The solicitor who acted in the transfer had acted for the Gallacher family since 1966. He had since died, but there was no record on the file that he had met with Mrs Gallacher at the time of the disposition or taken her instructions, that he had sent her a terms-of-business letter, or that she had been sent a copy of the disposition. The defender, however, gave evidence of the solicitor having called in to see his aunt and his mother in April of 2007 and having taken her instructions. The disposition was collected from the solicitor by the defender and later returned, having been signed in his house after he had taken his mother and aunt on a day-trip to Largs. The medical evidence was divided but on the whole supported the view that Miss Gallacher lacked the necessary capacity to make the disposition. Lord Clarke so held.

Lord Clarke having been satisfied in respect of (i), there was no need to determine (ii). Nonetheless, Lord Clarke gave it brief consideration. There was clear evidence of facility on the part of Miss Gallacher, but insufficient evidence, or indeed averments, of circumvention on the part of the defender.

(22) Matossian's Exr v Matossian
[2016] CSOH 21, 2016 GWD 7-139

Audrey Matossian had three sons: Berj, Richard and Alex. Alex did not get on with his two brothers. Richard lived in Forfar and Alex lived in Blairgowrie. Mrs Matossian lived in Glasgow in one of the three properties which she owned in that city.

On 4 May 2007, when she was staying with Alex in Blairgowrie, Mrs Matossian called in at a solicitor's office in Coupar Angus and signed her will. Although Alex accompanied her, the solicitor ('the Couper Angus solicitor') saw her on her own and took her instructions. There had been previous meetings and correspondence. The will left the houses to Alex and the contents to the other brothers.

A week before, unknown to Alex, Mrs Matossian had been taken to Richard's house at Forfar by Berj. A different solicitor ('the Forfar solicitor') was present. There Mrs Matossian executed dispositions of two of the houses in favour, respectively, of Berj and Richard and, the title deeds for the third house apparently being lost, executed a 'deed of gift' in respect of that house in favour of Richard. Presumably the deeds were then registered. No consideration was paid but a liferent was reserved for Mrs Matossian in respect of the first two houses. This too followed previous meetings, though there had not been (and was not to be) any correspondence between the Forfar solicitor and Mrs Matossian.

When Alex found out what had happened, he instructed the Couper Angus solicitor to contact the Forfar solicitor to have the properties reconveyed to Mrs Matossian. His brothers, however, refused to co-operate, and matters had not progressed further by the time of Mrs Matossian's death on 27 December 2010.

As Mrs Matossian's executor-nominate, Alex raised this action against his brothers for reduction of the dispositions and the deed of gift. After a proof, decree was granted, on the grounds of facility and circumvention and also undue influence. At the time that Mrs Matossian signed the deeds she had been 79, in poor health, and forgetful. The Forfar solicitor acted primarily for the brothers. He did not see Mrs Matossian on her own or ask her whether she would like to have separate representation, even although the transactions were to her detriment and to the benefit of Berj and Richard. Nor did he advise her in relation to IHT and CGT liability.

All three brothers made a poor impression on the Lord Ordinary (Lord Uist) at the proof: 'The proof to which I listened consisted of the undignified spectacle of a family feud. Large portions of the evidence were irrelevant' (para 31). Nonetheless, Lord Uist was satisfied that decree should be granted (para 33):

> I conclude that when Mrs Matossian signed the three deeds on 25 April 2007 she was subject to facility and circumvention as well as undue influence at the instance of both Berj and Richard. The circumstances of the signing of the three deeds are eloquent of both facility and circumvention and undue influence, the requirements of each of which I have set out in full above. I am satisfied that on 25 April 2007 Mrs Matossian was suffering from weakness of mind, that acts of circumvention by Berj and Richard impetrated the execution of the three deeds and that she suffered lesion as a result. I infer circumvention from the whole circumstances of the execution of the deeds, as narrated above. Lesion consists in her having divested herself of her entire heritable estate for no consideration. I reject any evidence … to the contrary. So far as undue influence is concerned, I am satisfied that all the requirements, as set out above, have been established by the evidence. There was a relationship that

created a dominant influence (sons and mother), confidence and trust arose from that relationship, a material benefit was given to the prejudice of the grantor and there was an absence of independent advice and assistance.

Berj and Richard had counter-claimed for repayment of the money they had spent since April 2007 improving the houses. This was based on unjustified enrichment. The counter-claim, however, was rejected on the basis that, having committed a wrong, the two brothers were *male fide* possessors. Furthermore, it could not be said that Alex was enriched in the capacity in which he had brought the action, ie as executor-nominate of his late mother.

(23) Neville v Donald
[2016] CSOH 6, 2016 GWD 2-38

This was another challenge to a disposition, this time on grounds of fraud or forgery. Isabella Martin and her late husband were council-house tenants in Aberdeen. With the help of an interest-free loan of £18,150 from their nephew, Anthony Donald, they were able to buy the house from the council at a discount. The loan was secured by a standard security. As well as providing money, Mr Donald also expended time and money on the refurbishment of the house. On 24 February 2014 Mr Donald registered a disposition of the house which bore to be signed by Mrs Martin, who was sole owner following the death of her husband. Later, Mrs Martin, by now in a residential home, denied all knowledge of having signed the deed. The present action, to reduce the disposition, was raised on her behalf by her daughter.

The case for Mrs Martin was that the signature had either been forged or procured by deception. In the event that these averments, which he denied, were proved, Mr Donald had a counter-claim for (i) an order ordaining Mrs Martin to dispone the house to him in implement of an agreement to do so dating from 2003, or (ii) an award of £20,500, being the amount by which Mrs Martin had been enriched by the work he had carried out.

At procedure roll, each party attacked the relevancy and specification of the other's averments. A proof before answer was allowed.

(24) Scottish Parliamentary Corporate Body v The Sovereign Indigenous
Peoples of Scotland
[2016] CSOH 65, 2006 SLT 761, 2016 Hous LR 48, affd [2016] CSIH 81,
2016 SLT 1307, 2016 Hous LR 109

This was an action by the body that owns the Scottish Parliament to secure the removal of the so-called 'Independence Camp' from its land. The Camp had been set up at or just before St Andrews Day 2015, and its stated intention was to remain there until Scottish independence. Answers opposing the action were lodged by a group calling itself 'The Sovereign Indigenous Peoples of Scotland' and also by Arthur McManus Gemmell, designed as 'A Member of the Government of Scotland'. The arguments were various, and relied on a miscellaneous range of authorities including the Declaration of Arbroath, the Treaty of Union, the book of Deuteronomy, and the United Nations Declaration on the Rights of Indigenous People of 2007. (Article 25 of the Declaration, on which some reliance was based, says: 'Indigenous peoples have the right to maintain and strengthen their distinctive spiritual relationship with their traditionally owned or otherwise occupied and used lands, territories, waters and coastal seas and other resources and to uphold their responsibilities to future generations in this regard.') A separate hearing was devoted to the argument that to grant the order would be to interfere with the rights to freedom of expression and freedom of assembly as enshrined in arts 10 and 11 of the ECHR: see [2016] CSOH 113, 2016 SLT 862, 2016 Hous LR 87. All defences were rejected, both at first instance and then, on appeal, by the Second Division.

So far as property law is concerned, the main issue was the title of the petitioner, and its right to exclude trespassers. In the first respondent's view (CSOH, paras 11 and 12):

any right of property vested in the petitioner could not be equated to the right in property held by a private individual. Since the Scottish Parliament had been paid for by the Scottish taxpayer, any land or property which it owned through the petitioner belonged to the people of Scotland and was owned in common by them. The petitioner was the embodiment of the Scottish Parliament and was therefore required to act in the interests of the 'body public'. As a public body the petitioner was not able to assume private rights which were in conflict with the public interest and its purely administrative role meant that it could only exercise its property rights to a limited degree, and only for the public good. The open area around the Scottish Parliament building, upon part of which the Camp was located, comprised an area of common ownership, which the Scottish people had freely accessed for centuries. The attempt by the petitioner to seek an order of the court in the present action, if successful, would therefore constitute an act of dispossession. To put the matter another way, to grant the petitioner's request for an order would diminish the rights and freedoms historically enjoyed by the Scottish people.

The second respondent's argument was bolder still (CSOH, para 20):

The petitioner being a body corporate, and therefore an entity which could neither be seen nor touched, was not able to own or hold property. Nor could it exercise any other private law rights. An entity such as the petitioner was not governed by law, as laws were made to govern men. In any event, the ground on which the Camp was located was public land which the petitioner was incapable of acquiring a right to. Furthermore, any right which the petitioner claimed to have could be revoked by the people of Scotland, since under the Treaty of Arbroath it would take only 100 men to oppose the exercise of the right claimed by the petitioner. As it was said that there were more than 100 people present in court in support of the respondents, the claim by the petitioner should not be given effect to.

However, as the Lord Ordinary (Lord Turnbull) observed (CSOH, para 20): 'No legal foundation for any of these submissions was identified'. They were accordingly rejected.

Instead the court accepted, on the basis of an extract of title sheet number MID79950 (the authenticity of extracts being provided for by s 105 of the Land Registration etc (Scotland) Act 2012), that the petitioner was owner of the land and buildings where the Scottish Parliament is located (CSOH, para 26). Furthermore, 'the general law of land ownership in Scotland entitles the petitioner to have exclusive use of its property, to resist encroachment upon it and to otherwise regulate the use of its property' (para 35). Thus the petitioner was entitled to require the Camp to leave.

On appeal, a new argument for the respondents was that, as their activities were essentially recreational and educational, they were entitled to be on the land by virtue of s 1(3) of the Land Reform (Scotland) Act 2003 (CSIH, para 19). This confers on the public the right to be 'on' land (as opposed merely to 'cross' land) for purposes which are recreational or educational. This argument too was rejected. The primary purpose of being on the land was political and hence did not fall within s 1(3) (see CSIH paras 26 and 33).

LAND REGISTRATION

(25) Highland Ventures Ltd v Keeper of the Registers of Scotland
2016 GWD 22-403, Lands Tr

This is the first application for rectification under the Land Registration etc (Scotland) Act 2012. And because the title in question had been registered under the Land Registration (Scotland) Act 1979, it is also the first case to make use of the transitional provisions in sch 4 paras 17–24 of the 2012 Act. See **Commentary** p 186.

(26) Whiteley v Keeper of the Registers of Scotland
2016 GWD 10-199, Lands Tr

The facts disclosed by this case are remarkable. In the 1990s Milton Mill in Invergordon, Ross and Cromarty, was converted into flats for residential use. Peter Whitely bought a flat on the ground floor, flat 6, the disposition in his favour being recorded in the Register of Sasines on 25 April 1996. The flats on the first floor directly above flat 6 were flats 2, 3 and 4. The titles to flats 2, 3 and 4 were or came to be registered in the Land Register; the title to flat 6 remained in the Register of Sasines.

Much later, when Mr Whitely was trying to sell flat 6, he discovered that the title sheets for flats 2, 3 and 4 bore to be of the ground floor. The title plans showed the outline of each of the flats, and there was no mention of the flats being on the first floor and not the ground floor.

Mr Whitely applied to the Keeper for rectification of the title sheets of numbers 2, 3 and 4. His proposal was that the words 'being a first floor flatted dwellinghouse' be added after the postal address in the A (property) section. As the application was made before the coming into force of the Land Registration etc (Scotland) Act 2012, it fell to be decided on the basis of the Land Registration

(Scotland) Act 1979. The Keeper refused the application. Her reason for doing so was that:

> The title sheets for numbers 2, 3 and 4 all reflect the description in the underlying conveyancing. The Keeper can only give effect to these descriptions. She cannot improve upon the descriptions. There is accordingly no inaccuracy in the Register.

Mr Whitely appealed to the Lands Tribunal against the Keeper's decision. Neither the Keeper nor the 'interested parties' (ie the owners of flats 2, 3 and 4) were represented at the hearing.

The argument that the Keeper 'cannot improve upon' the Sasine description is a familiar one, and has much to be said in its favour. But here there was a problem which the Keeper seems to have overlooked. If the split-off dispositions for flats 2, 3 and 4 really did convey an area of land rather than merely the flats on the first floor, then their legal effect depended on whether they were registered before or after 25 April 1996, being the date on which the split-off disposition of flat 6 was registered.

If they were registered before 25 April 1996, then they had the effect of conveying, in each case, (i) the first-floor flat in question, and (ii) that part of flat 6 which was directly underneath. In the event that Milton Mill had further floors, the dispositions would have conveyed those floors as well insofar as they were above the flat in question; but that potential complication can be passed over here. The subsequent disposition to Mr Whitely of flat 6 would then have been *a non domino* and could not have passed ownership.

If, conversely, the dispositions were registered after 25 April 1996 they could only have conveyed the first-floor flat in question. This is because, by the time the dispositions were registered, the disponer was no longer the owner of flat 6 – it now belonged to Mr Whitely – and so could not pass a good title to it.

An inquiry as to the accuracy of the Register thus required an inquiry into the chronology of the original split-off writs. If flats 2, 3 and 4 were disponed first, then – ignoring for the moment the possibility of positive prescription operating in favour of Mr Whiteley – the Register was perfectly accurate in including flat 6 within the title sheets for flats 2, 3 and 4. It had never belonged to Mr Whiteley. But if flat 6 were disponed first, then the title sheets were inaccurate, Mr Whitely was the 'true' owner, and the Register fell to be rectified.

So far as the judgment in the case discloses, however, no inquiry as to chronology was ever made – whether by the Keeper, by Mr Whitely, or by the Lands Tribunal itself. Instead the Tribunal seems to have taken for granted that the disposition in favour of Mr Whitely of flat 6 was effective, on registration, to make him owner of flat 6. This was because it was a matter as to which 'there is no dispute' (para 21). Accordingly, the Tribunal was 'satisfied that Mr Whiteley, and not the interested parties, is the true owner of the subjects described in his Sasine title and that he is therefore entitled to rectification of the registered titles in the manner sought' (para 22).

Another matter which goes unexplored in the Tribunal's judgment is the changes in ownership in respect of flat 6. On the Tribunal's view, Mr Whitely became owner of flat 6 on the recording of his disposition on 25 April 1996. Taking that to be true, it is important to ask what happened next. We know from the Tribunal's judgment that first registration in the Land Register occurred on 13 May 2004 in respect of flat 2, on 15 June 2005 in respect of flat 3, and on 24 October 2007 in respect of flat 4. Take the case of flat 2. When title to flat 2 was registered for the first time in the Land Register, on 13 May 2004, the person registered as proprietor would have become owner not only of flat 2 but also, due to the Midas touch (ie s 3(1)(a) of the Land Registration (Scotland) Act 1979), of the part of flat 6 that was directly underneath. Mr Whitely, however, continued in (natural) possession of flat 6 and so – assuming no further conveyancing in respect of flat 2 – would have reacquired ownership of the relevant part of flat 6 by positive prescription on 13 May 2014. By the time that he was seeking rectification, therefore, Mr Whiteley was the actual owner of that part of flat 6 and not merely the 'true' owner. The inaccuracy on the Register was thus 'actual' and not merely 'bijural'. (For this terminology, see K G C Reid and G L Gretton, *Land Registration* (2017) para 2.8.)

The story of flat 3 is different. Prescriptive reacquisition by Mr Whitely of the relevant part of flat 6 would not have been completed until 15 June 2015. But by then Mr Whitely would already have reacquired the property due to the transitional provisions in the Land Registration etc (Scotland) Act 2012. Paragraph 17 of sch 4 provides that, in a case where, immediately prior to the designated day (8 December 2014), there was an inaccuracy on the Register which the Keeper could have rectified, then as from that day, parties have such rights as they would have had if rectification had taken place. (For discussion, see Reid and Gretton, *Land Registration* paras 11.9–11.11.) Again, therefore, Mr Whitely became the 'actual' owner of the relevant part of flat 6, but this time only on 8 December 2014, and the inaccuracy on the Register became 'actual' rather than 'bijural'. The position for flat 4 is the same.

(27) Tock v Keeper of the Registers of Scotland
9 November 2016, Lands Tr

The original boundary between two estates in Oyne, Aberdeenshire – the Logie and the Pittodrie estates – was a burn (para 52). The Logie estate lay to the west of the burn and the Pittodrie estate to the east. The current dispute concerned two areas of land which had been split off from these estates. Mr and Mrs Tock owned area A, which had been split off from the Logie estate in 1953. Mr and Mrs Mearns (together with Alan Mearns Electrical Ltd) owned Area B, which had been split off from the Pittodrie estate in 1992. Area A was still held on a Sasine title; Area B was subject to a first registration when it was bought by Mr and Mrs Mearns in 2012.

The parties were in dispute as to the boundary between their respective properties. The title sheet for Area B showed the western boundary as the burn. This was consistent, probably, with the 1992 disposition.

The description in the 1953 split-off disposition in respect of Area A began: 'ALL and WHOLE that piece of ground on which the dwelling house known as Nursery Cottage is built .. and as present occupied and possessed by Thomas Donald as tenant thereof'. There was a reference to a plan on which the subjects were shown shaded in blue; but the plan came with the warning that, though it was believed to be correct, it was not warranted.

Mr and Mrs Tock disputed the boundary as shown in the title sheet for Area B. There was a dyke lying several feet to the east of the burn. In their view, this, and not the burn, marked the correct boundary between the properties. That would mean that the long, thin strip of ground between the burn and the dyke was part of Area A and not, as the title sheet currently indicated, part of Area B. For this view the original split-off writs gave distinctly mixed support. In the 1953 disposition of Area A, only part of the strip was shaded blue. By contrast, all of the strip appeared to be included in the 1992 disposition of Area B. The best that could be said was that the Sasine titles overlapped.

The parties were on bad terms. As the Tribunal commented (para 50):

> The respective diary entries of Mr Tock and Mrs Mearns record several distressing scenes of conflict. We heard in passing of one or more interdict orders, a criminal prosecution and we saw for ourselves one CCTV camera on the disputed area and elsewhere a sign warning of another nearby. A letter from a Chief Superintendent of Police Scotland states that since 6 March 2015 Mrs Tock has contacted the police on at least 119 occasions regarding a civil land dispute. This background has led us to assess the factual evidence with particular care.

On 18 August 2013 Mr and Mrs Tock applied to the Keeper for rectification of the title sheet of Area B to the effect of removing the disputed strip. The Keeper refused the application on 19 December 2013. On 8 July 2014 the Tocks appealed to the Lands Tribunal. As this was before the coming into force of the Land Registration etc (Scotland) Act 2012, the appeal was decided on the basis of the Land Registration (Scotland) Act 1979 alone. That approach had been approved in *Wight v Keeper of the Registers of Scotland* 2015 SLT (Lands Tr) 195 (for criticism, see *Conveyancing 2015* pp 28–30).

The foundation of the Tocks' title was the split-off disposition of 1953. The description (quoted above) was not, said the Tribunal, a description with fixed boundaries. Hence it was *habile* for the purposes of prescription. Whether, therefore, the Tocks were entitled to the strip depended on whether they had possessed it for the ten years required for positive prescription. A proof was heard at the end of which the Tribunal concluded that the Tocks had possessed the strip for part, but not for all, of its length. The title sheet for Area B was therefore inaccurate to the extent that the Tocks had possessed. Given the finding as to possession, there could be no question of Mr and Mrs Mearns enjoying the protection against rectification of a proprietor in possession (ie under s 9(3) of the 1979 Act). Accordingly, the Tribunal ordered the rectification of the title sheet to the extent of removing the relevant part of the disputed strip.

(28) Craigmyle v Keeper of the Registers of Scotland
2016 GWD 26-482, Lands Tr

The Craigmyles had owned 0.2981 hectares in Banchory, Aberdeenshire, since 1987. In 2005, neighbours of the Craigmyles disponed an area of land to developers. For reasons which are unclear, the disposition included a triangular area of land which belonged to the Craigmyles. This led to a first registration in the Land Register under title number KNC15640, and the inclusion of the triangular area in the title. The subjects were developed for residential housing, and the access road to the development incorporated the triangular area.

In August 2006 the Craigmyles applied to the Keeper for rectification of KNC15640 so as to exclude the triangular area. The Keeper's initial response was to refuse, on the basis that no inaccuracy had been demonstrated, but eventually – in 2009 – the existence of the inaccuracy was accepted. As the developers were in possession there could be no question of rectification. The Craigmyles therefore sought payment of indemnity from the Keeper under s 12(1)(b) of the Land Registration (Scotland) Act 1979. Eventually, the claim was formulated as (i) £400,000 in respect of the triangular area, and (ii) £124,272.41 in respect of the costs of pursuing the claim (which were due under s 13(1)). The costs were so high because negotiations with the Keeper on the claim were so prolonged, and fruitless. At one stage the Craigmyles had recourse to an FOI request in order to obtain a copy of the valuation carried out for the Keeper by the district valuer. Meanwhile, the Keeper denied any liability.

Negotiations having broken down, the Craigmyles brought this appeal against the position adopted by the Keeper. By this time the Keeper had, finally, accepted that she was liable, and the hearing was concerned with quantifying the claim. In particular, it was concerned with determining how essential was the triangular area for access to the development site and whether it was correct to view it, as the Craigmyles urged, as a ransom strip. After hearing expert evidence on both sides, the Tribunal concluded that the area was indeed a ransom strip. On the basis of *Stokes v Cambridge Corporation* (1962) 13 P&CR 77 it awarded one third of the development gain, which, it was agreed on both sides, was about £1.2 million. The resulting figure of £400,000 was the sum which the Craigmyles were seeking. The Tribunal also awarded the costs of pursuing the claim.

In a postscript to its Opinion, the Tribunal expressed some criticism as to the conduct of Registers of Scotland in this case:

> Mr Craigmyle described in evidence the lengthy process by which we have reached the present position. It involved him having to resort to Freedom of Information requests at certain points and it is plain that there were times at which the respondent, or some members of her staff, were dismissive of his claim and sought to prevent it progressing. In doing so they misjudged not only the merits of the claim but the tenacity of the claimant. A less well resourced victim of an error in the Register, in terms of intellect and finance, may well have given up, which would have led to a loss going unindemnified. We realise, of course, that the respondent and her staff have to take a view on claims. No doubt they receive some, perhaps many, unmeritorious ones. But failure to engage is not only unfair in the case of

a meritorious claim but can lead to consequences in expenses. In the present case, had the respondent engaged in negotiation with the Craigmyles when she received Ms Paton's report, as Mr Craigmyle expected her to do, there must be at least some prospect that the claim would have settled and that all the subsequent expense would have been saved.

(29) Chief Land Registrar v Caffrey & Co
[2016] EWHC 161 (Ch), [2016] PNLR 23

This is an English case but it is of some interest in Scotland. The defendants, a firm of solicitors, acted for clients in the discharge of a mortgage. The clients produced a signed discharge, explaining that the lender had its own solicitors. The defendants presented the discharge for registration without having checked their clients' story by contacting either the bank or the solicitors. When the Land Registry requested evidence of authority to sign, the clients produced a power of attorney which the defendants forwarded to the Registry. Later, it turned out that both the discharge and the power of attorney had been forged by the clients. As a result, the Land Registry had to pay compensation to the bank. In this action the Chief Land Registrar sought to recover the amount paid from the defendants. One of the grounds of action was that the defendants owed a duty of care to the Land Registry, and had breached that duty. The action was undefended.

It was argued for the Chief Land Registrar (i) that in applying for registration, the defendants were representing to the Land Registry that they had taken sufficient steps to satisfy themselves as to the validity of the discharge, and (ii) that, as they knew the Land Registry would rely upon such representations, they had a duty to take reasonable care that the representations were true.

As the action was undefended, the court took the factual basis and inferences pled under (i) as true, though noting that they could be challenged. It then turned to consider the question of law raised by (ii): did solicitors presenting a deed for registration have a duty of care to the Land Registry? The court was 'narrowly persuaded ... on the peculiar facts of this case' that they did (para 59). But there were also significant grounds for doubt (paras 57 and 58):

> It is clear that there are cases where a person who, exercising a particular skill, makes a statement to a person intended to rely on it assumes a duty to that person to make such statements with reasonable care. The question is whether the present is one of them. What jars with me here is the idea that, in making the representations which are alleged here, and which I must assume, the solicitors were acting as professionals exercising their skill. They were certainly professional conveyancers exercising that skill. But they had no particular qualifications for making the statements that are to be attributed to them. They were not detectives, for example. Moreover, the statements were not made to a layman, but to the Claimant's professional staff engaged in running the registration system, who might be expected to have systems for checking matters themselves. Indeed, the registry staff raised a requisition on the question of the authority of the person signing the discharge form to bind the bank. They did not just blindly accept whatever the Defendant told them.

So far as Scotland is concerned, the issue of a duty of care to the Keeper has now been settled by statute. Section 111 of the Land Registration etc (Scotland) Act 2012 imposes on solicitors (and on their clients) a duty to 'take reasonable care to ensure that the Keeper does not inadvertently make the register inaccurate'. For discussion, see K G C Reid and G L Gretton, *Land Registration* (2017) paras 15.2–15.4. The facts of *Chief Land Registrar v Caffrey & Co*, however, raise some interesting questions as to what the standard of care might be. Solicitors, as the court says, are 'not detectives'.

[Another aspect of this case is digested at (65) below.]

COMMUNITY RIGHT TO BUY

(30) Coastal Regeneration Alliance Ltd v Scottish Ministers
[2016] SC EDIN 60, 2016 GWD 29-523

The pursuer was (and is: see http://coastalregenerationalliance.org/) a company limited by guarantee which had been set up as a community body for the purposes of the community right to buy. The community in question comprised Prestonpans, Cockenzie and surrounding areas. On 12 November 2015 the pursuer applied to the Scottish Ministers for registration of community interests in land in respect of two different areas of land at Cockenzie, East Lothian, both owned by Scottish Power Generation Ltd ('SPG').

In considering applications, Scottish Ministers are required by s 38(1) of the Land Reform (Scotland) Act 2003 to be satisfied on a number of matters including (i) that a significant number of the members of the community have a substantial connection with the land, (ii) that there is within the community a level of support sufficient to justify registration, and (iii) that it is in the public interest that the community interest be so registered. In the present case, the Scottish Ministers were so satisfied.

But there was a problem. Unknown, apparently, to the pursuer, by the time that the applications were made SPG had been in negotiations for the sale of the two areas for well over a year. That automatically made the applications 'late', and so subject to the additional matters set out in s 39 of the 2003 Act. For the Act distinguishes between timeous and late applications – between cases where a community body, at an early stage, indicates by registration its wish to buy the land, and the case where the interest of the body, and often its actual formation, are only triggered when an owner is looking to sell, perhaps for development. The effect of s 39 is to raise the threshold for late applications, and so to prevent the community right to buy from turning into a merely general right of pre-emption. According to para 1 of the *Community Right to Buy Guidance*, published by the Scottish Government in 2009, late applications are to be accepted only in 'exceptional circumstances'.

More precisely, where an application is late, the Scottish Ministers require to be satisfied as to the three additional matters set out in s 39(3), namely:

(a) that there were good reasons why the community body did not secure the receipt of an application before the owner of the land or, as the case may be, the creditor took the action, or gave the notice, such as is mentioned in subsection (1) above;

(b) that the level of support within the community for such registration is significantly greater than that which Ministers would, by virtue of subsection (2) of that section, have considered sufficient for the purposes of subsection (1)(d) of that section had the application been received before that action was taken or, as the case may be, the notice was given; and

(c) that the factors bearing on whether it is or is not in the public interest that the community interest be registered are strongly indicative that it is.

The Scottish Ministers were satisfied as to (b) but not as to (a) or (c). Accordingly, they issued decision letters rejecting both applicants. The pursuer appealed to the sheriff under s 61.

Various grounds of appeal were advanced. One was that the pursuer did not know of SPG's negotiations. Another was that, in making their decision, the Scottish Ministers were relying on matters which were neither in s 39 nor in the official *Guidance*. In doing so they had set the bar too high for bodies like the pursuer which were run by local residents.

In considering the appeal, the sheriff (N A Ross) emphasised that his task was not to make a fresh decision on the evidence. Rather it was to consider the reasonableness of the decision by the Scottish Ministers. Only if that decision was unreasonable in the *Wednesbury* sense, or if on a consideration of the merits it was plainly wrong, could it be overturned. That was the approach taken a decade ago in another appeal in relation to a late application for registration of a community interest in land, *Holmehill Ltd v The Scottish Ministers* 2006 SLT (Sh Ct) 79 (*Conveyancing 2006* Case (85)). It was clearly the correct approach.

Applying that approach to the two s 39 requirements as to which the Scottish Ministers had not been satisfied, it could not be said that their decisions were unreasonable or plainly wrong. In respect of requirement (a) (good reasons for the lateness of the applications), the community is likely to have known of the negotiations by SPG even if the pursuer did not. But in any event, lack of knowledge was not of itself a good reason for lateness (para 52):

> The *Guidance* and the scheme of the 2003 Act clearly indicate the opposite. It is not legitimate to make an application to thwart a disposal. In the event that the community were not attempting to thwart a disposal, and were unaware of the disposal, the 2003 Act provides no relief or defence. It would have been straightforward to provide one. There is nothing illogical in the 2003 Act failing to provide for knowledge – if a site is truly of great community importance, it is not illogical to require the community to take early steps to protect their own interests. To prevent a landowner from selecting a purchaser, and agreeing their own price and timetable, is a significant restriction on their property rights, much more than subjecting their land to a registered interest. Where there is genuine unfairness towards the community, for example if the community had been making strong efforts to purchase and had been unfairly

thwarted, the 2003 Act allows this to be remedied under the 'good reason' test. The defender has decided, however, that this is not such a situation. The community was active in protecting local interests from, according to the information available to the defender, at least 2010. The legislation was passed in 2003. Yet it was not until March 2015 that approval was sought for the Articles, and not until August 2015 that first applications were made. These are the true circumstances in which 'good reason' for lateness was being assessed by the defender, and it is difficult to describe their logic as flawed.

As for requirement (c) (strongly indicative that registration is in the public interest), while it was true that the pursuer had a number of plans for the sites – open space, a respite home, a garden centre, allotments, farmers markets, and so on – the proposed sale by SPG, to an offshore energy provider, would also result in public benefit. Furthermore, the Scottish Ministers had found the pursuer's plans to be vague and underdeveloped. In summary, the sheriff's views were as follows (para 65):

> The 2003 Act represents a balancing exercise between competing interests. It creates some interference with the owner's right of unrestricted disposal, but gives the landowner some increased protection when the landowner has actually taken steps to deal with his property. As the Guidance points out, the community interest is not necessarily the same as the public interest. The right to attempt to buy is given, but is not absolute. I cannot say that the defender's view, that the facts were not strongly indicative of the public interest, was not one they were entitled to reach.

The present case was decided under s 39 in its original form. It should be noted that s 39 has now been amended, with effect from 15 April 2016, by s 42 of the Community Empowerment (Scotland) Act 2015. The most important change is the replacement of the 'good reasons' test in requirement (a) with a new series of tests which, in essence, require that the community body should have taken steps towards preparing the application (or acquiring the land) at a time which, in the opinion of the Scottish Ministers, was sufficiently in advance of the owner opening sale negotiations or taking other action with a view to the transfer of that land. The effect is to exclude applications which are put together only in response to a prospective sale.

RESIDENTIAL RIGHT TO BUY

(31) Lee v Highland Council
2016 GWD 30-529, Lands Tr

A public-sector tenant sought to buy her property at 59 Dunain Road, Inverness. The application was refused because the area had been designated a 'pressured area' (as to which see Housing (Scotland) Act 1987 s 61B, and *Conveyancing 2010* pp 52–53); in such areas the right to buy is suspended. The tenant then applied to the Lands Tribunal. Her application failed: *Lee v Highland Council* 2015 GWD 38-601 (*Conveyancing 2015* Case (42)). She then submitted a new application to the

Council, and, when that was refused, she applied, once again, to the Tribunal. The Council pled that the previous decision of the Tribunal founded a plea of *res judicata* against her. That plea was upheld and accordingly the application failed.

(32) Clark v South Ayrshire Council
2016 GWD 32-578, Lands Tr

Like the previous case, this involved an application to buy a property (84 Kincaidston Drive, Ayr) in an area that had been designated as a 'pressured area'. When the landlord refused the application the tenants applied to the Lands Tribunal. We quote the Tribunal (para 3): 'The appellants do not dispute that their home is within … a "pressured area", nor do they take any legal points about the effect of that status. All that is said is that refusal of the right to purchase "is unfair and unjust as this does not apply to other areas or [to] people with a lesser occupancy time".' This argument did not persuade the Tribunal.

(33) Thomson v South Ayrshire Council
9 November 2016, Lands Tr

This case was similar to the previous one, but it was slightly more developed. We quote the Tribunal (para 13):

> We … accept the likelihood ventured by the respondents that any other tenants who had succeeded in purchasing their property within a pressured area were likely to have done so because their tenancy of the specific property would have commenced prior to 30 September 2002. Section 61B did not apply to such cases and so any such tenants continued to have the right to purchase. There was no question of the council unlawfully discriminating against the applicant.

(34) McCallum v City of Edinburgh Council
2016 GWD 24-450, Lands Tr

In August 2015 the local authority granted to the applicant a tenancy of a property in Tron Square, Edinburgh. In October 2015 the tenant sought to exercise the right to buy. The local authority agreed to give him the benefit of its discretion (see s 61(10)(b)(iv) of the Housing (Scotland) Act 1987) to regard him as having been in occupation for the qualifying period even though he had in fact not been: this related to the fact that he had been in the army between 1983 (at which time he had been a council tenant) and 2005. It calculated the discount at £15,000 on the basis that this was a post-2002 tenancy and accordingly subject to the lower discount rate of the 'modernised' right to buy, as opposed to the more generous rate of the 'preserved' right to buy.

The applicant raised the present action to require the local authority to sell to him at the 'preserved' rate. In the Tribunal's words (para 15):

> The applicant's position was that as the respondents had conceded continuity of occupation after the coming into effect of the 2002 Order, he was entitled to purchase

on the preserved terms. Section 61(2)(c) allowed for the occupancy of armed forces accommodation to contribute to the right to purchase. He contended that he had never 'given up' a tenancy which is what was required to lose the preserved rights under the 2002 Order [ie the Housing (Scotland) Act 2001 (Scottish Secure Tenancy etc) Order 2002, SSI 2002/318].

Held: that the terms of article 4 of the 2002 Order were clear and that the applicant was not entitled to a discount at the 'preserved' rate.

(35) Caven v Irvine Housing Association
2016 GWD 23-433, Lands Tr

In 2015 a tenant applied to buy her property at Goldie Crescent, Nithsdale, Dumfries, which she had tenanted since 2003. At that time the right to buy in respect of that property was subject to a ten-year suspension, ie until 2012, in terms of s 61A of the Housing (Scotland) Act 1987, and there was later a further ten-year suspension, ie until 2022. At the beginning of her tenancy she had been told (para 4 of the Tribunal judgment):

> Your tenancy will be a Scottish Secure Tenancy and a copy of our tenancy agreement is available on request. You will have the modernised Right to Buy your new home, however, in accordance with legislation, you will not be able to exercise your Right to Buy until 30th September 2012 at the earliest, and this date could be extended.

Inevitably, her application failed, but the Tribunal expressed a degree of sympathy for her (para 6).

(36) Simpson v Hillcrest Housing Association Ltd
2016 GWD 38-682, Lands Tr

Tenants wished to buy their housing association property at 143 Charles Avenue, Arbroath. They made an informal approach, but were told that the housing association was not subject to the 'right to buy' legislation. Eventually they applied to the Tribunal. The Tribunal rejected the application, on the ground that the tenants had never in fact made a formal application to buy the property, and by now it would be too late anyway, because the 'right to buy' was abolished by the Housing (Scotland) Act 2014 s 1 with effect from 1 August 2016. As the Tribunal explained (para 8):

> We are satisfied that the inquiry made to the respondents sometime prior to 18 July 2016 was not an application to purchase in statutory form. Indeed neither does the applicants' letter dated 19 October 2016 seeking to describe itself as a formal document meet the statutory criteria as a formal application to purchase. It is not in statutory form and does not contain the information prescribed by s 63(1)(b) or (c). The application form prescribed by the 2011 Order [ie the Right to Purchase (Application Form (Scotland) Order 2011, SSI 2011/97] runs to several pages and contains, amongst other things, a declaration of accuracy of certain particulars. The applicants' letter does not do this.

LEASES

(37) Gray v MacNeil's Exr
2016 SLT (Sh Ct) 250

John Gray and his wife Michelle Gray ran a petrol station and chip shop on South Uist, the property belonging to the latter's father, Donald MacNeil. Relations between Mr Gray and his father-in-law eventually turned sour, and Mr MacNeil cut off the electricity supply. Mr Gray sued. He claimed (i) the return of the chip shop equipment, or its value, and (ii) damages for breach of lease, for he asserted, but Mr MacNeil denied, that he had been operating the chip shop on the basis of a 15-year lease agreed between the parties. The alleged lease, however, had been undocumented. This was a case complicated on its facts, but also raising difficult questions as to the effects of an oral lease. The pursuer was successful in respect of the first claim but not in respect of the second. See **Commentary** p 126.

(38) Gyle Shopping Centre General Partners Ltd v Marks and Spencer plc
[2016] CSIH 19, 2016 GWD 10-205

This was the most recent, and perhaps last, stage in the long-running Great Primark Crisis at Edinburgh's Gyle Centre. The owner of the shopping centre was the pursuer. There were numerous units leased out, but two of them had special status, namely the lease to Morrisons plc and the lease to Marks and Spencer plc. These leases were for 127 years, and were both recorded in the Register of Sasines. The tenants had special rights in the running of the centre as a whole. Moreover these two leases included not only the physical stores themselves but also *pro indiviso* shares of the extensive car-parking areas.

 The owner wished to grant a new lease to Primark plc. This new lease was to include not only some parts of the existing retail structure, but also part of what was the car-parking area. The Primark store would thus involve a certain element of new build. Morrisons plc had no objection, but Marks and Spencer plc did object. The owner raised the present action.

 Battle was joined on three main fronts. One was whether Marks and Spencer plc had in fact already consented to the development. It was held that it had not consented. A second was whether the original inclusion of *pro indiviso* lease shares of the car-parking area was valid. If not, then the defender could not object. It was held that the inclusion was valid. So on the first two fronts the owner (the pursuer) failed.

 The third front concerned a provision in the lease (clause 24) that 'works' in the development could not be 'unreasonably' objected to: the owner argued that the Primark development constituted 'works' and that the objection of Marks and Spencer plc was unreasonable. In the Outer House this third line of argument succeeded. For the protracted first-instance case, see [2014] CSOH 59, 2014 GWD 18-352 and [2014] CSOH 122, 2015 SCLR 171 (*Conveyancing 2014* Case (34)), and [2015] CSOH 14, 2015 GWD 6-127 (*Conveyancing 2015* Case (56)). Marks and Spencer plc reclaimed. By the time the case reached the Inner House, the proposed Primark development had been abandoned, but the litigation continued, notwithstanding, because both parties advised the court that 'a similar problem was likely to arise in the future' (para 18).

The Inner House has reversed the first-instance decision. Thus Marks and Spencer plc's right to object has been upheld. The Inner House took the view that clause 24 could not be interpreted in such a broad way as to run contrary to the 'well-established principles of Scottish land law' (para 46).

We confess, however, to being uncertain whether the decision is based on property law or on contract law: both elements seem to sit together, rather awkwardly. At places the court seems to be saying that the proposed development would take away the defender's real right in part of the car-parking area, and that would not be possible without a partial renunciation of the lease, or variation of the lease, duly recorded or registered. For instance, at para 49 it is said by Lady Paton that:

> any changes in or alterations to such a lease require a formal written (or electronic) deed, such as a minute of variation, duly recorded or registered. In this way clarity, certainty, and accessibility for the public is achieved, in that anyone searching the registers – for example, a potential purchaser, or a potential assignee of a lease – is able to ascertain the precise nature and extent of the lease. Questions relating to the authenticity of the granter's title, the area of land leased (including boundaries), the parties to the lease, and the term of the lease, are certain, clear, and publicly available.

At other places the court seems to be saying that the rules of property law merely constitute the background to the interpretation of clause 24, ie the parties must be presumed not to have intended to contravene property law rules, but that this is simply a presumption, and that if clause 24 had been differently worded, the pursuer would have been successful. For instance, at para 51 it is said that 'any intention by contracting parties to dispense with the well-settled and accepted conveyancing requirements relating to real rights in land would, in our opinion, require to be very clearly expressed' and at para 56 it is said that 'a study of the contract discloses nothing suggestive of an intention to change well-established law'. But we would respectfully observe that contracts cannot change property law.

One or two other *dicta* in the case merit comment. At para 47 it is said that 'Scots law governing land tenure and leases is based upon written titles registered either in the Land Register (formerly the Register of Sasines), or in the Books of Council and Session, or in both.' (And cf para 55.) If the suggestion is that the registration of a deed in the Books of Council and Session can achieve real effect, ie proprietary effect, we would respectfully disagree. We think the point too clear for citation of authority.

In the same paragraph it is said that 'alterations in title generally require a written deed duly registered or, following the introduction of digitalisation, an alteration in the electronic land register'. This sentence is generally correct up to the word 'registered'. But the word 'or' introduces a muddle. 'Alteration' of the land register (which, by the way, is not required by the primary legislation to be kept in electronic form – see the Land Registration etc (Scotland) Act 2012 s 1(4)) – is not an *alternative* to a registered deed. For real rights in land to be changed the general principle remains what it has been ever since the Registration Act 1617: deeds are needed (whether electronic or paper, or even, for those who like to do things in style, parchment) and must be registered.

What conclusions can be drawn from this case? Perhaps the only firm one is that the arrangement entered into for the car-parking area was valid as a real right. Each of the two major stores had a one-third share of that area, being a share by way of lease. As to the other one third, it remained unleased. In respect of the shared areas the landlord thus had 100% ownership, of which one third was unencumbered by the leases.

Beyond that, we doubt whether firm conclusions can be drawn. For instance, suppose that clause 24 had contained stronger wording, what would the consequences have been? Would the real right held by the defender have been reduced in extent, and if so would that have had conveyancing consequences, and if so of what type?

(39) Apcoa Parking (UK) Ltd v Crosslands Properties Ltd
[2016] CSOH 63, 2016 GWD 14-268

A multi-storey car-park at Kingsgate Shopping Centre in Dunfermline, Fife, was owned by the defender and was occupied and managed by the pursuer, in terms of missives concluded in 2007. The missives incorporated a draft lease for 25 years. No formal lease had ever been entered into; the litigation took place on the basis of the draft lease.

The car-park suffered from serious defects, and the question was whether liability for repairs rested with the pursuer (occupier and manager) or the defender (owner). The lease provided (clause 5) procedural machinery about repairs which, the pursuer averred, had not been followed. The defender argued that any failure to follow that procedure did not matter (para 14):

> The parties did not stipulate that compliance with the contract procedure was essential. It is impermissible to construe the wording of clause 9.3 to mean 'subject to the developer implementing its obligations under clause 5'. That would amount to rewriting the contract.

It was **held** by the Lord Ordinary (Lord Woolman) that compliance with the contractually-envisaged procedure was not an optional matter and that accordingly the pursuer's case was relevant.

(40) AWG Business Centres Ltd v Regus Caledonia Ltd
[2016] CSOH 99, 2016 GWD 22-407

Defects were discovered in the concrete decking of the car-parking area within an office block, Riverside House, Riverside Drive, Aberdeen. The dispute was as to who was liable to pay for the repairs. There was a lease and there was a sublease. The former, ie the head lease, imposed repairing costs on the tenant, and the sublease required the subtenant to reimburse the tenant, ie the tenant of the head lease. Thus either (i) the landlord was liable or (ii) the head tenant was liable but with a right of reimbursement against the subtenant. In this action to determine allocation of liability, the head tenant was the pursuer and the two defenders were, first, the subtenant and, in the second place, the landlord.

The position of the subtenant was evidently a difficult one, but it sought to rely on an exception ('exception (c)') as to repairing liability to be found in the head lease. The head tenant would not be liable for 'any expenditure incurred in respect of or pertaining to the initial construction of the Building or the Service Systems or any part thereof by the Landlord'. The problem with the concrete derived from the original construction of the building. The subtenant argued, in the words of the Lord Ordinary (Lord Tyre) (para 12):

> It was important to give content to the phrase 'or pertaining to' in exception (c).
> Those words made clear that the exception required to be construed broadly and covered not only the initial construction cost but also matters which 'pertained to' the initial construction. ... Costs incurred to remedy latent defects in design or construction pertained to the initial construction. As the building had only recently been constructed, it may be presumed that the original parties to the head lease were alive to the possibility of the existence of latent defects, yet no provision was made for any collateral remedy for the tenant in the event that it was liable for remedial costs. In all the circumstances it would offend against commercial common sense to construe the lease as imposing such liability on the tenant.

The Lord Ordinary did not agree, saying that (para 15):

> The first defender's contention places too much weight upon the words 'or pertaining to'. These words can be given content as a reference to costs such as professional fees associated with the construction of the building but not strictly costs of construction. To interpret them as contended for by the first defender would impose a substantial and continuing liability of uncertain extent upon the landlord in respect that it could be argued that any expense, whenever incurred, arising from a design flaw or indeed from a design decision was expenditure 'pertaining to' the initial construction of the Building. That would not be consistent with a lease such as the present one which bears the hallmarks of intending to impose a full repairing and insuring obligation upon the tenant.

Moreover, he said (para 16), referring to *Arnold v Britton* [2015] AC 1619 (*Conveyancing 2015* (Case (51)), an English case which adopted a stricter approach to contractual interpretation than has prevailed in recent years:

> It would not be consistent with the *Arnold v Britton* approach to construe the lease on the basis of what a reasonably prudent tenant might have wished to achieve, or by attempting to assess what would have been a good or bad bargain from either point of view. The proper approach is rather to identify the parties' intention by reference to what a reasonable person having all the background knowledge available to the parties would have understood them to be using the language in exception (c) to mean.

This case concerned repairs to common parts. In a valuable article on the case, 'Repairing obligations for common parts' (2016) 61 *Journal of the Law Society of Scotland*, online edition: www.bit.ly/2gJRoM6, Matthew Farrell observes that:

> Repairing obligations that apply to the common parts are often overlooked. Matters such as extraordinary repairs, the common law obligations implied into the lease, payment obligations and the repairing standard are all usually dealt with in the repairing clause for the lease, but are nowhere to be seen in the repairing clause for the common parts.

(41) Fyffe v Esslemont
2016 GWD 33-586, Land Ct

A tenant must not change the use of the property that has been agreed, whether expressly or by implication. Such a change is breach of contract, which goes by the curious name of 'inversion of possession'.

In this case there was a lease of a farm, Muirton of Corsindae, Aberdeenshire. The landlord averred (para 1) that:

> Over a number of years, despite the Applicant's objections, the Respondent has been using the Farm buildings and the yards around those buildings for non-agricultural purposes, principally through the vehicle of Monarch Conservatories Scotland Ltd ('Monarch'), a sizeable construction business, and that the on-going conduct of the non-agricultural business of Monarch is 'the principal activity now carried on at the Farm'.

The landlord sought declarator in the Land Court that, as a result, the tenancy was at an end as a tenancy under the Agricultural Holdings (Scotland) Acts. In other words, the claim was that the tenancy was now a non-agricultural tenancy, the result of which would have been loss of security of tenure etc.

This was an unusual invocation of the concept of 'inversion'. The substance of the action was based on an English Court of Appeal decision, *Wetherall v Smith* [1980] 1 WLR 1290, in which it was held that if an agricultural holding ceased to be used (whether wholly or mainly) for agricultural purposes it would then cease to be covered by the agricultural holdings legislation. The Land Court accepted that approach, while emphasising that minor deviations from agricultural use might not be relevant. A proof was allowed.

(42) McDonald v McDonald
[2016] UKSC 28, [2016] 3 WLR 45

This was an English case but, as a decision of the Supreme Court in an area where there would seem to be no relevant differences between English law and Scots law, it is likely that it would be followed in Scotland.

If a public-sector landlord of residential property seeks to remove a tenant, the tenant can invoke the protections of the Human Rights Act 1998, and in particular article 8 ('Right to respect for private and family life'): see in particular *Manchester City Council v Pinnock* [2010] UKSC 45, [2011] 2 AC 104. What has been less clear is whether the same is true for private-sector residential tenancies.

Mr and Mrs McDonald had a daughter with serious psychiatric problems. She was unable to work. They bought a property and let it to her, the rent being met through housing benefit. The purchase was financed by a mortgage, and the intention was that the housing benefit (routed through the rent) would fund the mortgage payments. Eventually, however, the parents got into financial difficulties, and the secured lender decided to enforce the mortgage. The first step was to remove the daughter so that the property could be marketed with vacant possession. An action against her was raised, in the name of her parents. Her defence was that eviction would violate her article 8 rights.

The Supreme Court, affirming the decision of the Court of Appeal (see [2014] EWCA Civ 1049, [2015] Ch 357), **held** that the defence should be dismissed. That the decision means that the ECHR can *never* be invoked in a private-sector tenancy is, however, not quite certain. We quote selectively from the Opinion issued by Lord Neuberger and Lady Hale, with whom the other justices concurred (paras 40–42):

> [A]lthough it may well be that article 8 is engaged when a judge makes an order for possession of a tenant's home at the suit of a private sector landlord, it is not open to the tenant to contend that article 8 could justify a different order from that which is mandated by the contractual relationship between the parties, at least where, as here, there are legislative provisions which the democratically elected legislature has decided properly balance the competing interests of private sector landlords and residential tenants. In effect the provisions of the Protection from Eviction Act 1977, section 89 of the Housing Act 1980 and Chapters I and IV of the 1988 Act [ie the Housing Act 1988], as amended from time to time, reflect the state's assessment of where to strike the balance between the article 8 rights of residential tenants and the A1P1 rights of private sector landlords when their tenancy contract has ended.
>
> To hold otherwise would involve the Convention effectively being directly enforceable as between private citizens so as to alter their contractual rights and obligations, whereas the purpose of the Convention is … to protect citizens from having their rights infringed by the state. To hold otherwise would also mean that the Convention could be invoked to interfere with the A1P1 rights of the landlord, and in a way which was unpredictable. Indeed, if article 8 permitted the court to postpone the execution of an order for possession for a significant period, it could well result in financial loss without compensation – for instance if the landlord wished, or even needed, to sell the property with vacant possession (which notoriously commands a higher price than if the property is occupied).
>
> This conclusion does not mean that a tenant could not contend that the provisions of the 1988 Act did not, for some reason, properly protect the article 8 rights of assured shorthold tenants.

So can a private-sector tenant ever invoke article 8? The answer is absolutely no, maybe.

(43) Regent Quay Development Co Ltd v Tyco Fire & Integrated Solutions (UK) Ltd
[2016] CSOH 97, 2016 GWD 21-382 affd [2016] CSIH 73, 2016 GWD 31-555

This case was about whether a break notice served by a tenant on the landlord was valid. The tenant originally took a lease of two units (numbers 3 and 4) at Glover Pavilion, Aberdeen Science and Technology Park. Later it was agreed that the tenant would also take a third unit (unit 1), and accordingly the lease was amended so as to be a lease of the three units. Various other amendments were made at the same time. The ish was 2021 but the tenant had the option to break the lease in 2016. It decided to exercise the option, and its law agents served notice to that effect on the landlord. The landlord asserted that the notice was invalid. If that was the case, the time for exercising the break option would have expired, with the consequence that the lease would continue until 2021. The tenant raised the present action, seeking declarator that the break option had been validly exercised.

The break notice was in the following terms:

> *Tyco Fire and Integrated Solutions (UK) Limited*
> *Units 3 & 4, The Glover Pavilion, Aberdeen Science and Technology Park, Aberdeen*
> *('the Premises')*

We act for Tyco Fire & Integrated Solutions (UK) Limited (Company Number 01952517) of Tyco Park, Grimshaw Lane, Newton Heath, Manchester M40 2WL, formerly known as Wormald Ansul (UK) Limited, its name having been changed conform to Certificate of Incorporation on Change of Name dated 29 December 2005, hereinafter referred to as the Tenant of the Premises, subject to (1) lease between Regent Quay Development Company Limited and Wormald Ansul (UK) Limited dated 24 February and 9 March and registered in the Books of Council and Session on 31 March, all months in 2004 ('the Lease'); and (2) minute of variation of lease between Regent Quay Development Company Limited, Tyco Fire and Integrated Solutions (UK) Limited and Wormald Ansul (UK) Limited dated 27 October and 8 November, both dates in 2011, and registered in the Books of Council and Session on 28 June 2012 ('the Minute of Variation of Lease').

Pursuant to clause 4.2 of the Minute of Variation of Lease, on behalf of and as instructed by the Tenant, we HEREBY GIVE YOU NOTICE to terminate the Lease over the Premises on the fifth anniversary of the Effective Date on giving not less than six months prior written notice of termination. Without prejudice we consider that date will be 31 August 2016 and that the lease will terminate on that date but please confirm that you agree.

We also act for all group companies of the Tenant and to the extent that this notice is required to be served by any one or more of such companies in addition to or in substitution for the Tenant, you should consider this notice served for and on behalf of such company or companies.

Please sign and date the endorsement on the accompanying copy of this notice and return to us by way of receipt.

The landlord attacked the notice on two grounds (para 9):

The first was the reference in the heading to Units 3 and 4 only, which were defined for the purposes of the notice as 'the Premises', thereby creating confusion by attributing a new meaning to a defined term. The second error, to be found in the first paragraph of the letter, lay in defining 'the Lease' by reference to the original lease only, as opposed to the original lease as varied by the minute of variation. The cumulative effect of those errors was that the notice given by the pursuer in the second paragraph of the letter applied to the Lease (as re-defined, for the purpose only of the notice, to mean the original lease) over the Premises (as re-defined, for the purposes only of the notice, to mean only Units 3 and 4). As there was no provision in the Lease for exercise of the break clause in respect of part only of the subjects let, the notice purported to do something that the pursuer was not entitled to do, and was therefore invalid.

The Lord Ordinary (Lord Tyre) took the view – surely correctly – that the second objection was without merit. The alleged error simply did not exist. The first objection, concerning the heading, required more careful consideration, because here there was clearly an error. Following the approach established in the leading case of *Mannai Investment Co Ltd v Eagle Star Life Assurance Co Ltd* [1997] AC 749, the Lord Ordinary rejected the landlord's argument (para 16):

> I am satisfied that the reasonable recipient would not have been perplexed in any way by the error in the letter heading. The operative element of the notice is sufficiently clear and unambiguous to avoid any such perplexity, and the fact that the ingenuity of lawyers can suggest theoretical ambiguities is not to the point.

The landlord appealed to the Inner House. In rejecting the appeal, Lady Smith reinforced the approach taken by the Lord Ordinary (para 16):

> As was observed by senior counsel at the close of his submissions, the point is a short, sharp one and is capable of determination by what might be termed a matter of first impressions. To flesh that out a little, that is not to adopt a casual approach but it is a matter of assessing what would have been the impression immediately made on the reasonable recipient who would have been informed by knowledge of the relevant context 1. That recipient would, in this case, have been the reasonable commercial landlord who would, before opening the notice, have known:
>
> - that, by 11 January 2016, the date for the expiry of the lease entered into in 2004 was long since past and by that time, parties' contractual rights and obligations were contained in the whole terms of the 2004 and 2011 documents read together (the original lease read together with the Minute of Variation);
> - that Tyco were tenants of units 1, 3 and 4 under contractual terms which were unitary in relation to those premises;
> - that Tyco had never had any right to terminate their tenancy in relation to individual units;
> - that clause 4.2 of the Minute of Variation provided only for termination of Tyco's whole tenancy;
> - that, to exercise the clause 4.2 right, Tyco required to provide written notice at least six months prior to 31 August 2016 but the notice did not need to be in any particular form;

- if Tyco were going to exercise the break option, it would be sensible to service the clause 4.2 notice well in advance of the end of February 2016 – notice in the course of January 2016 would not be at all surprising; and
- that if Tyco were, after 31 August 2016, to be tenants of unit 1 only, parties would require to enter into a new agreement as the terms of their existing agreement were not divisible and made no allowance for partial severance of the tenancy.

Against that background, what would the reasonable landlord have understood as being the meaning of the letter received? We accept that (s)he would, no doubt, observe that the heading of the letter – not the notice itself (which is contained in paragraph 2 of the letter) – refers to only two of the leased units. But on proceeding to read the whole letter, it would be clear that the heading was simply incomplete; what the tenant plainly intended was to intimate that the right to terminate conferred in clause 4.2 was being exercised. That was, for the purpose of the landlord/tenant relationship, the operative part of the letter. It was not as if any part of the letter sought to open negotiation for the termination of Tyco's tenancy of only two units and retention of a tenancy of unit 1. We can accept that (s)he might have paused in respect of the definition of 'the Lease' in paragraph one. However, that pause would, we consider, have been a brief one. We agree with the Lord Ordinary that, on reading the letter as a whole, there would have been no real doubt. It was simply too improbable that Tyco were serving notice under a lease which had expired, particularly given the specific reference to the then current break option clause in paragraph 4.2 of the Minute of Variation. Regent's approach in submissions focusses unduly on the words and involves a failure to stand back and consider what the words mean when considered in the overall context in which they were used. The meaning of what is said can be unambiguous despite the use of the wrong words (*Mannai Investment Co Ltd*, Lord Hoffmann at p 774D); this is, we consider, such a case.

(44) Balgray Ltd v Hodgson
[2016] CSIH 55, 2016 SLT 839

Like the previous case, this was a dispute as to the validity of a notice served by a tenant on a landlord. The tenancy was an agricultural one and it took the form, then common, of a lease to a limited partnership, of which the farmer was the general partner and the landlord the limited partner. Under this arrangement the provisions of the agricultural holdings legislation could be circumvented, because the landlord could simply dissolve the tenant (the partnership) and thus bring the tenancy to an end. The position was, however, changed by s 72 of the Agricultural Holdings (Scotland) Act 2003, which enables the general partner (ie the farmer) to serve a notice on the landlord, the effect of which is to transfer the tenancy to the farmer himself.

Mr Hodgson tenanted two farms, Blindhillbush and Ravenscleugh, in Dumfriesshire. The landlord of the latter was Mr Paterson, while the landlord of the former was not Mr Paterson personally but a Paterson family company (Balgray Ltd), of which Mr Paterson was director and secretary. Mr Hodgson's solicitors served two s 72 notices, one for each farm. They were in the same general terms. Both of them were addressed to Mr Paterson. There was no dispute as to the validity of the Ravenscleugh notice. But as to the Blindhillbush notice, Balgray Ltd raised an action for declarator that the notice was invalid, in that it had not been validly served on the landlord.

At first instance the Land Court found in favour of the farmer. 'Mr Jardine Paterson had admitted that he was not in any doubt as to what the notice was intended to mean nor, objectively assessed, could anyone in his position have been' (para 17). The pursuer appealed, and the Inner House has reversed the decision of the Land Court. Following *Ben Cleuch Estates Ltd v Scottish Enterprise* [2008] CSIH 1, 2008 SC 252 (*Conveyancing 2007* Case (47)) it **held** that a notice addressed to the wrong person is not a valid notice.

(45) Dolby Medical Home Respiratory Care Ltd v Mortara Dolby UK Ltd [2016] CSOH 74, 2016 GWD 19-344

A ten-year lease of Monitor House, Kerse Road, Stirling was entered into in 2007. The tenant granted to Mortara Dolby UK Ltd a 'license' to occupy, and trade from, part of the property.

The lease had a break option which the pursuer exercised in 2012, thereby bringing the lease to an end, and also, consequentially, the licence. There was then a dispute about dilapidations between the tenant and the landlord, the latter claiming £641,171.37. The dispute was eventually settled at a figure of £275,000. The tenant raised the present action to recover part of this sum from the defender, on the basis of the terms of the licence agreement, which provided (clause 8) that the licensee (ie the defender) was bound to meet 75% of 'the cost of maintaining and repairing the common parts'.

The defender denied liability on the basis that the 'obligations under the licence only applied during its currency, not at termination. As it had maintained the premises while in occupation, it had discharged its duties' (para 12). The Lord Ordinary (Lord Woolman) rejected that defence (para 14):

> In my view it [clause 8 of the licence agreement] clearly contemplates that Mortara has a dilapidations' liability. If the parties had intended to draw a distinction between currency and termination, I would have expected that to be clearly expressed. I therefore hold that Mortara's share amounted to 75 per cent of the cost of maintaining and repairing the common parts.

The defender also argued that the pursuer's averments about quantum were irrelevantly pled: as to this the Lord Ordinary held that these 'issues are properly dealt with after evidence has been led' (para 24).

(46) Trustees of the Tonsley 2 Trust v Scottish Enterprise [2016] CSOH 138, 2016 GWD 31-554

This case concerned the lease of a unit at Euromed Business Park, Strathclyde Business Park, Bellshill, Lanarkshire, which ran from 1994 to 2013. The tenant, the defender in the action, had admittedly failed to comply with its upkeep obligations, and in this action, raised after the ish, the landlords sought payment in respect of dilapidations. Central to the case was the snappily-worded, Vigorously Capitalised, clause 3.38.2:

> At the expiration or sooner determination of the Period of this Lease without any warning away or process of removal to that effect to remove from and leave void and redd the Premises in such good and substantial repair and condition as shall be in accordance with the obligations on the part of the Tenant contained in These Presents together with all fixtures and fittings (excepting Tenant's fixtures and fittings) and improvements and additions which now are or may at any time hereafter be in or about the Premises save such as the Tenant has been required to remove pursuant to Clause 3.38.1.3; Provided always that (a) if at such expiration or sooner determination the Premises shall not be in such good and substantial repair and condition then at the option of the Landlord either (i) the Tenant shall carry out at its entire cost the works necessary to put the Premises into such repair and condition or (ii) the Tenant shall pay to the Landlord the sum certified by the Landlord as being equal to the cost of carrying out such work and if the Tenant shall pay to the Landlord the sum as certified together with any surveyor's fees incurred by the Landlord in connection with such Certificate within fourteen days of demand the Landlord shall accept the same in full satisfaction of the Tenant's liability under this sub-clause *quoad* the work referred to in this proviso and (b) if the Landlord elects to require the Tenant to carry out the works foresaid and the Tenant defaults in doing so the Landlord shall be entitled to carry out such works at the entire cost of the Tenant and whether such works are carried out by the Tenant or in default by the Tenant as aforesaid, by the Landlord there shall in addition be paid to the Landlord by the Tenant a sum equivalent to the rent which the Landlord would have received had These Presents subsisted until the date that all such necessary works had been completed to the satisfaction of the Landlord such sum to be paid on a date being seven days from the date of the Landlord informing the Tenant that all such works have been so completed.

There were two defences. The first was that the lease provided for the service of a certificate about dilapidations, and the defender argued that what had been served did not amount to certification. The Lord Ordinary (Lord Doherty) commented (para 26) that:

> What constitutes 'certifying' or a 'certificate' is dependent upon the commercial or legal context in which the certification clause appears ... Generally, unless the contract provides otherwise, a certificate need not be in any particular form ... Nor is it necessarily a prerequisite of a certificate that it be final and conclusive.

The second argument by the defender was that the landlord had not, since the ish, restored the property and was not intending to do so, and so there was nothing for the landlord to recover. Following the decision of the Inner House in @*Sipp (Pension Trustees) Ltd v Insight Travel Services Ltd* [2015] CSIH 91, 2016 SLT 131 (*Conveyancing 2015* Case (52)), this defence was dismissed.

(47) Van Lynden v Gilchrist
[2016] CSIH 72, 2016 SLT 1187

At issue was a holiday chalet, one of a number built on the Ballimore Estate, Otter Ferry, Argyll. The Estate lies on the western side of the Cowal Peninsula and on the eastern side of Loch Fyne. The chalet was 10 metres × 8 metres in extent, and was connected to services such as electricity, water and sewerage.

The legal background was as follows. In 1969 the then estate owner granted a 31-year lease to a company. Among its terms was an obligation to build a number of holiday chalets. These were then to be sublet. Clause 9 provided, so far as relevant, that:

> All buildings and works erected by the Tenants on the land shall be removed at the termination of this lease and the subjects of lease will be returned to the Proprietor in the condition in which they were received.

The present dispute involved the sublease of chalet number 25, which was granted in 1970. This was to expire, with the head lease, on 1 March 2000. In terms of the sublease, the subtenant was to erect a chalet – referred to as a 'bungalow' – within a year. At the end of the sublease, he was then to have a range of options as to the chalet, which were set out in clause 15:

> On any termination of this sub-let otherwise than by the Sub-Tenant as aforesaid the Sub-Tenant shall be bound within one month from said termination to exercise one of the following three alternative options namely: — (Primo) to remove the said bungalow at his own expense, (Secundo) to call on the Company to purchase the said bungalow at a price of Three thousand five hundred pounds in which case the Company hereby binds and obliges itself so to purchase the said bungalow and to pay the price within one month or (Tertio) to call on the Company to act as his agent for the sale of the bungalow in which case the Company shall make reasonable endeavour to sell the said bungalow at the market price thereof to a purchaser acceptable as Sub-Tenant hereunder but the Sub-Tenant shall be bound to accept the terms of any such sale negotiated by the Company, and the Company shall be entitled to receive from the purchaser the price of the said bungalow and deduct therefrom a commission of eight per cent of the price thereafter within fourteen days accounting to the Sub-Tenant for the balance less any sums due hereunder by the Sub-Tenant.

The years passed and, when the subtenant died, the sublease was assigned to his son, Colin Gilchrist. Meanwhile the head lease also changed hands, coming ultimately to be held by Baron and Baroness van Lynden as trustees for the firm of Ballimore Farms. Finally, ownership of the estate also changed, the new owner being Baroness van Lynden.

On 1 March 2000 both the head lease and sublease came to an end, and a dispute arose as to the fate of the chalet. Mr Gilchrist wished to exercise his option under clause 15 of the sublease to remove the chalet – something which could, it seems, be done in sections and without the need for complete demolition. Baroness van Lynden resisted this claim, arguing that the chalet had acceded to the land and hence was her property. She raised an action against Mr Gilchrist in which she sought declarator that she was the chalet's owner, and interdict against dismantling or removing it.

At first instance, the action failed and the defender was assoilzied: see [2015] CSOH 147, 2015 SLT 864, *Conveyancing 2015* Case (65). According to the Lord Ordinary (Lord Philip), clause 15 conferred on the defender an option to remove the chalet which he was entitled to exercise. Insofar as the pursuer had property rights in the chalet, the terms of the head lease and sublease were such that she (and her predecessors) must be taken to have given them up.

In commenting on the Lord Ordinary's decision, we set out a number of grounds on which it appeared to be open to challenge: see *Conveyancing 2015* pp 163–66. The decision was appealed, and the arguments before the First Division were rather different, and much narrower, than those which had been made before the Lord Ordinary.

The main point of dispute was a simple one. It was accepted by both sides that the chalet had acceded to the land and so was the property of the pursuer, as owner of the land. It was also accepted that it was open to the parties to confer a right of severance, or in other words a right to remove the chalet, at least if this was done expressly. The defender's case was that such a right had been conferred by clause 15 of the sublease. The pursuer's case (echoing a point made in our earlier commentary) was that clause 15 imposed obligations on the subtenant but did not confer rights. The defender was bound to remove the chalet (or perform one of the alternative duties); but he was not *entitled* to do so. If the obligation was enforceable by the pursuer, it could also be waived by the pursuer. That was what had happened in the present case.

The pursuer's argument attracted support in the First Division. Nonetheless, on the crucial issue of interdict against removal of the chalet, the court found for the defender. Was, Lord Brodie asked, the removal of the chalet a wrong which the pursuer was entitled to interdict? He concluded that it was not (para 33):

> The matter falls to be tested as at 29 February 2000 immediately before the termination of the head lease and the sublease when the reclaimer obtained the interim interdict which she now seeks to be made perpetual. As at that date the respondent may be taken to have intimated his exercise of the option which he was bound to exercise in terms of cl fifteenth of the sublease by removing the bungalow at his own expense. At least in a question with the mid-landlord (then Ballimore Farms) how could that be said to be a wrong? Rather it was the fulfilling of an obligation owed to Ballimore Farms as the respondent's landlord. Equally, how could the removal of chalet 25 as one of the 'buildings and works' erected in terms of cl ninth of the head lease be regarded as a wrong, whether in a question between Ballimore Farms as head tenant and the reclaimer as proprietor and head landlord, or as between the respondent as Ballimore Farms' subtenant and the reclaimer as proprietor, when that is exactly what cl ninth provided for (admittedly together with the removal of other buildings and works which I have assumed were also erected albeit there was no evidence about that)? It is true, as was mentioned in the course of discussion, that an obligation, at least if conceived exclusively in favour of one party to a contract, may be waived by that party, but in the present case there was no suggestion that any obligation had been waived. Counsel for the reclaimer's submissions on cl ninth of the head lease and cl fifteenth of the sublease proceeded upon the basis that the obligations they imposed were extant.

The point, however, was evidently a narrow one, and Lady Clark dissented, emphasising that clause 15 imposed obligations on the defender rather than conferring rights, and pointing to the difficulty of reconciling clause 15 with the obligations undertaken by the head landlord in clause 9 of the principal lease.

(48) Cooper v Marriott
2016 SLT (Sh Ct) 99

The tenant paid a deposit of £550 in respect of a tenancy of a flat at Albion Place, Edinburgh. The landlord did not pay this into an approved scheme in terms of the Tenancy Deposit Schemes (Scotland) Regulations 2011, SSI 2011/176. After the tenant had moved out, in 2015, he claimed an award against the landlord, which, under the Regulations, can be up to three times the amount of the deposit. The landlord pled, in the words of the sheriff (Tom Welsh QC) (para 1):

> (i)   The tenancy was not protected by the 2011 Regulations at all in this case, because the property was not 'the principal home' of the tenant during the duration of the lease, in terms of s 12(1)(b) of the Housing (Scotland) Act 1988.
>
> (ii) Further, even if the tenancy was protected by the Regulations the present application is time barred in terms of regulation 9(2) because a new tenancy was created in June 2014 in respect of which no deposit was made.
>
> (iii) Further, even if the application is not time barred and is competently before the court, the sanction provision in the regulations is unenforceable, at the instance of the tenant, by reason of his own dishonesty and illegality.

As to the first, the tenant asserted that the flat was indeed his principal home, but the issue of fact did not have to be determined because the sheriff considered the landlord's defence to be irrelevant in law (para 8):

> I am not persuaded s 12 of the Housing (Scotland) Act 1988 is relevant to this case, as it deals with 'assured tenancies'. I am dealing here with 'a short assured tenancy' which is regulated by s 32 of the 1988 Act. I do not consider the question of the tenant's 'principal home' to have any bearing on the case. Accordingly, I consider the 2011 Regulations apply to the tenancy and that it is a relevant tenancy within the meaning of reg 3(3).

As to the second, the sheriff said (para 8):

> I consider that the applicant's tenancy was continued after 14 June 2014 on the principle of tacit relocation. After that date the parties to the contract were the same. The property was the same. The only change was that the landlord abated the rent by £50 because of a problem with the water supply. I have no reason to think this was anything other than an extension of the original lease.

As to the third, the landlord alleged that the tenant had, when in the property, been engaged in dishonesty in relation to council tax and in relation to social security, and so was barred by the principle of *ex turpi causa non oritur actio*. For this the landlord's authority was a consultation paper issued by the Law Commission for England and Wales. The sheriff commented, at para 8, that the consultation paper 'has no application to Scots Law'. It may be added that, whereas the tenant had been able to obtain professional legal representation, the landlord had only lay representation, by his 'partner', a term presumably not being used in its commercial sense. The sheriff held that the allegations of dishonesty had not been substantiated, but that even if they had been they had no bearing on the relationship between the tenant and his landlord.

The landlord's representative added (para 7) that if there was, contrary to her submissions, liability, 'the landlord had been a good and honest landlord who did not understand the Regulations. He was "an amateur landlord". The flat was his only investment and he was not a professional landlord. Any sanction should be at the lower end of the scale.' The sheriff noted (para 11) that 'the Regulations do not recognise the status of "amateur landlord". Landlords who rent to the public are covered by the Regulations whether they are large commercial concerns or single property, buy to let landlords.' That is certainly true, but it may be remarked that the effect is arguably that the 2011 Regulations, like so much public regulation, in practice bear on a business more heavily the smaller it is.

The sheriff awarded to the tenant a sum equal to double the deposit (minus £50 for certain damage to the furnishings). This award was, of course, in addition to the requirement to return the deposit itself.

(49) Russell-Smith v Uchegbu
[2016] SC EDIN 64, 2016 GWD 31-553

Four students took a tenancy of a flat in Drummond Street, Edinburgh, the term being from 1 September 2015 to 31 July 2016. They paid a deposit of £1,550. The owner, the defender in this action, failed to pay this sum into an approved deposit scheme, contrary to the requirements of the Tenancy Deposit Schemes (Scotland) Regulations 2011, SSI 2011/176. Eventually she did so, but only after the present action had been raised. The defender admitted liability, so the case was about quantum. The sheriff (Tom Welsh QC) made an award of £1,853, consisting of two elements (para 9):

> Firstly, the lease lasted 334 days, for 270 days of which, the deposit was unprotected and the tenants deprived of protection from the scheme and the proper information. In my judgment, to mark the fact that the defender breached the regulations for a sustained period of time which subjected the tenants and the deposit to a risk the Regulations are designed to avoid, the proportionate and appropriate starting point for sanction in these circumstances is £1550 divided by 334 multiplied by 270. This produces a figure of £1253. Secondly, to that sum I will add a weighting to reflect the fact that the landlady was repeatedly officially informed of her obligations and still failed to comply … I will set the financial penalty to reflect this second factor at £600.

We rather think that the first element is a new approach not seen in previous cases.

A novel feature of this case was that there were four joint tenants but only three of them raised the action. This led to a legal issue that the legislation does not cover and had not been considered in earlier case law. The defender argued that any award should accordingly be reduced by one quarter. The sheriff rejected that approach, and held that there should be no reduction, but that the three students who received the sum of £1,853 would be liable to the fourth student to pay him one quarter of it.

(50) Procurator Fiscal v Colvin Houston Ltd
4 July 2016, Kilmarnock Sheriff Court

The Tenancy Deposit Schemes (Scotland) Regulations 2011, SSI 2011/176, are enforceable by a civil action by the tenant against the landlord. The present case is noteworthy, and indeed perhaps surprising, because (i) the action was not against the landlord, but against an agent, and (ii) the action was not civil but criminal.

The defender had failed to pay deposits into an approved scheme. The prosecution, requested by the trading standards department of North Ayrshire Council, was under the Consumer Protection from Unfair Trading Regulations 2008, SI 2008/1277. The case has not been reported, so we have few details, but it appears that the prosecution argument was that the failure was an 'unfair commercial practice' in that it 'contravene[d] the requirements of professional diligence' (reg 3(3)), that latter phrase being defined (reg 2(1)) as 'the standard of special skill and care which a trader may reasonably be expected to exercise towards consumers which is commensurate with either (a) honest market practice in the trader's field of activity, or (b) the general principle of good faith in the trader's field of activity'.

The defender pled guilty, and a fine of £500 was imposed. Because of the guilty plea, the question of whether the 2008 Regulations can indeed be made use of in this context was not properly tested, and accordingly the assertions in various media sources that the case creates a 'precedent' are somewhat overstated. The case is innovative partly in that it invokes the criminal law and partly in that it targets the agent rather than the landlord. As to the latter, there exists a precedent of sorts in an English case, *Draycott v Hannells Letting Ltd* [2011] 1 WLR 1606, albeit that the circumstances there were not quite the same.

Information about the prosecution can be found in such sources as www. scottishlegal.com/2016/07/04/north-ayrshire-council-trigger-landmark-landlord-case/ and www.landlords.org.uk/news-campaigns/news/tenancy-deposit-schemes-could-landmark-case-lead-more-prosecutions.

STANDARD SECURITIES

(51) 3D Garages Ltd v Prolatis Co Ltd
[2016] SC EDIN 70, 2017 SLT (Sh Ct) 9

As part of a settlement of a commercial dispute, the pursuer granted to the defender standard securities over five properties. All were in security of sums due by the pursuer, not to the defender, but to David Gill. In other words, the creditor was not the same person as the holder of the securities. The pursuer raised the present action to have it declared that the standard securities were, for this reason, invalid and unenforceable. The action failed. See **Commentary** p 145.

(52) Outlook Finance Ltd v Lindsay's Exr
[2016] SC LAN 58, 2016 Hous LR 75

In an action to enforce a standard security, there were two defences. One was that the standard security contained an error in the description of the property, an error that had been carried forward to the calling-up notice. The other defence was that the creditor had failed to comply with the 'pre-action requirements' (Conveyancing and Feudal Reform (Scotland) Act 1970 s 24A) in that the basis for the calculation of the amount due was opaque. The first defence was dismissed, but the second defence was upheld. See **Commentary** p 192.

[Another aspect of this case is digested at (69) below.]

(53) McLeod v Prestige Finance Ltd
[2016] CSOH 69, 2016 Hous LR 43 affd [2016] CSIH 87, 2016 GWD 39-690

A heritable creditor raised an action to enforce a standard security. The defender, a party litigant, put forward dubious defences, and, after he walked out of the hearing, decree passed against him. He then raised this action to reduce the decree. He lost in the Outer House, and reclaimed. He lost again. See **Commentary** p 197.

(54) Landmark Mortgages Ltd v Stirling
[2016] CSIH 89, 2016 GWD 39-697

The pursuer held a standard security over the defender's property and in 2014 served a calling-up notice, later raising an action to enforce the security. The action was defended. The sheriff held in favour of the pursuer. The defender appealed to the sheriff principal, who refused the appeal. The defender appealed to the Inner House, which has once again refused the appeal.

The defender, who was a party litigant, lodged a remarkable 32 grounds of appeal. One was that the calling-up notice had not been validly served. This ground failed. The case has some useful discussion on the way calling-up notices can validly be served.

Another concerned an error in the description of the property. In the standard security the property's postal address, 233 Talla Road, Glasgow, had been mis-typed as 223 Talla Road, Glasgow. The property was in the Land Register and it seems that the standard security had included the correct title number. How serious an error this was did not come before the court for decision, since the creditor had, as part of the enforcement action, sought rectification (ie a change from '223' to '233') under s 8 of the Law Reform (Miscellaneous Provisions) (Scotland) Act 1985, and the sheriff had granted the crave. Unsurprisingly the defender argued, but without success, that the sheriff should not have done so.

The grounds of appeal were generally weak and the court had no difficulty in rejecting all 32 of them. One was based on the Law of Property (Miscellaneous Provisions) Act 1989, which does not apply in Scotland.

The dispute had been running for a long time. The lender had first served a calling-up notice in 2011, and had then launched an enforcement action, which, as in the present case, had worked its way up from the sheriff, then to the sheriff principal, and then to the Inner House, where, in 2013, the lender had abandoned the action (because it accepted that it had failed to comply with the correct enforcement procedures), thus going back down the slithery snake to the bottom of the board, beginning again in 2014, as above. Whether the game is now over remains to be seen, for the defender informed the Inner House (see para 55) that she now says that she never signed the standard security, and that accordingly she intends to raise an action of reduction.

(55) GE Money Secured Loans Ltd v MacBride
[2016] SC HAM 62, 2016 GWD 31-548

The pursuer raised an action to enforce a standard security, and in April 2010 obtained decree. Seemingly, nothing was done to enforce the decree until 2014, when a charge for ejection was served. (Whether a decree to enforce a standard security should, as a matter of sound legal policy, be allowed to hang over a debtor's head indefinitely might be open to debate.) The debtors responded with the assertion that the original action had never been properly served on them, and sought to open up the decree. In addition, they argued that even if the decree had been validly obtained, no attempt should have been made to enforce it, since the route that the creditor had taken to obtain the decree had been the one which was later held invalid by the Supreme Court in *Royal Bank of Scotland plc v Wilson* [2010] UKSC 50, 2011 SC (UKSC) 66 (*Conveyancing 2010* pp 129–49), which had been decided in November 2010. The attempt at enforcement in 2014 meant, pled the debtors, that they were entitled to damages against the creditor, and they claimed the sum of £50,000. (The Opinion issued at this stage of the case does not reveal how the figure of £50,000 was arrived at.) If the view is taken that the decision of the Supreme Court did not invalidate decrees already granted (assuming them to have been in other respects in order), and such is our view, it is not easy to see that the damages claim could have had a sound basis in *Wilson*. However, the claim was not dismissed, and it appears that a proof is to be held.

(56) Promontoria (Chestnut) Ltd v Ballantyne Property Services
[2016] SC EDIN 74, 2016 GWD 35-633

Clydesdale Bank plc made loans to a property firm, Ballantyne Property Services, the loans being secured over six properties owned by the firm. The transactions took place from 2008 to 2011. It appears that the loans were all due to mature in 2015. In 2014 the bank assigned the loans and the securities to Promontoria (Chestnut) Ltd. In 2015 Promontoria (Chestnut) Ltd requested payment, the total being £1,803,954.84. The property firm did not pay, and shortly thereafter proceedings began to enforce the standard securities, the defenders being the firm plus its two partners.

The defence was that an employee of Clydesdale Bank plc had, in 2007, promised that when the loans matured they would be renewed. Specifically, the defenders pled (see para 10 of the judgment) that:

> Mr Heslop told the Third Defender that the clause would not be enforced at the end of the 5 year term. Mr Heslop stated to the Third Defender that the facility would be renewed at the end of the 5 year term. Mr Heslop said additionally, 'Imagine the public outcry if Clydesdale Bank ever pulled in its business loans, it will never happen'. On a proper construction of those statements by Mr Heslop the Bank thereby made a legally binding promise to the Defenders to extend the facility at the end of the 5 year term.

The sheriff (Tom Welsh QC) dismissed the defence as irrelevantly pled, so that the question of what had or had not been said in 2007 was never actually the subject of evidential determination (para 13):

> I considered that the averments made by the defenders, quoted above, singularly failed to state the relevant words of the promisor which either, clearly and unambiguously demonstrated the Bank's intention to be legally bound to extend the loan facilities beyond 5 years and not to enforce the standard securities or, alternatively, amount to words which are capable, on a reasonable construction, by a reasonable recipient, of bearing the meaning contended for. ... [T]he words pled do not indicate a clear and unambiguous intention on the part of the Bank to extend the specific loan facilities beyond 5 years and not to enforce its 6 securities ... The words, even if proved, could never in my opinion, amount to a clear and unambiguous legally binding promise, on behalf of the Bank, to extend the specific loan facilities in question beyond 5 years and not to enforce the 6 specific standard securities in this case, in the event of default.

Whether this is a sound approach to the law of promise, or whether it places the hurdle too high, will not be discussed here. Nor will we discuss whether a statement by an individual employed by one company, Clydesdale Bank plc, could bind a separate company, Promontoria (Chestnut) Ltd; this issue seemingly was not raised in the case.

(57) @Sipp (Pension Trustees) Ltd v Campbell
21 December 2016, Kilmarnock Sheriff Court

A standard security was granted to the pursuer in its capacity as trustee of a certain trust. The pursuer raised the present action to enforce the security. The defence was no title to sue, in that the pursuer was raising the action as trustee of a different trust. In substance the beneficial interests seem to have been essentially the same, but there had been a reorganisation that meant that the identity of the trust was no longer the same as it had been at the time that the standard security had been granted. The defender argued that 'a company which is trustee of trust A has a separate legal personality from the same company as trustee of trust B' (p 7 of the judgment of Sheriff David W Hall.) Accordingly, argued the defender, title to sue would have required an assignation of the standard security from

@Sipp (Pension Trustees) Ltd (in its original trust capacity) in favour of itself (in its current trust capacity). The pursuer denied that a trust involves separate legal personality. @Sipp (Pension Trustees) Ltd was the pursuer and @Sipp (Pension Trustees) Ltd was the holder of the standard security. Everything was therefore in order. The sheriff agreed with the pursuer's argument.

(58) Peters v Belhaven Finance Ltd
2016 SLT (Sh Ct) 156, 2016 Hous LR 35

A secured creditor enforcing by sale has no economic interest in selling at any figure higher than the amount needed to clear off the secured debt (including interest and expenses). For this reason the law imposes a duty to obtain a fair price. In the present action the pursuers sought damages for breach of this duty. In addition to its interesting facts, the case sheds some light on the wording of the provisions of the Conveyancing and Feudal Reform (Scotland) Act 1970. See **Commentary** p 189.

(59) Chiswell v Chiswell
[2016] CSOH 45, 2016 GWD 10-186

Mr and Mrs Chiswell owned a house. A security over it was granted to Northern Rock Asset Management. In 2010 Mr Chiswell was sequestrated. In the following year the marriage broke down. Mrs Chiswell left, Mr Chiswell remaining in the house together with the children of the marriage. The heritable creditor obtained decree authorising it to sell the property. In 2013 Mr Chiswell raised the present action, the core of it being that his signature on the standard security had been forged and that accordingly the security should be reduced. 'The background', said the Lord Ordinary (Lady Wolffe) at para 6, 'is that the pursuer left the arrangements of the couple's financial affairs to his wife and that a number of her business ventures had been loss-making'. From this, it might be supposed that the wife had become insolvent and brought her husband down with her, but in fact it rather seems that only he, not she, was sequestrated.

The pursuer concluded for the reduction of the standard security. Oddly, the conclusion was for reduction in toto, rather than merely reduction in respect of the pursuer's half-share of the property. The Lord Ordinary noted (para 38):

> There was no suggestion that there was anything wrong with Mrs Chigwell's signature. There is no basis for reduction of the standard security *quoad* the first defender's own one-half *pro indiviso* share of the Subjects. Her grant is not said to be vitiated by any forgery. Accordingly, only partial reduction of the standard security would be appropriate; that is, only *quoad* the pursuer's one-half share. Counsel for the pursuer accepted during the course of the case that this was an error and that the conclusion for reduction would be restricted to the pursuer's half share.

The trustee in sequestration was not involved in the action and had not consented to its being raised. Although by this time the pursuer had been discharged from his sequestration, it must be borne in mind that the discharge of a bankrupt does not itself affect the property that fell under the sequestration: such property remains subject to the disposal of the trustee, for the benefit of the creditors, notwithstanding the debtor's discharge.

The core of the defence was lack of title to sue: even if the action had any merit in fact, the proper pursuer would be the trustee, not Mr Chiswell. Even if Mr Chiswell were to succeed in the reduction, what would be the effect? His half-share would be disencumbered, it is true, but what help to him would that have been? Because of his sequestration his share of the house was a lost cause anyway. To this undoubtedly forceful line of argument the pursuer replied, in the words of the Lord Ordinary (para 22):

> The pursuer currently occupies the Subjects with his three children. But for the standard security ... there could be no removal of the pursuer except by the trustee. The trustee in sequestration has taken no steps to remove the pursuer or his children from the family home. It is a family home for the purposes of s 40 of the 1985 Act. [Bankruptcy (Scotland) Act 1985 s 40, since replaced by Bankruptcy (Scotland) Act 2016 s 113.] An action on behalf of the trustee in sequestration and a court decree would be required in order to remove the pursuer and his family from the Subjects. In the event that the orders sought by the pursuer were not granted, the pursuer and his family would be removed from their family home as a result of a forged standard security about which they had no knowledge until November 2011. In any event, removal from their family home is not otherwise guaranteed. In the event that the pursuer succeeds in this action, he intends to negotiate the purchase of any interest that the trustee has in the Subjects. The sheriff court decree and standard security are preventing him from doing so.

So the pursuer did have some sort of interest. But was it enough? The Lord Ordinary adopted the approach taken by Lord McCluskey in *Dickson v United Dominions Trust Ltd* 1988 SLT 19 at 22: 'the bankrupt cannot be allowed to litigate in such a way that he competes with the creditors, or the trustee as representing them, for any part of the assets sequestrated; and accordingly where such a competition exists or may exist the bankrupt will have no title to sue'. In the present case there was no 'competition' between the pursuer on the one hand and the trustee, and general creditors, on the other hand. Indeed, success in this action would benefit the general creditors. Accordingly the plea of 'no title to sue' was dismissed.

We confess that when we first considered this case we thought that the 'no title to sue' plea was good, but the Lord Ordinary's argument – which contains an extensive review of the authorities – seems correct.

We end with two thoughts. Sometimes in sequestration the trustee, though unwilling to embark on speculative action himself, will consent to the bankrupt's doing so. Such consent risks nothing and occasionally gains something. Why that had not happened in this case we do not know. The other thought concerns the state of the title. A trustee in sequestration can, and sometimes does, complete title in his own name. Nothing is said in the case as to whether that had happened. If it had happened, it would have furnished another possible basis for the 'no title to sue' plea.

(60) Alexander v West Bromwich Mortgage Co Ltd
[2016] EWCA Civ 496, [2017] 1 All ER 942

In this English case, Mr Alexander borrowed money from the defendant, secured by a mortgage. The loan offer said that the loan term was 25 years, and the interest rate would be 1.99 percentage points over Bank of England base rate. Despite this the lender upped the interest rate to 3.99 percentage points over Bank of England base rate and asserted the right to demand repayment in full at any time on one month's notice. Mr Alexander raised an action for declaration (ie declarator) of the terms of the loan. At first instance, he lost: [2015] EWHC 135 (Comm), [2015] 2 All ER (Comm) 224 (*Conveyancing 2015* Case (71)). He appealed, and the Court of Appeal has now found in his favour. See **Commentary** p 149.

SEXUAL PROPERTY

(61) Courtney's Exrs v Campbell
[2016] CSOH 136, 2016 GWD 31-564

Mr Courtney and Ms Campbell entered into a relationship in 2009. In 2010 Ms Campbell bought a property in Glenrothes, and the couple lived there until the relationship came to an end in 2013. There was no marriage, nor was there an engagement to be married. Later Mr Courtney died, and his executors raised the present action against Ms Campbell, in which they sought payment of £150,000. It was said that this was the amount that the deceased had contributed, in part towards the purchase price and in part towards the improvement of the property. The argument was that she had been unjustifiably enriched by these payments, on the basis that the money had been expended on the assumption that the relationship would be a long-term one. Reliance was placed on such cases as *Shilliday v Smith* 1998 SC 725.

The action was dismissed on the ground that a claim in unjustified enrichment is normally available only where there is no other remedy, and that another remedy existed in the form of s 28 of the Family Law (Scotland) Act 2006, which allows for a claim to be made by one cohabitant against the other when the relationship comes to an end. A s 28 claim, however, has to be made within 12 months of the end of the relationship, and in this case that deadline had passed.

In fact there had already been a case on the same point, and with the same outcome: *Jenkins v Gillespie*, 8 September 2015, Alloa Sheriff Court (unreported). This was drawn to general attention in an article by Michael Hughes, 'The subsidiarity exclusion: cohabitation and unjustified enrichment' 2016 SLT (News) 7. The Lord Ordinary (Lord Beckett) said (para 47): 'I cannot reach any conclusion on the basis of the unreported case of *Jenkins v Gillespie*' but gave no reasons. One suspects that the earlier case may, however, have had some weight. For some discussion of *Courtney's Exrs v Campbell*, see Alison Edmondson, 'Timed out? Alternative financial claims by cohabitants' (2016) 61 *Journal of the Law Society of Scotland* Nov/17.

SOLICITORS

(62) NRAM plc v Steel
[2016] CSIH 11, 2016 SC 474, 2016 SLT 285

In this case a bank had standard securities over three properties owned by a company. When the company sold one of the properties, the bank discharged that security, being paid the bulk of the proceeds. At the same time it discharged the securities over the other two properties. Some years later, when the company went into insolvent liquidation, the bank claimed that the discharges of the latter two securities had been a mistake caused by the negligence of the debtor company's law firm, and it sued for damages. In the Outer House the action failed: [2014] CSOH 172, 2015 GWD 10-191 (*Conveyancing 2014* Case (63)). The pursuer reclaimed, and the Inner House has now, by a two-to-one majority, reversed the decision, ie has found in favour of the pursuer, awarding damages of £369,811.18, plus interest and expenses. The case is being appealed to the Supreme Court. See **Commentary** p 175.

(63) Gordon v Campbell Riddell Breeze Paterson LLP
[2016] CSIH 16, 2016 SC 548, 2016 SLT 580

The pursuers owned three fields in Killearn, Stirlingshire, all let to the same tenant. They instructed their solicitors to serve notices to quit. The three notices were served on 8 November 2004, to take effect on 10 November 2005. The tenant did not remove, and the pursuers raised an action, in the Land Court, for removing. The action failed. The reason was that the notices had been fatally defective. They had designed the tenant as 'the Firm of Messrs A & J C Craig and John C Craig, sole proprietor of and trustee for said Firm'. Although at one stage the field had indeed been let to the firm of Messrs A & J C Craig, that had been long ago, and the current tenant was John Campbell Craig as an individual. We pause to note that it is a familiar fact that there cannot be a partnership with only one partner, so the designation just quoted perhaps should have rung an alarm bell.

The owners sought damages from their law agents for professional negligence. The defence was negative prescription. The present action had been raised on 17 May 2012. The issue boiled down to whether the five-year period had begun to run in November 2008, when the Land Court had issued its ruling, in which case the present action had been raised timeously, or whether the period had begun to run in November 2004, when the invalid notices were served, or perhaps November 2005, in either of which cases the action had been raised too late. The Lord Ordinary (Lord Jones) held that any claim that the pursuers may have had had been extinguished by negative prescription: see [2015] CSOH 31, 2015 GWD 12-216, *Conveyancing 2015* Case (74). The pursuers reclaimed, but without success.

(64) Price v Scottish Legal Complaints Commission
[2016] CSIH 53, 2016 GWD 22-408

Mr and Mrs Price owned a property, 'Ewenburn', in Gwydyr Road, Crieff, Perthshire. Mr Price took the view that the property had, in relation to a part of a neighbouring property ('Ardlarich'), (i) a servitude right of pedestrian and vehicular access and (ii) a servitude of parking. He said that (i) had been constituted by deed, and that (ii) had been constituted by prescription. He (and perhaps Mrs Price, but she does not seem to make any appearance in the story) asked the neighbouring owner, a school, to grant a deed of servitude in respect of both access and parking. (If the access servitude had already been granted by deed, it is not clear why he wished it to be granted again.) This seems to have been prompted by the fact that the school was about to sell the property.

The school was willing to grant a deed for a servitude of access but not of parking. There was also lack of agreement as to who should pay for any deed to be granted, Mr Price taking the view, it seems, that all expenses should fall on the school. Discussions broke down and in the end no deed of any kind was granted. Mr Price lodged a complaint with the Scottish Legal Complaints Commission against the school's law firm, Messrs Miller Hendry. This was rejected as was a subsequent appeal to the Inner House. See **Commentary** p 184.

(65) Chief Land Registrar v Caffrey & Co
[2016] EWHC 161 (Ch), [2016] PNLR 23

Owners of a property in England forged a discharge of the mortgage over it, and their solicitors – the defendants – arranged for the discharge to be registered in the English Land Registry. The owners then borrowed money on mortgage from another lender. The first lender was paid indemnity by the Land Registry, and in the present action the Chief Land Registrar sought to recover that sum from the law firm that had acted for the fraudulent owners. In English law there is no equivalent to s 111 of the Land Registration etc (Scotland) Act 2012, but the court held that the law firm was liable at common law. See **Commentary** p 202.

[Another aspect of this case is digested at (29) above.]

(66) Purrunsing v A'Court & Co
[2016] EWHC 789 (Ch), [2016] 4 WLR 81

A fraudster impersonated the owner of a property in London, and sold it. The transaction completed. The buyer sought registration, but the Land Registry smelt a rat and rejected the application. Thus the true owner kept the property. Meanwhile the fraudster and the money had disappeared to the Middle East. The buyer, who had been swindled out of the purchase price, sued both (i) his own law firm and (ii) the law firm that had acted for the fraudster. It was held that both firms had been negligent and that both firms were jointly and severally liable to the buyer. See **Commentary** p 199.

(67) Rosbeg Partners Ltd v L K Shields (A Firm)
[2016] IECA 161, [2016] PNLR 30

We mention this Irish case as a horror story. The plaintiff bought property in Dublin in 1994. The purchase was completed. The transaction triggered first registration. The Irish Land Registry had certain minor title queries, and correspondence dragged on between the buyer's law firm and the Land Registry. In 2007 the plaintiff received an offer to buy the property at a price of €10 million. But the title was – 13 years after the original purchase – still unregistered. This fact derailed the sale because the buyer wished a rapid transaction and was not prepared to wait for the registration issues to be resolved. Shortly afterwards the Irish property market crashed. The owner sued its law firm for damages, on the basis that had the title been registered a sale at €10 million would have taken place before the market crashed.

The action was successful. The present value of the property was €1.5 million, and accordingly the law firm was liable to pay damages for the difference between €10 million and €1.5 million, ie €8.5 million. A further €1.5 million was awarded by way of interest, making the law firm liable for €10 million, plus costs.

JUDICIAL RECTIFICATION

(68) Nickson's Trs Ptrs
[2016] CSOH 119, 2016 SLT 1039

For the purposes of judicial rectification, s 8(1) of the Law Reform (Miscellaneous Provisions) (Scotland) Act 1985 distinguishes three types of document: (i) documents intended to 'express' an agreement (eg written contracts such as missives); (ii) documents intended to 'give effect' to an agreement (eg dispositions in implement of missives); and (iii) documents, not falling within either of the first two types, intended to create, transfer, vary or renounce a right. Documents of the first two types fall within para (a) of s 8(1); documents of type (iii) fall within para (b). The conditions for rectification under the two paragraphs are not the same.

At the margins it can be difficult to decide into which category a particular document falls. In *Nickson's Trs Ptrs* the document at issue was a deed of appointment executed by trustees with the purpose of bringing a discretionary *mortis causa* trust to an end. The Lord Ordinary (Lord Turnbull) classified this as a type (iii) document on the ground that it was 'a unilateral deed, not an agreement' (para 37). The conclusion is plausible, although the reasoning seems wrong, for many type (ii) deeds (such as dispositions) are also unilateral.

On Lord Turnbull's view, the rectification application was therefore governed by para (b) of s 8(1). This permits rectification where the court is satisfied that:

> (b) a document intended to create, transfer, vary or renounce a right, not being a document falling within paragraph (a) above, fails to express accurately the intention of the grantor of the document at the date when it was executed.

Was that test met in the present case? In what sense did the deed of appointment fail to express accurately the intentions of the trustees who had granted it?

The immediate purpose of the deed was to wind up a trust and appoint its capital to the husband of the testator. That purpose was achieved. But there was also a further purpose which was not achieved by the deed in its current form. That purpose was to transfer to the husband the testator's unused nil-rate band for IHT. It was not achieved because the trustees overlooked the need to wait three months from the testator's death before executing the deed. The purpose of the application for rectification was to insert into the deed of appointment a provision postponing its effect until the three-month period was over.

The previous decision closest to the present facts was *Bank of Ireland v Bass Brewers Ltd* 2000 GWD 20-786 and 2000 GWD 28-1077 (*Conveyancing 2000* pp 118–19). A company granted a standard security to the Bank of Ireland. There was a pre-existing floating charge with a negative pledge clause. The charge-holder granted a letter of consent in respect of the standard security. It was assumed, wrongly, that this would allow the standard security to rank before the floating charge. When this turned out not to be the case, the Bank sought to have the letter rectified so as to add a ranking provision. It is important to note the nature of the error for which rectification was being sought. This was not, as usually in rectification cases, an error in expression. It was, rather, an error in expectation. There had been no error as to the words, but as to the legal effect of the words. Rectification was nonetheless allowed by the Lord Ordinary (Lord Macfadyen).

Writing at the time of *Bank of Ireland* we speculated as to the future for this new departure (*Conveyancing 2000* p 119):

> It is not clear how far the principle goes. In *Bank of Ireland* it was at least debatable that the words used in the letter had the legal effect intended. The drafting might be classified as a narrow miss. The position may be different if the miss is less narrow. If a conveyancer uses words which no reasonable person would imagine could have the legal effect intended, a court might be reluctant to carry out the necessary corrective conveyancing. Section 8 confers a purely discretionary power, and it is not a power which the court is bound to exercise.

The miss in the present case was less narrow, and the court was not willing to rectify the deed in the manner requested by the petitioners (para 51):

> In the present case the trustees intended to create a right by executing the deed of appointment. They had no intention of delaying the creation of that right as they were unaware of any benefit in doing so. The deed of appointment expressed accurately the intention of the trustees at the date when it was executed, since their intention was to create a right to the trust fund absolutely in favour of Lord Nickson. The legal result of the deed being executed was that the trust funds were made available to him, exactly as the trustees had intended.

It was true that the trustees would now wish to have a provision inserted which would delay the start of the deed. But that was an 'associated or consequential legal right beyond that to be effected by the document' (para 48). It was not the primary purpose of the deed. There was no basis here for rectification.

(69) Outlook Finance Ltd v Lindsay's Exr
[2016] SC LAN 58, 2016 Hous LR 75

Heritable creditors raised an action by way of summary application seeking declarator that they were entitled to enter into possession of the subjects and warrant permitting the exercise of other remedies. During the course of the action it was discovered that the description in the standard security was defective and that the defect had been copied into a calling-up notice served by the lender. The pursuer accordingly amended its pleadings to as to seek rectification of the standard security and calling-up notice under s 8 of the Law Reform (Miscellaneous Provisions) (Scotland) Act 1985.

In the event, the court decided that the defect was not material. But, since the matter had been argued, the sheriff set out his views on the issue of rectification. The defender had questioned the competency of rectifying a calling-up notice. The answer depended on whether such a notice fell within s 8(1)(b) of the 1985 Act, ie was 'a document intended to create, transfer, vary or renounce a right'. The origins of the rectification provisions lay in the Scottish Law Commission's *Report No 79 on Rectification of Contractual and Other Documents* (1983), and the Commission made clear that it wanted them to apply to a wide range of documents (para 35). Furthermore, a calling-up notice could be said to create rights, notably the right to enforce the standard security in the event of non-compliance with the notice (para 37). Therefore, concluded the sheriff (D O'Carroll), rectification of such a notice was competent. However, this could not be done in the course of a summary application. Rather it would have been necessary to raise a separate ordinary action.

[Another aspect of this case is digested at (52) above.]

SPECIAL DESTINATIONS

(70) Hill v Hill
[2016] CSOH 10, 2016 GWD 3-66

Mr and Mrs Hill bought a house in Foxbar, Paisley, their title being registered in the Land Register in 1989. There was a standard survivorship destination. The parties' relationship deteriorated, and in June 1991 Mrs Hill executed a codicil to her will, evacuating, or bearing to evacuate, the destination in relation to her half-share, and bequeathing her half-share to the couple's son, Mr Hill junior. Mrs Hill died the following month. There was then a 'nomination' of the half-share in favour of the son. In March 1992 the son registered his title to the half-share in the Land Register. Between 1991, when Mrs Hill passed away, and 1995, both Mr Hill and the son, Mr Hill junior, resided in the property, but in the latter year Mr Hill junior moved out. To what extent Mr Hill senior occupied the house after 1995 is not clear. It seems that the house may have been unoccupied for substantial periods after 1995.

Eventually Mr Hill junior raised against his father an action of division and sale in Paisley Sheriff Court. Mr Hill senior responded by raising the present action in the Court of Session, the essence of the action being to have it found that the evacuation of the special destination had been invalid, and that accordingly he, Mr Hill senior, was the sole owner of the property. The court found in favour of Mr Hill senior. See **Commentary** p 203.

BOUNDARIES, ENCROACHMENT AND PRESCRIPTION

(71) McLernon v Rutherford
25 January 2016, Paisley Sheriff Court

A boundary dispute was referred by the court by consent to Professor Robert Rennie as a person of skill. He found in favour of the defender. His report was challenged by the pursuer, but the challenge was rejected by the court.

The titles had been registered under the Land Registration (Scotland) Act 1979 and one of the issues was the status of the underlying Sasine writs. In the course of his judgment the sheriff (R D M Fife) quoted with approval the following remark made by Sheriff Principal Bruce Kerr QC when the case was at an earlier stage:

> ... the effect of the Land Registration (Scotland) Act 1979 was to set up a system which might in some cases have the effect of altering a pre-existing boundary and in that event the title sheet now produced by the Keeper under reference to the OS maps supersedes deeds which may previously have been recorded in the Register of Sasines.

At one level this was, of course, perfectly true. If the Keeper drew the boundary in the wrong place, the effect of the Keeper's 'Midas touch' was to give legal force to her error: 1979 Act s 3(1)(a). But in such a case the Register was then 'bijurally' inaccurate and could therefore (s 9) be rectified by reference to the Sasine titles, provided that certain conditions were satisfied.

(72) McNaughton v Major
[2016] CSOH 11, 2016 GWD 3-77

Circumstances in which it was **held** that a person with a superiority title to property was in civil possession of that property, for the purposes of positive prescription, where the persons in natural possession occupied the property due to his agreement and were paying him a small weekly sum. See **Commentary** p 210.

INSOLVENCY

(73) Brown v Stonegale Ltd
(Joint Administrators of Oceancrown Ltd v Stonegale Ltd)
[2016] UKSC 30, 2016 GWD 20-359

If a person – whether a natural person or a company or otherwise – makes a gratuitous alienation in the run-up to insolvency (sequestration, liquidation etc) the alienation may be challenged for the benefit of the creditors. It quite often happens that a gratuitous transfer of value is dressed up in such a way as to disguise its true nature (eg a sale, but at undervalue, etc), so that on the surface it does not look like a gratuitous alienation. Conversely, it is also quite common, when a challenge is made of what was on the surface a gratuitous alienation, for the grantee to argue that there are reasons why in reality it was not. The next case, *Mahmood's Tr v Mahmood*, is an example of the latter, whilst the present case is an example of the former.

This case – a set of three actions to reduce gratuitous alienations – will chiefly be of interest to insolvency lawyers, but nevertheless has some interest too for conveyancers.

The Pelosi family had numerous properties in the Glasgow area, letting them out. There were six commercial properties in the portfolio, all let out to a vehicle-hire business. There were also 120 residential properties ('unfit for human habitation' – see [2013] CSOH 189 para 2). The family acted through a variety of companies, including Oceancrown Ltd, Ambercrest Ltd, Ambercroft Ltd, Lakecrown Ltd, Loanwell Ltd, Questway Ltd, Strathcroft Ltd and Stonegale Ltd.

Most or perhaps all of the properties had standard securities over them, initially in favour of Anglo-Irish Bank (which collapsed in 2009) and later, following assignations of the securities, by Hadrian Sàrl (a Luxembourg bank in the Banco de España group). The total lending involved was about £17 million. Most of the companies shared joint and several liability.

Following the economic downturn, the companies were in financial difficulties and were all, other than Stonegale, eventually placed in administration. The present case was an action (or strictly speaking three actions) by the administrators to reduce, as gratuitous alienations, the dispositions (granted in 2010) of four of the properties, namely 110 Glasgow Road, 210 Glasgow Road, 260 Glasgow Road, all in Rutherglen, and 64 Roslea Drive, Glasgow. (It appears that there may have been other, connected actions, possibly concerning other properties, but if so we have no specific information about them.) The three properties in Glasgow Road, Rutherglen were disponed to Stonegale Ltd, and 64 Roslea Drive, Glasgow was disponed to N R Pelosi personally (and was soon sold on, to a Mr Lazari).

As well as the four properties just mentioned, the Pelosis sold a fifth property (also in Glasgow Road, Rutherglen, namely No 278) to a public-sector company, Clyde Gateway, for about £2.4 million. This was a price much higher than valuation. 'The reason for the difference between that valuation and the sum paid by Clyde Gateway was not explored at the proof. Either the valuation was unduly low, or, for whatever reason, Clyde Gateway, which is a publicly funded organisation involved in the regeneration of the east end of Glasgow in connection with the Commonwealth Games, paid well over the market price': [2013] CSOH 189 at para 10.

The family saw the sales as an opportunity to get value out of the hands of the companies that were in financial difficulty and into the hands of Stonegale Ltd. They adopted a circuitous route to achieve this aim, disguising what they were doing. They told the bank that all five properties were being sold, and said that £2.4 million was the collective price for all. A letter to the bank's law firm from the Pelosi family's law firm set forth the following prices: 278 Glasgow Road (£762,000); 210 Glasgow Road (£934,000); 260 Glasgow Road (£450,000); and 110 Glasgow Road (£200,000). It is unclear whether this letter mentioned the fifth property, 64 Roslea Drive, Glasgow, which was being disponed to N R Pelosi, but it seems likely that it did so, for the bank's law firm proceeded to include that property in the list that it sent to the bank, the 'price' at which it was being 'sold' being stated as £68,000. The bank was asked for discharges of the standard securities on the basis that it would be paid the sale proceeds of the properties. It granted the discharges. As Lord Brodie was later to comment ([2015] CSIH 12, 2015 SCLR 619 at para 11), 'Had AIB known that a sum in excess of £2.4 million was being paid for 278 Glasgow Road, it would not have discharged the securities over the other properties unless both the true purchase price of 278 Glasgow Road and the value of the other properties was paid to AIB'.

To help conceal what was happening, the only actual sale (278 Glasgow Road) was done as a back-to-back transaction, with the property being 'sold' to another Pelosi company, Strathcroft Ltd, at a 'price' coinciding with valuation (£762,000), and then immediately resold to the real buyer, Clyde Gateway. The securities were thus cleared off not only the property that was actually being sold (278 Glasgow Road, to Clyde Gateway) but also off the four properties that were not being sold, but rather disponed gratuitously and kept in the family.

In the action the defender produced a document (the details of which are unclear) which was said to show that the transfers had in fact been made for value. The Lord Ordinary rejected this document as a fabrication. He also rejected the argument made for the defender (para 28) that 'the alienating company received a value for that disposal – here in the form of the commensurate reduction in their indebtedness to the bank. There was no detriment to the general body of their creditors.' See [2013] CSOH 189, 2014 GWD 2-27 (*Conveyancing 2013* Case (71)).

The defender reclaimed, unsuccessfully: [2015] CSIH 12, 2015 SCLR 619 (*Conveyancing 2015* Case (85)). The opinion of the Inner House confirmed the approach taken by the Lord Ordinary. The properties had been transferred gratuitously to keep them out of the hands of the creditors, which the law does not allow. 'The transactions under consideration were devices for the diversion of assets from creditors, facilitated by a misrepresentation to the banker of the companies which were involved' (para 32).

The state of knowledge of the Pelosi family's law firm, at the time that it wrote to the bank's law firm (see above), is a most interesting question, but was not a point at issue in this litigation. Reconstruction of that state of knowledge might not be easy, especially given that the relevant staff member said that he kept no file notes of his telephone conversations: see [2013] CSOH 189 para 13.

After losing first in the Outer House and then in the Inner House, the defenders appealed to the Supreme Court. In a fairly short judgment by Lord Reed, with whom the other Justices concurred, the appeal was dismissed. Lord Reed (at para 17) confirmed what the courts below had been saying: 'The purpose and effect of those transactions was to divert assets away from the companies' creditors: exactly what section 242 [of the Insolvency Act 1986] is intended to prevent. That they were gratuitous alienations is plain and obvious.'

(74) Mahmood's Tr v Mahmood
[2016] CSOH 164, 2016 GWD 39-699

This case is of no great importance from the standpoint of legal doctrine, but its facts – which are convoluted – may interest conveyancers.

Tariq Mahmood was the owner of a shop and post office at Balmore Road, Glasgow. His brother, Arshud Mahmood, had been the previous owner, and had disponed it to him in 2007, in exchange for assuming liability on a debt. Tariq Mahmood then leased the property back to Arshud Mahmood, who in turn subleased it to Adeel Mahmood, son of Tariq Mahmood. In 2009 Tariq Mahmood disponed the property to Adeel Mamood, the disposition bearing to be dated 17 September 2009. It was registered on 27 January 2010. The disposition bore to be for 'love, favour and affection'. On 8 January 2010 Tariq Mahmood was sequestrated, the trustee being the Accountant in Bankruptcy. On looking into the affairs of the bankrupt, the trustee discovered the recent transfer, and sought to recover the property as having been a gratuitous alienation, in terms of s 34 of the Bankruptcy (Scotland) Act 1985 (since replaced by s 98 of the Bankruptcy (Scotland) Act 2016).

Given that the disposition expressly stated that it was gratuitous ('love, favour and affection') the trustee's case was evidently a strong one. But, as in the preceding case, the defender, Adeel Mahmood, pled that in fact the disposition had not been gratuitous. In the words of the Lord Ordinary (Lord Tyre) (para 4), the defender averred that 'an oral agreement was reached between the debtor and the defender in about April 2007 that until his 25th birthday on 9 September 2009, the defender would transfer his monthly salary to the debtor's account. He would then become entitled to have the subjects transferred to him in consideration of the payments that he had made.'

The proof unearthed a strange story, to which we return below, but ultimately the pursuer won because the Lord Ordinary was unpersuaded by the defender's assertion that the transfer was not gratuitous (para 25):

> I am not ... persuaded that the transfer ... by the debtor [Tariq Mahmood] to the defender was made in return for payments of the defender's post office salary during the period between April 2007 and September 2009. I do not find it credible that the parties agreed in 2007 that the subjects would be transferred at a specific date in the

future in exchange for advance monthly payments which at the time of the alleged agreement could reasonably have been expected to amount to more than half as much again as the value of the property. I accept that arrangements entered into between family members are not necessarily comparable with contracts entered into by unconnected parties. However, the evidence in the present case disclosed no reasonable explanation of why the parties should have agreed that payments would continue for a lengthy period after the debtor had effectively received the full value of the subjects. Even if the agreed date of transfer was to be the defender's 25th birthday, payments could have been stopped before then. … The fact that the defender's monthly salary was paid into an account in the debtor's name – or, more accurately, into an account in the name of the debtor's business – does not of itself prove that the payments were made in return for a consideration or, if so, what that consideration was. It is equally consistent with an arrangement in terms of which the defender's salary was a contribution to family expenditure at a time when there appears to have been little else coming into the debtor's bank account. In the absence of any contemporaneous evidence of the alleged 2007 agreement, and having regard to its inherent unlikelihood, I hold that the defender has failed to discharge the onus of proving that the monthly payments into the debtor's account were made in return for a subsequent transfer of the subjects into his name.

But on the road to this conclusion, the proof was a truly remarkable one. We quote the Lord Ordinary at paras 6 to 7:

On 1 September 2009, the debtor telephoned his solicitor, Mr Michael Ramsay, to instruct him to prepare documentation for the transfer of the subjects to the defender. … Mr Ramsay worked in a branch office in Maryhill Road. His secretary there was Ms Janice Watt. On receipt of the debtor's call, Mr Ramsay made notes on a memorandum entitled 'Money Laundering and POCA – Sources of Funds'. He noted the client name as 'Tariq & Adeel Mahmood' and the nature of the transaction as 'Transfer of title. No consideration'. Mr Ramsay gave evidence at the proof although his memory of the transaction was vague. He did recall being told that money had been changing hands between the debtor and the defender via a bank account, and that they now wanted the appropriate conveyancing documentation prepared. Mr Ramsay proceeded to produce a disposition for signature by the debtor.

It is necessary to note at this stage that the productions lodged for the proof included two different dispositions of the subjects by the debtor in favour of the defender. Both bore to have been signed on 17 September 2009. The first disposition, a copy of which was lodged on behalf of the defender, narrated that the subjects were being disponed 'for certain good and onerous causes'. It was signed by the debtor and witnessed by Mr Ramsay. The date (17 September 2009) and place (Glasgow) of signing, and the full name and address of the witness, appear to have been completed by Ms Watt. The conveyancing file … also lodged, contains what appears to be the original of this document, but with two diagonal red lines scored through it which are absent from the copy produced by the defender. The second disposition, a copy of which was lodged on behalf of the pursuer, and the original of which is also on the conveyancing file, narrated that the subjects were being disponed 'for love, favour and affection'. It was signed by the debtor and witnessed by Ms Watt. The date of signing (17 September 2009) and the full name and address of the witness appear to have been completed by Ms Watt. The place of signing (Glasgow) is in Mr Ramsay's handwriting. Both dispositions have backings bearing the date '2009'. It is not suggested by anyone that the debtor's and witnesses' signatures on these two documents are other than genuine. However, the defender, the debtor and Mr Ramsay were all clear in their recollection that the debtor did not sign two dispositions on 17 September 2009.

The defender and Tariq Mahmood, the debtor, as well as Mr Ramsay all concurred in their testimony before the court that the disposition that was signed on 17 September was 'for certain good and onerous causes' and the Lord Ordinary accepted this.

We continue the story in the words of the Lord Ordinary (para 9): 'No disposition was recorded promptly after the meeting on 17 September 2009. I note, however, that an inhibition was served on the debtor on 22 September 2009 and registered in the Register of Inhibitions and Adjudications on 25 September 2009.' In the event the disposition with the 'love, favour and affection' narrative was registered in the Land Register on 27 January 2010. 'Indemnity was not excluded in respect of the inhibition registered against the debtor on 25 September 2009 after Mr Ramsay provided a letter confirming that the disposition had been delivered on 17 September 2009' (para 13).

So why two dispositions? Back to the Lord Ordinary (paras 10 and 11):

> The debtor's evidence in relation to the signing of the second disposition, ie the one bearing the narrative 'for love, favour and affection' was as follows. In early January 2010 he received a phone call from Ms Watt asking him to come to the office to sign a document relating to the transfer of the subjects. He called in on his way to another appointment. Ms Watt passed a document to him under the glass screen at the reception counter and asked him to sign it. Only the bottom of the document was passed through; Ms Watt did not explain what it was or invite him to read it. He signed it without reading it as he was in a hurry. Ms Watt said that she would fill in the details and as he left he saw her beginning to do so. Mr Ramsay was not present. The debtor now believed that the deed he signed in early January was the disposition containing the 'love, favour and affection' narrative. At no time had he given instructions to Mr Ramsay to prepare a second disposition. Nor did he ever tell Mr Ramsay that he had transferred the subjects to the defender for no consideration.
>
> Mr Ramsay was unable to provide an explanation of how it had come about that a second disposition was drafted and signed. He acknowledged that the transaction had not been handled expeditiously. He could not recall why the disposition 'for certain good and onerous causes' had been scored through; perhaps some problem had come to light after the transaction had been completed. It might be that the file had fallen asleep and then, when it was reactivated, he had felt it necessary to prepare another disposition but had inserted an incorrect narrative. He could not remember when or why the second disposition was signed but was certain that it had not been signed on the date which it bore, ie 17 September 2009. He could not explain how an incorrect date had come to be inserted: it might have been an error on the part of Ms Watt. He thought that the use of the narrative 'for love, favour and affection' had been an error for which he was responsible.

What did Ms Watt say? We quote from para 15:

> Ms Watt's evidence was that she had witnessed the disposition containing the narrative 'for love, favour and affection' on the date which it bore, ie 17 September

2009. She would not have entered an incorrect date in a disposition. She had no recollection of telephoning the debtor in January 2010 to ask him to come in to sign a deed, nor of presenting him with a deed to sign in Mr Ramsay's absence. If a disposition had been signed in January 2010 she would not have inserted the date 17 September 2009. She had no specific recollection of this transaction.

The Lord Ordinary was not convinced. We quote from para 22:

> The difficulty with Ms Watt's evidence is that both dispositions contain the date '17 September 2009' entered in her handwriting. I can see no reason why both dispositions would have been signed and witnessed on the same day, and I accept the evidence of the defender, the debtor and Mr Ramsay that they were not. It must therefore be the case that, contrary to her recollection of events which happened some years ago, Ms Watt entered an incorrect date in at least one of the deeds. As I have found that the 'certain good and onerous causes' disposition was signed and witnessed on 17 September 2009, it must follow that it was the 'love, favour and affection' disposition that was signed and witnessed on another date.

The Lord Ordinary was not 'able to reach a conclusion as to why an incorrect date may have been inserted, although I observe that delivery of any disposition after 25 September 2009 would have constituted a breach of the inhibition registered against the debtor on that date' (para 22).

The story is a disturbing one: two dispositions for one transaction, one bearing a date that cannot have been true, and with the suggestion that the mis-dating may have been linked to the inhibition against the granter.

(75) Fortune's Tr v Medwin Investments Ltd and Cooper Watson Ltd
[2016] CSIH 49, 2016 SLT 923

Mr Fortune was sequestrated in December 2010. He owned numerous properties. The trustee in sequestration neither sold these properties nor completed title in his own name. In March and April 2014 Mr Fortune (i) granted standard securities over four of these properties to Medwin Investments Ltd, (ii) granted dispositions of another three to the same company, and (iii) granted dispositions of another five properties to Cooper Watson Ltd. All these deeds were registered in the Land Register. Both companies were aware of Mr Fortune's sequestration.

The trustee in sequestration then raised two actions, one against Medwin Investments Ltd and the other against Cooper Watson Ltd, seeking reduction of these various deeds. Difficult issues concerning the interface of bankruptcy law and conveyancing law were involved. It was held by the Lord Ordinary (Lord Jones) that all the deeds fell to be reduced: see [2015] CSOH 139, 2015 GWD 34-552 (*Conveyancing 2015* Cases (87) and (88)). The complex issues in this case are extensively discussed at pp 180–86 of that volume.

The defenders reclaimed, and the decision of the Outer House has been affirmed, the Inner House adopting essentially the same approach as had been adopted by the Lord Ordinary.

The case is mainly about s 44(4) of the Conveyancing (Scotland) Act 1924. This protects buyers of heritable property from a bankrupt where the property remains in the name of the bankrupt. What, roughly speaking, the provision says is that, if three years have passed since the opening of the sequestration, a buyer (or a grantee of some other deed) is protected even though the trustee has not consented. Obviously, this provision does not often apply, for usually, by the time that the third anniversary of the sequestration arrives, the trustee has already sold the property, or has completed title in his own name *qua* trustee. (It should always be borne in mind, in considering the way that sequestration law and property law interact, that the fact that the debtor has been discharged has no effect on the property that fell under the sequestration.) But whilst s 44(4) does not come into play often, its potential application cannot be said to be rare, because it is a curious, and to us inexplicable, fact that the trustees in sequestration do sometimes allow years to pass without either selling the heritable property, or completing title in their own name *qua* trustee.

What was held in the Outer House, and has now been confirmed by the Inner House, is that s 44(4) does not apply to buyers, or other grantees, who are aware that the property is sequestrated property. In other words, s 44(4) requires good faith. The decision can be taken as settling a matter that hitherto had been far from clear.

MISCELLANEOUS

(76) South Lanarkshire Council v Aviva Insurance Ltd
[2016] CSOH 83, 2016 GWD 21-368

Though not a conveyancing case, this may be of interest to conveyancers. It arose out of the collapse of Scottish Coal Co Ltd, a company that has appeared more than once in the present series: see *Scottish Coal Co Ltd v Danish Forestry Co Ltd* [2009] CSOH 171, 2010 GWD 5-79 (*Conveyancing 2009* Case (9)) affd [2010] CSIH 56, 2010 SC 729 (*Conveyancing 2010* Case (3)); *Joint Liquidators of the Scottish Coal Co Ltd* [2013] CSOH 124, 2013 SLT 1055, rev [2013] CSIH 108, 2014 SC 372 (*Conveyancing 2013* Case (67)).)

The Scottish Coal Company, being insolvent, was unable to comply with its obligations to restore its open-cast mine at Broken Cross Muir, Lanarkshire. The company had, before the mining operations could begin, obtained an insurance bond from Aviva Insurance Ltd, and, following the company's collapse, the local authority called upon Aviva to pay £3,117,724 by way of restoration costs. Aviva declined to pay, partly on the basis of how the bond should be interpreted, and partly on the basis that the formal demand by the local authority was not valid. It failed on both counts. Decree in full was granted in favour of the pursuer.

(77) Jack v Jack
[2016] CSIH 75, 2016 Fam LR 177

Partnership property is a concept defined in s 20 of the Partnership Act 1890. But the 'definition' is rather vague – perhaps unavoidably so. Often, indeed usually, what is or is not the property of a partnership is perfectly clear. Property may be held by a partnership in its own name, and if so it is clear that the property is partnership property. (Even heritable property can be held directly by a partnership, in terms of s 70 of the Abolition of Feudal Tenure etc (Scotland) Act 2000, though in practice this seldom happens.) Or property can be held expressly in trust for a partnership, and once again it is clear that such property is partnership property. But it is also possible for property to be partnership property merely on the basis that the facts and circumstances lead to that conclusion. For instance, (i) title to land is in the name of James Macdonald, but (ii) the land is farmed by the partnership of Messrs J & H Macdonald, and (iii) there is no lease to the partnership, and so no rent is paid to James, and (iv) the annual accounts of the partnership, approved by the partners, say that the land is a partnership asset, and so on. Or the facts and circumstances might point the other way. For instance, James might lease the farm to the partnership, in which case the lease would be partnership property but not the land itself.

The present case was a divorce action in which the question of whether land was partnership property was relevant to the claims of the divorcing parties. The title to Torebanehill, West Lothian was in the sole name of Mr Jack, having been passed to him by his father. He was in partnership with his wife. Mrs Jack asserted, but he denied, that the land was partnership property.

At first instance ([2015] CSOH 91, 2015 Fam LR 95 (*Conveyancing 2015* Case (94)) it was held that the farm was not partnership property. The wife reclaimed, and the decision has been affirmed. A major factor was that the land was not included as a partnership asset in the accounts. Whereas the discussion of the law when the case was at first instance was sketchy, the discussion in the Inner House was ample. This will no doubt establish itself as a major case on the 'what counts as partnership property?' question. The decision was delivered by Lord Drummond Young.

(78) Argyll and Bute Council v Gordon
2016 SLT (Sh Ct) 196, 2016 SCLR 192

'Elder law' is a neologism that has swum across the Atlantic from west to east, and whilst there are those who do not like it, it seems to have come to stay. One aspect of elder law concerns liability for care-home costs. The local authority has longstop liability, but old people who can afford to pay are expected to do so. There are rules about assessing ability to pay, one of the most important elements being whether the person concerned has capital, and, if so, how much. And very often 'capital' means heritable property. The rules are to be found in the National Assistance (Assessment of Resources) Regulations 1992, SI 1992/2977, as amended, under which the threshold figure is (currently) £26,250. In other words, if the capital of the person in care is under that figure, care is provided free of charge, but the local authority can charge for care to the extent that the capital is over that figure.

Capital can be quickly eaten up by care charges, and for that reason there may be a wish to transfer capital to relatives or friends. A factor here is the feeling that those who have been provident and saved for their old age are – in a sense

– penalised, while those who have been feckless are – in a sense – rewarded. The legislation has provisions to check certain types of transfer. In fact, and rather oddly, it has two. One is reg 25 of the 1992 Regulations, providing that 'a resident may be treated as possessing actual capital of which he has deprived himself for the purpose of decreasing the amount that he may be liable to pay for his accommodation'. The other is s 21 of the Health and Social Services and Social Security Adjudications Act 1983, which provides that:

> Where a person avails himself of part III accommodation; and that person knowingly and with the intention of avoiding charges for the accommodation has transferred any asset … to some other person … not more than six months before the date on which he begins to reside in such accommodation; or transfers any such asset to some other person … whilst residing in the accommodation; and either the consideration for the transfer is less than the value of the assets; or there is no consideration for the transfer, the person … to whom the asset is transferred by the person availing himself of the accommodation shall be liable to pay to the local authority providing the accommodation … the difference between the amount assessed as due to be paid for the accommodation … and the amount which the Local Authority receive from him for it.

The broad thrust of the 1983 Act and the 1992 Regulations is thus similar, but the wording is not the same, and there are two particular differences that are notable. One is that the 1983 Act has a six-month time-limit, whereas the 1992 Regulations have no time limit. To that extent the 1992 Regulations are more powerful. But in another respect the 1983 Act is the more powerful of the two, for whereas the 1992 Regulations merely say that the consequence is that the elderly person's notional capital is deemed to include the alienated capital, the 1983 Act goes further and makes the transferee directly liable to the local authority.

In the present case Mrs Duncan-Jones owned a house in Kilmartin, Argyll. On 3 June 2005 she went into residential care. On 7 June 2005 she concluded missives for the gratuitous transfer of her house to friends, Mr and Mrs Gordon. (To have missives where there is a donation is unusual. We do not know the reason.) Title was transferred later in the year. The property was unencumbered. (For the effect of encumbrances in cases of this type, see *Cunningham v East Lothian Council* [2011] CSOH 185, 2011 GWD 39-792, *Conveyancing 2011* Case (78).)

From the date of her admission to residential care until 10 January 2010 Mrs Duncan-Jones paid the care charges out of her own resources, the total paid in the period being £167,000. At the latter date her resources were exhausted, and from then on the costs fell on Argyll and Bute Council, this continuing until her death on 4 January 2013. The Council then claimed from Mr and Mrs Gordon in respect of the costs of care from 10 January 2010 to 4 January 2013, founding on s 21 of the 1983 Act. The sum claimed was £42,750. This was much less than the value of the Kilmartin house, even at the time of the donation in 2005: deductions were made to reach this figure, but the judgment does not go into details on this point.

The Council raised the present action in the sheriff court, and the Gordons proposed a defence on the merits (see below). The Council argued that the sheriff court could not consider this defence, but had to grant decree automatically, and that if the Gordons wished their defence to be heard they would have to raise an action of judicial review in the Court of Session. At this stage of the case it was this procedural point that was at issue, and the sheriff (Peter J Braid) agreed with the defenders that he did not have to grant automatic decree in favour of the pursuer, but could consider the defence. Accordingly the case was continued for a proper hearing about the substantive issues.

The defence was that the precondition of liability, that Mrs Duncan-Jones had donated the property 'knowingly and with the intention of avoiding charges for the accommodation', had not been satisfied. The defenders presented to the court an account that suggested that her motivation had been quite different: that the gift made sense in the context of the relationship between the parties and that she had had a reasonable expectation of being able, notwithstanding the gift, to defray the accommodation charges out of her own resources. The defenders pled (para 12):

> The possibility of transferring [the heritable property in question] to the defender and her late husband was first considered by Mrs Duncan-Jones in late 2004 and again in early 2005, all before Mrs Duncan-Jones was admitted to hospital and thereafter to residential care. Mrs Duncan-Jones and her late husband were extremely close to the defender and her family. [The property] forms part of Poltalloch Estate, owned by the defender's family. Mrs Duncan-Jones wished the cottage to be returned to the estate. Robert James Nicholas Linzee Gordon was diagnosed as suffering from multiple sclerosis in November 2002. His condition deteriorated quickly and he and the defender considered moving to Poltalloch. Mrs Duncan-Jones wished to make [the property] available to them to live in and the transfer of the property was effected for that purpose. At the time of the transfer Mrs Duncan-Jones was 85 years old. She had substantial capital resources in addition to the cottage. It was not envisaged by Mrs Duncan-Jones or her advisers that she would require to remain in residential care for such a period that her capital would be exhausted.

Whether that defence will be upheld remains to be seen: the next stage of the case will be a proof.

A curious feature of the case concerns the following clause in the missives (para 12):

> The seller declares that she is taking up a place in a retirement home. While she will be fully funded from her own resources for the foreseeable future, it is a possibility, which the purchasers will accept, that the local authority might need to take steps to try to reduce the conveyance in order to recover costs which they have paid for the sellers to stay in residential/nursing home accommodation. The purchasers will be bound to accept the property in the full knowledge of this risk. For the avoidance of doubt, any two year limitation of missives will not apply to the terms of this clause.

It might be supposed that this clause would weigh against the defenders: it shows that they were aware of the accommodation charges issue. But in fact it may weigh the other way. In the first place, under the legislation what matters is the state of mind of the transferor, not the state of mind of the transferee. In the second place the clause indicates that the deceased had expected to be able to pay for her own accommodation.

A minor postscript is that, whilst the missives clause mentions the possibility of reduction, in fact the applicable legislation does not refer to that possibility. Reduction might be a possibility if the local authority were to proceed on the basis that the person in care was or had become insolvent, for then the transfer might be open to challenge under the general law of gratuitous alienations. But as far as we know that course tends not to be adopted in practice. For consideration of this aspect, see *Conveyancing 2000* pp 120–23, discussing *Yule v South Lanarkshire Council* 2001 SC 203, itself a case discussed in the present action.

❧ PART II ☙

STATUTORY DEVELOPMENTS

STATUTORY DEVELOPMENTS

Succession (Scotland) Act 2016 (asp 7)

Two provisions of this Act, in force since 1 November 2016 (see **Succession (Scotland) Act 2016 (Commencement, Transitional and Saving Provisions) Regulations 2016, SSI 2016/210**), have implications for conveyancing.

Section 2 evacuates special destinations in the event of divorce or the termination of a civil partnership. This replaces s 19 of the Family Law (Scotland) Act 2006 which was to the same effect: see *Conveyancing 2005* pp 72–74.

Section 24 replaces s 17 of the Succession (Scotland) Act 1964, which is now repealed. Section 17 had protected acquirers in good faith and for value in the event of (i) reduction of a confirmation of executors, or (ii) the seller having received the property from an executor in error. Section 24 reproduces both protections, albeit in different language, and adds a third to take account of the new procedure, in ss 3 and 4 of the Act, for judicial rectification of wills: acquirers are now also protected in the event of (iii) the property having been distributed in accordance with the former provisions of a will which was rectified after the distribution.

Land and Buildings Transaction Tax (Amendment) (Scotland) Act 2016 (asp 11)

This Act amends the Land and Buildings Transaction Tax (Scotland) Act 2013 so as to impose additional tax of 3% on purchases of second homes. See **Commentary** p 214.

Land Reform (Scotland) Act 2016 (asp 18)

The work of the LRRG

The origins of the Land Reform (Scotland) Act 2016 lie in the Land Reform Review Group ('LRRG') set up by the Scottish Government in July 2012 and chaired by Dr Alison Elliot. (For background, see *Conveyancing 2012* 94–96 as well as the LRRG's website: www.scotland.gov.uk/About/Review/land-reform.) An initial call for evidence resulted in almost 500 responses, ranging from a couple of paragraphs to 266 pages from Scottish Land and Estates (www.scotland.gov. uk/Publications/2013/07/2790, and, for an analysis, www.scotland.gov.uk/ Publications/2013/05/4519). An interim report was published by the LRRG in May

2013 (www.gov.scot/Resource/0042/00426905.PDF) and was widely castigated by the land-reform lobby for what was seen as a lack of ambition. A year later that criticism was met to some degree by the LRRG's final report, *The Land of Scotland and the Common Good* (www.scotland.gov.uk/Resource/0045/00451087. pdf), which was published in May 2014: see *Conveyancing 2014* pp 98–102.

As the title chosen for the final report indicated, the idea underlying the LRRG's work was that of the 'common good'. (Not in the technical sense of that term in Scots law, for which see p 165 below.) This was said to describe 'a comprehensive and complex concept which brings into its embrace questions of social justice, human rights, democracy, citizenship, stewardship and economic development' (p 235). The LRRG continued (p 236):

> Land is a resource not just for the present generation, but also generations to come. It is also home to other species. Care of the land therefore calls for a strong sense of stewardship. Finally, successful economic development is also a critical element of the common good: the way in which land is used to generate economic activity and sustainable livelihoods is, and will be, crucial to an economically successful Scotland. The Review Group therefore regards the common good as the general outcome which informs and drives land reform. It has guided decisions about which recommendations the Group should support, without the suggestion that any single action will realize the common good.

Among the 62 recommendations was a call for more statistical information as to patterns of land ownership, and for a speeding-up of the task of getting land on to the Land Register. The Crown Estate Commissioners should cease to operate in Scotland, and Crown rights should be pared back. Community control over land and buildings should be encouraged and extended. The law of riparian rights should be reformed to reflect the public interest. So should the law of common good in the narrow, technical sense of that expression. Crofting law should be modernised and simplified. The exemption from non-domestic rates for agricultural, forestry and other land-based businesses should be reconsidered. The idea of a land value tax should be explored. In the interests of transparency, non-EU companies should be barred from acquiring land in Scotland, though it was accepted that the gains from such a measure would be modest. There was a proposal to empower local authorities to make a 'compulsory sale order' over vacant or derelict land. Particularly controversial was the suggestion that there should be an upper ceiling on the amount of land which could be owned by any one person. Finally, the report argued that, rather than proceeding by piecemeal reform, the Government should devise a 'National Land Policy', with a permanent 'Scottish Land and Property Commission' to 'provide a single, overall and integrated focus on the different aspects of Scotland's system of land ownership, including land information, property law, land use, fiscal measures and land markets' (p 238).

The Scottish Government's response

In welcoming the LRRG report the Scottish Government announced an immediate 10-year target for completion of the Land Register (see *Conveyancing 2014* p 88), a policy which went much further than the LRRG's recommendation. Further, some of the LRRG's concerns about community involvement were met by the Community Empowerment (Scotland) Act 2015 (see *Conveyancing 2015* pp 75–78), while the Scotland Act 2016 s 36 transferred administration of the Crown Estate in Scotland from the Crown Estate Commissioners to the Scottish Government (as to which see p 105 below). Beyond that, the Government proceeded to consult on some, but by no means all, of the LRRG's recommendations. *A Consultation on the Future of Land Reform in Scotland* (www.scotland.gov.uk/ Publications/2014/12/9659) was published on 2 December 2014. The ministerial preface gave as the aspiration 'a fairer and more equitable distribution of land in Scotland where communities and individuals can own and use land to realise their potential. Scotland's land must be an asset that benefits the many, not the few'. 1,269 responses to the consultation were received, mainly (82%) from individuals. A summary of the responses was published in May 2015: see www. gov.scot/Publications/2015/05/4885; the responses themselves can be found at www.gov.scot/Topics/Environment/land-reform/consultation.

The Land Reform Act

A Bill based on the consultation document and hence, indirectly, on parts of the LRRG report was introduced to the Scottish Parliament on 22 June 2015. The Bill also included provisions on agricultural holdings which derived from the recommendations of a separate Agricultural Holdings Legislation Review (www. gov.scot/Resource/0046/00468852.pdf). The Stage 1 proceedings were conducted by the Rural Affairs, Climate Change and Environment Committee. As well as oral evidence, the Committee received 200 written submissions (www.scottish. parliament.uk/parliamentarybusiness/CurrentCommittees/91072.aspx). The Bill was passed on 16 March 2016 and received Royal Assent on 22 April 2016 (www. parliament.scot/parliamentarybusiness/Bills/90675.aspx).

For discussion of the Act, see Malcolm Combe, 'Land reform: back, and here to stay' (2016) 61 *Journal of the Law Society of Scotland* May/18 and, for a more detailed account by the same author which considers some of the background, 'The Land Reform (Scotland) Act 2016: another answer to the Scottish land question' 2016 *Juridical Review* 291.

The Act is in ten main parts, not all of which were in force at the time of writing.

Part 1: a Land Rights and Responsibilities Statement

Part 1 (ss 1–3) requires the Government to issue and keep under review a 'land rights and responsibilities statement' having regard to certain criteria such as human rights, community empowerment, diversity of land ownership, and sustainable development (s 1). In implement of the Act (s 2(2)), a draft statement was published for comment on 16 December 2016: see Scottish Government, *Land Rights and Responsibilities Statement: a consultation* (2016; www.gov.scot/ Resource/0051/00511857.pdf). This comprises a Vision and six Principles, as follows:

Vision for a strong relationship between the people of Scotland and the land of Scotland

The ownership, management and use of land and buildings in Scotland should contribute to the collective benefit of the people of Scotland. A fair, inclusive and productive system of land rights and responsibilities should deliver greater public benefits and promote economic, social and cultural rights.

Principles

1. The overall framework of land rights, responsibilities and associated public policies governing the ownership, management and use of land, should contribute to building a fairer society in Scotland and promote environmental sustainability, economic prosperity and social justice.
2. There should be an increasingly diverse and widely dispersed pattern of land ownership and tenure, which properly reflects national and local aspirations and needs.
3. More local communities should be given the opportunity to own buildings and land which contribute to their community's wellbeing and future development.
4. The holders of land rights should recognise their responsibilities to meet high standards of land ownership, management and use, acting as the stewards of Scotland's land resource for future generations.
5. Information on land should be publicly available, clear and detailed.
6. There should be wide community engagement in decisions about land.

The Vision and each of the Principles are glossed on pp 19–28 of the consultation document. The consultation closes on 10 March 2017. The Land Rights and Responsibilities Statement should not be confused with the Land Use Strategy (as to which see p 104 below), the National Peatland Plan, the Scottish Rural Development Plan, the Scottish Forestry Strategy, the Play Strategy (www.gov.scot/Publications/2016/03/9995), or the Strategic Vision for the Uplands.

Part 2: the Scottish Land Commission

Part 2 (ss 4–38) establishes a Scottish Land Commission (Coimisean Fearainn na h-Alba), to comprise five ordinary Commissioners and a sixth 'Tenant Farming Commissioner' (s 4). The functions of the Commissioners are 'on any matter relating to land in Scotland (a) to review the impact and effectiveness of any law or policy, (b) to recommend changes to any law or policy, (c) to gather evidence, (d) to carry out research, (e) to prepare reports, and (f) to provide information and guidance' (s 22(1)). In the exercise of these functions, Commissioners must 'have regard to' the Land Rights and Responsibilities Statement (s 22(3)(a)(i)). The first Commissioners are Andrew Thin, Professor David Adams, Megan MacInnes, Lorne MacLeod, Dr Sally Reynolds, and, as Tenant Farming Commissioner, Dr Bob McIntosh. None is a lawyer. The Scottish Land Commission is based in Inverness and will begin work on 1 April 2017, by which time all of the provisions in part 2 of the Act will be in force: see **Land Reform (Scotland) Act 2016 (Commencement No 2 and Transitory Provisions) Regulations 2016, SSI 2016/250.**

Part 3: information about control of land

The presupposition underlying part 3 (ss 39–43) is that the public has the right to know who owns, controls and benefits from land, and that the right to privacy does not extend to such matters. In the form in which the Bill was introduced to Parliament, part 3 attracted sharp criticism for not doing enough to increase transparency: see Rural Affairs, Climate Change and Environment Committee, *Stage 1 Report on the Land Reform (Scotland) Bill* (www.scottish.parliament.uk/ parliamentarybusiness/CurrentCommittees/94538.aspx) paras 177–221. As a result, additional sections (ss 39–42) were introduced by Government amendment at Stage 3 requiring the Scottish Ministers to make provision by regulations for the collection and publication in a public register of information as to the persons who have controlling interests in owners and tenants of land. The intended target is presumably companies, especially those incorporated abroad, and also trusts. As s 41 requires, a public consultation was launched in September 2016 and closed in December 2016: see Scottish Government, *Improving transparency in land ownership in Scotland: a consultation on controlling interests in land* (www. gov.scot/Publications/2016/09/6681) and, for further discussion, p 167 below.

Section 43 adds new ss 48A and 48B to the Land Registration etc (Scotland) Act 2012. Once in force, and once regulations have been made by the Scottish Ministers, this will allow the Keeper to request information from those who own land, or are applying for registration, as to the category of person or body into which a proprietor falls. For the moment the purpose and scope of these provisions remain unclear: see K G C Reid and G L Gretton, *Land Registration* (2017) para 8.20.

Part 4: engaging communities in decisions relating to land

Section 44, the only provision in part 4 of the Act, requires the Government to issue guidance to those who own and control land as to the need to engage local communities in respect of decisions which might affect them. No sanction is provided for ignoring the guidance other than the prospect that it is taken into account, under s 56(4), where an application to buy land is made under part 5 of the Act. Section 44 came into force on 1 November 2016 (see **Land Reform (Scotland) Act 2016 (Commencement No 2 and Transitory Provisions) Regulations 2016, SSI 2016/250**) but, at the time of writing, draft guidance was still awaited.

Part 5: right to buy land to further sustainable development

Rights of community organisations to buy land have been a feature of land reform legislation ever since the Land Reform (Scotland) Act 2003. See p 100 below. To the community right to buy and the crofting community right to buy introduced by the 2003 Act, the Community Empowerment (Scotland) Act 2015 has recently added the community right to buy abandoned, neglected or detrimental land (see *Conveyancing 2015* pp 75–76) although the relevant provisions – a new Part 3A inserted into the Land Reform (Scotland) Act 2003 by s 74 of the 2015 Act – are not yet in force. Part 5 (ss 45–73) of the 2016 Land Reform Act now adds a right to buy land in order to further sustainable development, although once again the provisions are not yet in force. The Government's target is to have 1 million acres of land in community ownership by 2020 (see eg *Stage 1 Report* para 248).

The procedure proposed in part 5 is familiar from earlier models. Like the crofting community right to buy and the right to buy abandoned, neglected or detrimental land (but unlike the community right to buy), the new part 5 right does not require a willing seller. It applies to most types of land though there are some exceptions including owner-occupied homes (s 46). The right can only be exercised by 'community bodies' (s 49). Those bodies are defined as (i) companies limited by guarantee, (ii) Scottish charitable incorporated organisations ('SCIOs'), or (iii) community benefit societies under the Co-operative and Community Benefit Societies Act 2014. Alternatively the right can be exercised by a person nominated by such a body: s 54(1). An application to buy is made to the Scottish Ministers, having first been approved by the community by means of a ballot (ss 56(3)(h) and 57) and registered in a new register maintained by the Keeper, the Register of Applications by Community Bodies to Buy Land (s 52). In reaching a decision, the Scottish Ministers have a broad duty to consult (s 5).

In terms of the criteria set out in s 56(2), an application is not to be accepted unless the Scottish Ministers are satisfied that:

(a) the transfer of land is likely to further the achievement of sustainable development in relation to the land,
(b) the transfer of land is in the public interest,
(c) the transfer of land –
   (i) is likely to result in significant benefit to the relevant community (see subsection (11)) to which the application relates, and
   (ii) is the only practicable, or the most practicable, way of achieving that significant benefit, and
(d) not granting consent to the transfer of land is likely to result in harm to that community.

The criteria for accepting an application were criticised by some as over-strict (see eg *Stage 1 Report* paras 247 and 258), and were obviously designed partly with article 1 Protocol 1 of the European Convention on Human Rights in mind. They were made somewhat less strict by amendment during the Bill's passage by (i) the addition of the words 'or the most practicable' to para (c)(ii), and (ii) the deletion of 'significant' before 'harm' in para (d). The question of whether part 5 is ECHR-compatible is explored (without reaching any firm conclusion) by Douglas Maxwell in articles published in (2016) 61 *Journal of the Law Society of Scotland* Jan/22 and in (2016) 41 *European Law Review* 900.

There is no definition of 'sustainable development' (something which some have criticised) but para 143 of the Bill's *Policy Memorandum*, drawing on the work of the Labour Government's Land Reform Policy Group of 1998, states that:

Sustainable development is defined as development that is planned with appropriate regard for its longer term consequences, and is geared towards assisting social and economic advancement that can lead to further opportunities and a higher quality of life for people whilst protecting the environment. Sustainable development requires an integrated approach to social, economic and environmental outcomes. Sustainable communities are more self-reliant, with increasing economic independence and a better quality of life, while conserving or enhancing their environment. Contrasted with unsustainable communities, where populations are declining, local economic and social activity is inhibited and the natural heritage is damaged.

Provision is made for valuation of the land being bought (s 65), and for the making of Government grants towards the purchase (s 68). There is a right of appeal to the sheriff court (s 69) or, in respect of the valuation, to the Lands Tribunal (s 70).

Parts 6–10

The remainder of the Act is of less interest to conveyancers other than those involved in agricultural leases (an area of law which we do not seek to cover in this series). The provision in part 6 (ss 74–76) to end the exemption for shootings and deer forests from non-domestic rates (an exemption which dates from 1995) is controversial and was not supported by the *Stage 1 Report* in the absence of 'a thorough, robust and evidence-based analysis of the potential impacts of ending the ... exemption (including what impact imposing the exemption had in 1995)' (para 310). Part 6 was brought into force on 28 June 2016: see **Land Reform (Scotland) Act 2016 (Commencement No 1 and Transitional Provision) Regulations 2016, SSI 2016/193**.

Prompted by the difficulties encountered in building Portobello High School on common-good ground – difficulties which in the end required to be solved by a special Act of Parliament (see *Conveyancing 2014* p 71) – part 7 (s 77) amends s 75 of the Local Government (Scotland) Act 1973 with effect from 28 June 2016. Previously, s 75(2) provided that where a local authority wanted to dispose of 'land forming part of the common good with respect to which a question arises as to the right of the authority to alienate', the local authority could do so with the authorisation of a court. But, as the Inner House pointed out in *Portobello Park Action Group Association v City of Edinburgh Council* [2012] CSIH 69, 2013 SC 184 (discussed in *Conveyancing 2012* pp 172–75), there was no equivalent mechanism where a local authority wished to keep the land but appropriate it for a different purpose. The effect of the amendment is to allow a court to give consent to such appropriation.

Part 8 (ss 78–82) is about the controversial subject of deer management: see *Stage 1 Report* paras 353–391. The provisions were brought into force on 28 June 2016: see **Land Reform (Scotland) Act 2016 (Commencement No 1 and Transitional Provision) Regulations 2016, SSI 2016/193**.

The LRRG concluded that, in general, the provisions on access rights in part 1 of the Land Reform (Scotland) Act 2003 were working well and that only minor amendments were needed. Part 9 (ss 83 and 84) introduces some amendments which came into force on 31 December 2016: see **Land Reform (Scotland) Act 2016 (Commencement No 4 Transitional and Saving Provisions) Regulations 2016, SSI 2016/372**. A new subsection (7A) is added to s 28 (s 84). The effect is that where a declarator is sought as to whether a person has exercised access rights responsibly, the application must be served on the person in question. The other amendments are all to the provisions on core paths (s 83). A replacement s 20(1) makes clear (as the previous version did not) that local authorities are free to review their existing core paths plan when they consider it appropriate to so do (and must do so if so required by Ministers). New provision is made for consultation on any amendments which result from the review.

Part 10 (ss 85–123) contains far-ranging and controversial provisions in relation to agricultural holdings. See *Stage 1 Report* paras 400–561. Many but not all of the provisions were brought into force on 23 December 2016: see **Land Reform (Scotland) Act 2016 (Commencement No 3 Transitory and Saving Provisions) Regulations 2016, SSI 2016/365.**

Private Housing (Tenancies) (Scotland) Act 2016 (asp 19)

Background

The private rented sector ('PRS') in Scotland has more than doubled in size in the past ten years and now covers 13% of homes (around 330,000). This increase in size has been matched by an increase in attention by Government and Parliament. Developments in the last few years have included (i) HMO regulation (2000), (ii) landlord registration (2006), (iii) a new repairing standard (2007), (iv) tenancy deposit schemes (2012), (iv) tenant information packs (2013), (v) a much-enhanced jurisdiction for what was formerly the Private Rented Housing Panel but is now (see p 91 below) the Housing and Property Chamber of the First-tier Tribunal (2014), and (vi) a registration system for letting agents (2014; see p 88 below). To this pattern of reform and change, the Private Housing (Tenancies) (Scotland) Act 2016 is an important addition. This introduces a new and mandatory PRS tenancy known as a 'private residential tenancy'. This will replace the assured and short assured tenancies which, since 1989, have been the only form of PRS tenancy available for ordinary houses.

The Act follows on from *A Place to Stay, A Place to Call Home: A Strategy for the Private Rented Sector in Scotland* (www.scotland.gov.uk/Publications/2013/05/5877), published in 2013 (see *Conveyancing 2013* pp 89–90), and from the work of the Government's PRS Tenancy Review Group, which reported in May 2014 (www.scotland.gov.uk/Topics/Built-Environment/Housing/privaterent/government/Tenancy-Review/report). The Act was the subject of two pre-legislative consultations by the Scottish Government, one in October 2014 (www.gov.scot/Publications/2014/10/9702) and the other in March 2015 (www.gov.scot/Publications/2015/03/6142). There were 2,500 responses to the first consultation and 7,689 to the second, although most of the latter were in support of one of four organised campaigns. The responses are summarised at www.gov.scot/Publications/2015/03/1968 and www.gov.scot/Publications/2015/08/3653.

The Bill was introduced to the Scottish Parliament on 7 October 2015, was passed on 17 March 2016, and received Royal Assent on 22 April 2016. Full details of its Parliamentary passage can be found at www.parliament.scot/parliamentarybusiness/Bills/92310.aspx. For the most part the Act is not yet in force, although a few provisions were commenced on 31 October 2016 by the **Private Housing (Tenancies) (Scotland) Act 2016 (Commencement No 1) Regulations 2016, SSI 2016/298**.

Two articles by George Clark describe the main features of the Act: see (2016) 140 *Greens Property Law Bulletin* 4, and (2016) 141 *Greens Property Law Bulletin* 1. A consultation document, *Consultation on proposals for regulations and policy supporting the Private Housing (Tenancies) (Scotland) Act 2016* (www.gov.scot/Publications/2016/10/8046) was published by the Scottish Government on 3 October 2016. This sought responses, by Boxing Day, on the statutory terms of tenancies, the form and content of the prescribed notices to be used by tenants and landlords under the new tenancy, the content of the model tenancy agreement, and whether there should be an option of serving documents electronically.

Private residential tenancies

Once the relevant provisions are in force, the only permitted PRS tenancy will be the new 'private residential tenancy' (ss 1, 2), and it will no longer be competent to enter into assured or short assured tenancies (sch 5 paras 1, 2, amending the Housing (Scotland) Act 1988). In most cases, existing tenancies will be unaffected. Special rules apply, as usual, for eg student lets, holiday lets, and lets by residential landlords (s 1(1)(c) and sch 1).

Security of tenure

A key feature of current short assured tenancies, which make up 94% of all PRS tenancies, is that the landlord is entitled to require the tenant to remove at the contractual ish. This will no longer be the case with private residential tenancies (s 44). Instead, tenants will have security of tenure and can only be removed if the landlord is able to establish, to the satisfaction of the Housing and Property Chamber of the First-tier Tribunal (which subsumed the Private Rented Housing Panel on 1 December 2016: see p 91 below), that one of the eighteen grounds for eviction set out in schedule 3 has been satisfied (ss 50 and 51). The grounds are:

1. landlord intends to sell;
2. property to be sold by lender;
3. landlord intends to refurbish;
4. landlord intends to live in property;
5. family member intends to live in property;
6. landlord intends to use for non-residential purpose;
7. property required for religious purpose;
8. tenant no longer an employee;
9. tenant no longer in need of supported accommodation;
10. tenant not occupying let property;
11. breach of tenancy agreement;
12. rent arrears of three consecutive months;
13. criminal behaviour;
14. anti-social behaviour;
15. association with person who has relevant conviction or engaged in anti-social behaviour;

16. landlord has ceased to be registered;
17. HMO licence has been revoked; or
18. overcrowding statutory notice.

Some of these grounds are at the discretion of the Tribunal in whole or in part while others are mandatory.

As always, termination requires to be preceded by what is now called a 'notice to leave' (ss 50(1)(a) and 52(3)) which must state the eviction ground that is said to apply (s 62(1)(c)). The normal period of notice is 84 days but is reduced to 28 days where the tenant has occupied for six months or less or where the eviction ground is based on the conduct of the tenant (s 54).

A revised version of the tenant information pack (as to which see *Conveyancing 2013* p 59) was published by the Scottish Government in December 2016: see www.gov.scot/Publications/2016/12/4614. It will need to be revised again once private residential tenancies are in operation.

Rent control

An element of rent control is a feature of the present law in respect that the First-tier Tribunal has power to fix a market rent, in certain circumstances, for both assured and short assured tenancies: see Housing (Scotland) Act 1988 ss 24 and 34. Equivalent provision is made in the Act in respect of the new private residential tenancy. While landlords are able to increase the rent, they cannot do so more than once a year (s 18). Tenants must be sent a rent-increase notice specifying the new rent (s 22). If they are unhappy with the new rent they can request a rent officer at Rent Service Scotland (www.gov.scot/Topics/Built-Environment/Housing/privaterent/advice) to set an open-market rent using the assumptions laid down in s 32 (ss 24 and 25)). There is a right of appeal to the First-tier Tribunal (ss 28–30).

A (controversial) novelty in the Act is the special provision made for 'rent pressure zones'. On application by a local authority, the Scottish Ministers can designate an area as a 'rent pressure zone' for a period of up to five years (ss 35–37 and 39). This is for areas where (s 40(3)):

  (i) rents payable within the proposed rent pressure zone are rising by too much,
 (ii) the rent rises within the proposed zone are causing undue hardship to tenants, and
(iii) the local authority within whose area the proposed zone lies is coming under increasing pressure to provide housing or subsidise the cost of housing as a consequence of the rent rises within the proposed zone.

The expression 'rising too much' is not defined.

Following the designation of an area as a 'rent pressure zone', rents are not to be increased by a percentage greater than the consumer price index rise since the last rent increase + 1 percentage point + X (being a number prescribed by the Scottish Ministers) (s 38). On application by the landlord, a rent officer can award a further increase in consequence of improvements (s 42). Information on recent rent levels can be found in *Private Sector Rent Statistics, Scotland, 2010 to 2016* (www.gov.scot/Publications/2016/11/3295) published on 8 November 2016. This shows a 14.8% cumulative increase in average rents from 2010 to 2016 for 2-bedroom properties – which is more than 2% above CPI – although there is considerable regional variation.

Model tenancy agreement

As under the present law, landlords in private residential tenancies must provide their tenants with a written tenancy agreement and certain other information (ss 10–13). In order to assist with this, the Scottish Government has prepared, and has been consulting on, a draft of a model tenancy agreement: see *Consultation on proposals for regulations and policy supporting the Private Housing (Tenancies) (Scotland) Act 2016* pp 55–83. This contains both mandatory and discretionary clauses, and could also be supplemented by additional clauses as the parties choose. The legislative basis of the mandatory clauses is ss 7 and 8 of the Act. As a minimum, these must include the clauses set out in schedule 2, which deal with receipts for rent paid in cash, rent increases, notification as to adult residents (other than the tenant), restrictions on subletting, and rights of access for repairs and inspection. The Scottish Government will also prepare a legal commentary on the model agreement, written in plain English.

Despite all of this, a private residential tenancy, even if for more than 12 months, is valid without writing provided that a person occupies the property as the person's only or principal home (s 3(1)). Thus s 1(2) of the Requirements of Writing (Scotland) Act 1995, which says that leases for more than 12 months must be in writing, is disapplied to PRTs.

Bankruptcy (Scotland) Act 2016 (asp 21)

This is a consolidation Act, replacing the Bankruptcy (Scotland) Act 1985, and bringing together in one place provisions which previously appeared in other legislation. As well as the Bankruptcy (Scotland) Act 1985, this includes the Bankruptcy (Scotland) Act 1993, the Bankruptcy and Diligence etc (Scotland) Act 2007, the Protected Trust Deeds (Scotland) Regulations 2013, SSI 2013/318, and the Bankruptcy and Debt Advice (Scotland) Act 2014. The Act is based on a draft Bill produced by the Scottish Law Commission: see *Report No 232 on the Consolidation of Bankruptcy Legislation in Scotland* (2013). The Report contains a Table of Derivations (pp 188–209) and a Table of Destinations (pp 210–43). The Act came into force on 30 November 2016: see **Bankruptcy (Scotland) Act 2016 (Commencement) Regulations 2016, SSI 2016/294**. The Act is supplemented by the **Bankruptcy (Scotland) Regulations 2016, SSI 2016/397**, and by the **Bankruptcy (Scotland) Act 2016 (Consequential Provisions and Modifications) Order 2016, SSI 2016/1034** (which deals with certain matters reserved to Westminster).

For discussion of the Act, see articles by Alan McIntosh (2016) 61 *Journal of the Law Society of Scotland* Aug/24, and by Graham Fisher (2016) 61 *Journal of the Law Society of Scotland*, online edition: www.bit.ly/2dymwgo.

Registration of letting agents

Part 4 (ss 29–62) of the Housing (Scotland) Act 2014 introduced a registration system for those, including solicitors, who act as letting agents for private-sector residential tenancies. This followed, and indeed was modelled on, earlier schemes for the registration of private-sector landlords (Antisocial Behaviour etc (Scotland) Act 2004 part 8) and property factors (Property Factors (Scotland) Act 2011). The change acknowledged both the size of the private-rented sector – it has doubled in the last ten years and now stands at around 13% of the housing stock – and also the problems which some agents cause. The official Policy Memorandum listed some of them (para 211): 'agents going out of business and losing all monies held on behalf of landlords and tenants; the use of poorly drafted and legally inaccurate tenancy agreements; and tenants being charged illegal premiums for accessing privately rented accommodation'. For further details, see *Conveyancing 2014* p 70.

The primary legislation is now supplemented by the **Letting Agent Registration (Scotland) Regulations 2016, SSI 2016/432**, which comes into force on 31 January 2018. This prescribes additional information to be included in the application for registration and on the register itself (regs 3 and 4). It also provides that applicants require to have a qualification at level 6 or above of the Scottish Credit and Qualifications Framework which includes training on matters such as the legal obligations relating to letting agency work, the rights and responsibilities of landlords and tenants, managing repairs, and handling money (regs 5–7).

As of 31 January 2018, letting agents will be subject to the Code of Practice provided for by s 46 of the Housing (Scotland) Act 2014 and set out in the schedule to **Letting Agent Code of Practice (Scotland) Regulations 2016, SSI 2016/133**. The Regulations were preceded by a public consultation: see *Conveyancing 2015* p 93 and, for an analysis of the responses, www.gov.scot/Publications/2016/01/6999. The Law Society was active in trying to ensure that solicitors who undertake letting agency work could avoid being regulated again, and differently, in respect of matters on which, as solicitors, they were already regulated. There were some victories. Solicitors, for example, are exempt from the requirement to obtain indemnity insurance (r 32(o)). On the other hand, and despite concerns about client confidentiality, solicitors, like other letting agents, must inform the local authority if client landlords are failing to meet their legal obligations (r 31).

Asset transfer requests

Part 5 (ss 77–97) of the Community Empowerment (Scotland) Act 2015 came fully into force on 23 January 2017: see **Community Empowerment (Scotland) Act 2015 (Commencement No 4 and Transitory Provision) Order 2016, SSI 2016/363**. This allows 'community transfer bodies' to request certain public bodies to sell or lease heritable property to them (s 79). See *Conveyancing 2015* p 76. The term 'community transfer bodies' has the same meaning as is provided for the community right to buy by s 34 of the Land Reform (Scotland) Act 2003 (as amended): see **Asset Transfer Request (Designation of Community Transfer Bodies) (Scotland) Order 2016, SSI 2016/361**. The relevant public bodies are listed in schedule 3 to the Act and include local authorities, the Scottish Government, the Scottish Courts and Tribunal Service, the Scottish Police Authority, Scottish Natural Heritage, and Scottish Water.

Following a public consultation (see www.gov.scot/Publications/2016/03/8947 and, for an analysis of responses, www.gov.scot/Publications/2016/11/5724), the Scottish Ministers have made Regulations on a number of topics. The procedure for making, and responding to, an 'asset transfer request' is set out in the **Asset Transfer Request (Procedure) (Scotland) Regulations 2016, SSI 2016/357**, with minor amendments in the **Community Empowerment (Miscellaneous Amendments) (Scotland) Regulations 2016, SSI 2016/411,** reg 2. In considering requests, public bodies are required to assess the community body's proposals against the current use or any other proposal, and must agree to the request unless there are reasonable grounds for refusal (s 82). There is a right of appeal against refusal, or the imposition of conditions, to the Scottish Ministers (s 85). Further details are given in the **Asset Transfer Request (Appeals) Scotland Regulations 2016, SSI 2016/359** as amended by the **Community Empowerment (Miscellaneous Amendments) (Scotland) Regulations 2016, SSI 2016/411,** reg 4.

On agreeing to an asset transfer request, public bodies issue a notice specifying the terms and conditions on which they are prepared to transfer ownership (s 83). It is then for the community transfer body to make a formal offer. If no contract is concluded within six months of the offer, the community transfer body may appeal to the Scottish Ministers (ss 83(5)–(7) and 90). Further details are given in the **Asset Transfer Request (Appeal Where No Contract Concluded) (Scotland) Regulations 2016, SSI 2016/360** as amended by the **Community Empowerment (Miscellaneous Amendments) (Scotland) Regulations 2016, SSI 2016/411,** reg 5.

In order to assist community bodies, and in the interests of transparency more generally, each schedule 3 body must establish, maintain and publicise – including on a website – a 'Register of Land' which, to the best of the body's knowledge and belief, lists all land owned or leased by the authority (s 94). The **Community Empowerment (Registers of Land) (Scotland) Regulations 2016, SSI 2016/362,** as amended by the **Community Empowerment (Miscellaneous Amendments) (Scotland) Regulations 2016, SSI 2016/411,** reg 6, sets out a list of types of land that do not need to be included in the Register. This comprises roads, railway stations and other parts of railway systems, operational canals, bus stations, reservoirs, land occupied by masts used for electronic communications, land used in connection with covert police operations, mineral rights, and souvenir plots. None of these is likely to be of much interest to community bodies.

The Scottish Government has issued guidance on the procedure both for community transfer bodies (www.gov.scot/Publications/2016/11/3688) and also for public authorities (www.gov.scot/Publications/2016/11/1889).

Energy performance in non-domestic buildings

Buildings account for over 40% of the carbon emissions in the UK. New buildings can be made more energy-efficient by appropriate provisions in the building regulations. For existing buildings, however, the task is much harder. An initial step was taken on 4 January 2009, in partial transposition of the Energy Performance of Buildings Directive (Directive 2002/91/EC). This requires the production of an energy performance certificate ('EPC') on the sale or lease of all buildings, domestic or non-domestic: see the Energy Performance of Buildings (Scotland) Regulations 2008, SSI 2008/309, discussed in *Conveyancing 2008* pp 47–48. Since then the 2008 Regulations have been subject to a series of amendments: see (i) the Energy Performance of Buildings (Scotland) Amendment Regulations 2012, SSI 2012/190; (ii) the Energy Performance of Buildings (Scotland) Amendment (No 2) Regulations 2012, SSI 2012/208; (iii) the Energy Performance of Buildings (Scotland) Amendment (No 3) Regulations 2012, SSI 2012/315 (all described in *Conveyancing 2012* p 67); and (iv) the Energy Performance of Buildings (Scotland) Amendment Regulations 2013, SSI 2013/12 (described in *Conveyancing 2013* pp 58–59).

While, however, EPCs disclose the current energy performance of a building, they do not of themselves require the carrying out of improvements. Two new legislative initiatives seek to promote improvements, at least to a small degree. First, the **Building (Energy Performance of Buildings) (Scotland) Amendment Regulations 2016, SSI 2016/71** will, when they come into force on 31 December 2020 (or on 1 January 2019 for buildings occupied and owned by public authorities), require the inspection of accessible parts of all air-conditioning systems at regular intervals not exceeding five years.

Secondly, and much more importantly, the **Assessment of Energy Performance of Non-domestic Buildings (Scotland) Regulations 2016, SS1 2016/146** seek to force owners to improve the energy efficiency of non-domestic buildings by means of an 'action plan' which must be commissioned and exhibited whenever a building or building unit of more than 1,000 square metres is sold, or is leased to a new tenant (reg 2(1)). This is in addition to the requirement to produce an EPC. The Regulations were made under s 63 of the Climate Change (Scotland) Act 2009, and came into force on 1 September 2016. The requirement is normally waived for buildings completed after 4 March 2002 as, due to the building regulations by then in force, such buildings should already be reasonably energy-efficient (reg 2(2)). Helpful guidance can be found at www.gov.scot/Topics/Built-Environment/Building/Building-standards/S63.

Action plans are produced by 'section 63 advisers' – qualified members of organisations approved by the Scottish Ministers under reg 13. A sample plan is given on p 19 of Scottish Government, *Improving Energy Performance and Emissions in existing Non-Domestic Buildings: A guide for Building Owners* (2016; www.gov.scot/Resource/0050/00503633.pdf). The plan contains a programme for the implementation of measures to improve energy performance and reduce emissions of greenhouse gases (reg 6(1)). The range of 'improvement measures' (set out sch 1) is, however, fairly modest: installing draught stripping to doors and windows; upgrading lighting controls; upgrading heating controls; installing an insulation jacket to a hot water tank; upgrading low energy lighting; installation of insulation in an accessible roof space; and replacement of a boiler. This is deliberate. The Regulations aim low in the hope of encouraging the owner to carry out the necessary work. Apart from the last, all the other improvements should recoup the capital cost by energy savings over a seven-year period.

In principle, the work prescribed in the action plan must be carried out in three and a half years (42 months: see regs 3 (definition of 'compliance period') and 8) – a figure arrived at by attributing half a year to obtaining statutory permissions and three years to carrying out the work. The obligation falls on the owner (reg 8(1)); if the action plan is issued in connection with a sale, this means the obligation is on the new owner. On completion of the work, a new EPC is needed (to record the improvements) as well as a 'document of confirmation improvement' (reg 9) which, in effect, is an updated version of the action plan. All documentation involved in the process, including the initial action plan, must be registered in the Scottish Energy Performance Certificate Register (www. scottishepcregister.org.uk/) (reg 14).

In recognition of the fact that energy can be saved by behavioural change as well as by improvements, owners are allowed to postpone carrying out the work prescribed in the action plan as long as they obtain, and register, an annual 'display energy certificate' reporting annual energy use (regs 8(2), (3) and 11). In such cases the plan will elect for 'operational rating' rather than 'building improvements' (reg 8(3)(a)).

Local authorities have the duty of enforcing the Regulations within their area (reg 20). Non-compliance can result in a penalty charge of £1,000 (reg 22).

First-tier Tribunal: Housing and Property Chamber

The First-tier Tribunal was established by the Tribunals (Scotland) Act 2014. With effect from 1 December 2016, the Tribunal has been divided into five 'chambers': Mental Health, Housing and Property, Health and Education, General Regulatory, and Tax: see **First-tier Tribunal for Scotland (Chambers) Regulations 2016, SSI 2016/341.** The Housing and Property Chamber is based at 1 Atlantic Quay, 45 Robertson Street, Glasgow G2 8JB (www.housingandpropertychamber.scot/). Normally, it comprises a legal member either sitting on his or her own or with the addition of a maximum of two ordinary members: see **First-tier Tribunal for Scotland Housing and Property Chamber and Upper Tribunal for Scotland (Composition) Regulations 2016, SSI 2016/340**. The Rules of Procedure can be found in sch 1 of the **First-tier Tribunal for Scotland Housing and Property Chamber (Procedure) Regulations 2016, SSI 2016/339.** Thus far, the Housing and Property Chamber has taken over the functions of the Homeowner Housing Committees and Homeowner Housing Panel (in relation to disputes with factors under the Property Factors (Scotland) Act 2011) and of the Private Rented Housing Committees and Private Rented Housing Panel (in relation to disputes in the private-rented sector, including repossessions): see **First-tier Tribunal for Scotland (Transfer of Functions of the Homeowner Housing**

Committees) Regulations 2016, SSI 2016/335; First-tier Tribunal for Scotland (Transfer of Functions of the Homeowner Housing Panel) Regulations 2016, SSI 2016/ 336; First-tier Tribunal for Scotland (Transfer of Functions of the Private Rented Housing Committees) Regulations 2016, SSI 2016/337; and First-tier Tribunal for Scotland (Transfer of Functions of the Private Rented Housing Panel) Regulations 2016, SSI 2016/338. The functions of the Lands Tribunal will follow in due course.

A new tenant information pack is prescribed by the **Tenant Information Packs (Assured Tenancies) (Scotland) Amendment Order 2016, SSI 2016/334**, to take account of the transfer of functions.

New conservation bodies

Conservation bodies are bodies which are able to create and hold conservation burdens under s 38 of the Title Conditions (Scotland) Act 2003. A conservation burden is a personal real burden which preserves or protects the natural or built environment for the benefit of the public. The first list of conservation bodies, prescribed by the Title Conditions (Scotland) Act 2003 (Conservation Bodies) Order 2003, SSI 2003/453, was amended by the Title Conditions (Scotland) Act 2003 (Conservation Bodies) Amendment Order 2004, SSI 2004/400, the Title Conditions (Scotland) Act 2003 (Conservation Bodies) Amendment Order 2006, SSI 2006/110, the Title Conditions (Scotland) Act 2003 (Conservation Bodies) Amendment (No 2) Order 2006, SSI 2006/130, the Title Conditions Scotland) Act 2003 (Conservation Bodies) Amendment Order 2007, SSI 2007/533, the Title Conditions (Scotland) Act 2003 (Conservation Bodies) Amendment Order 2008, SSI 2008/217, the Title Conditions (Scotland) Act 2003 (Conservation Bodies) Amendment Order 2012, SSI 2012/30, and the Title Conditions (Scotland) Act 2003 (Conservation Bodies) Amendment Order 2013, SSI 2013/289. The **Title Conditions (Scotland) Act 2003 (Conservation Bodies) Amendment Order 2016, SSI 2016/371,** further amends the list by adding Chapelton Community Interest Company and Tornagrain Conservation Trust.

The complete list of conservation bodies is now:

All local authorities
Aberdeen City Heritage Trust
Alba Conservation Trust
Castles of Scotland Preservation Trust
Chapelton Community Interest Company
Dundee Historic Environment Trust
Edinburgh World Heritage Trust
Glasgow Building Preservation Trust
Glasgow City Heritage Trust
Highlands Buildings Preservation Trust
Inverness City Heritage Trust
New Lanark Trust
Perth and Kinross Heritage Trust
Plantlife – The Wild-Plant Conservation Charity

Scottish Natural Heritage
Sir Henry Wade's Pilmuir Trust
Solway Heritage
St Vincent Crescent Preservation Trust
Stirling City Heritage Trust
Strathclyde Building Preservation Trust
Tayside Building Preservation Trust
The John Muir Trust
The National Trust for Scotland for Places of Historic Interest or Natural Beauty
The Royal Society for the Protection of Birds
The Scottish Wildlife Trust
The Trustees of the Landmark Trust
The Woodland Trust
Tornagrain Conservation Trust
United Kingdom Historic Building Preservation Trust

PART III
OTHER MATERIAL

OTHER MATERIAL

Registers of Scotland

KIR underway

Keeper-induced registration ('KIR') is now underway in three different parts of the country. The properties being targeted are those with straightforward titles in research areas, ie in housing estates and other developments which are subject to uniform burdens which have already been examined by Registers of Scotland ('RoS'). For more about KIR, see p 158 below.

Fees to remain unchanged

In September 2016 Keith Brown MSP, the Cabinet Secretary for the Economy, Jobs and Fair Work, announced that the fees charged by RoS will remain the same for the time being, and that the 25% discount for applications for voluntary registration will be maintained until at least March 2019.

Digital discharges, standard securities, and dispositions

Conveyancing is set to be transformed in 2017 with the replacement of paper discharges, standard securities, and dispositions with digital equivalents. For details, see p 152 below.

Online requests for plan assistance service

An enhancement to the online reports portal will enable plan assistance service ('PAS') requests to be submitted online from early in 2017. The system will provide notifications at each stage of the process, and also make it possible to monitor the progress of inquiries online.

First registrations: encumbrances over a lesser area

Where, on first registration, some lesser area within the plot being registered is or will be subject to a registered encumbrance such as a servitude, there must be submitted with the application a plan or description sufficient to enable the Keeper to delineate the boundaries of that area on the cadastral map: see Land Registration etc (Scotland) Act 2012 ss 23(1)(d), 25(1)(c) and 28(1)(b). On 8 November 2016 RoS announced an extra-statutory concession in respect of pre-existing encumbrances. In future, only those applications for registration of a deed creating a *new* encumbrance will be rejected where insufficient information has been provided.

Register of Sasines closed to standard securities

Since 1 April 2016 it has ceased to be possible to register standard securities in the Register of Sasines: see Land Registration etc (Scotland) Act 2012 s 48(2) and Registers of Scotland (Voluntary Registration, Amendment of Fees, etc) Order 2015, SSI 2015/265, art 3. All standard securities must now be registered in the Land Register. That means that if the plot of land is still held on a Sasine title, the registration of the security must be preceded or accompanied by a first registration of the plot. No additional registration fee is charged for a voluntary registration which accompanies the registration of a standard security: see SSI 2015/265 art 4(5).

Corporate plan 2016–19: new target times for registration

In RoS's new *Corporate Plan 2016–19* the target time for most registrations is 20 days (see para 54). In the case of first registrations this halves the previous target, of 40 days, and is an incidental benefit of the introduction of 'tell me don't show me'.

Last 1979 Act applications completed

According to the RoS *Annual Report 2015–16* p 17, the last two applications under the Land Registration (Scotland) Act 1979 which were still outstanding were despatched on 31 March 2016. Most of the others had been completed in the course of the previous year. A particular problem for RoS had been the record number of applications received immediately before the introduction of the 2012 Act.

Official: RoS not leaving Meadowbank House

On 19 September 2016 the Keeper issued a formal denial of a story published in the previous day's *Sunday Post* to the effect that RoS were leaving Meadowbank House. They are not. But they *are* changing offices in Glasgow, moving in February 2017 from Hanover House, Douglas Street to St Vincent Plaza, 319 St Vincent Street, Glasgow G2 5LP.

ScotLIS

ScotLIS (Scotland's Land and Information System) is an online system that will allow professionals and members of the public to find out comprehensive information about any piece of land or property in Scotland with a single inquiry. See www.ros.gov.uk/about-us/scotlis. Based in Registers of Scotland, ScotLIS is expected to be up and running by the autumn of 2017. In due course it will replace Registers Direct. ScotLIS is underpinned by Land Register data, and searched via different layers on the cadastral map. As well as allowing access to the Land Register and Register of Inhibitions, it will, in time, include a great deal of other information such as school catchment areas, mining reports, flood risks and crime statistics. Some of the information will be free, others will not. For further details, see Stewart Brymer and Iain McKay, 'What is ScotLIS?' (2016) *61 Journal of the Law Society of Scotland* Jan/34. (See also p 169 below.)

Revocation of Rule B8.2 (ARTL Mandates)

Rule B8.2 of the Law Society's *Rules and Guidance* has been revoked with effect from 1 September 2016. This required that solicitors obtain a mandate signed by the client in a specified form and then register that mandate with the Keeper prior to taking certain steps to deal with property rights under ARTL. According to the Law Society's website, 'the rationale for revocation is primarily that the rule conveys no benefit to clients and may increase costs; is no longer effectively enforced; is unnecessary given the increased awareness of the ARTL system; and its maintenance is inconsistent with progress by the Registers towards e-enablement.' Nonetheless, solicitors will continue to need clear, written authority to sign a deed electronically on behalf of a client, and this issue will become of increasing importance with the rush towards digital deeds which is expected to occur in 2017: see p 152 below and, for a discussion of mandates, para 19.7 of K G C Reid and G L Gretton, *Land Registration* (2017).

New edition of Scottish Standard Clauses

The first edition of the Scottish Standard Clauses was published in December 2014. A revised, second edition has now been issued and came into effect on 3 May 2016. It is available at www.lawscot.org.uk/media/816883/Scottish-Standard-Clauses-Edition-2-.pdf.

Styles of commercial lease

The Property Standardisation Group (www.psglegal.co.uk) is engaged in 'putting a kilt' on the suite of commercial leases produced, for England and Wales, by Model Commercial Lease (www.modelcommerciallease.com). The first lease to be adapted is the lease of part of an office building; others will follow. The styles are intended to achieve a reasonable balance between the parties, and hence to provide a useful starting-point for negotiations. The styles aim for plain English, and make use of short clauses.

Happy Valley and Aberdeen fraud

Two long-running disputes, neither of which reflected well on Scottish conveyancing practice, came to an end during 2016. The first concerned the unfortunately-named Happy Valley housing estate in Blackburn, West Lothian where, it turned out, a small number of houses had been built partly on land not belonging to the builder and where the builder subsequently became insolvent. The second, concerning property in Queen's Gardens, Aberdeen, involved the fraudulent alteration of a disposition which may have been carried out by a solicitor (but not the solicitor who acted for the purchaser). The second, but not the first, has resulted in reported litigation: *Pocock's Tr v Skene Investments (Aberdeen) Ltd* [2011] CSOH 144, 2011 GWD 30-654 (discussed in *Conveyancing 2011* pp 126–29).

The cases prompted an investigation on behalf of the Law Society by Sheriff Principal Edward Bowen QC. His report, on *Consumer Protections in Conveyancing Cases*, was published in February 2015 (www.lawscot.org.uk/media/439009/ Law-Society-report-Consumer-Protections-in-Conveyancing-Cases.pdf): see *Conveyancing 2015* pp 108–10. An immediate change made as a result of his recommendations was to rename the Guarantee Fund the 'Client Protection Fund'. Other recommendations require legislation and have not so far been implemented.

According to *The Herald* of 17 April 2016 it was a pay-out from the Client Protection Fund, to the tune of £780,000, which brought the Aberdeen fraud case to an end. Meanwhile, joy was restored to Happy Valley by a payment from the Master Policy which allowed the disputed strip of land to be transferred to the home-owners affected: see JLSS online news for 21 June 2016.

Community right to buy

Extension of community right to buy

It is more than a decade since the community right to buy, in part 2 of the Land Reform (Scotland) Act 2003, came into force. Restricted to rural areas in its first incarnation, it was extended to the whole of Scotland, with effect from 15 April 2016, by s 36 of the Community Empowerment (Scotland) Act 2015 (amending s 33 of the Land Reform (Scotland) Act 2003). The 2015 Act also made some important technical changes: see ss 36–61, summarised in *Conveyancing 2015* pp 76–77. New guidance for landowners and community bodies has now been issued by the Scottish Government: see www.gov.scot/ Publications/2016/03/8496. There are also 'quick information' guides for both community bodies (www.gov.scot/Publications/2016/02/7321) and for landowners and creditors (www.gov.scot/Publications/2016/02/8289), as well as an information leaflet (www.gov.scot/Publications/2016/02/8782).

The 2003 Act also contains, in part 3, a crofting community right to buy. This too was modified by the Community Empowerment (Scotland) Act 2015 ss 62–73. A consultation on new secondary legislation (www.gov.scot/ Publications/2016/03/2558) was launched on 1 March 2016, with responses requested by 20 June 2016. It covered matters such as application forms, the conduct of ballots, forms of notice, and procedures for compensation.

Two further community rights to buy have been added in the last year or two but neither is yet in force. These are the right to buy abandoned, neglected or detrimental land contained in part 3A of the Land Reform (Scotland) Act 2003 (inserted by s 74 of the Community Empowerment (Scotland) Act 2015: see *Conveyancing 2015* pp 75–76), and the right to buy land to further sustainable development contained in part 5 of the Land Reform (Scotland) Act 2016 (see p 81 above). In relation to the first of these, the Scottish Government has been consulting on secondary legislation on matters such as the meaning of 'eligible land', and the prohibitions or suspensions of rights that follow receipt of an application: see www.gov.scot/Publications/2016/03/9764 and, for the 51 responses, www.gov.scot/Publications/2016/09/7330.

So far, around 500,000 acres of land is in community ownership. The Scottish Government's target is to have 1 million acres in community ownership by 2020.

Possible implications for missives

With the extension to the whole country of the community right to buy in part 2 of the Land Reform (Scotland) Act 2003, there is the potential for *any* sale to be affected by a community buy-out. Hitherto, however, such buy-outs have been very rare (see below). Nonetheless, there may possibly be implications for missives, at least in some cases.

It is competent to apply for the registration of a community interest in land at any stage before missives of sale have been concluded in respect of the target land (Land Reform (Scotland) Act 2003 s 39(4A), (5)). The thing most to be feared, from a seller's point of view, is an application which is made immediately pre-missives. This will stop the transaction in its tracks even if, before finding out about the application, the parties had proceeded to conclude missives. Admittedly, such 'late' applications are subject to the additional requirements set out in s 39(3) and so are more likely to be rejected. A recent example of a rejection is *Coastal Regeneration Alliance Ltd v Scottish Ministers* [2016] SC EDIN 60, 2016 GWD 29-523 (Case (30) above). Nonetheless, the seller will have to wait for the Scottish Ministers' decision, which must normally be made within 30 days (s 39(2)(b)), before taking stock of the situation. The Property Standardisation Group has recently added a new clause – clause 7.5 – to its offer to sell in order to deal with the problems of late applications for registration of a community interest in land: see www.psglegal.co.uk and, for explanatory background, an article published at (2016) 61 *Journal of the Law Society of Scotland* July/34.

Buy-outs in the shadow of the legislation: a new protocol

There were only 21 community buy-outs in the first decade of the legislation: see *Impact Evaluation of the Community Right to Buy* (2015; www.gov.scot/Publications/2015/10/8581) para 1.29. But other purchases will have taken place in the shadow of the legislation. Indeed, the (inevitable) complexities of the legislation make negotiated sales particularly attractive. With that in mind, representative organisations of community owners and private landowners – Community Land Scotland and Scottish Land and Estates – have agreed a protocol for negotiated sales: see www.communitylandscotland.org.uk/find-out-more/resources/. This includes detailed flowcharts, with notes, for both landlord-initiated and community-initiated purchases. There is also a summary of the legislation, and case studies of negotiated purchases which have taken place in, for example, Findhorn, Barvas, Carloway, and Scalpay.

Scottish Land Fund relaunched

The most obvious barrier to community buy-outs is money. Here significant assistance is provided by the Scottish Land Fund. This was relaunched by the Scottish Government on 1 April 2016 and will run until 2020. The Fund is administered by the Big Lottery and Highland and Islands Enterprise: see www.biglotteryfund.org.uk/scottishlandfund. On average, the Fund pays for 80% of acquisition costs, but community bodies must, as a minimum, find 5% of their funding from other sources.

In its previous incarnation, the Fund awarded a total of £9 million over three years to 52 communities, assisting in the acquisition of more than 90,000 acres of land. An independent evaluation can be found at www.gov.scot/Publications/2016/07/1628. The Government has committed £10 million to the relaunched Fund in each of its first two years, thus more than trebling the amount previously available.

Diversity of landownership: social, economic and environmental outcomes

A research study on *The impact of diversity of ownership scale on social, economic and environmental outcomes* (www.gov.scot/Publications/2016/07/1094) was commissioned by the Scottish Government to examine the local impacts of differing scales of rural landownership on social, economic and environmental outcomes. In three separate case-studies, the study considered pairs of parishes – one dominated by one or more large landowner(s) and a nearby comparator parish that had once been so dominated but in which the land had come to be fragmented. The results are of considerable interest in the context of the Government's drive to achieve greater fragmentation of ownership. The study suggests that the scale of landownership is only one factor among many in promoting sustainable development.

The main findings were as follows (pp 1–2):

> Land ownership scale is one of a myriad of factors that influence the economic, social and environmental development of rural communities. The complexity of ownership motivations, societal, policy and economic interactions in driving community development means that it is too simplistic to conclude that scale of land ownership is a significant factor in the sustainable development of communities.
>
> There was a wide range of land ownership scales and degrees of land ownership fragmentation within the selected case studies and different local community development pathways that have resulted in quite different local sustainable development outcomes. Whilst it therefore may be tempting to conclude that the different local outcomes were related to land ownership factors, the research findings confirm that interactions of other factors have a very strong bearing on local development.
>
> Indeed the key historical (and current) forces of change in the case studies were often reported by research participants as not being directly related to land ownership, instead being driven by a range of general socio-economic factors: regional economic growth, mechanisation, reduced land based workforce, mobility of people,

housing developments, tourism growth, infrastructure, communications, commuters, second homes, ageing populations, improved standards of living etc.

The types of change faced by communities are heavily influenced by location – more specifically accessibility of urban areas. Changes in land-based employment, demography and housing development were influenced by proximity to urban areas. Accessible areas had population growth and housing developments driven by urban based employment and commuting opportunities, whilst more remote areas had less population growth, higher shares of employment in farming, forestry, a growing reliance on the tourism sector and higher proportions of housing stock used as second homes and tourism accommodation. Choices made by land owners clearly influence the availability of land for housing development, but so do local and national policies (eg council/social housing, planning permission).

Overcoming barriers to community land-based activities

Following a study published in 2015 which sought to identify the barriers to community land-based activities (see *Conveyancing 2015* pp 111–13), a new report by the James Hutton Institute on behalf of the Scottish Government, *Good practice in overcoming barriers to community land-based activities* (2016; www.gov. scot/Publications/2016/07/7298), considers ways in which such barriers might be overcome. The findings are based on an interview survey of 20 representatives of private and third-sector landowners. The report puts forward a number of 'good practice principles' (p 5):

Good practice principles for private landowners

  (i) Ensuring clarity and transparency regarding engagement processes (eg regarding intentions, through an agreed discussion format and recording discussions).
 (ii) Ensuring supportive behaviour and attitude (ie respect, honesty and responsiveness, plus commitment to community engagement).
(iii) Fostering positive relationships through direct communication, and building a 'track record' of community engagement.
(iv) Involving expertise and specialist knowledge, and ensuring that professional land management advisors adhere to good practice principles.
 (v) Reflectivity in land ownership and management (ie promoting a transparent estate development strategy, including community engagement, recognising the public interest in decision-making, identifying surplus land/assets and make available for community land-based activities, etc).

Good practice principles for communities

  (i) Ensuring positive and early engagement with the relevant landowner(s) (eg presenting proposals, and seeking up-to-date information and views).
 (ii) Undertaking strategic and critical thinking (ie regarding community dynamics, capacity, governance, and needs, in addition to the role of asset ownership and alternatives).
(iii) Establishing a 'sustainable development' plan, demonstrating community visioning, land use assessments and resource planning.
(iv) Achieving a unified community voice, through active participation in local democracy and dialogue.

    (v) Building community capacity, positive engagement behaviours and knowledge (eg of valuation processes, negotiation practices, business planning, etc).

    (vi) To work with objective and highly skilled community advisors (including development officers and land agents), in order to support the progress of land-based activities (eg in seeking funding, devising business plans, commissioning feasibility studies, transacting land sales, etc).

These principles are discussed and developed on pp 38–45 of the report. Other matters considered include success factors, and challenges facing private landowners. The research has particular relevance to the requirement, in s 44 of the Land Reform (Scotland) Act 2016, that the Government issue guidance to those who own and control land as to the need to engage local communities in respect of decisions which might affect them.

Land Use Strategy

The first Land Use Strategy was laid before the Scottish Parliament in 2011, in implement of s 57 of the Climate Change (Scotland) Act 2009. It comprised a Vision, Three Objectives, and Ten Principles for Sustainable Land Use. They are reproduced in full in *Conveyancing 2011* pp 75–76. That, however, was far from being the end of the matter because s 57(6) of the Act requires that a revised Land Use Strategy be prepared every five years. For this the preparations have been extensive. An interim review of the workings of the Strategy was published in 2014: see *Conveyancing 2014* p 104. Meanwhile there were progress reports, stakeholder workshops, regional land-use pilot projects, and finally a public consultation the results of which are summarised at www.gov.scot/Publications/2016/03/6371. The final document was published on 22 March 2016: see *Getting the best from our land: A Land Use Strategy for Scotland 2016–2021* (www.gov.scot/Publications/2016/03/5773). This was accompanied by a second document (www.gov.scot/Publications/2016/03/6493) which explained how the consultation responses were taken into account in the final version of the revised Strategy.

    As the final document records (p 4), the comments made in the review reflected 'the changing landscape of ideas since 2011'. Nonetheless, it was decided that the 2011 Land Use Strategy could be carried forward, unaltered, for the next five years. The original Vision, Three Objectives, and Ten Principles for Sustainable Land Use are, however, now supplemented by Nine Policies. These are (pp 14–37):

1. We are committed to better understanding and managing Scotland's natural resources to enable their fair, wise and productive use, and to conserve stocks of ecosystem services for future generations. We will do this by promoting an ecosystem approach to managing our natural capital.
2. The Land Use Strategy 2016–2021 sits alongside and has informed the National Planning Framework 3, Scottish Planning Policy and the National Marine Plan to support Scotland's Economic Strategy 2015. Relevant sectoral strategies (eg forestry and agriculture) will take account of the Land Use Strategy.

3. We will undertake a programme of information and awareness-raising. This will provide:
   - more detail and clarity on the relevance of the Land Use Strategy to the planning system;
   - information about the added value the Land Use Strategy can bring, particularly to development planning; and
   - information on the use of an ecosystems approach in Strategic Environmental Assessment (SEA), which in turn supports development.
4. We will undertake a review of the Scottish Forestry Strategy.
5. We will develop and consult on the draft of a first Land Rights and Responsibilities Statement which will contain principles to guide the development of public policy on the rights and responsibilities in relation to the ownership, use and management of land.
6. We will continue to encourage those holding public data to make it open and available for others to use and will facilitate access to that data via the Land Use Data Directory. We will explore the development of models and Geographic Information System (GIS) tools to enable assessments of land use/management change.
7. We will encourage the establishment of regional land use partnerships.
8. We will develop and implement a package of measures to facilitate the step change to climate friendly farming and crofting. This will promote carbon efficient agriculture, environmental benefits and increasingly integrated land use.
9. We will continue to develop a targeted approach in the current SRDP Agri-Environment Climate Scheme and will utilise more localised map-based ecosystems assessments to inform funding decisions as appropriate and as these become available across Scotland.

Future management of the Crown Estate

As a recent consultation document – *A Consultation on the Long Term Management of the Crown Estate in Scotland* (www.gov.scot/Publications/2017/01/8661) – reminds us (pp 7–8 and 59–60), the Crown Estate in Scotland comprises some 3,000 individual assets, including the seabed within territorial waters, around half of the foreshore, and 37,000 hectares of rural land. As well as salmon-fishing rights, there are 5,000 licensed moorings and 800 aquaculture sites. The Crown Estate is owned by the Crown but managed, on a UK basis, by the Crown Estate Commissioners, and all profits are paid to the Treasury. That, however, is about to change. While ownership will remain undisturbed, the power of administration is shortly to be transferred to the Scottish Ministers by virtue of s 90B of the Scotland Act 1998, a provision which was added by s 36 of the Scotland Act 2016. Thereafter, all profits from the Crown Estate in Scotland will be paid into the Scottish Consolidated Fund, although this will be largely fiscally neutral as there is to be a baseline deduction from the Scottish Government's block grant from Westminster equal to the net profit generated by Crown Estate assets in the year before the transfer (p 45). The sums in any case are modest. In 2015/16 the gross revenue from the Crown Estate in Scotland was £14 million, yielding a net profit of around £6.6 million (p 42).

The consultation mentioned above is concerned with arrangements for the long-term management of the Crown Estate in Scotland. As this will require legislation by the Scottish Parliament, it is unlikely to be in place before 2019 or 2020 (p 13). Three options for future management are put forward in the paper (para 2.2). The Crown Estate could be (i) managed at a national (ie all-Scotland) level, or (ii) managed at a local level by local authorities or community bodies, or (iii) there could be some combination of the two depending on the type of asset. In this connection it is worth recalling that the Smith Commission of November 2014, in recommending (para 32) that 'responsibility for the management of the Crown Estate's economic assets in Scotland, and the revenue generated from these assets; should be 'transferred to the Scottish Parliament' also recommended (para 33) that 'following this transfer, responsibility for the management of those assets' should be 'further devolved to local authority areas such as Orkney, Shetland, Na h-Eilean Siar or other areas who seek such responsibilities'. In the event that option (iii) were to be pursued, a possible division of assets suggested in the paper (para 2.4) would be for local councils or communities to manage foreshore rights, leasing for wave and tidal energy, and certain ports and jetties, and for a national body to manage offshore renewable leasing, rights over cables and pipelines, gas storage and mineral rights, and rights to naturally occurring gold and silver.

The consultation document touches on a number of other topics, including whether Crown assets should continue to be managed on a fully commercial basis or whether account should be taken of wider socio-economic or other benefits (para 1.2). The document was published on 4 January 2017 and responses were requested by 29 March 2017.

Meanwhile, a short-term administrative solution is also needed, as the target date for the transfer of management powers is April 2017. On this, too, the Scottish Government has been consulting. The Government's proposals were set out in *Crown Estate – Consultation on Proposals for Establishing the Interim Body to Manage the Crown Estate Assets in Scotland Post-Devolution* (www.gov. scot/Publications/2016/06/8344), published on 30 June 2016, with an analysis of the responses (www.gov.scot/Publications/2016/10/7117) following on 24 October 2016. The plan is that, in the first years, the Crown Estate in Scotland should be administered on an all-Scotland basis by a body corporate, separate from the Scottish Government, to be known as Crown Estate Scotland (Interim Management).The necessary statutory instrument – the Crown Estate Scotland (Interim Management) Order – was approved by the Scottish Parliament on 30 November 2016 and is expected to gain Privy Council approval early in 2017.

Commercial harvesting of seaweed

At present, seaweed is harvested only on a small scale. To assess whether that might be changed, Marine Scotland has carried out a Strategic Environmental Assessment ('SEA') of wild-seaweed harvesting to investigate the sustainability and potential environmental and cumulative impacts of large-scale mechanical extraction of wild seaweed, in particular kelp forests. Its report, *Wild Seaweed*

Harvesting: Strategic Environmental Assessment – Environmental Report (www. gov.scot/Publications/2016/11/6869), was published on 22 November 2016. Consultation responses are invited by 15 February 2017.

The report begins by explaining the ecological role of seaweeds (p 2):

> Seaweeds and seagrasses play a key role in marine and coastal ecosystems. Some are able to modify the environment (ie 'ecosystem engineers') and support high levels of marine and coastal biodiversity. As primary producers, they are also critical for supporting food webs which in turn contribute to fish and shellfish productivity. … Seaweeds and seagrasses also provide a number of ecosystem services, including natural hazard protection and climate regulation. Kelp forests and seagrasses are known for their capacity to weaken waves and reduce currents. Beach-cast seaweeds provide nutrients to dune habitats which in turn stabilise local sediments and contribute to coastal protection. In terms of climate regulation, seaweeds and seagrass habitats are important carbon stores and some may act as carbon sinks.

On commercial harvesting, the report's conclusion is largely negative (p 6):

> The SEA has confirmed that significant adverse effects can occur as a result of large-scale (ie industrial) mechanised harvesting of seaweeds (namely kelps and wracks). Although there is no evidence that small scale artisanal hand cutting or gathering of living and beach-cast seaweeds at discrete locations has significant environmental effects, there is the potential for significant cumulative effects as a result of multiple harvesting activities. However, we do not know what the cumulative effects of a large number of small-scale activities being undertaken within the same geographic location or the cumulative effects of potential small scale harvesting operations in conjunction with large scale industrial operations would be. These would need to be considered in the cumulative assessments of individual licence applications.

Scottish Vacant and Derelict Land Survey 2015

The Scottish Government conducts an annual survey of vacant and derelict land based on returns from local authorities. 'Vacant' land is land which is unused for the purposes for which it is held and is viewed as an appropriate site for development; the land must either have had prior development on it or preparatory work must have taken place in anticipation of future development. 'Derelict' land (and buildings) is land which has been so damaged by development that it is incapable of development for beneficial use without rehabilitation. The annual surveys may be watched with greater attention following the introduction of a community right to buy abandoned, neglected or detrimental land by s 74 of the Community Empowerment (Scotland) Act 2015.

Key findings from the 2015 survey (published in May 2016: www.gov.scot/ Publications/2016/05/1596) include (pp 7–8):

- There has been a large upward revision to the total amount of derelict land reported for 2014, from 8,509 to 10,753 hectares. This increase was mainly due to the addition of 2,217 hectares of land that became derelict in East Ayrshire due to the liquidation of Scottish Coal and ATH Resources causing several surface coal mines to fall out of use.

- The total amount of derelict and urban vacant land in Scotland decreased by 458 hectares or 3.5%, from 13,132 hectares in 2014 to 12,674 hectares in 2015. Of those, 2,309 hectares (18%) were classified as urban vacant and 10,365 hectares (82%) were classified as derelict.
- The local authority with the highest amount of recorded derelict and urban vacant land is East Ayrshire, containing 2,536 hectares (20% of the Scotland total). Highland has the second highest amount with 1,342 hectares (11%), North Ayrshire is third with 1,333 hectares (11%), followed by North Lanarkshire with 1,266 hectares (10%).
- For those sites where the previous use is known, 38% of derelict land recorded in 2015 had been previously used for mineral activity (3,768 hectares), 19% for defence (1,941 hectares), and a further 18% for manufacturing (1,835 hectares). The most common previous use for urban vacant land, where previous use is known, was agriculture (19%, or 382 hectares) and the second most common previous use was residential development (18%, or 355 hectares).
- 3,250 hectares (28%) of derelict and urban vacant land in 2015 was reported to be developable in the short term, with an expectation of development within five years. A total of 3,053 hectares (26%) of derelict and urban vacant land is seen by local authorities as being uneconomic to develop and/or is viewed as suitable to reclaim for a 'soft' end use (ie non-built use).
- The most common new use for derelict land was residential, with 43% (88 hectares) of the derelict land that was brought back into use since the previous survey reclaimed for this purpose. The second most common new use was for mineral activity, accounting for 31% (63 hectares). For urban vacant land the most common new use was residential, with 45% (67 hectares) of the land reclaimed for this purpose.
- Of the 356 hectares of land reused in 2015, a total of 66 hectares involved some form of public funding, either a full or partial contribution.

Scottish House Condition Survey 2015

Key findings from this informative annual study (published in December 2016: http://www.gov.scot/Publications/2016/12/1539/0) include the following:

- In 2015 37% of Scottish homes were in EPC band C or better and half had an energy efficiency rating of 65 or higher. [A is best, G is worst; D is 55–68.] This is similar to 2014.
- In the last year the average energy efficiency rating of older properties (pre-1919) increased 3.2 points to reach 54.8.
- Based on modelled energy use the average Scottish home is estimated to produce 7.3 tonnes of CO_2 per year. Carbon emissions for older properties (pre-1919) have decreased in the last year from 102 kg per square metre of floor area to 93 kg/m2 in 2015, a reduction of nearly 10%.
- The level of disrepair remained unchanged in the last year. In 2015, 73% of all dwellings had some degree of disrepair, however minor. Disrepair to critical elements stood at 52%, 33% of dwellings had some instances of urgent disrepair, and in 8% of the housing stock some extensive disrepair was present.
- Levels of damp and condensation remained similar to 2014 levels. Around 9 out of 10 properties were free from any damp or condensation, an improvement of around 3 percentage points since 2013.

- Compliance with the tolerable standard in 2015 remained similar to 2014: 2% (or 42,000) of all dwellings fell below the tolerable standard. This represents an improvement of nearly 2 percentage points since 2012.
- Across the stock as a whole, Scottish Housing Quality Standard (SHQS) compliance remained similar to 2014 levels. In 2015, just under 44% (43.8%) of Scottish homes failed to meet the SHQS, compared to 47.5% in the previous year.
- The SHQS failure rate in the social sector was 38%, not allowing for abeyances and exemptions. This has fallen from 60% in the last 5 years. 26% of properties did not meet the Energy Efficient criterion.

Housing Statistics 2015–16

The annual survey of housing discloses a marked decline in new houses supplied by housing associations, and a further and final rise in council house sales, of 14%, ahead of the abolition of the right to buy on 1 August 2016. Full details can be found in *Housing Statistics for Scotland 2016: Key Trends Summary* (www.gov. scot/Publications/2016/09/5806). In summary, the figures show:

Housing Supply (Private and Public Sector)

- *New housing supply*: New housing supply (new build, refurbishment and conversions) decreased by 82 homes (0.5%) between 2014–15 and 2015–16, from 17,077 to 16,995 units. Private-led new builds increased by 408 homes (3%), rehabilitations increased by 233 homes (104%) and conversions increased by 40 homes (6%), whilst housing association new builds decreased by 744 homes (24%) and local authority new builds decreased by 19 homes (2%).
- *New house building*: In 2015–16, 15,854 new build homes were completed in Scotland, a decrease of 355 homes (2%) on the 16,209 completions in the previous year. During the same time-period the number of homes started rose by 664 homes (4%) from 16,246 to 16,910, the highest annual number of starts since 2008–09.
- *Affordable housing*: In 2015–16, there were 6,518 units completed through all Affordable Housing Supply Programme (AHSP) activity, a decrease of 551 units (8%) on the previous year.

Local Authority Housing

- *Local authority housing stock*: At 31st March 2016, there were 316,553 local authority dwellings in Scotland, a small decrease of 452 units (0.1%) from the previous year.
- *Sales of local authority dwellings*: Sales of public authority dwellings (including local authorities with total stock transfers) rose by 14% in 2015–16, from 1,835 to 2,088. This is the third consecutive annual increase after years of declining numbers of sales. The increases are likely to be due to the announcement in 2013 that right to buy was to be ended for all tenants.
- *Vacant stock*: At 31st March 2016, local authorities reported 6,181 units of vacant stock, of which 37% consisted of normal letting stock. This represents 1% of all normal letting stock, and is down from 6,515 the previous year.
- *Lettings*: During 2015–16 there were 26,258 permanent lettings made, a decrease of 3% compared to 27,006 lettings in the previous year. Lets to homeless households represented 38% of all lets made by local authorities in 2015–16, a total of 9,913 lettings to homeless households, which is a decrease of 5% on the 10,390 lettings in 2014–15.

- *Evictions*: Eviction actions against local authority tenants resulted in 1,300 evictions or abandoned dwellings in 2015–16 (859 evictions, 441 abandoned dwellings). This is up by 7%, or 85 actions of evictions or abandonments, on the 1,215 in 2014–15.
- *Housing lists*: Household applications held on local authority or common housing register lists decreased by 5% or 8,211 households to 167,122 at March 2016, the eighth consecutive annual decrease.

Local Authority Housing Assistance and Licensing

- *Scheme of assistance*: There were 10,753 scheme of assistance grants paid to householders in 2015–16, 1,527 (17%) more than in 2014–15. Spend on scheme of assistance grants totalled £31.8 million, £2.3 million (8%) more than in 2014–15. The majority of grants in 2015–16 were for disabled adaptions, 6,482 grants totalling £23.1 million.
- *Houses in multiple occupation*: In 2015–16, 8,852 applications were received in respect of the mandatory licensing scheme for houses in multiple occupation. At 31st March 2016 there were 15,034 licences in force, representing an increase of 1% over the previous year.

Leading pipes through tenement buildings

Section 19 of the Tenements (Scotland) Act 2004 empowers the Scottish Ministers to make regulations allowing owners within a tenement to lead pipes, cables and other equipment through one another's flats and through the common parts. The background is explained in paras 10.6–10.8 of the Scottish Law Commission's *Report No 162 on the Law of the Tenement* (1998). Thus far, no regulations have been made under s 19, and the provision has lain unused. That may be about to change. On 21 January 2016 the Scottish Government issued a consultation document on draft Tenements (Scotland) Act 2004 (Heating Services) Regulations (www. gov.scot/Publications/2016/01/3668). These would allow the leading of pipes in relation to the provision of district heating services. District heating is provided by pipes carrying hot water or steam in communal areas. Neighbours would have to be notified in writing. In the event of their objecting, and an attempt at reaching agreement having failed, an application could be made to the sheriff under s 6 of the Act. The consultation closed on 14 April 2016 and the outcome is still awaited.

High hedges: revised guidance to local authorities

Since the High Hedges (Scotland) Act 2013 came into force, on 1 April 2014 (see *Conveyancing 2013* pp 163–67), local authorities have been dealing with applications by unhappy home-owners seeking to have neighbours ordered to cut back or cut down their hedge. Where an application is refused, the applicant has a right of appeal to the Scottish Ministers. Reports of the appeals can be found by inserting the case reference 'HHA' into the search engine at www. dpea.scotland.gov.uk/casesearch.aspx?T=1.

In order to assist local authorities in their deliberations, the Scottish Government has issued a revised version of a booklet first published in 2014:

see *High Hedges (Scotland) Act 2013: Revised Guidance to Local Authorities* (www. gov.scot/Publications/2016/05/9087).

Eco-fiasco, or the Great Green Deal Disaster

There is always something fascinating and even aesthetically satisfying in observing a much-heralded and hugely expensive governmental initiative slide impressively down the launch slipway, amid the flashing cameras of the assembled media, and thence descending elegantly beneath the waves, to settle gracefully on the seabed, never to be heard of again, except in the billionth footnote to the statistics of the National Debt. It is a traditional phenomenon, as much loved by the good folk of this country as Father Christmas, First Footing, the Easter Hare, and Halloween (except by those grumpy, never-pleased, boring, scroogish killjoys, the taxpayers).

Such was the Green Deal (for which see eg *Conveyancing 2013* pp 150–55). In July 2016 the House of Commons Committee of Public Accounts published a report, *Household Energy Efficiency Measures: Eleventh Report of Session 2016–17* (www.publications.parliament.uk/pa/cm201617/cmselect/cmpubacc/125/125. pdf). We quote selectively from pages 3 and 5 of the report. 'Wildly optimistic…' 'Overly complex …' 'The Department did not act on warnings …' 'The Department did not take account of lessons from international experience …' 'Abysmal …' 'The scheme cost taxpayers £17,000 for every loan arranged …' We could go on, but won't, because we know that readers will be eager to study the report for themselves, first fortifying themselves, we would respectfully urge, with a rational modicum of tax-paid uisge-beatha.

Books

Craig Anderson, *Property: A Guide to Scots Law* (W Green 2016; ISBN 9780414038646)

Neil Collar, *Planning*, 4th edn (W Green 2016; ISBN 9780414019331)

Kenneth S Gerber, *Commercial Leases in Scotland: A Practitioner's Guide*, 3rd edn (W Green 2016; ISBN 9780414054264)

Lord Gill, *Agricultural Tenancies*, 4th edn (W Green 2016; ISBN 9780414015012)

Mark Higgins, *The Enforcement of Heritable Securities*, 2nd edn (W Green 2016; ISBN 9780414018976)

Kenneth G C Reid and George L Gretton, *Conveyancing 2015* (Avizandum Publishing Ltd 2016; ISBN 9781904968757)

Ann Eileen Atkinson Stewart and Euan Fraser Fitzpatrick Sinclair, *Conveyancing Practice in Scotland*, 7th edn (Bloomsbury Professional 2016; ISBN 9781780438665)

Articles

James Aitken and Andy Duncan, 'A positive start for LBTT' (2016) 144 *Greens Property Law Bulletin* 5

Craig Anderson, 'Compromise agreements and heritable property' 2016 SLT (News) 169 (considering *DWS v RMS* 2016 GWD 22-402)

Katherine Anderson, 'Written title to land in Orkney and Shetland' 2016 *Juridical Review* 191

Mike Blair, '"A look over the horizon?" – securities over agricultural leases' (2016) 144 *Greens Property Law Bulletin* 1

Mike Blair, 'Agricultural holdings law and the Land Reform (Scotland) Act 2016' (2016) 143 *Greens Property Law Bulletin* 1

Ewen Brown, 'Dilapidations: enforcing the bargain' (2016) 61 *Journal of the Law Society of Scotland* Feb/32 (considering *@Sipp (Pension Trustees) Ltd v Insight Travel Services Ltd* [2015] CSIH 91, 2016 SLT 131)

Scott Brymer, 'Checklists – you simply cannot (or at least should not) live without them' (2016) 141 *Greens Property Law Bulletin* 3

Stewart Brymer, 'Home reports – an assessment' (2016) 143 *Greens Property Law Bulletin* 3

Stewart Brymer, 'Looking forward – with one eye on the past' (2016) 142 *Greens Property Law Bulletin* 2 (considering *Whitely v Keeper of the Registers of Scotland* 2016 GWD 10-199)

Stewart Brymer, 'When things go wrong in a conveyancing transaction' (2016) 140 *Greens Property Law Bulletin* 1

Stewart Brymer and Iain McKay, 'What is ScotLIS?' (2016) 61 *Journal of the Law Society of Scotland* Jan/34

Stewart Brymer and James Ness, 'Using your secure digital signature' (2016) 61 *Journal of the Law Society of Scotland* March/48

David Cabrelli, 'Implying terms in law: *Belize* no more?' (2016) 20 *Edinburgh Law Review* 338 (considering *Marks and Spencer plc v BNP Paribas Securities Services Trust Company (Jersey) Ltd* [2015] UKSC 72, [2016] AC 742)

Daniel J Carr, 'Reduction for forgery and equitable exceptions: *Chalmers v Chalmers*' (2016) 20 *Edinburgh Law Review* 235 (considering *Chalmers v Chalmers* [2015] CSIH 75, 2016 SC 158)

George B Clark, 'Private residential tenancies: the Private Housing (Tenancies) (Scotland) Bill' (2016) 140 *Greens Property Law Bulletin* 4 and (2016) 141 *Greens Property Law Bulletin* 1

Malcolm Combe, 'Land reform: back, and here to stay' (2016) 61 *Journal of the Law Society of Scotland* May/18

Malcolm Combe, 'The environmental implications of redistributive land reform' (2016) 18 *Environmental Law Review* 104

Malcolm Combe, 'The Land Reform (Scotland) Act 2016: another answer to the Scottish land question' 2016 *Juridical Review* 291

R Craig Connal, 'Has the Rainy Sky dried up? *Arnold v Britton* and commercial interpretation' (2016) 20 *Edinburgh Law Review* 71 (considering *Arnold v Britton* [2015] UKSC 36, [2015] AC 1619)

Stephen Cranston, 'Radical and effective? The Land Reform (Scotland) Bill' (2016) 141 *Greens Property Law Bulletin* 7

Matthew Farrell, 'Repairing obligations for common parts' (2016) 61 *Journal of the Law Society of Scotland*, online edition: www.bit.ly/2gJRoM6 (considering *AWG Business Centres Ltd v Regus Caledonia Ltd* [2016] CSOH 99, 2016 GWD 22-407)

Ken Gerber, 'Landlords still' (2016) 61 *Journal of the Law Society of Scotland*, online edition: www.bit.ly/1PfGTLB (considering compensatory payments for loss of rent in respect of long leases converted into ownership under the Long Leases (Scotland) Act 2012)

Stephen Goldie, 'Deeds of conditions: emerging stronger' (2016) 61 *Journal of the Law Society of Scotland* April/32 (considering *Marriott v Greenbelt Group Ltd*, 2 Dec 2015, Lands Tribunal)

Jonathan Hardman, 'Necessary and balanced? Critical analysis of the Legal Writings (Counterparts and Delivery) (Scotland) Act 2015' 2016 *Juridical Review* 177

Gordon Junor, 'Interpreting repair obligations in commercial leases' 2016 SLT (News) 17 (considering *@Sipp Pension Trs v Insight Travel Services Ltd* [2015] CSIH 91, 2016 SLT 131)

Gordon Junor, '*Khosrowpour* – revisited and reviewed – but not homologated' (2016) 84 *Scottish Law Gazette* 53 (considering *Khosrowpour v Mackay* [2016] CSIH 50, 2016 GWD 21-366)

Gordon Junor, 'Solicitors duties to other than clients – differing perspectives?' (2016) 84 *Scottish Law Gazette* 27 (considering *NRAM plc v Steel* [2016] CSIH 11, 2016 SC 474)

Gordon Junor, 'Surviving special destinations' (2016) 84 *Scottish Law Gazette* 14 (considering *Hill v Hill* [2016] CSOH 10, 2016 GWD 3-66)

Charles Keegan, 'The Keeper steps in' (2016) 61 *Journal of the Law Society of Scotland* Nov/9 (considering Keeper-induced registration)

Chris Kerr and John King, 'Lessons learned and new initiatives' (2016) 142 *Greens Property Law Bulletin* 4 (considering aspects of the Land Registration etc (Scotland) Act 2012)

John King and Ross Mackay, 'Altered deeds? Mind the rules' (2016) 61 *Journal of the Law Society of Scotland* Dec/10 (warning against unauthenticated post-subscription alterations)

John King and Frances Rooney, 'Plans reports: an evolving scene' (2016) 61 *Journal of the Law Society of Scotland*, online edition: www.bit.ly/25N1Wgh

Frankie McCarthy, 'The Private Housing Tenancies (Scotland) Bill and the ECHR' (2016) 61 *Journal of the Law Society of Scotland* Jan/5

Ross Mackay, 'That's fine in theory, but ...?' (2016) 142 *Greens Property Law Bulletin* 5 (considering aspects of the Land Registration etc (Scotland) Act 2012)

Roddy MacLeod, 'Contentious executries: problems with succession to heritable property' 2016 SLT (News) 61 (considering *Hill v Hill* [2016] CSOH 10, 2016 GWD 3-66 and *Matossian v Matossian* [2016] CSOH 21, 2016 GWD 7-139)

Douglas Maxwell, 'Disputed property rights: Article 1 Protocol No 1 of the European Convention on Human Rights and the Land Reform (Scotland) Act 2016' (2016) 41 *European Law Review* 900

Douglas Maxwell, 'Human rights and land reform' (2016) 61 *Journal of the Law Society of Scotland* Jan/22

Sophie L Noble, 'The role of the Keeper and the 2012 Act' (2016) 143 *Greens Property Law Bulletin* 7

Rachel Oliphant, David McFarlane and Margaret King, 'Silberburn: sold on the right to buy' (2016) 61 *Journal of the Law Society of Scotland* May/36 (describing a successful exercise of the community right to buy)

Wendy Quinn, 'Deeds of conditions: not dead yet' (2016) 61 *Journal of the Law Society of Scotland* Feb/20 (considering *Marriott v Greenbelt Group Ltd*, 2 Dec 2015, Lands Tribunal)

Megan Rea, 'Is possession 9/10 of the law? Making a prescriptive claimant application' (2016) 144 *Greens Property Law Bulletin* 3

Robert Rennie, 'Land registration – who is in charge?' (2016) 142 *Greens Property Law Bulletin* 7

Lorna Richardson, 'Commercial common sense revisited: further developments in contract interpretation and commercial leasing' (2016) 20 *Edinburgh Law Review* 342 (considering *@Sipp (Pension Trustees) Ltd v Insight Travel Services Ltd* [2015] CSIH 91, 2016 SLT 131)

Lorna Richardson, 'The limits of statutory personal bar: leases and the Requirements of Writing (Scotland) Act 1995' (2016) 20 *Edinburgh Law Review* 66 (considering *Gyle Shopping Centre General Partners Ltd v Marks and Spencer plc* [2014] CSOH 122, 2015 SCLR 171)

Frances Rooney, 'Controlling interests: problem questions' (2016) 61 *Journal of the Law Society of Scotland* Oct/34 (considering the Scottish Government's consultation on controlling interests in landowners)

Frances Rooney and Sarah Duncan, 'Cutting the RoS bouncebacks' (2016) 61 *Journal of the Law Society of Scotland*, online edition: www.bit.ly/1JYbdFX

Frances Rooney and Sarah Duncan, 'The Keeper is coming' (2016) 61 *Journal of the Law Society of Scotland*, online edition: www.bit.ly/21z75nT (considering Keeper-induced registration)

Frances Rooney and Sarah Duncan, 'Title out of nothing' (2016) 61 *Journal of the Law Society of Scotland* Feb/34 (considering registration of *a non domino* dispositions)

Mark Shepherd, 'Conflict of interest: the questions still to come' (2016) 61 *Journal of the Law Society of Scotland* Feb/42 (considering rule B2.1.4, on conflict of interest in conveyancing transactions)

Andrew Stevenson, 'Land attachment revisited' (2016) 84 *Scottish Law Gazette* 38

Ann Stewart, 'Convenient but necessary?' 61 *Journal of the Law Society of Scotland* Nov/36 (considering *Asa International Ltd v Kashmiri Properties (Ireland) Ltd* [2016] CSIH 70, 2016 GWD 27-493 and *Johnson, Thomas and Thomas v Smith* [2016] SC GLA 50, 2016 GWD 25-456)

Ken Swinton, 'Dealing with abandoned property' (2015) 83 *Scottish Law Gazette* 64

Ken Swinton, 'Free standing servitude rights to park – some reflections on *Johnston, Thomas and Thomas v Smith*' (2016) 84 *Scottish Law Gazette* 49

Ken Swinton, 'Pertinents and the Land Register' (2016) 84 *Scottish Law Gazette* 18

Andrew Todd, 'The end of deeds of conditions?' (2016) 61 *Journal of the Law Society of Scotland* Jan/20 (considering *Marriott v Greenbelt Group Ltd*, 2 Dec 2015, Lands Tribunal)

Andrew Todd and Robbie Wishart, 'Common areas – keep Pandora's box shut' (2016) 61 *Journal of the Law Society of Scotland* Oct/26, with a response by Registers of Scotland at Dec/11

Janis Voyias, 'Unlocking doors: demystifying squatting' (2016) 61 *Journal of the Law Society of Scotland* Sept/24

PART IV
COMMENTARY

COMMENTARY

ENFORCING REAL BURDENS:
THE IMPORTANCE OF MUTUAL FENCES

The law

For a real burden still to be 'live' there must be someone with a title to enforce – or, to say the same thing in another way, there must be a benefited property. Without a benefited property, no real burden can exist. But how is one to know whether a benefited property exists?

There is no difficulty in the case of burdens created on or after 28 November 2004; for not only must the benefited property or properties be identified in the constitutive deed, but the deed must then be registered against the benefited property (as well as against the burdened property). These requirements stem from the Title Conditions (Scotland) Act 2003.[1] The pre-2004 common law, however, was more lax.

Before 2004, benefited properties were sometimes identified in the constitutive deed. But there was no requirement to do so. In the absence of identification, the common law would help in certain cases by implying that neighbouring properties were benefited. But the rules were complex and not well understood. They were swept away by the Title Conditions Act and replaced by new rules set out in ss 52–57 of that Act. The new rules, while better and simpler than the rules they replaced, are also complex and not well understood.

All of this creates problems in dealing with pre-2004 burdens. The burdens glisten menacingly on the Register. But many, on closer scrutiny, turn out to be unenforceable. Any enforcement rights held by superiors were, of course, abolished with the feudal system on 28 November 2004.[2] But, as just mentioned, any implied enforcement rights held by neighbours were also abolished on that day or, in the case of one particular type of implied right, on the day occurring ten years later.[3] Sometimes, of course, a burdens writ conferred *express* non-feudal enforcement rights and, if so, the rights continue unimpaired. But in the absence of express rights, a pre-2004 burden survives if and only if one (or more) of the

---

1 Title Conditions (Scotland) Act 2003 s 4(2)(c), (5).
2 Except when, as hardly ever, they were preserved, as non-feudal rights, by a notice under ss 18–18C of the Abolition of Feudal Tenure etc (Scotland) Act 2000 which was registered before the appointed day. No notice had been registered in the present case.
3 Title Conditions (Scotland) Act 2003 s 49. For the latter case, see *Conveyancing 2013* pp 131–39. The ten-year abolition could be avoided by registration of a notice under s 50.

replacement rules in ss 52–57 applies to the effect of identifying a benefited property. For, in the absence of a benefited property, the burden is extinguished.

Of the replacement rules in the Title Conditions Act, only two are usually of importance. These are the rules set out in s 52 and in s 53. Section 52 is merely a restatement, in slightly simplified terms, of the former common law. Section 53 is wider, vaguer, and harder to understand. It is a rule in need of case law. Unfortunately, cases so far have been few and far between. For that reason, but not just for that reason, the new case of *Thomson's Exx*[1] is to be welcomed.

The facts

There is nothing out of the ordinary in the facts of *Thomson's Exx*. In that lies some of its value.

By a feu disposition recorded in 1947, a Mrs Piggott acquired 3.965 acres of land in Newton Mearns, Glasgow. A decade or so later she divided the land into five plots. One (number 1 Old Humbie Road) she kept for herself. The others (numbers 3, 5, 7, and 9 Old Humbie Road) she sold. The conveyancing was done by feu disposition, two of the deeds (of numbers 7 and 9) being recorded on 22 January 1958 and the other two (of numbers 3 and 5) being recorded on 1 October 1960. At the time of the sale the plots were unbuilt-on.

In feuing the plots, Mrs Piggott more or less repeated burdens which had been imposed, on the whole area, by the 1947 feu disposition by which she acquired. In the case of the feu disposition of number 9 (with which this case is concerned), the burdens imposed were the following:

> And also with and under the following further real burdens, obligations and others videlicet: (First) my said disponee and his foresaids shall be bound to erect and maintain in all time coming in good order and repair on the plot of ground hereby disponed a dwellinghouse with relative offices, which may include a garage, of the value of at least Two Thousand Five Hundred Pounds conform to plans and specifications which must be submitted to and approved of in writing by me or my successors as the proprietors of the remainder of the said piece of ground of which the plot hereby disponed forms part before building operations commence; And it is hereby specially provided and declared that the said dwellinghouse shall be used as a private residence for the occupation of one family only and my said disponee and his foresaids shall not use or permit the use of the subjects for the purpose of any manufacture, trading or business or for any other purpose which in the opinion of me or my successors as proprietors of the remainder of the said piece of ground may be deemed to be a nuisance or annoyance to the neighbouring proprietors or tenants or likely to affect detrimentally the amenity of the district for residential purposes; And the said plot of ground so far as not occupied by buildings as aforesaid shall be laid out and used as garden or amenity ground in connection with the said house; (Second) my said disponee and his foresaids shall forthwith enclose the said piece of ground, so far as not already done, with suitable and substantial fences of a height, material and pattern to be approved by me or my foresaids in writing; and it is hereby

---

1 2016 GWD 27-494. This is a decision of the Lands Tribunal, the Tribunal comprising R A Smith QC and D J Gillespie FRICS.

declared that the fence along the west boundary of the said plot of ground hereby disponed shall be erected to the extent of one half of its width on the adjoining ground [ie number 7] and shall be mean and common to my said disponee and his foresaids and the adjoining proprietor and, as such, shall be maintained at the joint expense of my said disponee and his foresaids and the adjoining proprietor, but no part of the cost of erection or maintenance of any of the said fences shall be recoverable from me or my foresaids.

The burdens were followed by an irritancy clause, but no provision was made as to rights to enforce.

The burdens imposed in the feu dispositions of numbers 3, 5 and 7 Old Humbie Road were substantially the same as the burdens just quoted, with only small variations.[1]

As the law stood in 1958, at the time the feu disposition was granted, the burdens on number 9 would have been enforceable by Mrs Piggott, as feudal superior, but by no one else. No enforcement rights were conferred expressly on neighbours in the deed; and none would have been implied, under the rules then in force, because of the absence of any notice in the deed of the existence of a common scheme of burdens applying to the group of houses in Old Humbie Road.[2] On 28 November 2004, the superior's rights were extinguished.[3] Unless new rights were simultaneously created in favour of neighbours, the burdens in the feu disposition would have been extinguished too. Whether new enforcement rights were created depended on s 52 and s 53 of the Title Conditions Act.

Sections 52 and 53

The Tribunal application

The application to the Tribunal, by the owner of number 9 Old Humbie Road, was for a determination that the burdens in the first of the two conditions in the 1958 feu disposition were unenforceable due to the lack of a benefited property.[4] The applicant's case, in other words, was that neither s 52 nor s 53 applied. In the event of the application being unsuccessful – as indeed turned out to be the case – the applicant asked to be allowed to amend the application so as to seek variation or discharge of the condition. The background was that planning permission had been obtained for the erection of a second house, which would be contrary to the first of the two conditions in the feu disposition. The application was unopposed, so that the Tribunal did not have the advantage of hearing counter-arguments.

---

1 Two are mentioned in the Lands Tribunal's Opinion. First, in the case of the two later feus (ie numbers 3 and 5), the plans were to be approved 'by me and my successors as the proprietors of the *dominium directum* of the plot of ground hereby disponed'. Secondly, the burdens imposed on number 3 were expressly declared to be enforceable by the owner of number 5.

2 The facts fall within the first of the two cases identified by Lord Watson in *Hislop v MacRitchie's Trs* (1881) 8 R (HL) 95 at 103: see K G C Reid, *The Law of Property in Scotland* (1996) paras 399 and 400.

3 Abolition of Feudal Tenure etc (Scotland) Act 2000 s 17(1).

4 The application was thus made under s 90(1)(a)(ii) of the Title Conditions (Scotland) Act 2003.

Common scheme

A prerequisite for both s 52 and s 53 is that the burdens were 'imposed under a common scheme' affecting other properties. A threshold question, therefore, was whether the burdens in the 1958 feu disposition of number 9 were part of a common scheme which also affected one or more of the other properties feued by Mrs Piggott. That in turn required an investigation of the neighbouring titles.

The answer, however, was hardly in doubt. As the applicant's counsel conceded, 'the requirements for a common scheme included at least two properties being subject to the burdens, that the burdens affecting the properties be identical or substantially similar or in some sense equivalent, and probably also for the burdens to derive from a common source'.[1] All three requirements were fulfilled in respect of the burdens imposed by Mrs Piggott on numbers 3–9 Old Humbie Road. They were plainly a common scheme.

The applicant had sought to resist this conclusion by pointing to certain doubts expressed, *obiter*, in an earlier decision of the Lands Tribunal, *Smith v Prior*.[2] Something more was needed, argued the applicant, than the three requirements mentioned above – some sort of indication that the properties were part of a community.[3] This argument, however, is mistaken. It confuses what is needed to establish a common scheme (the current question) with what is needed to meet the further requirements of either s 52 or s 53 (a different question, discussed below). These are separate matters. So long as the burdens are similar or the same, there is a common scheme.

The Tribunal had no hesitation in rejecting the argument.[4] A 'scheme' suggests merely 'some sort of planned or systematic regulation by the superior over a certain area'.[5] The remarks in *Smith v Prior* 'were both *obiter* and expressly guarded given the absence of full argument'.[6] They had to be read in the light of 'subsequent interpretations and learned discussion of the Act'.[7] The Tribunal continued:[8]

> Here there does appear to have been such a 'scheme' in mind, despite it only taking the form of successive feu dispositions. If more were needed, we note that the properties 3, 5, 7 and 9 all required to be of a value of at least £2,500 at the time of the feu dispositions in 1958 and 1960. It seems to us that this is a significant common characteristic, and if

---

1 This tripartite test comes from K G C Reid, *The Abolition of Feudal Tenure in Scotland* (2003) para 5.2.
2 2007 GWD 30-523. There is so little authority on the meaning of common schemes that it is surprising that the Tribunal's attention was not drawn to the only decision of the Court of Session on the subject, namely *Russel Properties (Europe) Ltd v Dundas Heritable Ltd* [2012] CSOH 175, 2012 GWD 38-749, discussed in *Conveyancing 2012* pp 113–18.
3 Paragraphs 16–20.
4 Paragraphs 28–38.
5 Paragraph 28.
6 Paragraph 29.
7 Paragraph 29. Here the Tribunal appears to be referring to the criticism of *Smith v Prior* in *Conveyancing 2007* pp 79–80.
8 Paragraph 38.

not a 'uniform' plan, at least embodied an intention that the relevant residential area should attain a certain quality of amenity. Other common conditions point in a similar direction. So we are satisfied there is a common scheme in this case.

Section 52

But the existence of a common scheme is not enough, in itself, to make burdens mutually enforceable among the properties affected by the scheme. Both s 52 and s 53 insist on the fulfilment of a further requirement, although the requirement is different in each case.

In the case of s 52, repeating the former common law, the requirement is that the deed imposing the burden (in this case, the 1958 feu disposition of number 9) contains notice of the existence of the common scheme.[1] The idea is that, by reading the burdens writ and nothing else, the burdened proprietor can know not just what burdens affect the property but also that other properties in the area are subject to the same burdens with the result that there will be mutual rights of enforcement. For the purposes of testing this requirement it is necessary to consult the deed itself rather than relying on the transcription of burdens which, in the case of registered property, appears on the title sheet.

In the present case, as so often, the burdens writ was silent as to a common scheme. Hence no enforcement rights could arise under s 52.[2]

Section 53

The additional requirement in s 53 is quite different. In order for s 53 to apply, the properties subject to the common scheme, or some of them, must be 'related' to one another. More precisely, enforcement of the burdens against number 9 Old Humbie Road was only possible by the owners of such, if any, of numbers 3, 5, and 7 Old Humbie Road as were 'related' to number 9.

The difficulty, of course, was to know what was meant by 'related'. Plainly it must mean more than that the properties were subject to the same burdens, because 'relatedness' is a requirement additional to the presence of a common scheme. The Act fights shy of giving a definition, but s 53(2) does at least contain a number of hints in the form of a non-exhaustive list of factors which may indicate 'relatedness'. The factors, which have a miscellaneous or even random appearance, are as follows:

(a) the convenience of managing the properties together because they share –
  (i) some common feature; or
  (ii) an obligation for common maintenance of some facility;
(b) there being shared ownership of common property;
(c) their being subject to the common scheme by virtue of the same deed of conditions; or
(d) the properties each being a flat in the same tenement.

---

1 The requirement, set out in s 52(1), is that the burdens writ 'expressly refers to the common scheme or is so worded that the common scheme is to be implied'. Some exceptions are set out in s 52(2).
2 Paragraphs 39–40.

The status of these factors has never been very clear.[1] If all are satisfied, then presumably the properties are 'related'. But that will be rare. What is the position if only one of the factors is satisfied, or maybe two? Are all the factors of equal weight? How much hangs on the significance of the factor when set against the burdens as a whole? And finally, what is the position where none of the factors is satisfied? Does that mean that the properties cannot be 'related'? Or, given that the factors are non-exhaustive, can properties be 'related' by virtue of factors that are not on the statutory list?

The houses in the present case formed a row of detached houses with substantial gardens. Each was custom-built, by the first feuar of the plot, and they were of different designs. Only in a very loose sense could they be regarded as forming a housing estate. Nonetheless, two of the four statutory factors were satisfied at least in some degree. For in terms of the burdens imposed both on number 9 and number 7, the boundary fence between them was to be common property ('mean and common') (factor (b)), and it was to be maintained by the owners of both properties (factor (a)(ii)).[2] Yet, taking the burdens as a whole, these were minor matters – and they had nothing to do with the burdens which were at issue in the application to the Tribunal (ie the building and use restrictions). Were they, nonetheless, enough to establish that the properties were 'related'? In respect of numbers 7 and 9, the Lands Tribunal thought that they were:[3]

> We think there is sufficient to infer that numbers 7 and 9 are related to each other in that they are contiguous and the common boundary feature is in shared ownership and gives rise to a legal relationship in that context. The relationship is not so slight so that it can be ignored for practical purposes. The focus of section 53 is to identify whether the properties themselves are related, not whether any particular title condition in issue is related to any particular head of sub-section (2) eg the common features or common property. There is no suggestion of a test that the common features etc require to be of a certain importance in relation to the conditions in issue ... In our view there is a sufficient relationship between numbers 7 and 9 on the statutory criteria so that they form a group of related properties for the purpose of the 1958 Williams feu disposition.

The relationship, however, depended on the common fence. If *Othello* is the tragedy of the handkerchief, this was a drama about a fence. But there was no common fence between number 9 and any of the other properties, from which it followed that these other properties were not 'related' within the meaning of s 53. Hence the burdens affecting number 9 were enforceable by the owner of number 7, the next-door property, but by no one else.

Although this is a decision on particular facts, it is also of wider importance. In treating properties as 'related' when the only connection between them was

---

1 For discussion, see K G C Reid, 'New enforcers for old burdens', in R Rennie (ed), *The Promised Land: Property Law Reform* (2008) 71, 82–85.
2 A boundary fence is a 'facility': see Title Conditions (Scotland) Act 2003 s 122(3).
3 Paragraph 48.

a mutual fence, it adopts an expansive view of 'related', and, mutual walls and fences being common, one which will apply to a large number of titles. To be expansive was a conscious policy choice of the Tribunal based on what was taken to be the intention of Parliament as evidenced by statements in Parliament by the relevant Minister.[1]

Even after *Thomson's Exx*, s 53 remains an unsatisfactory provision. It is to be reviewed by the Scottish Law Commission.[2] Meanwhile there will continue to be many cases where its applicability is in doubt. But those doubts are reduced by the new decision.

Postscript: the 1947 feu disposition

The application in *Thomson's Exx* concerned only the 1958 feu disposition of number 9 Old Humbie Road. But it may be of interest to say something also about the original 1947 feu disposition, which applied to the whole development (ie to what became numbers 1, 3, 5, 7 and 9 Old Humbie Road). This is not something that was touched on in the Lands Tribunal's Opinion.

As already mentioned, the burdens in the 1958 deed were largely copied from the 1947 deed. In particular, the 1947 deed, like the 1958 deed, restricted building to a single dwellinghouse. That restriction evidently caused problems for the feuars of the individual plots in the late 1950s, and minutes of waiver were obtained from the over-superior (ie the granter of the 1947 feu disposition). But, so far as the Tribunal's judgment discloses, the co-feuars did not consent to the waiver. In other words, the minute of waiver in relation to number 9 was granted by the over-superior but not by the owners of the other properties affected by that feu disposition (ie numbers 1, 3, 5 and 7 Old Humbie Road). If that is so, then it was a mistake, albeit one very commonly made at the time; for, under the law then in force, the co-feuars would have had an implied right to enforce the 1947 burdens against one another.[3] Thus, while the 1947 conditions were duly varied vis-à-vis the over-superior, they were not varied vis-à-vis the co-feuars.

On 28 November 2004, the enforcement rights of both over-superior and co-feuars in respect of the 1947 feu disposition were, of course, extinguished.[4] But the question would then arise as to whether the enforcement rights of the (former) co-feuars (ie the owners of numbers 1, 3, 5 and 7) were re-created by either s 52 or s 53 of the Title Conditions Act. This was an entirely separate

---

1 Paragraph 44. In fact the evidence for this is rather frail. The Tribunal relied on the rather imprecise statement by the Deputy First Minister (Jim Wallace QC MSP) that 'houses on a typical housing estate would be related properties' but not 'scattered properties in rural areas': see Scottish Parliament, *Official Report*, Justice 1 Committee, 10 December 2002. The passage is quoted in para 5.8 n 3 of K G C Reid, *The Abolition of Feudal Tenure in Scotland* (2003). As already mentioned, the houses in the present case were far from constituting a typical housing estate.

2 Scottish Law Commission, *Annual Report 2015* (Scot Law Com No 244, 2016) 16.

3 Even though, as mentioned earlier, there would have been no right to enforce the burdens contained in the individual feu dispositions granted by Mrs Piggott. The facts fall within the second of the two cases identified by Lord Watson in *Hislop v MacRitchie's Trs* (1881) 8 R (HL) 95 at 103: see K G C Reid, *The Law of Property in Scotland* (1996) paras 399 and 401.

4 Abolition of Feudal Tenure etc (Scotland) Act 2000 s 17(1); Title Conditions (Scotland) Act 2003 s 49(1).

question from enforcement rights in respect of the 1958 feu disposition: it is clear from the wording of ss 52 and 53, as well as from general principles, that each burdens writ must be considered on its own.[1] In *Thomson's Exx* the Lands Tribunal found that s 53 applied to the 1958 burdens. In the case of the 1947 burdens, however, it was s 52 that applied. This was because (i) the burdens were imposed under a common scheme (the 1947 feu disposition), and (ii) the very fact that the 1947 deed applied to all five properties gave notice to the owners of each of the existence of the common scheme.[2] Thus, whereas the 1958 burdens were found by the Tribunal to be enforceable against the owner of number 9 by the owner of number 7 (only), the 1947 burdens were (and for all we know still are) enforceable by the owners of each of numbers 1, 3, 5 and 7.

LEASES AND STATUTORY PERSONAL BAR

Property law disputes sometimes arise between members of the same family. Partly this is because families can begin to feud about all sorts of things, including property. But it is also because arrangements between family members are often undocumented or not properly documented since, when they are entered into, any suggestion of such documentation could be taken to indicate lack of trust, and also on account of the feeling that there is no need to incur professional fees. And of course in the great majority of cases arrangements between family members do not result in litigation. But sometimes they do. A case in Lochmaddy Sheriff Court, *Gray v MacNeil's Exr*,[3] was a bitter family dispute that was not only factually complex but also raised a difficult question about the law of leases.

The story in outline

Daliburgh, or Dalabrog in the Gaelic, in the southern part of South Uist, has not, as far as we can recall, hitherto made any contributions to the law reports of Scotland. That omission has now been made good.

Donald MacNeil owned the Burnside Petrol Filling Station. His daughter Michelle helped him in the business. She was married to John Gray (the pursuer in the action); they had five children. The seven Grays lived in a house (Burnside Chalet) on land belonging to Donald MacNeil, he himself living in another house (Burnside Cottage) on the same property. Evening meals meant cooking for eight, for he would usually eat with the Grays. By this time he was a widower, his wife Flora having passed away in 1996. In 2004/05 the three of them, that is to say Donald MacNeil, John Gray and Michelle Gray, concerned that the petrol station was no longer trading satisfactorily, decided to add a chip shop to the

---

1 On this point the Lands Tribunal in *Thomson's Exx* seemed uncertain: see para 42 ('It is not impossible that numbers 1 and 9 could be said to be part of a common scheme should the "modified" 1947 feu disposition and 1958 Williamson feu disposition be taken together').
2 Reid, *Abolition of Feudal Tenure* para 5.15.
3 2016 SLT (Sh Ct) 250.

site. This would require some capital to set up, and Mr Gray 'obtained a £11,000 loan from the Royal Bank of Scotland' and 'grants from Western Isles Enterprise and Western Isles Council. In total the pursuer obtained approximately £50,000 in funding.'[1] He also 'attended a fish fryer course in Leeds'.[2]

Mr and Mrs Gray and Mr MacNeil agreed, in general terms, that the Grays would run the chip shop and would also pay staffing and maintenance costs for the petrol station. No monetary rent for the chip shop would be paid. But exactly what was agreed was later to be bitterly disputed.

The chip shop needed equipment, which Mr Gray bought, and we list the items here,[3] partly because they feature in the litigation, partly because such matters seldom enliven the pages of the law reports, but mainly because some readers of this series may understandably be contemplating the idea of career diversification:

- Frank Ford fish frying range with griddle
- fish fridge
- stainless steel fridge
- bold chipping machine
- 28lb potato rumbler
- Wet Well Bain Marie
- eclipse counter
- serve over refrigerated counter
- fish and chip filtration machine
- stainless steel table with cut away corner
- stainless steel shelving
- water tanks and boiler unit
- signage
- uniforms and safety shoes
- utensils (including two batter trays)
- gas tank
- three picnic benches
- white marquee
- chip barrel and basket
- four 80 ltr black bins
- industrial microwave
- radio
- kettle
- new motor for the fish frying range.

The chip shop proved reasonably profitable, and matters went on satisfactorily until 2008, when relations between Mr Gray and his father-in-law began to sour. As time went on, relations between Mr Gray and Mrs Gray also began to sour, and they separated in 2011, though there seems to have been no divorce. In 2012 relations between Mr Gray and his father-in-law came to a

---

1 Paragraph 7 of the findings-in-fact.
2 Paragraph 6 of the findings-in-fact. This is not a course currently offered by Edinburgh University, but clearly a market exists.
3 Paragraph 12 of the findings-in-fact.

crisis. The former accused Mr MacNeil of sexual offences and contacted the police. The latter accused Mr Gray of having a 'female' in his house with him, which Mr Gray denied. In October 2012, following an alleged physical attack by Mr Gray on Mr MacNeil, the latter disconnected the chip shop's electricity supply. As from May 2013 Donald MacNeil's grandson, Donald John MacNeil, ran the chip shop and garage. In 2014 a curious document was entered into, which we give in full here, not because it proved to be crucial in the litigation, but because it is a remarkable document, a strange blend of testament and *inter vivos* contract.

> I Donald MacNeil, residing at Burnside, Daliburgh, Isle of South Uist in order to settle the succession to my means and estate after my death do hereby transfer ownership of my business interest, known as, D & F MacNeil, Burnside Filling Station to my grandson Donald John MacNeil, presently residing at Burnside Chalet, [address] with effect from First of April Two Thousand and Fourteen.
>
> Furthermore I am granting my aforementioned grandson an indefinite lease of the shop premises in order that he can continue his business interest and that being the operation of a fish and chip shop. Lease of the shop area is deemed to have commenced on First of May Two Thousand and Thirteen. I am transferring ownership of all business assets including electrical equipment, furnishings and fittings and any other items pertaining to the shop to my grandson Donald John MacNeil with immediate effect.
>
> I grant my grandson Donald John MacNeil with an indefinite lease of the premises known as Burnside Chalet.
>
> The above testament is not intended to revoke a prior will but serves to modify it.

> | | |
> |---|---|
> | Donald MacNeil | [signature] 31.5.14 |
> | Donald John MacNeil | [signature] 31.5.14 |
> | Iain Macdonald, Accountant | [signature] 31.5.14 (witness) |

> I hereby agree with the terms of the above statement:

> | | |
> |---|---|
> | Roderick MacNeil | [signature] |
> | Donald MacNeil | [signature] |

Thereafter Mr Gray sued Mr MacNeil (senior) (i) for delivery of the chip shop equipment, which failing, its value, and (ii) for damages for breach of an alleged lease, for Mr Gray's account was that the agreement reached in early 2005 had been for a 15-year lease, and that accordingly by cutting off electric power in 2012 the lease had been breached. During the action, the original defender passed away, and his executor replaced him. His executor was his son, Roderick MacNeil,[1] so that the new defender was the pursuer's brother-in-law.

---

1 One of the bones of contention in this family feud was another MacNeil property in the island, called the Old School House. It appears that this property, which was used as self-catering accommodation, had been earmarked for Roderick MacNeil to live in when he retired from the priesthood. The property was not the subject of the present litigation, so details are patchy. It seems that the property was at first owned by Donald MacNeil, was transferred by him to Michelle Gray, and was later transferred by Michelle Gray to herself and her husband. At the time of the litigation a bank was enforcing a standard security over the Old School House. See para 6 of the sheriff's note.

The first claim: the equipment

Given that the equipment had originally belonged to the pursuer, it still belonged to him unless something had happened to pass ownership from him. There were averments from the defence that the equipment had acceded to the property, but this argument was not seriously developed, and accordingly failed.[1] The defender at one stage took the view that he owned the equipment because the pursuer (allegedly) owed him money. But this was legally unstateable, and was not formally asserted as a defence. Ownership can, of course, be transferred from X to Y in satisfaction of a debt owed to Y by X (in other words *datio in solutum*) but this involves mutual agreement to that effect, and there was no suggestion that there had been any such agreement.

Another question was whether the equipment had perhaps been transferred to Donald MacNeil (the grandson) by the odd document, quoted above, of 31 May 2014. The sheriff[2] considered that the wording of that document was too unspecific.[3] But in any event, even if it could be construed as purportedly transferring the equipment, it would have been to that extent void, since the defender had no title to the equipment, and *nemo dat quod non habet*.[4] (Or, for those who prefer a different form, with the same meaning, and as formulated by Ulpian himself,[5] *nemo plus juris ad alium transferre potest quam ipse haberet.*[6])

The pursuer craved delivery, or payment of the value. There were procedural problems about the former, and so the sheriff granted decree for the value. The value was disputed: in the end the sheriff adopted the depreciation figure given by an accountant who had appeared as a witness, which was that the equipment had depreciated by 50%. Given that the original value was estimated (albeit with imperfect certainty) at £32,061.93, the sheriff concluded that '£16,000 was a reasonable valuation of the chip shop equipment'.[7] The alternative would have been a removal-and-sale valuation, which would have been less; the approach to valuation adopted by the sheriff seems to us right.

The second claim: the lease

The pursuer claimed that the parties had agreed on a 15-year lease, this having been done orally, and that the landlord had forcibly ended the lease by cutting

---

1 See paras 46 and 48.
2 Christopher Dickson.
3 Paragraphs 55 and 56 of the note.
4 Paragraph 55 of the note.
5 Not only (many would say) the greatest of the Roman jurists, but also one known to have visited Scotland. On his visit see eg Tony Honore, *Ulpian* (2nd edn 2002) pp 21–22. The connection between the two facts is obvious. Why oh why is there still no Ulpian tartan? Professor R R M Paisley points out to us that Papinian also visited Scotland, so clearly a further tartan will be needed. On Papinian's visit, see Cassius Dio, *Historia Romana* 77:14 (using the standard modern numbering).
6 Digest, 50, 17, 54.
7 Paragraph 58 of the note.

off the power supply. For this he sought damages. The sheriff was of the view that if the pursuer was entitled to damages the appropriate sum would have been £141,117.[1] But had the pursuer established that there was a valid 15-year lease?

The pursuer had two hurdles to climb over. The first was factual: there was no documentation, so what, if anything, had been agreed? The defence asserted that there had in fact been no agreement for a lease. The second hurdle was legal. A lease for 15 years requires to be in writing, and the agreement (if any) had been oral.

The factual hurdle

The first hurdle required evidence as to what had happened back in early 2005. The original defender (Mr MacNeil senior) gave evidence on commission before his death, denying that a lease had been agreed. The pursuer gave evidence to the contrary. What turned out to be crucial was the evidence of the pursuer's estranged wife, Michelle Gray, who said that a 15-year lease had indeed been agreed. The sheriff accepted the pursuer's account. But there was still the question of the validity of an oral lease.

The legal hurdle

Writing is required for 'the creation, transfer, variation or extinction of a real right in land' says s 1(2)(b) of the Requirements of Writing (Scotland) Act 1995. Subsection (7) says that 'in this section "real right in land" means any real right in or over land, including any right to occupy or to use land or to restrict the occupation or use of land, but does not include … a tenancy … if the tenancy or right is not granted for more than one year.' This does not expressly state, but clearly indicates, that writing *is* required for a tenancy for *over* a year.

The agreement between the pursuer and defender was for a tenancy for 15 years and was oral. So it was not valid. Or was it? The provisions of s 1 of the 1995 Act have a major qualification: what has come to be called 'statutory personal bar'. Where there has been agreement, but not in writing, and one party has acted in reliance on the agreement (plus certain other conditions), then the other party 'shall not be entitled to withdraw from the contract … and the contract … shall not be regarded as invalid'.[2] The standard example would be where Alice and Bob agree the sale of land but the agreement is not in writing, or perhaps it is in writing but there are no signatures. If a disposition is then granted, all is well and good, but suppose that Alice (or Bob) seeks to back out before a disposition is granted. The agreement is *prima facie* invalid. But if it can be shown that the agreement has been relied upon (etc) then it is thereby validated. One might put it thus: for certain types of agreement (eg sale of land) a contract can be entered into either (i) by formal writing or (ii) by

---

1 Paragraph 84 of the note.
2 Requirements of Writing (Scotland) Act 1995 s 1(3). Presumably 'shall not be regarded as invalid' is just a verbose form of 'shall be valid'.

informal (including oral) agreement, followed by reliance (plus certain other conditions).

Statutory personal bar applies to contracts for real rights, such as missives.[1] It does not apply to deeds that constitute, transfer or vary real rights, such as dispositions. For instance, if a disposition has not been signed, whole cartfuls of personal bar will not validate it.

The way the 1995 Act draws the distinction is as follows: personal bar can validate 'a contract or unilateral obligation for the creation, transfer, variation or extinction of a real right in land' (s 1(2)(a)(i)) but cannot validate 'the creation, transfer, variation or extinction of a real right in land' (s 1(2)(b)). That works well enough for most conveyancing transactions. But, as many authors have observed, it does not work well for leases, because a lease falls under *both* headings: it is a contract (to state the obvious) and it has real effect, assuming that, in the case of a short lease it is followed by possession, or, in the case of a long lease it is followed by registration.[2] As Lord Drummond Young put it more than a decade ago, in *Advice Centre for Mortgages v McNicoll*: 'On one hand, a lease is itself a contract for the creation of an interest in land. On the other hand, it creates an interest in land.'[3] He went on to say:[4]

> [W]here it can be inferred that the intention of the parties to a lease is that possession should be taken by the tenant on the faith of the lease document, or the lease document should be registered, thus creating real rights in the tenant, that document will create an interest in land and will accordingly fall within subs (2)(b) of s 1. In that event the personal bar provisions contained in subss (3) and (4) will not apply.

As Angus McAllister has observed: 'Since it is difficult to envisage missives of let that are not intended to create a real right in land, it follows, on this analysis, that the statutory form of personal bar cannot operate to cure informalities in missives of let.'[5] And of course the same comment would apply equally to an oral agreement.

An alternative view is that one can draw the same distinction between an agreement for a lease and a lease, as one can between an agreement for a disposition and a disposition. Thus if there is an agreement (eg missives) calling for a subsequent separate document of lease, such agreement, if not in writing, would, on this view, be capable of validation by personal bar.[6] But that has yet to be tested in litigation. And it is not clear that it really makes much sense. One cannot easily make a contract/lease division, for a lease *is* a contract. Indeed, it is one of the nominate contracts. It is a strange contract

---

1   For a case this year in which an attempt was made to set up missives through personal bar, see *Reilly v Brodie* [2016] SC EDIN 36, 2016 GWD 15-280 (Case (2) above).
2   See in particular Angus McAllister, *Scottish Law of Leases* (4th edn, 2013) ch 2; Robert Rennie et al, *Leases* (2015) ch 3; Elspeth Reid and John Blackie, *Personal Bar* (2006) ch 10. These discussions all bring the problem into focus.
3   *Advice Centre for Mortgages v McNicoll* 2006 SLT 591 at para 19.
4   Paragraph 19. We have substituted '(2)(b)' for '(2)(c)', which was evidently a slip.
5   McAllister, *Scottish Law of Leases* p 32.
6   This seems to be the view taken by Reid and Blackie, *Personal Bar* para 10-06, and cf para 7-08 where a distinction is drawn between a 'contract to lease' and 'the lease itself'.

because it can bind those not party to it.[1] But it is still a contract, albeit with bulging muscles.

Lord Drummond Young's approach was followed in *Gyle Shopping Centre General Partners Ltd v Marks and Spencer plc*[2] and both those cases were accepted as authoritative in *Gray v MacNeil's Exr*. We quote the sheriff:[3]

> In the present case the pursuer's averments are clear that what was agreed ... in early 2005 was a lease of the chip shop for 15 years. There was no averment that could be construed as meaning that this was an agreement for a lease (ie an underlying agreement), which could fall within s 1(2)(a)(i) of the 1995 Act ... There was no evidence of a separate underlying agreement. Both s 1(2)(a)(i) and 1(2)(b) refer to a 'real right in land'. The meaning of that phrase 'is any real right in or over land, including any right to occupy or to use land or to restrict the occupation or use of land'. In my view both the pursuer and Mrs Gray were of the view that the pursuer had verbally agreed a lease and that the clear intention of the parties to the lease was that possession and occupation of the chip shop would be taken by the pursuer on the faith of that lease. In other words, all the parties thought the verbal lease would create a real right in land. Accordingly, what we are left with is a single agreement which was, on the one hand, a contract for the creation of a real right in land (s 1(2)(a)(i)) and, on the other hand, was capable of creating a real right in land (s 1(2)(b)). In such circumstances, the verbal lease could not be described as creating purely personal rights (see *The Advice Centre for Mortgages* at para 18 and *Gyle Shopping Centre* at para 14). Therefore, according to *The Advice Centre for Mortgages* and *Gyle Shopping Centre*, the verbal lease falls within s 1(2)(b) rather than s 1(2)(a)(i). This leads to the unfortunate result that the pursuer cannot rely on s 1(3) and (4).

So the pursuer's argument that there was a lease failed. As will be noted, the sheriff reached that conclusion with regret.

Some reflections

Gray v MacNeil's Exr contains extensive discussion of the personal bar issue and is on that account valuable. It confirms that a lease for more than a year cannot be set up by personal bar.[4] It neither shuts not widens the possibility that an agreement to grant a lease, the latter to be a separate juridical act from the agreement, might qualify for protection by the personal bar provisions of the 1995 Act.

---

1 Not at common law (which follows the Roman law), but by one or other of two statutes: the Leases Act 1449 and the Registration of Leases (Scotland) Act 1857, the latter of which applies both to the Land Register and to the Register of Sasines. The 1449 Act applies to short leases, but not to long ones (though formerly it did so), and the 1857 Act applies to long leases, but not to short ones.
2 [2014] CSOH 122, 2015 SCLR 171. For discussion see Lorna Richardson, 'The limits of statutory personal bar' (2016) 20 EdinLR 66.
3 Paragraph 77 of the note.
4 The difficulties in this area are about whether a *lease* can be set up by statutory personal bar. As for *assignations of leases*, the same difficulties do not apply, for there the contract/deed distinction is clear enough. For such a case this year see *Reilly v Brodie* [2016] SC EDIN 36, 2016 GWD 15-280 (Case (2) above), though as a matter of fact in that case the invocation of personal bar failed for other reasons.

It does not seem that it was suggested that the agreement could not have been a lease, because there was no true rent. It will be recalled that the 'rent' was payment of the staff and the upkeep of the premises. Probably there was no problem here. A rent does not have to be a money rent. For instance, it was once common for the rent of agricultural property to be paid in grain. Still, the 'rent' in this case is not one for which we can offhand think of a precedent. This point, if it has any substance, would have aided the pursuer, for it would have meant that the 15-year contract would not have been a contract of lease, and so the requirements of form in s 1 of the Requirements of Writing (Scotland) Act 1995 would not have been applicable.

This reflection indicates a possible oddity in the law. An unwritten contract to possess land for more than a year is invalid if it is a contract of lease. But if it is not a contract of lease, such an unwritten contract would seem to be valid.[1]

The law is not in a satisfactory state. In the first place it is obscure, and in the second place it is uncertain what the rules ought to be. Part of the problem may lie in unanswered questions about the nature of a lease in Scots law, and part may lie in uncertainties as to why and when writing should, as a matter of policy, be required for a juridical act. If the policy of the 1995 Act is that personal bar should be able to validate personal rights but not real rights, then why should not the Gray/MacNeil lease have been validated as a personal right (binding the parties) but not as a real right (binding singular successors)? After all, there is nothing unthinkable in the idea of a lease that is simply a contract, without real effect. At common law (following Roman law) all leases were thus, and even today it can happen, for instance when a lease for over 20 years is granted but not registered.[2]

SERVITUDES

Implied access rights

Introduction

A person owns adjacent properties. Access to the first property is commonly taken by means of the second. The first property is disponed. The disposition is silent on access rights. What then? Can access to the first property continue to be taken over the second property? Is there, in other words, a servitude over the second property in favour of the first? That, in essence, was the issue before the Inner House in *ASA International Ltd v Kashmiri Properties (Ireland) Ltd*.[3]

---

1 Because the default rule is that contracts do not require to be in writing: Requirements of Writing (Scotland) Act 1995 s 1(1). It is true that s 1(7) refers not only to a 'tenancy' but also to a 'right to occupy or use land', but the subsection is expressly about 'real' rights, so what must have been in contemplation was such rights as proper liferent.

2 Because, as mentioned above, a lease can have real effect only by virtue of one or other of two statutes, the Leases Act 1449 and the Registration of Leases (Scotland) Act 1857, and the former does not (nowadays) apply to leases for more than 20 years.

3 [2016] CSIH 70, 2016 GWD 27-493. The court comprised Lady Paton, Lord Drummond Young and Lord Malcolm, with Lord Drummond Young delivering the Opinion of the court.

Normally, a servitude is created either expressly (in which case the deed must, today, be registered against both dominant and servient tenements)[1] or by positive prescription. But there is also a third way which is far less common than the other two. When a disposition splits off land from a larger property, the law will sometimes imply a servitude or servitudes into the disposition. Such servitudes can be in favour of the land being disponed, or in favour of the land being kept, or indeed both.

Relatively speaking, implied servitudes are new to Scots law. They entered the law only with the decision of the House of Lords in *Cochrane v Ewart*[2] in 1861 – a decision which applied in a Scottish case a body of law which was already well developed in England. Whether because of the manner in which it entered the law, or because of concerns at the absence of publicity surrounding implied servitudes, or for other reasons, the law of implied servitudes has been only grudgingly applied in Scotland. Most cases in which it is pled have failed.[3] In that respect *ASA International* is no exception. Yet *ASA International* is different from previous cases in one important respect. The court attempts, for the first time, to articulate what it takes to be the policy considerations underlying implied servitudes. As we will see, however, the considerations identified by the court do not suggest a bright future for the law in this area.

The facts

The parties in *ASA International* owned two adjacent terraced townhouses in Coates Crescent on the western edge of Edinburgh's New Town. The pursuer (and appellant) owned number 6; the defender (and respondent) owned number 7. Both were used as offices. At the rear of both properties was a (public) lane, William Street South East Lane. The most convenient way of accessing the lane from number 6 was by means of a gate which led from the back garden of number 6 to the back garden of number 7 (now used as a car park) and hence into the lane. From the lane there was then ready access to William Street, which was the next street down from, and parallel with, Coates Crescent. William Street could also be reached from number 6 by leaving the building by the front entrance in Coates Crescent and walking along one of the streets at right angles (Walker Street or Stafford Street). But the route over the rear garden of number 7 was a shortcut. The route was also the quickest way to reach car-parking spaces owned as part of number 6 which were at the rear of number 9 Coates Crescent.

The titles to numbers 6 and 7 Coates Crescent were entirely separate but for a brief few years, between 1989 and 1994, the properties were owned by the same person, National Mutual Life Assurance Society. In 1994 National Mutual disponed number 6 to a predecessor in title of the pursuer while retaining number 7. In due course number 7 passed into the ownership of the defender. Prior to the split-off of number 6 in 1994, and for many years after, those working

---

1 Title Conditions (Scotland) Act 2003 s 75.
2 (1861) 4 Macq 117.
3 See eg *Gow's Trs v Mealls* (1875) 2 R 729; *McLaren v City of Glasgow Union* (1878) 5 R 1042; *Shearer v Peddie* (1899) 1 F 1201.

in number 6 made regular use of the shortcut over number 7 in order to go to William Street (for example, to buy lunch) or to reach the parking at the rear of number 9. If matters had carried on as they were, an access right would probably have been established by prescription. But in 2010, four years short of the prescriptive period, the defender rebelled and blocked access to number 7 by erecting a fence across the gate. Hostilities ensued.[1] The pursuer took down the fence. The defender reinstated it, and added for good measure two one-tonne sand bags at the point where access had previously been taken. The pursuer took down the fence again and used a Land Rover to drag the sand bags away. The defender built a temporary block-work wall and installed CCTV. The pursuer demolished the wall with a sledgehammer. The police were called in. Eventually, an action was raised in which the pursuer sought declarator of the existence of a servitude of pedestrian access over the rear ground at number 7 as well as interdict against interference with the access.

The law

The outlines of the law were set out in the case which introduced implied servitudes to Scotland, *Cochrane v Ewart*.[2] In what has become a well-known passage, the Lord Chancellor, Lord Campbell said this:[3]

> My Lords, I consider the law of Scotland as well as the law of England to be, that when two properties are possessed by the same owner, and there has been a severance made of part from the other, anything which was used, and was necessary for the comfortable enjoyment of that part of the property which is granted, shall be considered to follow from the grant, if there are the usual words in the conveyance.

He added:[4]

> When I say it was necessary, I do not mean that it was so essentially necessary that the property could have no value whatever without this easement, but I mean that it was necessary for the convenient and comfortable enjoyment of the property as it existed before the time of the grant.

In these passages the Lord Chancellor set out two requirements. In the first place, the putative right must have been 'used' before severance of the two properties; and in the second place, the right must be 'necessary for the comfortable enjoyment' of the property which is being disponed. As the language indicates, the second requirement is tailored to servitudes in favour of the property being disponed (ie to servitudes of implied grant); a sterner test of virtual or quasi-necessity applies to servitudes in favour of the property being retained (ie to servitudes of implied reservation).[5] But in *ASA International*

---

1 The details that follow come from the closed record.
2 The standard modern account of the law is in D J Cusine and R R M Paisley, *Servitudes and Rights of Way* (1998) ch 8.
3 (1861) 4 Macq 117 at 122.
4 At 123.
5 On this distinction see eg *Murray v Medley* 1973 SLT (Sh Ct) 75.

the alleged servitude was in favour of the property being disponed, or in other words in favour of number 6 Coates Crescent.

As the Inner House acknowledged in *ASA International*, the two requirements set out in *Cochrane v Ewart* are not of equal importance. It is the second requirement that matters most, and in some cases it may even be possible to dispense with the first.[1] The evidence in the present case – there had been a proof before the sheriff – was that the shortcut had been in regular use prior to severance in 1994. The only remaining question, therefore, was whether a right to use the shortcut was necessary for the comfortable enjoyment of number 6.

The decision

At first instance, the sheriff was not persuaded that the shortcut was necessary for number 6's comfortable enjoyment, and so granted decree of absolvitor. The view of the Inner House, on appeal, was the same. The pursuer's case, indeed, seems to have been a weak one. Even without the shortcut, access to and from the building at number 6 could be taken both from the front and from the rear. The front door led straight out into Coates Crescent. The rear door led out to a path which finished at the back door to a garage, which belonged to number 6, and the garage in turn led to William Street South East Lane. It is true that this rear exit was awkward to use, at least if a car was parked in the garage. Unquestionably it was much easier to use the shortcut through the adjoining property at number 7. But the fact remained that access *was* possible at the rear. Furthermore, the front access was easy – indeed was the main entrance to the building; and while William Street – apparently the destination of choice for employees – was further if the building was left from the front rather than from the rear, it still could not be said to be far. It is hard, therefore, to disagree with the Inner House's conclusion that the evidence fell 'well short' of satisfying the requirement of comfortable enjoyment.[2] Furthermore, the result is consistent with previous decisions which, in general, decline to allow a second access by way of implied servitude when a perfectly good means of access already exists.[3]

The policy considerations

In deciding the case, the Inner House took the unusual step of laying down a number of policy considerations:[4]

> First, when property is divided, it is always possible to create servitudes by express grant. If a servitude right is important, it can generally be expected that the matter will be raised in negotiation and that an appropriate clause will be inserted into the disposition. The question of an implied grant only arises where no express provision has been made. Secondly, claims for implied rights inevitably involve a degree of

---

1 Paragraph 20.
2 Paragraph 32.
3 *Gow's Trs v Mealls* (1875) 2 R 729; *McLaren v City of Glasgow Union* (1878) 5 R 1042. Compare *Wall v Kerr*, 30 July 2015, Airdrie Sheriff Court, Case (9) above, where the existing access was found to be markedly inferior to the one sought by implication.
4 Paragraphs 17 and 18.

uncertainty, and if an expansive approach is taken to the creation of such rights there is a risk that a substantial number of dubious or even extravagant claims may be made. Thirdly, and more importantly, servitude rights are real rights created over heritable property. In this area of the law certainty has always been regarded as crucial, because of the perpetual existence of such rights. Fourthly, perhaps the most important factor is that real rights bind the whole world, and will be binding on any future purchaser of the servient property. Any such purchaser should be able to discover the existence of real rights easily. Normally this is achieved by express grant and the recording of the relevant deeds in the Land Register. Implied rights, however, do not appear in the Land Register.

From these policy factors the court drew two broad conclusions. First, 'the law should be slow in recognizing the creation of servitudes in this manner'.[1] Secondly, 'there are strong policy reasons for restricting the recognition of such rights to cases where their existence is reasonably obvious from the surrounding facts and circumstances. Cases where the right is reasonably necessary for the enjoyment of the dominant tenement can be said to fall into the latter category.'[2]

In a general way, it is hard to disagree with the four – or really three, for numbers two and three come to the same thing – policy factors set out by the court. But they are all reasons for *not* allowing implied servitudes, and take no account of the counter-arguments, of the potential utility of such servitudes. Moreover, precisely the same objections – with the possible exception of the first – apply to servitudes created by prescription. Indeed, on this kind of reasoning, the case against prescriptive servitudes is stronger still. For if implied servitudes are at least to be 'reasonably obvious from the surrounding circumstances', and hence potentially visible to future acquirers of the servient tenement, this will often not be true of prescriptive servitudes. Indeed the court expressly contrasts the visibility of a right which is 'reasonably necessary for the enjoyment of the dominant tenement'[3] with the mere fact of a right having been used (as is needed to establish a servitude by prescription), 'which may not be obvious to a purchaser when he acquires the property especially if the use is not constant'.[4] Yet it may be assumed that in its remarks the court was not intending to limit the recognition of prescriptive servitudes.

As appears from later in the judgment, the main purpose of the court's policy analysis was to counter certain loose *dicta* in some of the older case law which had been relied upon by counsel for the pursuer.[5] Whether it will have any broader effect – whether, in other words, it will make courts less willing to recognise implied servitudes in the future – remains to be seen. It is to be hoped not. Implied servitudes are neither perfect nor frequent, but they have

---

1 Paragraph 17.
2 Paragraph 18. In fact, just because a right 'is reasonably necessary for the enjoyment of the dominant tenement' does not mean that it will always be 'reasonably obvious from the surrounding facts and circumstances'. For example, underground pipes may be reasonably necessary or even essential without being at all obvious to third parties.
3 Paragraph 18.
4 Paragraph 21.
5 Paragraphs 22–28.

their place. That place should not be lost by what might be regarded as slightly one-sided reasoning employed in *ASA International*.

Permissible types of servitude

Introduction

What sort of right[1] can be a servitude? The answer depends, in the first place, on how and when the servitude was created (or purported to be created). Traditionally, servitudes were restricted to those which were 'known to the law',[2] but that rule was disapplied by s 76 of the Title Conditions (Scotland) Act 2003 to any servitude created by express provision in a registered deed on or after 28 November 2004. There are thus two broad possibilities. For express servitudes created on or after 28 November 2004, a servitude can encompass any right which satisfies the general characteristics of a servitude. But for other servitudes – in other words, for servitudes created by prescription, by implication, or by express deed before 28 November 2004 – the 'known-to-the-law' rule continues to apply. Each possibility may be considered in turn.

Express servitudes created on or after 28 November 2004

Section 76 did not abolish all restrictions as to content. On the contrary, even in the case of express servitudes created on or after 28 November 2004 the general characteristics of a servitude must be observed.[3] In particular, in order to qualify as a servitude a right must (i) be positive in nature, (ii) be praedial, ie confer benefit on the dominant tenement, and (iii) not be repugnant with ownership.[4] But what s 76 did do was to abolish the 'known-to-the-law' rule. Today it is no objection that the right has not been recognised as a servitude before. Section 76 is a green light for the invention of new types of servitude. Conveyancers are invited to use their imaginations. The extent to which conveyancers have actually done so, since 2004, is, however, less clear. Certainly no exotic servitude has so far come before the courts. By way of encouragement, therefore – if encouragement is needed – we mention a new case from England.

   Regency Villas Title Ltd v Diamond Resorts (Europe) Ltd[5] concerned land used for the purposes of a timeshare development. Originally the land was owned together with an immediately adjacent property which contained sporting and leisure facilities such as tennis courts, a swimming pool, and a golf course. In 1981 the timeshare land was split off. The conveyance conferred on the grantee and its successors and lessees the right:

---

1 Or, looked at from the perspective of the servient tenement, obligation.
2 Cusine and Paisley, *Servitudes and Rights of Way* para 2.87. The Scots law of servitudes derives from the Roman law.
3 As to which see Cusine and Paisley, *Servitudes and Rights of Way* para 2.01.
4 The first and last of these were added by the Title Conditions (Scotland) Act 2003 ss 76(2) and 79; the second comes from the common law as, in origins, does the last.
5 [2015] EWHC 3564 (Ch), [2016] 4 WLR 61.

to use the swimming pool, golf course, squash courts, tennis courts, the ground and basement floor of Broome Park Mansion House, gardens and any other sporting or recreational facilities ... on the Transferor's adjoining estate.

Later a dispute arose as to whether the right so conferred was merely personal or whether it was an easement (in Scottish terms, a servitude) binding on successors. The judge noted that:[1]

There is no English (or Scottish) authority authoritatively determining whether or not an easement can exist to use (say) a golf course, swimming pool or tennis court, but in my judgment there is no legal impediment to the grant of such an easement, provided the intention to grant an easement, as opposed to a merely personal right, is evident on the proper construction of the grant.

Having construed the grant, the judge held that an easement was established.

How would these facts play out in Scotland? An immediate obstacle is the decision in *Patrick v Napier*[2] which refused to recognise as a servitude a right 'of angling or rod-fishing in the river Echaig'. But this was partly due to the distance between the alleged dominant tenement and the river in which the fishing rights were to be exercised. It might be a different matter if, as in *Regency Villas*, the properties were next-door. In particular, such immediate proximity might well be sufficient to satisfy the praedial requirement (ie the second of the characteristics mentioned above). That, certainly, was the view of Professor W M Gordon:[3]

It seems to be a mistake to suppose that one can settle in the abstract the question whether a particular right, of strolling, golfing or anything else, can or cannot be a servitude. If the right must benefit a dominant tenement the question whether it is an appropriate servitude can only be settled by considering it in relation to the tenement with which it is to be connected ... It is obviously a metaphor to say that a servitude is for the benefit of land and not for the benefit of the owner of the land. When it is possible to have a servitude right to a water supply to drive a mill, there seems nothing anomalous in, say, a hotel having a servitude right of fishing or golfing, although it may be questionable whether a private house should have it.

Admittedly, there is a practical difficulty. The value of a servitude of, say, swimming in a pool depends upon the servient owner maintaining the pool and keeping it full of water. He cannot be made to do so as part of the servitude although, in Scotland at least, such an obligation can be constituted as a real burden. It was doubts on this point that led Lord Scott, in the Scottish House of Lords case of *Moncrieff v Jamieson*,[4] to 'doubt whether the grant of a right to use a neighbour's swimming pool could ever qualify as a servitude'. Yet if the holder of a servitude of way can enter the servient property to maintain the road,

1 Paragraph 56. The judge was Charles Purle QC sitting as a High Court judge.
2 (1867) 5 M 683.
3 W M Gordon, *Scottish Land Law* (2nd edn, 1999) para 24-19.
4 [2007] UKHL 42, 2008 SC (HL) 1 at para 47.

then presumably the holder of a right to swim can enter the servient property to maintain or fill the pool. That, certainly, was the view of the judge in *Regency Villas*.

A right to swim or play golf may lie on the edge of what can be accepted as a servitude. But lying behind *Regency Villas* is a case which has considerable promise for Scotland. In *In re Ellenborough Park*,[1] decided in 1955, the Court of Appeal in England held that houses surrounding a private park could have an easement to use the park for walking and for other recreational purposes. More than swimming or golfing, such a right confers a clear benefit on the houses in question, 'for just as the [sole] use of a garden undoubtedly enhances, and is connected with, the normal enjoyment of the house to which it belongs, so also would the right granted, in the case supposed, be closely connected with the use and enjoyment of the part of the premises sold'.[2] In this sort of reasoning may lie a solution to the problem of amenity areas in housing estates where, whether deliberately (as in Greenbelt-type arrangements) or by inadvertence (as where an attempt to make the areas common property has failed due to an insufficient description), the areas do not belong to the householders.[3]

Other servitudes

For servitudes created in other ways, such as by prescription, the 'known-to-the-law' rule is unaffected by the Title Conditions (Scotland) Act 2003, and so remains in place. There is, more or less, a fixed list of permissible servitudes, many of which were already found in Roman law.[4] By limiting the servitude type, the idea is to limit the exposure, of those acquiring property, to servitudes which are unregistered and of which they may have no knowledge. Yet even here there is flexibility. As the sheriff emphasises in an important new case, *Johnson, Thomas and Thomas v Smith*,[5] 'References to servitudes "known to the law", and more especially to a supposed "fixed list", while convenient as a short-hand, may have tended to disguise the more subtle and flexible aspects of the common law principle.'[6] Certainly, 'the exercise does not begin and end by reading down the textbook list of recognised servitudes'.[7] The sheriff draws attention to a statement in Bell's *Principles* that a right can be a servitude if it is 'such a use or restraint as by *law* or *custom* is known to be likely and incident to the property in question, and to which the attention of a prudent purchaser will, in the circumstances, naturally be called'.[8] Servitudes 'by law' are those on the fixed list, as well as analogues of such servitudes. But there can also be servitudes 'by custom' by

---

1 [1955] Ch 131.
2 At 174 per Evershed MR.
3 See eg *Conveyancing 2015* pp 137–38.
4 For the possible contents of this list, see Cusine and Paisley, *Servitudes and Rights of Way* ch 3.
5 [2016] SC GLA50, 2016 GWD 25-456.
6 Paragraph 21.
7 Paragraph 26. The sheriff is S Reid.
8 G J Bell, *Principles of the Law of Scotland* (4th edn, 1839, repr Edinburgh Legal Education Trust, 2010) § 799 (our emphasis).

which is meant, not that custom constitutes the servitude, but that the activity in question 'should have been within the contemplation of the parties, thereby satisfying the policy concern protected by the common law principle'.[1] An example of a servitude by custom is the servitude of bleaching, first recognised by a case decided in 1779;[2] and as this example shows, a servitude by custom might have little or no resemblance to servitudes already on the textbook list.[3]

So much for the theory. The reality has been rather different. In truth, there has been a deep reluctance on the part of the courts to recognise new types of servitude. After the triumph of bleaching, in 1779, more than two centuries were to pass before another type of servitude, the servitude of projection (*jus projiciendi*), was admitted to the canon.[4] Others, meanwhile, had been refused.[5] In *Johnson, Thomas and Thomas v Smith*, the question has arisen once more. The servitude at issue was a free-standing right of parking.

Free-standing servitudes of parking

Introduction

Land belonging to the pursuer in *Johnson, Thomas and Thomas v Smith*[6] was used as a residential site for showmen's caravans. The defender's land, a long, narrow and vacant strip immediately adjacent to the pursuer's land, had been used by the pursuer for many years to park various types of vehicle, including articulated lorries, and for a variety of purposes, including the storing and repairing of amusement-arcade rides and equipment.[7] The pursuer claimed a servitude of parking by prescription. At debate two questions in particular required to be determined. Did Scots law recognise a servitude of parking? And even if it did, was the right being claimed by the pursuer too onerous – too 'repugnant with ownership' – to fall within such a servitude?

A servitude of parking?

We have already mentioned the considerations that apply in the recognition of new servitudes. But parking is in a special position because, a decade or so ago, the House of Lords in *Moncrieff v Jamieson*[8] accepted that parking could be implied as a right ancillary to a servitude right of way. And if parking could be ancillary to a servitude of way, then it seemed to follow that it could also be a servitude in its own right. In theory the matter was still an open one because it had not yet been judicially determined; but in practice, the logic seemed impossible to

---

1 Paragraph 28.
2 *Sinclair v Magistrates of Dysart* (1779) Mor 14519.
3 Paragraph 28.
4 *Compugraphics International Ltd v Nikolic* [2011] CSIH 34, 2011 SC 744, discussed in *Conveyancing 2011* pp 94–98. In fact, this servitude could be traced back to Roman law: see *Digest* 8, 2, 2 (Gaius).
5 Notably, and relatively recently, a servitude of signage: see *Romano v Standard Commercial Property Securities Ltd* [2008] CSOH 105, 2008 SLT 859, discussed in *Conveyancing 2008* pp 108–11.
6 [2016] SC GLA50, 2016 GWD 25-456.
7 As yet there has been no proof and the facts given are based on the pursuer's averments.
8 [2007] UKHL 42, 2008 SC (HL) 1.

resist. That, certainly, was the view that we expressed when discussing *Moncrieff* in our 2007 volume:[1]

> It must follow from the decision ultimately reached in *Moncrieff* that car parking can be *ancillary* to a servitude right of way. But can car parking also exist as a servitude *on its own*, as where, for example, the parking area is reached by a public road?[2] A majority of their Lordships – Lords Scott, Rodger and Neuberger[3] – considered the answer to be yes; and while the remaining judges (Lords Hope and Mance)[4] thought it unnecessary to reach a view, they too were supportive of the principle of a servitude. In the light of this decision, it must now be accepted that car parking joins the dozen or so rights which comprise the 'known' servitudes in Scots law.[5] Accordingly, a freestanding servitude of parking can be established by any means by which a servitude may be created, and could be so established even before 28 November 2004.

That view has now been confirmed by *Johnson, Thomas and Thomas v Smith*. As the sheriff put it:[6]

> [W]hile I acknowledge that *Moncrieff* does not represent a strictly binding judicial recognition of the existence of a free-standing servitude right, in my judgment the debate on this narrow issue is ended for all practical purposes by the overwhelming current of eminent *obiter dicta* in that case. It is futile to stand Canute-like against it. From *Moncrieff*, it is but a short skip in logic to conclude, by analogy with the ancillary right recognised in that case, that an independent free-standing servitude right is, at least, similar in nature thereto.

The result is to add a new servitude – the servitude of parking – to the list of 'known' servitudes in Scots law.

Repugnancy with ownership?

More difficult was the question as to whether the particular right of parking being claimed by the pursuer was so onerous as to be repugnant with the defender's ownership.

Servitudes which go beyond the fixed list must not be repugnant with ownership. This we know for sure because s 76 of the Title Conditions (Scotland) Act 2003 says so. The limitation was imposed as a control device on the new, and potentially exotic, servitudes which s 76 allows. Whether the same limitation applies to non-s 76 cases, including servitudes by prescription, was once uncertain,[7] but has been

---

1 *Conveyancing 2007* pp 110–11.
2 Lord Scott took for granted (at para 49) that, once a road is public, it can be used by anyone without the need for a servitude. On this issue see further *Conveyancing 2006* p 30.
3 Paragraphs 47, 72, 75 and 137.
4 Paragraphs 22, 24 and 102.
5 For an authoritative account, see Cusine and Paisley, *Servitudes and Rights of Way* ch 3.
6 Paragraph 33.
7 The Scottish Law Commission, for example, was in doubt on the point: see *Report No 181 on Real Burdens* (2000) para 12.24. A case in support of such a principle is *Dyce v Hay* (1852) 1 Macq 304. This concerned a right of access for the public, but the case is also regarded as of significance for the law of servitudes. In rejecting the supposed right, the Lord Chancellor (Lord St Leonards), at 309, thought the right to be 'entirely inconsistent with the [servient proprietor's] right of property; for no man can be considered to have a right of property, worth holding, in a soil over which the whole world has the privilege to walk and disport itself at pleasure.'

taken for granted in recent cases beginning with *Nationwide Building Society v Walter D Allan*.[1] The rule is the same in England, where it is known as the ouster principle. In Scotland the rule applies also to real burdens.[2]

The core idea of repugnancy is straightforward. While a servitude, necessarily, restricts the servient owner in the use of his property, such restriction must not be so severe as to remove most or all of the rights of ownership itself. If a servitude is to be merely a subordinate real right, something substantial must be left to the owner of the affected property. Moreover, a servitude must retain its own distinctive characteristics and not mutate into a lease or liferent or a real right of some unknown kind. Among the characteristics of a servitude is the characteristic of non-exclusive use: a servitude must not involve 100% occupation of the servient tenement or, at least in the normal case, of any part of that tenement. A right which allows exclusive use could not, therefore, be a servitude.

As with most general rules, however, the application to particular cases can be difficult. It is certainly difficult in the context of parking. Prior to *Johnson, Thomas and Thomas v Smith*, the repugnancy principle had been considered twice in relation to parking. In *Nationwide Building Society v Walter D Allan*,[3] a right to park two cars in an area which could accommodate six was held to be repugnant with ownership. That was a decision of the Outer House. In *Moncrieff v Jamieson*, by contrast, the House of Lords seemed untroubled by the repugnancy principle.[4]

The servitude said to have been constituted in *Johnson, Thomas and Thomas v Smith* was about as intrusive as parking can be, being unlimited as to the number and type of vehicles, and potentially covering, at all times, the whole of the burdened property.[5] Nonetheless, concluded the sheriff, it was not repugnant with ownership. This was said to follow from *Moncrieff v Jamieson*.[6] After all, explained the sheriff, building on remarks by Lord Scott in *Moncrieff*,[7] there was still something left for the servient owner:[8]

> He can build over the servient tenement, he can build under it, he can advertise on hoardings around it, or otherwise utilise the boundary walls. Indeed, he can park

1 2004 GWD 25-539. The other cases are *Moncrieff v Jamieson*; *Holms v Ashford Estates Ltd* [2009] CSIH 28, 2009 SLT 389; and *Johnson, Thomas and Thomas v Smith* itself. Compare Ken Swinton, 'Free standing servitude rights to park – some reflections on *Johnston, Thomas and Thomas v Smith*' (2016) 84 *Scottish Law Gazette* 49.
2 Title Conditions (Scotland) Act 2003 s 3(6). The common law was the same: see K G C Reid, *The Law of Property in Scotland* (1996) para 391.
3 2004 GWD 25-539.
4 For discussion, see *Conveyancing 2007* pp 109–10.
5 Paragraph 38.
6 *Nationwide Building Society* was not referred to in the sheriff's judgment.
7 *Moncrieff v Jamieson* para 59.
8 Paragraph 44. A similar approach was taken a few years before in relation to the effect of a right of access over an area used by the servient proprietor for parking: see *Holms v Ashford Estates Ltd* [2009] CSIH 28, 2009 SLT 389 at para 53 per Lord Eassie: 'it is not evident that the existence of a servitude right of access over Ms Mason's area of ground prevents use of that area for all purposes. As counsel pointed out, it might accommodate the parking of a motorcycle or a pedal cycle, or the setting out of potted plants and a seat whereby to enjoy the fresh air and sunshine, all compatibly with the pursuers' right of vehicular access.'

on it himself, or use it for any other purpose, provided he does not interfere to any material extent with the reasonable exercise of the servitude right by the dominant proprietor. The servient proprietor may not have physical occupation of the surface of the land when the servitude right is being exercised, but he remains the owner of the land, he remains in control of it, he remains in (legal) possession of it, and he is at liberty to exploit its residual uses.

The test being proposed seems to be one of exclusivity. So long as the possession of the dominant proprietor is not exclusive – so long as he leaves *something* for the servient proprietor – then the repugnancy principle is not breached.

The result of *Johnson, Thomas and Thomas v Smith* is attractive in some respects.[1] But it comes at the cost of reducing the repugnancy principle almost to nothing. Of course, it is possible to argue, as Lord Scott indeed does argue in *Moncrieff*,[2] that that is as it should be. But if that is correct, it renders largely ineffectual the principle's role as a control device in s 76.

SECURED LENDING

Must the security-holder be the same person as the creditor?

Introduction

In the normal case, where there is a standard security or other type of security right, (i) the person who is the debtor is also the owner of the property and (ii) the person who is the creditor is also the holder of the security. Thus James owns Blackmains. He borrows £100,000 from Bank of Forfar plc and grants the bank a standard security. He is both debtor and owner. The bank is both creditor and security-holder.

But must it always be like that? Would it be possible to split the two roles on the debtor side? Might it be possible to split the roles on the creditor side? Specifically: (i) Might it be possible for James to be the owner of the property, and thus the granter of the security, but someone else, say James Global, Solar and Galactic Enterprises Ltd, to be the debtor, the person that owes the money? And (ii) might it be possible for the person to whom the money is owed to be one person, Bank of Forfar plc, while the person who is the holder of the security is another, say Forfar Financial Group plc?

---

1   The case contains other things of interest, not least the suggestions: (i) that where the dominant tenement is subject to a use restriction in the form of a real burden, possession of the servient tenement in association with a use of the dominant tenement not authorised by the burden would not qualify as possession for the purposes of prescription (paras 35-27); and (ii) that, notwithstanding the principle *tantum praescriptum quantum possessum*, a person who acquires a servitude of parking by prescription is not limited to the type and number of vehicles he happens to have parked over the 20-year period but rather has a general servitude of parking, the exercise of which is then regulated by other rules such as the *civiliter* principle (paras 48-55). The second suggestion, at least, cannot be accepted without qualification, for the principle of 'no increase in the burden' presupposes that servitudes, whether constituted by deed or by prescription, are set at a certain level of use which cannot then be lawfully exceeded. See Cusine and Paisley, *Servitudes and Rights of Way* p 336; W M Gordon, *Scottish Land Law* (2nd edn, 1999) para 24-61.
2   *Moncrieff v Jamieson* para 59.

These questions have not been much discussed in our law. That is because they seldom arise in practice. But from time to time they do.

On the first question, the common law is that the debtor and the security-giver need not be the same person,[1] and there is nothing in the Conveyancing and Feudal Reform (Scotland) Act 1970 to depart from the common law. Thus James can grant a security over land that he owns in respect of a debt owed by James Global, Solar and Galactic Enterprises Ltd. This is sometimes called third-party security. If the company defaults, the security can be enforced and James will lose the property. That is not, however, the same as saying that James is personally liable. Suppose that the debt is £1 million and the property is sold for £700,000: James is not liable for the shortfall, because he has no personal liability at all. Of course matters could have been arranged so that James was a cautioner for the debt. In that case he would be liable for the shortfall. But it does not have to be done that way: there can be pure third-party security, in which James grants a security but has no personal liability.

What about the second question: does the creditor have to be the same person as the security-holder? That was the question for the court in *3D Garages Ltd v Prolatis Co Ltd*.[2]

3D Garages: the facts

Without pausing to inquire what sort of garage is *not* 3D,[3] we outline the facts of the case, admittedly of a complex and unusual nature. The pursuer was involved in commercial litigation in the English High Court. The action settled in 2011. The settlement agreement, dated 17 January 2011, involved at least 16 separate parties, including the pursuer in the current action, but not the defender. The settlement agreement bound the pursuer to pay £1.5 million within 12 months of the date of the agreement. To whom was the money to be paid? We do not know the exact wording, but in the present action the sheriff principal is presumably quoting when he says that under the agreement 'parties (10) to (16) shall pay to parties (1) to (9) (or David Gill as their nominee)'.[4] Who parties (10) to (15) were we do not know, but we do know that the current pursuer was party (16). So 3D Garages Ltd had bound itself to pay the money to nine separate parties or to their nominee, Mr Gill.[5]

---

1 Scots law is the same as Roman law: 'Dare autem quis hypothecam potest sive pro sua obligatione sive pro aliena': *Digest* 20, 1, 5 (Marcianus).
2 [2016] SC EDIN 70, 2017 SLT (Sh Ct) 9.
3 The answer is perhaps that those who set the company up were concerned about the possibility of 4D garages in Minkowski space. We merely speculate.
4 Paragraph 3.
5 The mind immediately wonders whether payment to any one of these ten (parties (1) to (9) plus Mr Gill) would have discharged the debt. Or was payment to be split into nine equal parts, unless paid to Mr Gill in a oner? One hopes that the settlement agreement covered such matters. And equally one wonders: who the proper claimant/pursuer was to be if payment was not made by 17 January 2012? Separate actions by the separate creditors? A single global action by Mr Gill? Again, one hopes that the settlement agreement covered such matters. We need not pursue these issues here, since they were not for consideration in the present action.

The £1.5 million was, said the settlement agreement, to be secured by the grant of standard securities over five properties, all in Berwickshire, that were owned by 3D Garages Ltd. The grantee of the standard securities was, said the settlement agreement, to be Prolatis Company Ltd.[1] Why? If there was to be a representative of the various creditors, why have two rather than one? In other words, why both Mr Gill, as creditor, and Prolatis Company Ltd, as security-holder? We have no idea. We trust that there was some sound and compelling reason, for on the surface it seems a prescription for confusion. The settlement agreement provided that Mr Gill had 'responsibility for registering the standard security … and he has the obligation to provide a release and discharge of the security'.[2] Since he was not the grantee of the securities, one wonders how he could have validly applied for their registration. One also wonders how, if the £1.5 million had in fact been paid, how someone who was not the holder could grant valid discharges. Presumably the answer to both questions would be 'mandate', but one feels like clutching very firmly at the bars of the fairground thrill-ride.

In the event, the £1.5 million was not paid by the deadline in January 2012. Whether any steps towards enforcement were taken is not known to us, but at all events the debtor, 3D Garages Ltd, went on the offensive and in 2013 the present action was raised in Duns Sheriff Court. The pursuer was unsuccessful before the sheriff,[3] and appealed to the sheriff principal, Mhairi Stephen QC.

The action

The action was for declarator that the standard securities were void and unenforceable, on the basis that the holder of the security was not owed the debt.[4] As summarised by the sheriff principal:[5]

> The appellants argue that the Conveyancing and Feudal Reform (Scotland) Act 1970 … provides that the person in whose favour a standard security is granted must also be the creditor in the obligation secured by the standard security. As these standard securities purport to be in security of debts owed to a third party (David Gill) they are not in conformity with that legislation and Scots law. They are therefore void and unenforceable. Only the creditor in respect of the debts secured by the standard security may enforce the right in security.

The case was fought out on the basis of the 1970 Act. It does not seem that the common law was considered. The difficulty of course is that the 1970 Act does not deal with the issue. It does not say that the creditor and the security

---

1 An entity registered in Cyprus. According to the Cyprus Corporate Registry its sole director is 'Argybar Nominees Ltd'. This sounds classically off-shore-ish.
2 Paragraph 4, quoting, we assume, from the deed. Presumably the singular 'standard security' includes all five standard securities.
3 We have no other details of the case at first instance.
4 In substance the action was one of reduction, yet at the time when the action was raised the sheriff court did not have jurisdiction in actions of reduction. (The position changed on 1 April 2015: see Courts Reform (Scotland) Act 2014 s 38.) This issue was not discussed in the sheriff principal's judgment.
5 Paragraph 5.

holder have to be the same person. Nor does it say the opposite – that they can be different persons. It is simply silent on the issue. That silence could be the basis of an argument either way round – ie as an implied 'permissible' or as an implied 'impermissible'. The sheriff principal interpreted the silence in the first way: 'There is no provision or requirement in the statute that the creditor in the standard security and principal obligation must be the same person.'[1] 'The statutory provisions do not restrict the ambit of the standard security to the narrow meaning contended for by the appellants.'[2] 'Accordingly, an analysis of the statutory provisions provides no obstacle to finding that the standard securities are both valid and enforceable.'[3] That seems to us a reasonable approach, though, as we have said, the 1970 Act leaves the issue open.

That was enough to dispose of the action. But the defender had a double-barrelled subsidiary argument:[4]

> The subsidiary argument advanced on behalf of the respondents is to the effect that in any event the respondents are the creditors in the principal obligation. The debt by virtue of the settlement agreement is transferred to the respondents in trust. The settlement agreement may also be construed as an assignation of the debt to the respondents.

The sheriff principal agreed with both barrels of the argument. We do not find this easy to follow. If the £1.5 million payment right had been transferred to Prolatis Company Ltd to hold in trust, that surely could have been done only by assignation.[5] The two barrels were a single barrel. The sheriff principal seems, however, to say that if X holds a right, and declares that he holds it in trust for Y, then the right is thereafter held by Y. That is not the law of Scotland. The result of the declaration is that X holds the right, in trust for Y. Furthermore, the argument, however it is formulated, makes little sense anyway. If the settlement agreement meant that the debt was owed to Prolatis Company Ltd, why did it say precisely the opposite? Though we suspect that the settlement agreement may have been muddled, we cannot believe that it was as muddled as that.

Born divided, or divided later?

In *3D Garages*, the division between the creditor and the security holder was from the beginning. That is how matters were set up. But there is also the possibility that a standard security is granted in the ordinary way, ie with no difference between the creditor and the security holder, and thereafter a division takes place. This could happen by (i) the security being assigned by creditor X to Y, but not the debt, or, conversely, (ii) the debt being assigned, but not the security. The first happened in *Watson v Bogue*[6] and the second in *UK Acorn Finance Ltd*

---

1 Paragraph 29.
2 Paragraph 30.
3 Paragraph 32.
4 Paragraph 39.
5 Assuming Scots law to be the applicable law. That is in fact not clear, but the case proceeded on that basis.
6 2000 SLT (Sh Ct) 125.

v Smith.[1] Oddly, the first of these cases was discussed in *3D Garages* but not the second, which is unfortunate because of the two the second is, we incline to think, the more relevant. It held that if the debt is assigned but not the security, the security-holder, even though no longer the creditor, can still enforce the security.

Proceeds of realisation

If the debt and the security are held by different persons, and the security-holder enforces and realises the property, the proceeds of realisation would be held, by the security-holder, in trust for the creditor in the debt. Thus says the 1970 Act,[2] and it may be that the common law is the same. The existence of a trust means that problems would not arise if, immediately after the realisation, the security-holder were to become insolvent.

Personal bar

Anyone looking at this case is bound to ask: how could 3D Garages Ltd be allowed to deny the validity of deeds that the company itself had granted? Is not personal bar applicable here? We imagine that few readers of this case will forbear to mutter – quietly, so as not to disturb their nearest and dearest – '*contra proprium factum nemo venire potest*'. The possible invalidity of the security rights could be put forward by competing creditors, and also by a future purchaser, *but not by the grantor*.[3] This line of argument was, however, not explored in the case.

And all in aid of ... what?

Finally, what was the purpose of the litigation? The sheriff principal thought that it was 'the avoidance of their obligations in terms of the settlement agreement'.[4] But this is not easy to make sense of. Even if the five standard securities had been null and void, the company's liability to pay £1.5 million would have remained. The existence of a security right, such as a standard security, is important to the creditor, because it enhances the probability of recovery. But it is much less important from the standpoint of the debtor. The debtor is bound to pay the money, security or no security, and failure to pay will end up with loss of assets, whether through diligence or through an insolvency process. The reduction of the standard securities would not have had the effect of the avoidance of its obligations. Debt is one thing, security for the debt another. There were two possibilities: that 3D Garages Ltd was solvent, or insolvent. (i) If it was solvent, it could, *ex hypothesi*, pay all its creditors in full, in which case the standard securities would have had little practical significance. (ii) If it was insolvent, it was destined to lose all its assets, including these five properties, and that would be true whether or not the standard securities were validly in place. In short, reducing the standard securities could be of no ultimate benefit to 3D Garages

---

1 2014 Hous LR 50 (*Conveyancing 2014* Case (55)).
2 Conveyancing and Feudal Reform (Scotland) Act 1970 s 27.
3 Compare – though the specific facts are different – *Boyd v Shaw* 1927 SC 414.
4 Paragraph 28.

Ltd. So why did the litigation take place? To this question there is no doubt a good answer, but we are not able to suggest what it might be.

Is a lender bound by the terms of the loan contract?

Introduction

The terms of (i) offers to lend and of (ii) lenders' standard terms (which the standard security, or, in England, the mortgage, will normally incorporate by reference) often say rather different things. The offer sets out the terms that have in fact been agreed, sometimes even doing so in plain English. By contrast, the standard terms are typically lengthy, have not, in any real-world sense, been agreed between the parties, and are seldom easy reading. Often they are what clients would call legalese, or the small print, or would so call them if they read them, which of course seldom happens. Indeed, it is to be feared that the standard terms are often not read by their legal advisers either.

The problem is not confined to secured loans. It arises in contracts of all sorts: there are often tensions or even downright conflicts between what the parties shook hands on and what the standard-form small print says. In some cases the small print may be kept out of action because for one reason or another it has not been validly incorporated into the contract. And in consumer cases, the small print may be kept out of action by consumer protection legislation (which, it must not be forgotten, can apply to loans secured by standard security). But there are always cases where the small print is deemed part of the contract, and that is typically the case in secured loans, because, as mentioned, the standard security (or mortgage) almost invariably has an express clause of reference and incorporation.

In secured loans, the conflict tends to be sharpest in relation to (i) the length of the loan and (ii) the interest rate. As to the former, the offer of loan will say, eg, '20 years' whereas the standard terms will often say 'repayable on demand' or 'repayable on 30 days' notice'. As to the latter, the standard terms will often say, roughly speaking, that the lender can vary the interest rate at will, thus often contradicting the loan offer, which says something different, namely what the parties have actually agreed.

That this state of affairs has persisted for so long is strange. But getting financial institutions to depart from their practices is extraordinarily difficult, and in anything other than a major commercial transaction almost impossible. *Alexander v West Bromwich Mortgage Co Ltd*[1] is the first case that we know of in which the issue has been litigated. It is an important decision.

Mr Alexander's buy-to-let tracker mortgage

Mr Alexander had a buy-to-let tracker mortgage. He took it out in the summer of 2008. It was for 25 years. For the first two years there was a fixed rate and thereafter it was to track the Bank of England base rate, plus 1.99%.

---

1 [2016] EWCA Civ 496, [2017] 1 All ER 942, reversing [2015] EWHC 135 (Comm), [2015] 2 All ER (Comm) 224 (*Conveyancing 2015* Case (71)).

After two years the lender told Mr Alexander that the interest rate would not be 1.99% over base but 3.99% over base. And as for the term, it told him that it was not for 25 years but was repayable whenever it wanted the money back. Mr Alexander raised the present action for declarator[1] of the position as agreed.

This was a test case. The report discloses that Mr Alexander was 'representative of the Property 118 Action Group'. So it was not only Mr Alexander who was treated in this way by the lender.

What was agreed about the interest rate?

The formal offer of loan, which Mr Alexander accepted, said what has just been outlined:[2]

> 6.29% fixed until 30.06.2010 … After 30 June 2010 your loan reverts to a variable rate which is the same as the Bank of England Base Rate, currently 5%, with a premium of 1.99%, until the term end …

The lender's Mortgage Conditions said:[3]

> Interest is payable by you … at the rate or rates specified in your Offer of Loan Letter which, except during any period in which interest is expressed to be at a fixed rate, may be varied by the Company at any time for any of the following reasons:
>
> - If there has been, or we reasonably expect there to be in the near future, a change in the Bank of England Base Rate or in interest levels generally;
> - If investment interest rates have increased or decreased;
> - To reflect market conditions generally;
> - To take account of changes in the law, or any decisions, determinations, precedent, compelling guidance, regulations or instructions issued by a relevant governmental body, ombudsman, regulator or similar person or any code of practice with which we intended to comply;
> - At the end of any period during which any fixed rate or concession or alternative rate (such as the Bank of England Base Rate) is in force;
> - To reflect a change in the way the property is used or occupied;
> - To make sure our business is carried out prudently, efficiently and competitively;
> - To make sure we can meet our obligations to third parties.
>
> If any of the above reasons is found to be invalid, we may still vary the interest rate for any of the remaining valid reasons.

What was agreed about the term of the loan?

The loan offer said that the term of the loan was 25 years, divided between 22 monthly payments at the initial fixed rate and 277 monthly payments at the

---

1 'Declaration' in English terminology.
2 Paragraph 10.
3 Paragraph 19.

tracker rate.[1] The lender's Mortgage Conditions said that the loan was repayable in full if:[2]

- we give you one month's notice requiring such repayment;
- any Payment remains unpaid for longer than one calendar month;
- you are in breach of any of the other obligations or conditions contained in these Mortgage Conditions;
- the Property becomes subject to a Compulsory Purchase Order;
- you are made bankrupt;
- you enter into an arrangement with or for the benefit of your creditors or propose to do so;
- you die or you become incapable of managing your affairs;
- you do anything which may damage or reduce the value of the property or you fail to perform any obligation (whether to pay money or otherwise) imposed upon you as the owner of the property;
- the Guarantor terminates or purports to terminate its obligations under the Mortgage Conditions or becomes insolvent or dies or becomes incapable of managing his affairs.

The conflict provision

The Mortgage Conditions said that:[3]

These Mortgage Conditions incorporate any terms contained in the Offer of Loan. If there are any inconsistencies between the terms in the Mortgage Conditions and those contained in the Offer of Loan then the terms contained in the Offer of Loan will prevail.

The decision at first instance

On interest rate, the first-instance decision was that there was no absolute inconsistency between what the loan offer said and what the Mortgage Conditions said. The former had the basic rule, and the latter had certain exceptions and qualifications which would apply in unusual circumstances. If this approach is right, it still left open the question of whether the interest that the lender chose to award itself, a rate far higher than had been agreed, did *in fact* 'reflect market conditions' etc. That factual question seems not to have been explored in the case. One wonders which side would have had the burden of proof.

The High Court took a similar approach to the question of the term. The offer contemplated the possibility that the loan might be paid off before the expiry of 25 years, and for the judge this fact,[4] combined with the fact that 'a term of 25 years is a long time and it is unrealistic to suppose that during that period the lender had no right to terminate the mortgage', persuaded him that the lender

---

1 Paragraph 11.
2 Paragraph 35. Terms of this sort are almost universal, and they are absurd. Why list all these possibilities when the first does for the lender everything it could want? Conceivably the others are meant as back-up in case the first falls foul of consumer protection legislation. As against that, such terms are used in non-consumer cases too.
3 Paragraph 18.
4 See in particular para 39 of the first-instance judgment.

was, despite the terms of the loan offer, entitled to demand repayment in full on one month's notice.

What the Court of Appeal has decided

The first-instance decision has been reversed by the Court of Appeal. The point, as seen by the appellate court, was fairly simple. The Mortgage Conditions were incompatible with the terms agreed by the parties at the outset, and, given the conflict provision (see above), the bank was bound by the terms originally agreed.

Reflections

Borrowers will be relieved by this decision, especially non-consumer borrowers, for consumer borrowers have various protections apart from the general law. But it will be borne in mind that an important aspect of the case was that the Mortgage Conditions had a provision saying that the terms of the loan offer would have priority. Had that provision not been there, the result might have been different for, generally speaking, a later document has priority over an earlier document, and the mortgage deed itself (or standard security) will be signed later than the date when the loan offer is accepted.

In our view, clients, especially in non-consumer cases, should be specifically warned where the lender's standard conditions provide for variable interest, and for repayment on demand.

AFTER ARTL: THE NEW E-CONVEYANCING

The vision

On St Andrew's Day 2016, Registers of Scotland published a consultation document which is of huge importance for the future of conveyancing. Entitled *Digital Transformation: Next Steps*,[1] it sets out a plan for the digitisation of standard conveyancing deeds. This is far from being a distant vision. On the contrary, the idea is that, within the next year or two, all dispositions, standard securities, and discharges – that is to say, nearly 90% of all deeds presented for registration – should be prepared, signed and registered electronically. With only limited exceptions, the ability to register paper deeds will be withdrawn.

This is no less than a revolution. For hundreds of years, conveyancers have prepared deeds in physical form, first on parchment, then on special deed paper, and finally on the thin and unattractive paper demanded by modern printers. If the RoS plan is realised, all of this will come to an end, and may have come to an end indeed by as early as the close of 2017 – the year of the 400th anniversary of the Registration Act 1617 and the setting up of the Register of Sasines.

The legislation is already in place to allow deeds to be produced and executed in electronic form. Since 11 May 2014 it has been competent to draft a deed within

---

1 Registers of Scotland, *Digital Transformation: Next Steps* (2016; www.gov.scot/Publications/2015/11/9619).

one's own computer system, to authenticate it on behalf of a client by means of an electronic signature,[1] and to deliver it by electronic means to the solicitor acting for the grantee.[2] But there the e-conveyancing stops. As matters currently stand, electronic deeds cannot be registered, other than within the ARTL system.[3] In effect, therefore, they cannot be used. The RoS proposals will change all that. A new system for e-deeds and e-registration will be put in place, and ARTL will close its electronic doors forever. It is unlikely to be missed.

The proposed new system

The new system will not be much like ARTL except in one important respect. Like ARTL, it will be a *system*, provided for conveyancers by RoS. To draft a deed, to complete the application form, and to achieve registration, it will be necessary to enter this system. None of this can be done by conveyancers working on their own.

How will the new system operate?[4] In developing the model, RoS has been in close touch with bodies such as the Law Society, the Council of Mortgage Lenders, and with some law firms. Nonetheless, certain details remain a little hazy and open for discussion – hence the RoS consultation. Work is most advanced in respect of digital discharges. Here is how the proposed system is described in the consultation document:[5]

> For discharges, we have designed a digital service run and maintained by the Keeper. Rather than simply registering a digital discharge, this service involves the Keeper providing an end-to-end service for creation, execution and submission of the digital deed. We think this offers a number of benefits to customers that would not otherwise be realised. We have opened up current Land Register data to automatically populate key parts of the deed, saving time and reducing errors. We have provided a standardised deed template, to help to ensure that errors of form do not invalidate the deed (for example by omitting relevant operative clauses). We have built the system to work with current digital signature solutions on the basis that, currently, citizens don't generally have their own digital signature and there is no significant market for the provision of such signatures. Crucially, the system will also interact through what is termed an API (application programming interface). This will provide time-saving and risk-reduction benefits by giving users the facility to re-use information already held in their case management systems. This service approach also allows the Keeper to receive data in a much more structured way and that can be used to automate parts of the registration process – meaning quicker service for customers. We intend to replicate this approach for dispositions and securities.

---

1 For practical guidance on the use of the Law Society's smartcard, see Stewart Brymer and James Ness, 'Using your secure digital signature' (2016) 61 *Journal of the Law Society of Scotland* March/48.
2 Requirements of Writing (Scotland) Act 1995 ss 9C and 9F: see *Conveyancing 2014* pp 140–46.
3 That will remain the position until regulations are made by the Scottish Ministers under RW(S)A 1995 s 9G(3). While this will be done in order to implement the RoS digital plan, we understand that the e-registration of discharges is likely to proceed under the ARTL rules.
4 For further details, see https://www.ros.gov.uk/about-us/digital-transformation.
5 *Digital Transformation* para 2.3.

A number of features of this approach are worthy of note. First, in the interests of ease of completion as well as to reduce errors of drafting, the system provides a standardised deed template which, when completed, is likely to look much like an ordinary deed. No doubt some conveyancers will mourn the loss of drafting autonomy.[1] While, however, this degree of standardisation is possible for the deeds currently selected – dispositions, standard securities, and discharges – it is unlikely to be possible for long leases and a number of other, more complex deeds. In such cases, the long-term plan is for solicitors to create the deeds themselves in electronic form and then join up in some way with the Keeper's system.

Secondly, the system will allow data already held by RoS to populate parts of the deed template, thus reducing the amount of information which the solicitor needs to supply. The consultation paper gives the example of the use of an advance notice to populate the disposition that follows:[2]

In the example of a digital disposition over the whole of a registered plot, a user might want to continue their registration activity from the information supplied in an advance notice. This means that the following is already known at the point of initiating the digital disposition:

• Title Number
• Purchasing parties
• Selling parties
• FAS (this is supplied from the user's access details).

The user would then be prompted to provide the following information in relation to the transaction:

• Consideration or value
• Date of entry
• Confirmation of compliance with LBTT
• Notification email addresses.

Thirdly, there is the promise of enabling the re-use of information already held in case management systems. In this connection, reference may also be made to 'Altis', the digital platform developed by the Law Society in association with the ESPC and BDP Estate Agency Software.[3]

Fourthly, the application form for registration will be completed and submitted online. The opportunity is to be taken to revise the existing form in the light of experience under the 2012 Act.[4] At present, the form is prescribed by

---

1 Although it may be that this autonomy will eventually be restored. Paragraph 1.17 of *Digital Transformation* states that: 'Ultimately, digital conveyancing will replicate the current paper process where the Keeper simply accepts digital documents in much the same way as she currently accepts paper documents. The drafting and execution of the deed would be left to the parties and the Keeper's role would be to accept (or not) the application for registration.'

2 *Digital Transformation* Annex B paras 5 and 6.

3 www.altislegal.com. See also (2016) 61 *Journal of the Law Society of Scotland* Feb/18.

4 *Digital Transformation* paras 2.5–2.9.

statutory instrument,[1] which makes incremental modification difficult to achieve. The intention is to replace it with a new, non-statutory form which can be readily adjusted as circumstances change.[2] The replacement form is likely to be shorter and simpler, and with the questions that baffle being reworded or replaced. The need for a signature will be dispensed with, on the basis that the form is being completed by an accredited RoS user acting through a RoS channel. The same form will also be used for paper applications, but in that case will need to be signed. The signature box, however, will be moved to the front of the form so that it will be difficult to miss, thus helping to eliminate one of the commonest reasons for rejection.

Fifthly, one happy consequence of the use of standardised deeds and pre-populated data is that errors, and rejection rates, are likely to be significantly reduced.

The projected timetable

The new system will be made available first for discharges, then for standard securities, and finally for dispositions. Unlike ARTL, it will apply to all dispositions, including first registrations and split-offs, although in the last two cases the electronic application will sometimes need to be supplemented by the paper submission of certain other material such as prior burdens writs.[3] Once a new deed-type is brought on-stream, there will be an initial period of six months during which applications for registration can be made either electronically or on paper. Thereafter, only electronic submission will be possible except in some unusual cases.[4] If an electronic system is merely optional, it is, RoS consider, likely to be little used. To achieve significant usage, compulsion will be necessary: that is the RoS thinking. If the experience with digital advance notices can be relied on, it should be workable. Whether it will be popular within the legal profession is another matter.

Digital discharges, piloted last year, are set to be introduced in the course of 2017.[5] Details of the system are already clear.[6] The borrower's solicitor sends an electronic request to the lender for a discharge. The lender executes the discharge and submits it directly to RoS, without returning it to the solicitor. RoS then give notice of the removal of the standard security to the borrower's solicitor and, if need be, to others such as the solicitor acting for a purchaser. In theory this could all be done within a single day.

---

1 Land Registration Rules etc (Scotland) Regulations 2014, SSI 2014/150, r 7, sch 1 pt 4.
2 Strictly, however, its use cannot be made compulsory, because the relevant general condition which must be complied with for the application to be accepted refers only to applications being made in 'the form (if any) prescribed by land register rules': see Land Registration etc (Scotland) Act 2012 s 22(1)(d). Once the new form is introduced there will be no prescribed form and so s 22(1)(d) will cease to apply.
3 *Digital Transformation* paras 1.21–1.25. The introduction of 'tell me don't show me' has considerably reduced the amount of additional material that needs to be submitted. In that sense it has been an important enabler of e-conveyancing.
4 *Digital Transformation* paras 1.8–1.11.
5 Over 100,000 discharges are registered every year, accounting for around 30% of registrations.
6 *Digital Transformation* para 1.5.

The current timetable is for digital discharges to be joined by digital standard securities and dispositions before the end of 2017.

Now that RoS have the technology to accept digital plans, digital advance notices will become available for transfers in part.[1] Indeed, as with other advance notices, it will normally be compulsory to use RoS's online system.[2] The changeover day is likely to be 1 April 2018.

Some issues of practice will need to be settled, but this may take time and cannot be done until the details of the new system are all clear. One matter worth mentioning now concerns the letter of undertaking that is generally offered by a seller's law firm in cases where the discharge of the seller's standard security is unavailable by the time of settlement. Assuming that this practice of giving an undertaking continues, it would presumably no longer be an obligation to deliver the discharge but rather an obligation that the discharge will be registered.

MISSIVES BY TEXT

Reilly v Brodie[3] concerned the sale of a fishery business, Selmuir Fly Fisheries, which operated from a leased site in Livingston. The owner of the business was Ross Reilly and the potential purchaser was Lee Brodie, who ran a fishing-tackle shop in Livingston. The subjects leased included a pond, pontoons and outhouses, and among the business assets were boats and fishing tackle.

The negotiations between the parties were conducted by a mixture of speech and text messages, and without the intervention of lawyers. On 1 October 2012 Mr Brodie moved into the premises and was still there at the time of the litigation. He did not, however, pay the price, which was said to be £15,000. On the basis that a contract of sale had been concluded, Mr Reilly raised an action for implement including, in particular, for payment of the price.[4] He relied in particular on a series of text messages which had been sent, mainly by Mr Brodie, between 30 September and 10 October 2012. These were as follows:

Mr Brodie, 30 September 2012
I will contact linda tom arrange a lease transferr and will need bank account details to pay money into.

Mr Brodie, 1 October 2012
Give me a shout when u get a min. Rent is due but not paying anything until we get some stuff sorted. I have instructed my lawyer to draw up a payment agreement for 15k. Should be ready today.

---

1 *Digital Transformation* paras 1.12 and 1.13.
2 For exceptions, see K G C Reid and G L Gretton, *Land Registration* (2017) para 10.10.
3 [2016] SC EDIN 36, 2016 GWD 15-280. The sheriff was T Welsh QC.
4 This was thus one of those rare cases in which a seller, instead of rescinding, reselling and seeking damages, seeks to have the buyer perform his obligations under the contract. There is some discussion of this remedy by the sheriff at para 11 but without mention of the leading modern authority, the decision of the Inner House in *AMA (New Town) Ltd v Law* [2013] CSIH 61, 2013 SC 608, discussed in *Conveyancing 2013* pp 124–31.

Mr Brodie, 1 October 2012
Kev and lewis will bring the agreement to your home later if your busy will give you til 1pm as there is no need to be ignoring people.

Mr Brodie, 3 October 2012
Not sure mate. should have in the office will be in a couple of hours. Lease should be with me today tom then will get things paid up mate.

Mr Brodie, 3 October 2012
Lease is at home mate will take care of payments tom.

Mr Brodie, 5 October 2012
Just made instant payment for loan and 1st payment for the business. I deducted 150 for the solicitors share as he still had to be paid for the work. Also deducted 300 as u took that extra on ur last week.

Mr Brodie, 5 October 2012
It was Kev that reminded me that u were due the business. Unless I get money in my hand from whoever is due it then it wount be counted for I have no record of it being paid back but my books show its down so I have to go with that.

Mr Brodie, 10 October 2012
Get that outboard back to the fisher. I am hold all funds just now as environmental health have told us to shut down for a few weeks due to you f**k ups. Spoke with my lawyer he said loss of earnings have to be taken from whatever money is due to you. They even know about a customer breaking a leg And all the f*****g septic waste if this costs me a fortune I wont let it lie.

Mr Reilly, 10 October 2012
How would they know any thing and what f**k ups was there? The out board that I have is my own personnel one.

Mr Brodie, 10 October 2012
My lawyer said he cant talk with you. U need to deal through a lawyer and have them send a letter to the fishery.

Mr Reilly, 10 October 2012
Ok that's fine.

Did these text messages form the basis of a contract of sale, and hence of an action which sought payment of the price? It was certainly arguable that they disclosed agreement as to the essentials of such a contract, namely parties, property and price. But there were (at least) two difficulties. One was the absence of formal missives. The other was the absence of any conveyancing.[1]

As a general rule, contracts for the sale of land require to be in formal writing, ie in writing subscribed by or on behalf of the parties.[2] That requirement was not met in the present case. But defects of form can sometimes be overcome by

---

1 See para 7 for the arguments brought on behalf of Mr Brodie.
2 Requirements of Writing (Scotland) Act 1995 ss 1(2)(a)(i) and 2.

personal bar.[1] If it could be shown that, to Mr Brodie's knowledge, Mr Reilly had acted in reliance on the contract and would be prejudiced by Mr Brodie's withdrawal, the contract would be binding on Mr Brodie. In the present case, however, the pursuer's averments were held insufficient to make out a case of personal bar.[2] Hence there was no contract of sale.

Furthermore, even if a contract of sale had been found to exist, the price would not have been due until the conveyancing had been done, that is to say, until there had been execution of an assignation of the lease and the promise, at least, of its delivery. The need for a 'lease' – or, more properly, for an assignation of the existing lease – was acknowledged in the text messages which were being relied on. The sheriff, taking up an argument presented on behalf of Mr Brodie, saw this requirement as a suspensive condition, but a more straightforward approach would be to treat delivery of an assignation as the counterpart obligation to payment of the price.[3] Either way it came to the same thing: absent a written assignation, there was no entitlement to the price.[4] On this ground too Mr Reilly's action failed.

KEEPER-INDUCED REGISTRATION

Background

Keeper-induced registration – 'KIR' as it is invariably referred to – means registration in the Land Register of hitherto-unregistered property, done at the discretion of the Keeper, and without the need for the consent, or even knowledge, of the owner, or of other parties having real rights in the property.[5] It is governed by various provisions of the Land Registration etc (Scotland) Act 2012, but the central provision is s 29(1) which states that: 'Other than on application and irrespective of whether the proprietor or any other person consents, the Keeper may register an unregistered plot of land or part of that plot.'

KIR was foreshadowed in the Land Registration (Scotland) Act 1979[6] which gave power to the Secretary of State to 'provide that interests in land of a kind or kinds specified in the order, being interests in land which are unregistered at the date of the making of the order other than overriding interests, shall be registered.' But it was an undeveloped provision and there was doubt whether it was an aircraft that could actually fly: nobody seems ever to have actually proposed the attempt. In addition to doubts about the provision from a technical point of view, there was little pressure, from a policy point of view, for its use.

---

1 RW(S)A 1995 s 1(3), (4). For discussion, see E C Reid and J W G Blackie, *Personal Bar* (2006) ch 7. For another case this year involving the unsuccessful invocation of statutory personal bar, see *Gray v MacNeil's Exr* 2016 SLT (Sh Ct) 250 (Case (37)).
2 Paragraph 14: 'A duty of candour applies … where a pleader seeks to plead an exception or statutory provision like this'.
3 For some of the issues involved in simultaneous performance where one of the parties is in breach, see *Conveyancing 2013* pp 126–28.
4 Paragraph 12.
5 See K G C Reid and G L Gretton, *Land Registration* (2017) paras 7.19–7.24.
6 Land Registration (Scotland) Act 1979 s 2(5).

For a long time, there was little interest in the idea of 'completing the Register', ie getting all properties into the Land Register. As for the Registers of Scotland, they had their hands full with first registrations, and would not have been in a position to contemplate completion of the Register.

Thus matters stood when the Scottish Law Commission was asked to review the law of land registration. The SLC recommended (i) that the triggers for first registration should be extended, and (ii) that the Keeper's discretion to refuse to consider applications for voluntary registration should be removed. These two changes (which were adopted in the Land Registration etc (Scotland) Act 2012) would accelerate the extension of Land Register coverage. But it was nevertheless the case that true completion of the Land Register would, even with these changes, not be carried out by the end of the 21st century, or even by the end of the 22nd. Why so long? The calculation was simple. The Register of Sasines was opened in 1617, yet even now, 400 years later, there are some properties for which, since that time, there has been no registrable deed. Some properties acquired before 1617 by burghs or by the old universities, as well as Crown property, have yet to make their first appearance in the Register of Sasines. Indeed, nowadays this type of situation is potentially more common, for today there are countless companies, some of which have property (for instance the head office) for which there is no registrable transaction for indefinite periods – perhaps centuries.

The SLC thought that the prospect of an indefinite delay in completing Land Register coverage was undesirable. Having two systems of land registration law in tandem is inefficient (for instance conveyancers have to be familiar with both), but more importantly the question is not just one of conveyancing convenience. The Land Register offers transparency as to ownership and as to boundaries which the Register of Sasines does not offer, and that transparency is of value to many constituencies, including government, government agencies and local authorities. 'Who owns Scotland?' is a question that can never really be answered without Land Register completion, and Land Register completion cannot happen without KIR. Indeed, it was the prospect of Land Register completion that seems to have been the chief motivation for Parliamentary time having been found for what is now the 2012 Act.[1] Had there been no provision for KIR, the 2012 Act might never have happened.

In recommending KIR, the SLC saw it as an endgame strategy,[2] something that would be used little or not at all for many years, a device that would be used for completing the last bits of the jigsaw. But in 2014 it was announced that completion of the Land Register was to be achieved by 2024. Now, the Land Register opened in April 1981, and by 2015, ie after 34 years, 59% of titles had been registered. To register the remaining 41% in just nine years was a tough target, and obviously there was no possibility that it could be attained by the

---

1 'Completion of the Land Register is considered to be the most important policy aim of the Bill' said the Scottish Government on introducing to Parliament the Bill that became the 2012 Act: see Policy Memorandum para 14, reproduced in Scottish Parliament, *Passage of the Land Registration etc (Scotland) Bill 2011* (2013, SPPB 174; available at www.scottish.parliament.uk/parliamentarybusiness/Bills/44469.aspx) 180.

2 Scottish Law Commission, *Report No 222 on Land Registration* (2010) para 33.49.

ordinary processes of first registration, even as enhanced by the 2012 Act. The 2014 announcement meant that KIR would have to be used early and aggressively, and not merely, as had been envisaged originally, as a mopping-up process to be used many years into the future.

KIR has now begun

The first tentative Keeper-induced registrations happened in 2015,[1] but only with a 'willing victim', the National Trust for Scotland: the first KIRed properties were the Georgian House in Edinburgh's Charlotte Square, and St Kilda. In the autumn of 2016 the KIR programme began in earnest. By the end of 2016 more than 600 properties had been KIRed. This was a proof-of-concept pilot operation, designed to see what problems would crop up in practice, and to train a core of RoS workers. Three areas were chosen for the pilot, in Edinburgh (in and around Murrayfield), Glasgow (in and around Bearsden) and Angus (in and around Craigie and West Ferry). During 2017 the KIR programme is to be scaled up, so as to become a significant part of RoS work. It is hoped to reach a figure of 20,000 by the end of March, and by the end of 2017 the number of KIRed properties may possibly reach as many as 100,000. During 2017 practitioners will begin to encounter KIR titles.

Research areas

The Keeper has the power to register any unregistered property. But the approach at this stage is that only properties in research areas are to be KIRed. A research area is a development where the properties are generally subject to the same real burdens, and where the titles are already familiar to the Keeper. These titles are the easiest from a KIR standpoint. The idea is to use these research areas to make rapid inroads into the stock of unregistered properties.

Private/public?

KIR is just as possible for properties owned by a public-sector body (and, indeed, for properties owned by the Crown) as it is for properties in private ownership. That has not happened thus far,[2] but eventually it is likely to happen, for although the Scottish Government has announced a target of 2019 for all public-sector properties to be in the Land Register, the chances of that fully happening via voluntary registration do not seem good.

Since voluntary registration incurs a fee (albeit currently with a 25% discount),[3] it may be that some public authorities (and here local authorities

---

1 Preceded by a consultation by the Keeper: see www.ros.gov.uk/about-us/what-we-do/our-business/consultations/keeper-induced-registration. See also Frances Rooney and Sarah Duncan, 'The Keeper is coming' (2016) 61 *Journal of the Law Society of Scotland*, online edition: www.bit.ly/21z75nT.

2 Not counting the National Trust for Scotland: see above.

3 Our own view, for what it is worth, is that this discount is not large enough.

seem the obvious possibilities) may choose not to go for voluntary registration but to sit back and wait to be KIRed, which costs nothing. But this is merely to speculate.

Fee?

As just mentioned, there is no fee for KIR.

Warranty

In the normal case the Keeper will grant warranty ('indemnity' in old money). This is a windfall to the owner, given that no fee has been charged. It is like a free title insurance policy.

Notification

When the pilot began in October 2016, we understand that RoS notified the owner when a property was KIRed. This is no longer done, for practical reasons including the fact that many or most owners turned out not really to understand what was happening, with resulting worry, correspondence and so on. Whilst we understand this approach, it must be observed that it is not easy to quadrate with s 41(1)(b) of the 2012 Act. There is also the point that in those cases (admittedly unusual – see below) where the KIR title sheet is in some substantial way not right, the owner, and the owner's solicitors, will usually not know about the problem until a transaction looms, and by that stage sorting matters out may run into time constraints.

Process and quality

There has been concern in the profession that KIR titles may be second-rate titles. Their quality remains to be seen. But our impression is that, at least for now, quality is likely to be high. In research areas the Keeper has good prior knowledge of the titles. Moreover, for each title a prescriptive progress is checked. Few problem cases have arisen thus far and, where they have, the tendency at least at present is to omit the title from KIR. For instance in early December 2016 one of us visited the KIR unit in Glasgow and noted that in one private housing-estate two properties lying at the edge of the estate had boundary issues: the gardens, as existing on the ground, apparently extended slightly beyond the original development boundary. The decision taken was to omit those two properties from KIR, at least for now.[1]

So we think it likely that, at least for the time being, KIR titles will be of good quality. The real test for KIR, from the point of view both of quality and of speed of processing, will come when the research areas have all been done, and KIR will have to be used for other types of property, often one-of-a-kind titles, both as to boundaries and as to burdens. But that is for the future.

---

1 Of course, these properties may in fact never be KIRed, because they may enter the Land Register by one of the normal routes – for instance, by reason of sale.

What if KIR is not done right?

Errors in KIR are, at least in the initial period, likely to be rare. If an error occurs, there are various possibilities, and we will not go through them all here. But the essential point is that *KIR does not change rights*. Take two examples:

> *Example 1.* Betty owns Whitemains on a GRS title. KIR happens, and the title sheet shows her as owning more than she in fact owns: say that a boundary strip, one metre by ten metres, has been wrongly included. The inclusion is at the expense of a neighbour, Alan, whose title is a GRS title.[1] No rights are changed. Whilst Betty appears, from inspection of the Land Register, to be owner of the strip, she is not. Alan remains owner of the strip.[2]

> *Example 2.* The first example was one of over-registration. This is an example of under-registration. Jill owns Blackmains on a GRS title. KIR happens, and the title sheet shows her as owning less than in fact she owns: say that a boundary strip, one metre by ten metres, has been left out. What is the consequence? Her right of ownership is unaffected. Her title to the main area is now a Land Register title. As for the boundary strip, she still owns it. Her title to the boundary strip remains a GRS title.

In the first case, the Land Register is inaccurate, for what it says (that Betty owns the strip) is false.[3] Hence it can be and should be rectified.[4] In the second case there is no inaccuracy, for nothing that the Land Register says is false. The position is simply that there is still some land that Jill owns on a GRS title. That issue can be resolved either by an additional KIR, or by a voluntary registration, or by registration as and when the property is disponed.

Returning to the first example, there could be a twist. If, before rectification could take place, Betty were to sell to a good-faith buyer (Duncan), then s 86 of the 2012 Act (realignment) could step in to give Duncan a good title to the strip. The result would be that Alan would lose title. Were that to happen, Alan would be entitled to compensation from the Keeper.[5] Such cases, however, are likely to be rare. Apart from anything else, s 86 can operate only if Betty (and not Alan) was in possession of the strip.

Servitudes and real burdens

The Keeper is unlikely to have information about prescriptive servitudes, whether as pertinents in favour of the property, or as encumbrances in favour of a neighbouring property. The fact that a KIR title sheet is silent on such matters does not, however, affect the validity of any prescriptive servitude. If valid before KIR, it remains valid after KIR.

---

1 In practice if Alan's title is a Land Register title the mistake would almost certainly not have happened, because in the KIR process the registered extent of Alan's title would have been noticed.

2 The position would have been significantly different under the Land Registration (Scotland) Act 1979, with its Midas touch (s 3(1)(a)). Under the 2012 Act there is no Midas touch (see in particular s 49(4) of the 2012 Act).

3 See the definition of 'inaccuracy' in s 65 of the Land Registration etc (Scotland) Act 2012.

4 LR(S)A 2012 s 80.

5 LR(S)A 2012 s 94. For realignment under s 86, see Reid and Gretton, *Land Registration* paras 12.8 ff.

On an ordinary first registration it is possible to fillet the D section, cutting out real burdens that are no longer valid, or, indeed, burdens that were never valid as real burdens in the first place. The Keeper is less likely to do such filleting as part of the KIR process.

Dealing with KIR titles

Relying on KIR titles

'A title sheet completed using the KIR process will be clearly marked in the title and easily identifiable to the user. Otherwise, it will essentially look the same as any other title sheet created through a first or voluntary registration. Conveyancers will be able to transact on a KIR title with the same certainty as any other Land Register title.' That statement from RoS[1] seems generally right to us.

Whether it will be common, on the first sale of a KIR property, for the buyer's law firm to check the underlying GRS title, to verify that the KIR process has been done right, remains to be seen. This is a matter more of practice than of law. Our own view, for what it is worth, is that checking the underlying GRS title would not be necessary in the normal case, but will be necessary if there is something in the title sheet which seems unsatisfactory or arouses suspicion.[2]

What if a transaction is pending?

If RoS are aware that a transaction is pending, KIR will not take place for that property. For instance, if the Keeper is considering KIRing a title, but an advance notice application comes in, the KIR process will be halted, with the result that the transaction will (in the normal case at least) proceed as an ordinary first registration.

Finding out that KIR has happened

The following, from RoS, provides a useful summary of what will happen when a transaction is begun in relation to a property that was in the GRS but has in fact now been KIRed:[3]

- If you ask for a plans report over an unregistered plot that has been registered under KIR powers, we will supply a level 3 plans report over the registered KIR title instead.[4]
- If you apply for an advance notice over a plot of land which has been registered under KIR powers then you will be informed this has occurred. We will tell you the title number for the plot of land and invite you to apply for an advance notice in relation to a deed over the registered plot.

---

1 (2016) 61 *Journal of the Law Society of Scotland* Nov/9.
2 Reid and Gretton, *Land Registration* para 16.6.
3 www.ros.gov.uk/about-us/land-register-completion/keeper-induced-registration/how-kir-works.
4 To be pedantic, the words 'unregistered plot' are not quite right because if KIR has happened, the plot is now a registered plot.

- Where KIR has occurred and a first registration application is submitted in relation to the same plot of land, we will internally convert the first registration application to a dealing, provided that it passes the usual checks at intake stage. Please note that these checks will include consideration of our current policy regarding title numbers in writs.
- If a legal report has been submitted over an unregistered subject the report will disclose the KIR title number.

REGISTRATION, REGISTRATION, REGISTRATION

Introduction

Every conveyancer is familiar with certain registers, such as the General Register of Sasines, the Register of Inhibitions, the Books of Council and Session, all of which are ancient, and the Land Register of Scotland, which is not. Sometimes the conveyancer has to consult the Companies Register. But there are (or, in some cases, soon will be) many others touching on conveyancing, for example:[1]

1. the Register of Landlords;
2. the Register of Letting Agents;
3. the Register of Land;
4. the Register of Common Good.
5. the Crofting Register;
6. the Register of Community Interests in Land;
7. the Register of Applications by Community Bodies to Buy Land;
8. the Register of Controlling Interests in Land;
9. the Register of Sites of Special Scientific Interest.

We live in an age of registration. So numerous are the registers, and so often are new ones created, that it would be a major research task to list them all. Perhaps there should be a National Scottish Register of Registers, registration in which would be a precondition of the validity of the register.

The nine registers mentioned above have all arrived since 2003 and some are so new that they are not yet in operation. Our account below is merely a bird's eye view. We divide them into two groups. The first four are kept by local authorities, so that there are not one but 32 registers in each case. The other five are kept by the Keeper.

The new local authority registers

(1) The *Register of Landlords* was established by the Antisocial Behaviour etc (Scotland) Act 2004.[2] The register is for private-sector landlords only. It is an offence to be a private-sector landlord without registration.[3]

---

1 No attempt is made to be exhaustive. For instance another new register is the Scottish Energy Performance Certificate Register under the Assessment of Energy Performance of Non-domestic Buildings (Scotland) Regulations 2016, SSI 2016/146, discussed at p 90 above. One which is longer established is Alan Barr's Official Register of Enemies.
2 Antisocial Behaviour etc (Scotland) Act 2004 s 82. See *Conveyancing 2004* pp 92–95.
3 AB(S)A 2004 s 93.

(2) The *Register of Letting Agents* derives from the Housing (Scotland) Act 2014.[1] The Register begins operation on 31 January 2018, and from 30 September 2018 it will be an offence to carry on business as a letting agent without registration.[2]

(3) The *Register of Land* was established by the Community Empowerment (Scotland) Act 2015.[3] Since 23 January 2017,[4] each local authority has been under an obligation to maintain a public register of all properties that it either owns or holds on lease.[5]

(4) The *Register of Common Good* is to be established by the Community Empowerment (Scotland) Act 2015, although the relevant provisions are not yet in force.[6] When they are, each local authority will have to maintain a public register of everything that is 'common good' property in its area. In practice almost all of this will be heritable property, but it is also possible for corporeal moveables to count as 'common good' assets.

Could the common good status of property concern a person transacting with a local authority, for example buying? For instance, suppose that the City of Edinburgh Council decided to sell off or lease[7] a public park that is near to where both authors live, namely the Meadows. If the Council were to obtain the consent of the court, then the disposal would be competent.[8] But what if the court's consent had not been sought, or worse, sought but refused? Would the title of a buyer or lessee be open to challenge as a result? This may be open to debate.[9] But unless an acquirer is confident in a negative answer to the question, it would be wise to instruct a search in the Register of Common Good. Hitherto, this has not really been a live issue, for there was no register in which to search.

The Keeper's new registers

In other, lesser, countries, the department responsible for land registration does not administer other registers. Her Majesty's Land Registry in England is an example.[10] We know of no other country with an organisation like Registers of

---

1 Housing (Scotland) Act 2014 s 29. See also the Letting Agent Registration (Scotland) Regulations 2016, SSI 2016/432, and p 88 above.
2 Or at least without having applied for registration: see Housing (Scotland) Act 2014 s 44; Housing (Scotland) Act 2014 (Commencement No 6 and Transitional Provision) Order 2016, SSI 2016/412, arts 2 and 3, sch.
3 Community Empowerment (Scotland) Act 2015 s 94.
4 Community Empowerment (Scotland) Act 2015 (Commencement No 4 and Transitory Provision) Order 2016, SSI 2016/363.
5 For exceptions, see Community Empowerment (Registers of Land) (Scotland) Regulations 2016, SSI 2016/362, as amended by the Community Empowerment (Miscellaneous Amendments) (Scotland) Regulations 2016, SSI 2016/411. See also p 89 above.
6 Community Empowerment (Scotland) Act 2015 s 102.
7 For long leases of common good land see *East Lothian District Council v National Coal Board* 1982 SLT 460.
8 Local Government (Scotland) Act 1973 s 75.
9 The subject is briefly touched on in Andrew Ferguson, *Common Good Law* (2006) p 129.
10 Or rather 'Land Registry' as it now brands itself: the 'the' has been booted out along with Her Majesty.

Scotland, which administers many registers, with land as the main but not sole subject.[1]

Despite the name, Registers of Scotland do not administer all Scottish registers. The Keeper is probably – we merely speculate – content not to have to administer the Register of Sex Offenders.[2] Many registers are kept by local authorities, and others, while centrally kept, are not in the Keeper's stable, such as the Register of Companies, or, more importantly, the Register of Tartans.[3] Below we mention five new or fairly new registers now in the RoS stable, though some not yet operational, and later on we mention some of the older ones.

(5) The *Crofting Register* was established by the Crofting Reform (Scotland) Act 2010.[4] Its importance is considerable, but we will not discuss it here as in this series we do not deal with crofting law. It should not be confused with the Register of Crofts or the Register of Crofting Community Rights to Buy, both of which are kept not by the Keeper but by the Crofting Commission.[5]

(6) The *Register of Community Interests in Land* has two divisions. The first concerns the community right to buy under the Land Reform (Scotland) Act 2003.[6] The second is the agricultural tenants' right to buy under the Agricultural Holdings (Scotland) Act 2003.[7] However, this second part of the register is being discontinued,[8] since in future the right to buy will not have to be preceded by registration. The registration of a property in the first division of the register is particularly significant because it means that power of sale is restricted and a transfer in breach of the restriction is of no effect.[9] A search in this register is therefore important, especially as the community right to buy now potentially applies to all land and not just to rural land.[10] We understand that at least some searchers provide this automatically.

(7) The *Register of Applications by Community Bodies to Buy Land* is governed by s 52 of the Land Reform (Scotland) Act 2016 although, at the time of writing,

---

1   See www.ros.gov.uk/about-us/registers-we-hold.

2   In fact – and contrary to popular belief – there is no such register, though the aims of the legislation might be better served if there were, as there is in some countries. Instead, there are rules whereby sex offenders must make notifications to the police: see Sexual Offences Act 2003 ss 80 ff.

3   Scottish Register of Tartans Act 2008 s 1. This is kept not by the Keeper of the Registers of Scotland but by the Keeper of the Records of Scotland.

4   Crofting Reform (Scotland) Act 2010 s 3. See www.crofts.ros.gov.uk.

5   Crofters (Scotland) Act 1993 s 41; Land Reform (Scotland) Act 2003 s 94.

6   Land Reform (Scotland) Act 2003 s 36. See also p 100 above.

7   Agricultural Holdings (Scotland) Act 2003 s 24.

8   Land Reform (Scotland) Act 2016 s 99.

9   LR(S)A 2003 s 40.

10 Here and elsewhere we look at matters from the standpoint of a buyer. But the position of the owner also needs to be borne in mind. The owner should know if the property has been made subject to a community right to buy, or has become a site of special scientific interest, etc. But there will be cases where this information is lost sight of, for instance if the owner is no longer capax, and an attorney or guardian is acting, or if the owner has taken the property by inheritance. Thus there may be situations in which a pre-sale search in one or more of the parallel registers may be advisable.

this register was not yet operational.[1] When it is, it will be used to register applications by community bodies to buy (i) land which is abandoned, neglected or detrimental,[2] or alternatively (ii) land which it is sought to acquire for the purposes of sustainable development.[3] The effect on a sale by the owner (other than to the community body) will be determined by statutory instrument.[4] No such instrument has yet been made but if, as seems likely, the effect is to invalidate the sale,[5] buyers of land, or at least of land that might potentially be abandoned, neglected or detrimental, will have to consider searching this register.

(8) The *Register of Controlling Interests in Land* is established by the Land Reform (Scotland) Act 2016.[6] The Land Register, and, insofar as still applicable, the Register of Sasines, show who owns land. The fact that the Land Register does so more readily and accessibly than the Register of Sasines was a major factor in the passing of the Land Registration etc (Scotland) Act 2012, because politicians are keen on the 'who owns Scotland?' question, and the new legislation was needed to accelerate the completion of the Land Register. But being able to find out who owns Blackmains is not enough for many. It may be, for example, that Blackmains is owned by a company in an offshore jurisdiction, a company about which it is hard to discover anything. The person or persons who ultimately benefit from the property, and the person or persons who ultimately make the decisions as to what happens to the property, may be hard or impossible to discover. The 2016 Act sets up a framework provision for obtaining information but without providing any details. In September 2016 the Scottish Government issued a consultation paper as to how these provisions should be fleshed out in secondary legislation.[7] This paper is itself fairly light on details, so that it is still unclear what the final shape of the scheme might be. It is unlikely, however, that buyers would have to search the new register. The concern for conveyancers acting for a buyer will be to check that registration takes place in the new register, if such registration is necessary.[8]

The consultation paper discusses what mechanisms should be adopted to ensure compliance. Should the duty of disclosure be upon the 'person

---

1 See p 82 above.
2 LR(S)A 2003 s 97F (inserted by the Community Empowerment (Scotland) Act 2015 s 74), amended by the LR(S)A 2016 s 53. See *Conveyancing 2015* pp 75–76.
3 LR(S)A 2016 s 52. See p 81 above.
4 LR(S)A 2003 s 97N; LR(S)A 2016 s 61.
5 For the Scottish Government's proposals as to the effect of registering an application to buy abandoned, neglected or detrimental land, see *Consultation on secondary legislation proposals relating to Part 3A of the Land Reform (Scotland) Act 2003 – the community right to buy abandoned, neglected or detrimental land as introduced by the Community Empowerment (Scotland) Act 2015* (2016; www.gov. scot/Publications/2016/03/9764) pp 17–22.
6 LR(S)A 2016 s 39.
7 *Improving transparency in land ownership in Scotland: a consultation on controlling interests in land* (2016; www.gov.scot/Publications/2016/09/6681). For discussion, see Frances Rooney, 'Controlling interests: problem questions' (2016) 61 *Journal of the Law Society of Scotland* Oct/34.
8 We say new register but among the questions put out to consultation is whether the Land Register might be used for this purpose: see *Improving transparency in land ownership in Scotland* pp 23–34. The preliminary view expressed in the consultation paper is that there should be a new register.

with controlling interest'? Should it be on the buyer? Should it be on the buyer's law firm? Or some combination? Should there be civil penalties for non-compliance? Or criminal penalties? Should disclosure (or certification that there is nothing to disclose)[1] be a condition of registration in the Land Register? What happens if a change of control happens at a time when there is no conveyancing transaction? The consultation asks such questions but one has the impression that clear and workable answers are proving elusive. Solicitors may be unhappy about some of the suggested possibilities. It seems likely that whatever the final shape of the legislation, there will be an upward push on conveyancing fees.

As will be clear already, the new register is not yet operational, and we suspect that it will be quite some time before it becomes so.

(9) The *Register of Sites of Special Scientific Interest* is regulated by the Nature Conservation (Scotland) Act 2004.[2] Designation as a SSSI has important consequences, consequences that affect singular successors. The register is searchable free online.[3] One curious provision of the legislation is that the seller must within 28 days *after* the sale[4] tell the buyer of the SSSI status.[5] The point of this is obscure: the time when a buyer wants to know such things is in advance.

The Keeper's old registers

Down in the Keeper's wine cellar, kept at a constant 13 degrees, are the older registers, some, indeed, too old to be good drinking. Those familiar to conveyancers are the General Register of Sasines, the Land Register, the Register of Inhibitions and the Books of Council and Session. The Register of Protests, which is for protests of dishonoured negotiable instruments, and the Register of Judgments, which is for the registration of certain foreign judgments, which are to be put into execution in Scotland, are sometimes categorised as parts of the Books of Council and Session, but sometimes as separate registers.

Lesser-known old registers administered by the Keeper are the Register of the Great Seal, the Register of the Cachet Seal, the Register of the Quarter Seal, the Register of the Prince's Seal, the Register of Service of Heirs, the Register of Crown Grants, the Register of Sheriffs' Commissions, and that golden oldie, the Register of Hornings.

---

1 Presumably (though this depends on how the legislation develops) in most cases there will be nothing to disclose. If Mr and Mrs McGlumphry buy a house, it seems likely that there will be nothing to disclose, though it is likely that there would need to be certification to that effect.

2 Nature Conservation (Scotland) Act 2004 s 22.

3 www.ros.gov.uk/services/registration/sssi. And see also www.snh.gov.uk/protecting-scotlands-nature/protected-areas/national-designations/sssis/.

4 To be precise, after the 'disposal'. Perhaps that means the date of the registration in the Land Register. The links between the Act's terminology, on the one hand, and general property law, on the other hand, are sometimes a little fuzzy.

5 NC(S)A 2004 s 42.

Parallel registration, and ScotLIS

When legislation creates property-related duties, which are to bind not only the current owner but singular successors as well, it might be thought that the natural home would be the Land Register (or Register of Sasines). And indeed that is often what legislation does provide. As one example out of very many that could be given, tree preservation orders are registered in the Land Register (or GRS). But legislation does not always take this approach, and indeed sometimes – as will be clear from the above – sets up specialist parallel registers. Why matters are sometimes done that way we do not know. It seems to us less efficient and hence more costly, to everyone involved.

But as and when ScotLIS comes into operation, the problem of parallel registers for property-related matters will be much ameliorated, since ScotLIS is intended to be a single portal.[1] If it works as planned, ScotLIS will be a major step forward.

TENEMENTS

Paying for repairs: roofs and roof lights

Introduction

Waelde v Ulloa[2] was a dispute about liability for repair to the roof and roof lights of a tenement. The sums involved were small: the total sum sued for was £180. But the legal issues were of considerable interest, and were treated with skill and care by the sheriff.[3]

The dispute concerned the tenement at 10 Strathearn Place, Edinburgh. Originally a single dwelling, this had been divided in the 1950s into three flats. The pursuer owned the top flat, and the defender the middle flat. Repairs had been carried out by the pursuer to the roof. In terms of the split-off writs, the roof was common property, and the owner of each flat was taken bound to pay a share of the cost of its maintenance.

The defender accepted liability for the cost of certain of the repairs but disputed liability in respect of repairs to (i) a skylight and (ii) the felt or metal flashing which lay between the outer edge of a velux window and the wall separating the building from the building next door. Both skylight and velux window served the pursuer's flat (only). They were not in place when the split-offs occurred but had been added later. Therefore, said the defender, they were not covered by the maintenance burden, either because they were not part of the roof at all or because they were not part of the roof at the time when the burden was imposed.

The case thus raised two important issues on which there was little or no previous authority. Are skylights and velux windows part of the roof? And do

1 For more on ScotLIS see p 98 above.
2 [2016] SC EDIN 30, 2016 GWD 11-221.
3 Sheriff Kenneth J McGowan.

maintenance burdens cover innovations that have been carried out since the burden was imposed?

Skylights as part of the roof?

Are skylights (or other roof lights) part of the roof? The sheriff thought not. 'It is true that it provided protection against water ingress in place of the roofing material which had preceded it. But its primary function was to provide light.' In short, it was more window than roof and, as such, did not fall within the burden of roof maintenance. To that extent the defender's argument succeeded.

This is certainly a possible view of matters. But the contrary view seems preferable. A key goal – perhaps *the* key goal – of the law of the tenement is to keep buildings wind and watertight. Viewed from this aspect, a skylight serves the same purpose as felt and slates. It is one of the things that stands between the flats and the weather. Its maintenance is for the benefit of everyone in the building. In short, it is more roof than window.[1] This view derives support from the Tenements (Scotland) Act 2004 where the word 'roof' appears to include roof lights.[2]

Although the defender prevailed on this point, it was the pursuer, not the defender, who was ultimately victorious. The pursuer's argument, with which the sheriff agreed, was as follows.[3] (i) If (as the sheriff held) the skylight is not part of the roof, then it is not the subject of any maintenance provisions in the titles. (ii) Accordingly, maintenance is or may be governed by r 4 of the Tenement Management Scheme.[4] (iii) Rule 4 provides that all flat-owners must contribute in equal shares to the maintenance of 'scheme property'. (iv) Rule 1.2 explains that there are three types of scheme property. (v) Type (a) scheme property is 'any part of the tenement that is the common property of two or more of the owners'. (vi) When the skylight was fitted, it became part of the roof by accession. (vii) As the roof was common property, so must be the skylight. (viii) Hence the skylight is type (a) scheme property. (ix) Hence maintenance of the skylight is a shared responsibility.

In response, the defender had drawn attention to r 1.3(b)(iii) of the Tenement Management Scheme which excludes skylights from 'scheme property'. But this exclusion only applies in respect of type (c) scheme property, whereas, due to accession, the skylight was type (a) scheme property.

In accepting that accession took place (step (vi) above), the sheriff reached a different conclusion from that of the sheriff principal in *Mehrabadi v Hough*,[5]

---

1 This was a matter on which the Scottish Law Commission changed its mind. Its original position was that roof lights should be maintained by everyone, but later it departed from that view in the interests of consistency with the treatment of ordinary windows: see *Report No 162 on the Law of the Tenement* (1998) para 5.8. The new policy was implemented to a certain extent by r 1.3(b)(iii) of the Tenement Management Scheme (set out in sch 1 of the Tenements (Scotland) Act 2004).

2 We say 'appears to' because it is not a matter of express definition; but the fact that skylights are expressly excluded from 'roofs' (by r 1.3(b)(iii) read with r 1.2(c)(iv) of the Tenement Management Scheme) seems to presuppose that a roof does (or, at its lowest, may) include skylights.

3 Paragraphs 42–59.

4 Tenements (Scotland) Act 2004 s 4(6).

5 11 January 2010, Aberdeen Sheriff Court: for discussion, see *Conveyancing 2010* pp 93–96.

a case concerning dormer windows. He was right to do so. At the same time, however, the sheriff preserved his view that the skylight was not part of the roof by saying that the skylight acceded to the roof as a matter of title (so that it became common property) but not as a matter of function (so that it did not become part of the roof).[1] This is a novel distinction but also, in context, a reasonable one.

The argument made, successfully, for the pursuer is a reminder of the importance of the Tenements (Scotland) Act 2004 and of the Tenement Management Scheme which it contains. It is a natural mistake, but a mistake nonetheless, to assume that repairs not covered by title provisions are not covered at all. That may of course be the case. But if the repair is to 'scheme property' then it is covered by r 4 of the Tenement Management Scheme. That was the position of the skylight in *Waelde v Ulloa*.

Post-burden innovations?

As already mentioned, both the velux window and the skylight were added after the split-off writs, and hence after the imposition of the real burden concerning the maintenance of the roof. The installation of each, but especially the first, involved a significant degree of disturbance to the roof.[2] On the sheriff's view, neither roof light was part of the roof itself. But the felt and flashing added at the time of the velux *was* part of the roof, and was also one of the disputed items on the repair bill. Was it therefore covered by the maintenance burden? That depended on whether a real burden to maintain a roof meant (i) the roof as it was at the time of the burden, or (ii) the roof as it is at the time of the repair. In *Mehrabadi v Hough*, a decision from Aberdeen Sheriff Court, the sheriff upheld the first of these views.[3] In *Waelde v Ulloa*, a decision from Edinburgh Sheriff Court, the sheriff has upheld the second.

In adopting the second view, the sheriff in *Waelde v Ulloa* accepted that there would have to be qualifications. For example, the burden would only apply to innovations which were of the same character as the original thing, and then only where the other proprietors had either agreed to the innovation or had acquiesced in it. But in the present case neither qualification applied. The sheriff's views are worth quoting in full:[4]

> For my own part, I do not see why a maintenance burden should be so restricted, at least in relation to burdened co-proprietors who have or are to be taken to have acquiesced in the alteration concerned. A hypothetical example would be a tenement building which, when first erected, had (i) a flat roof and (ii) a title burden imposing a shared maintenance obligation on the co-proprietors. As a result of the costs of repeat repairs to the flat roof, the proprietors agree to it being replaced by a pitched slate roof. Later, repairs are needed to the slate roof following storm damage. It seems

1 Paragraphs 46–59.
2 The details are given in paras 4 and 5 of the sheriff's Opinion.
3 This was at first instance: see the decision of June 2009 noted in *Conveyancing 2009* pp 10–11. The issue was not pursued in the subsequent appeal to the sheriff principal.
4 Paragraphs 28–31.

counter-intuitive to suggest that the co-proprietors should not be liable for their share of those costs in accordance with the maintenance burden.

I accept that there may be more difficult cases involving issues about what constitutes acquiescence and/or alterations which change the character of the part of the building in question, such as a dormer which may, depending on the precise design, itself consist of a 'roof' part; vertical 'walls'; and a glazed 'front'. Nevertheless, I am attracted by the idea that a 'roof' (or other strategic part of a building) should be taken to include parts added thereto which are of the same character; and that an obligation to contribute to the cost of maintaining it created by the type of burden in the present case should be treated as extending to the cost of maintaining same.

In particular, it is clear that the velux was *in situ* long before the defender bought his flat. Accordingly, it appears to me that he should be treated as having acquiesced in its presence. That being so, it is appropriate that the title burden should be interpreted in a way consistent with the factual situation as it exists now.

This is a valuable discussion of the issues. But, given the decision to the contrary in *Mehrabadi*, it cannot be regarded as settling the question. For that we will have to await a decision of a higher court.

Getting repairs done

Impasse

In *Waelde v Ulloa*, the dispute was about repairs that had already been carried out. But getting repairs done in the first place can also be a fertile source of disagreement. Titles in modern blocks of flats usually provide a mechanism for decision-making, although it may be ignored in practice. In the absence of something in the titles, the Tenement Management Scheme provides as a default rule that decisions as to repair can be made by a majority of owners. A majority, however, may not be easy to come by. And in two-flat tenements, a majority means unanimity, so that the desire of one of the owners to carry out repairs may be thwarted by the determination of the other that no repairs should be done. That was the situation in *Humphreys v Crabbe*, a decision of the Inner House.[1]

The dispute concerned a Victorian house at 84 and 86 Forsyth Street, Greenock. The house had been divided into two flats in the 1920s. The split-off writs left ownership of the roof with the upper flat but provided that the cost of maintenance should be shared equally. Norna Crabbe owned the lower flat and had done so for over sixty years. The upper flat had at one time been a Church of Scotland manse but was now in private ownership. The current owner was Helen Humphreys, who acquired the flat in 2010. The building seems to have suffered from neglect, and by the time Ms Humphreys became owner the roof was in serious disrepair. The sheriff's finding-in-fact was as follows:[2]

---

1 [2016] CSIH 82, 2016 GWD 35-634. The Extra Division comprised Lady Paton, Lord Malcolm and Lord Glennie, with Lord Glennie giving the Opinion of the court.
2 Paragraph 6.

The villa is in disrepair. The roof, chimneys, gutters, downpipes, fascias and soffits need to be repaired. Their state of disrepair results in water coming into number 84 [the upper flat]. A number of problems have occurred as a result of the disrepair of the villa during the pursuer's [Ms Humphrey's] time there. These have involved difficulties with gutters, slates, downpipes and smoke penetration. Birds have come in and out of the roof space and water has leaked in. The pursuer has been unable to sleep because of water dripping in. She has had to catch the water in buckets, and has eight buckets in place to do so. The birds have been able to gain access because soffits and fascias have fallen off.

Ms Humphreys presumably bought the flat with her eyes open. At any rate, as soon as she had concluded missives, she called in to see her new neighbour in the downstairs flat. As the Inner House explains, the meeting did not go well:[1]

> The sheriff described the tone of their first meeting, on the day after Ms Humphreys had concluded missives for number 84, as 'not pleasant'. Ms Humphreys took flowers to Ms Crabbe and introduced herself as the new owner of the property upstairs. Ms Crabbe would not accept the flowers 'on any account'. There was a discussion about the need to repair the property. There was no dispute about the need for repairs but Ms Crabbe declined to accept any responsibility for sharing in the cost. She blamed the need for them on the neglect of earlier owners.

Repairing the roof would involve the erection of scaffolding as well as certain other access requirements in respect of the lower flat. Ms Crabbe made clear that she would not consent to access except on the basis that Ms Humphreys met the whole cost of the repairs (other than betterment).[2] To this condition Ms Humphreys was, naturally enough, unwilling to agree. The result was impasse. Meanwhile, the rain continued to come in and the roof continued to deteriorate.

Break-through

Fortunately, in s 8 of the Tenements (Scotland) Act 2004, there was the means of breaking the deadlock. Where owners are unable to muster the necessary majority for repairs to be carried out – as Ms Humphreys could not – s 8 provides an alternative means of carrying out repairs. Section 8 is limited to such repairs as are needed to provide support and shelter for the building. Where a part of the building which provides support or shelter is in need of repair, any flat-owner can require the owner of the part in question to carry out the repair. The cost is then divided among the owners as if the repair had followed on from a regular decision – as if, in the present case, Ms Crabbe had agreed to the repairs. In the light of the maintenance burden, quoted above, that would mean that each owner must pay one half of the cost.

In the present case, the part requiring repair was the roof; and as this provided shelter for the building, the repair fell squarely within s 8. Furthermore, as the roof belonged to Ms Humphreys and not to Ms Crabbe, the duty, and the

---

1 Paragraph 5.
2 Paragraph 8.

right,[1] to carry out the repair rested with her. The consent of Ms Crabbe was not needed.

But in one respect the consent, or at least the co-operation, of Ms Crabbe was still required. The repair could not go ahead unless scaffolding could be put up, and the scaffolding would impinge on the flat belonging to Ms Crabbe. But here too the Tenements Act has an answer. Section 17 entitles owners in a tenement to take reasonable access over each other's properties for the purpose of carrying out repairs. The only requirement is that reasonable notice is given. As long, therefore, as Ms Humphreys gave reasonable notice to Ms Crabbe, she could proceed to have the scaffolding erected.

In these provisions of the Act lay a complete solution to the impasse. Furthermore, as they were matters of right rather than of judicial discretion, there was no need to invoke the aid of the court. In the event, Ms Humphreys thought that it would be of practical help to have her rights judicially declared. Section 6 of the Act provides a simple means of doing so, by summary application to the sheriff.[2] After a hearing lasting five days, the sheriff found for Ms Humphreys on all counts. In particular, the sheriff found: (i) that the proposed repairs were necessary under s 8 of the Act in order to provide shelter for the building; (ii) that, in terms of the real burden, the cost must be borne by Ms Humphreys and Ms Crabbe in equal shares; and (iii) that, on 21 days' notice, Ms Crabbe must allow access to contractors, including access for the purpose of erecting scaffolding.[3]

Appeal

Ms Crabbe appealed to the Inner House. Of her thirteen grounds of appeal, only one need be mentioned here.[4] As it appeared in the split-off writ for the lower flat, the maintenance burden read as follows:

> that the expense of upholding the roof of the said building and chimney stalks, rain water pipes and drains, and all other burdens, common or mutual to the said subjects shall be borne equally between the proprietor of the dwelling house before disponed and the proprietor of the dwelling house forming the upper flat of said building.

Ms Crabbe drew attention to the comma after 'all other burdens'. This meant, she said, that the phrase that followed ('common or mutual to the said subjects') must be read as applying, not only to 'all other burdens' but to 'the expense of upholding the roof of the said building' etc. And as the roof was *not* common or mutual, being owned solely by Ms Humphreys, it followed, Ms Crabbe argued, that she, Ms Crabbe, was not liable for the cost of its maintenance.

There was certainly something in this argument. If 'common or mutual to the said subjects' was intended to apply only to 'and all other burdens', then

---

1 As Ms Humphreys was the sole owner of the roof, she was at liberty to repair it.
2 The Inner House's judgment has a helpful discussion about the flexible nature of the s 6 procedure: see paras 33–35.
3 Paragraph 11.
4 A number of the others alleged procedural errors or irregularities, and complained of the conduct and/or alleged partiality of the sheriffs at various stages of the case.

the intervening comma should not be there – as indeed it was not there in the split-off writ for the upper flat. Yet if the argument were to be accepted, it would make a nonsense of the burden as a whole.

The Inner House did not accept the argument:[1]

> We reject this argument. In our view it places too much weight on the position in this burden of a single comma. We do not seek to downplay the potential significance of punctuation in a syntactical analysis of any particular provision whether that provision be in a contract or, as here, in a title deed or disposition; but where the draughtsman and parties intend a punctuation mark to be of particular significance in understanding the meaning of the provision, we would expect that intention to be evidenced by a careful and consistent use of the mark. In the present case, had the construction for which Ms Crabbe contends been intended, one might have expected to find the descriptive phrase 'common or mutual to the said subjects' closed off by another comma placed immediately after those words. That might at least have raised the argument that those words were intended to qualify not only 'all other burdens' but also the roof, chimney stalks, rain water pipes and drains. Without that second comma closing off those words, that argument does not get off the ground. But having said that the argument places too much weight on the position of one comma, we would not wish to rest our decision on the absence of another. Looking at the matter more broadly, it is clear that both dispositions are intended to provide for the expense of maintaining and repairing the roof, etc. to be borne equally between the proprietors of the top and bottom floor flats. We do not think any elaboration is required – the point is as simple as that.

The appeal, on this and all other grounds, was refused.

SOLICITORS

Liability to the other side

All solicitors have the awareness, worrying away at the back (or the front) of their minds, that the present transaction might be one for which they are sued by their own client. But occasionally there are also claims against a law firm, not by the client, but by the other side in the deal, and *NRAM plc v Steel*[2] was one such. And, to add spice, the action was not only against the law firm, Messrs Bell & Scott LLP, but against the partner in question, personally. Of such stuff bad dreams are made.

The story so far

There are some cases where, for one reason or another, the full story never quite comes out, and the court pronounces on what is really a fragmentary version of the full story. We think, as will appear, that this is such a case.

A company called Headway Caledonian Ltd (HCL) originally owned four units – numbers 1, 2, 3 and 4 – at Cadzow Business Park in Hamilton, Lanarkshire.

---

1 Paragraph 26.
2 [2016] CSIH 11, 2016 SC 474, 2016 SLT 285.

It had substantial borrowings from a bank whose name has had a convoluted history, but which is now NRAM plc.[1] These borrowings were secured against all four units by means of (i) standard securities, and (ii) an all-assets floating charge. HCL had bought the properties in 1997/98 and the standard securities had been in place since that time. The floating charge had been granted in 2002. Beginning in 2005 HCL began to sell the units. The first to be sold was unit 3, which happened in 2005. The other sales were slower, but all were completed in the course of 2007. The sale of unit 1 was completed in March 2007. Then in September/October 2007 the sale of unit 4 was completed, and finally in December 2007 the sale of unit 2 was completed. So by the end of 2007 all four units had been sold.

On the eve of the sale of unit 1, in March 2007, the total debt to NRAM was £1,221,850. Unit 1 sold for £560,000. By agreement, £495,000 was remitted to the bank, as a result of which the debt was reduced to £726,850. Units 4 and 2 realised £750,000 and £325,000 respectively. What happened to these two sums is not disclosed in the litigation. Clearly the money was not all used to pay off the debt. We know that by the time that the present action was raised the amount outstanding was £458,723.99, or £440,162.68 if certain debits fell to be taken into account.[2] So between March 2007 and 2010, when HCL went into liquidation, more than £200,000 of capital must have been repaid, though the source of that repayment is not known.[3] As for interest, HCL continued to pay interest until shortly before it went into liquidation in 2010.

What happened to the standard securities and the floating charge? In a case of this sort, the lender would typically discharge the securities held, one by one, so as to enable the properties to be sold on the basis of unencumbered titles, and, in return, would be paid all or a large part of the sum realised on sale. At the same time, certificates of non-crystallisation would be given, one by one for each sale. If that straightforward process had happened here, by the end of 2007 the amount owing to NRAM would have been paid off, because the total value of the units was substantially larger than the total debt. But that was not quite what happened. It had, it is true, happened for the sale of unit 3 in 2005. But for the other three units, the story becomes strange.

NRAM, at the time of the sale of unit 1, in March 2007, discharged not only the standard security over unit 1 (as one would expect), but also the standard securities over the other two units, whose sales were not to be completed until some months later. Why? To that we will return, but it was this event – the discharge of the standard securities over units 2 and 4 as well as the discharge of the standard security over unit 1 – that formed the basis of the present action. The bank claimed that these discharges were granted in error, an error induced by the negligence of HCL's law firm, and that had the

---

1 Formerly Northern Rock (Asset Management) plc. For something about the history of this bank and its name, see *Conveyancing 2009* pp 58–59 and *Conveyancing 2012* pp 77–78.
2 The difference between these figures does not matter for present purposes. For some discussion of the figures see para 51 of the case when at first instance: [2014] CSOH 172.
3 The question of what happened to the proceeds of the sales of units 4 and 2 is not explored in the case. Nor is the question of the repayment of over £200,000 of capital prior to liquidation.

discharges not been granted, it would have made a full recovery of all sums owed to it.

What about the floating charge? When unit 1 was sold, in March 2007, a certificate of non-crystallisation was granted (as one would expect), and the same happened later in the year for the sales of units 2 and 4. That was all in accordance with normal conveyancing practice – except for the mystery that the second two non-crystallisation certificates (for unit 4 and later for unit 2) did not bring about payment to the bank of the proceeds of sale, or such part thereof as might be agreed. To this puzzle we return below.

In the liquidation the bank was able to make a substantial recovery, but nevertheless overall there was a large shortfall. The shortfall, after deducting the amount recovered already from the liquidator, plus the further, smaller, amount that the bank could be expected to recover from the liquidator by the end of the winding-up process, was £369,811.18.[1]

The bank then raised the present action in delict to recover this shortfall from the law firm that had acted for HCL in 2007, plus the partner concerned, personally. At first instance the Lord Ordinary (Doherty) held against the bank.[2] The latter reclaimed, and the Inner House has, by a two-to-one majority, allowed the appeal.[3] Thus of the four judges who have considered the case so far, two have been in favour of the pursuer and two have been in favour of the defenders. The defenders sought from the Court of Session leave to appeal to the Supreme Court. This was refused. The defenders then applied direct to the Supreme Court for leave to appeal, and this has been granted. We understand that the hearing in London is scheduled for later on in 2017.

The mystery email

The central document in the litigation was an email that the solicitor acting for HCL had sent to the bank during the sale of unit 1, in March 2007.

> Subject: headway caledonian limited sale of Pavilion 1 Cadzow Park Hamilton (title nos LAN 6421 and LAN 124573)
>
> Helen/Neil
> I need your usual letter of non-crystallisation for the sale of the above subjects to be faxed through here first thing tomorrow am if possible to 0141 221 0123 marked for my attention – I have had a few letters on this one for previous other units that have been sold. I also attach discharges for signing and return as well as the whole loan is being paid off for the estate and I have a settlement figure for that. Can you please arrange to get these signed and returned again asap.
> Many thanks
>
> Jane A Steel
> Jane Steel
> Partner
> For Bell & Scott LLP

---

1 See [2014] CSOH 172 at para 83. This figure was accepted by the Inner House.
2 [2014] CSOH 172, [2015] PNLR 16, 2015 GWD 1-34 (*Conveyancing 2014* Case (63)).
3 [2016] CSIH 11, 2016 SC 474, 2016 SLT 285.

The heading of the email referred to unit 1 as being 'title nos LAN 6421 and LAN 124573'. These title numbers covered the three units that the company still had: 1, 4 and 2. Furthermore, the draft discharges attached were for the standard securities over all the units, ie not only unit 1 but also the units sold later in the year, namely 4 and 2.

When it received the email, the bank opened the attachments, printed them off, executed them, and returned them. They were promptly registered, the result being that all three units were disencumbered of the standard securities.

Just why the email, with its attachments, had been sent was investigated in the proof. No answers were obtained.

As for the floating charge, the bank granted this certificate, which, unlike the discharges of the standard securities, was restricted to unit 1:

PRIVATE AND CONFIDENTIAL[1]
FAO Jane Steel
Bell & Scott LLP. ...

Dear Sirs
Commercial Mortgage Account Number: C2/14150T-00260
Headway Caledonian Limited
Pavilion 1 Cadzow Business Park Hamilton
We Northern Rock plc, the holders of a Floating Charge dated 27 June 2002 hereby confirm we have taken no steps to Crystallise the said Floating Charge.
Northern Rock consent to the sale of the subjects and will release the subjects from the floating charge on delivery of the disposition to the purchaser.[2]

Yours faithfully
Martin Clarke
Manager – Loan Reviews ...

The delict case

In general, a law firm does not owe a duty of care to third parties, but, as is well known, there can be exceptions. NRAM's case against the defenders was set out in its pleadings:[3]

Due to the formalities of settling Scottish conveyancing transactions (the purchase price will only generally be released, in exchange for inter alia a discharge of the security over the sale subjects), executed Discharges were as a matter of course provided to the borrower's solicitors in advance of funds being made available to NR.[4] It was therefore necessary for NR to rely exclusively on the borrower's solicitor

---

1 Why the letter was headed 'private and confidential' we do not know. The normal purpose of a certificate of non-crystallisation is where a third party is transacting with the debtor company (as of course happened here). Were the certificate to be kept private as between the bank and the debtor company it would fail in its purpose, for the third party will not normally agree to complete the transaction without seeing the certificate.
2 The certificate uses the future tense, as if on delivery of the disposition the bank was to grant a further deed. But clearly that is not the meaning: the meaning is that on delivery of the disposition by HCL to the buyer the charge would cease to apply to unit 1.
3 Quoted in [2014] CSOH 172 at para 4.
4 NR is short for NRAM.

where direct requests were made, such as here, for discharge documentation. This was the process which NR followed for the partial discharge of unit 3. By way of further example, the same solicitor had in November 2005 requested the execution of a full discharge (drafted by her firm) of a security over other subjects owned by HCL (Macdonald Drive, Lossiemouth). This was provided to her in advance of funds being received for the redemption of the loan. Ms Steel was accordingly well aware that any request by her for discharge documentation from NR would generally be acted upon by them without question. She was also aware that it would be provided to her, and could be passed to the purchaser, in advance of redemption funds being transferred. This was on the implicit understanding that such funds would then be held by her to the strict order of NR and, in the absence of any contrary instruction, should be remitted to them forthwith ...

The members of the pursuers' CMT team[1] who received the email ... the members of the pursuers' Admin Team who were responsible for having the discharges executed and the signing officer who executed both discharges were misled into believing that the first defender would repay or arrange repayment of the whole borrowings on receipt by her of the executed discharges. They were misled into believing that the first defender would not deliver the discharges to the purchaser of unit 1 or would not otherwise cause or permit the discharges to be registered without effecting or arranging repayment of the whole borrowings. If they had not been misled in this way they would not have arranged for the discharges to be executed or returned to the first defender ... NR are content to execute the discharge documents in advance of funds being received by them only because they rely on the requesting solicitor not releasing those documents without receiving in exchange a sum sufficient to redeem the outstanding loan and thereafter to hold those funds to NR's order. The first defender knew that this was a common practice in transactions where a solicitor acts for a party selling heritable property in Scotland which is burdened by security. She knew that the pursuers were relying on her not to release the discharges or otherwise cause or permit their registration unless or until they were repaid in full ...

At first instance, the Lord Ordinary had been unpersuaded. He said:[2]

In some respects the email was vague and ambiguous. There was tension between the subject heading and the body of the email. The email did not state what the settlement figure was, or by whom the first defender had been provided with it. It cried out for clarification.

He continued:[3]

I have no real difficulty in concluding that it was not reasonable for a bank in the position of the pursuers to rely on the misstatement information without checking its accuracy; and that a solicitor in the position of the first defender would not foresee that such a bank would reasonably rely on that information without carrying out such a check. Any prudent bank taking the most basic precautions would have checked the information provided by seeking clarification from the first defender and/or looking at their file.

---

1 The meaning of 'CMT team' is not explained in the case.
2 [2014] CSOH 172 at para 77.
3 [2014] CSOH 172 at para 78.

By a two-to-one majority the Inner House has now reversed the decision of Lord Doherty.[1] We will not here explore the delictual doctrines at play in this area, but the core issue (regardless of whether the 'threefold' analysis or the 'assumption of responsibility' analysis is adopted) is whether NRAM's reliance on the email, ie its granting of complete discharges, was reasonable. In the view of the majority of judges, it was. We quote from Lady Smith:[2]

> The Lord Ordinary required, when applying the law to the facts, to give careful consideration to, and answer, the question of whether or not Ms Steel fell to be treated by the law as having assumed responsibility for the misstatements and their consequences. I readily accept that the particular circumstances weighed heavily in favour of NRAM's contention that, on the question of assumption of responsibility alone, they were, when the email was written and sent, owed a duty of care by Ms Steel. The representations made in an email which she 'signed' in her capacity as a solicitor, particularly those to the effect that the circumstances were such as to require the attached discharges to be signed, were within her area of professional skill. The information was supplied – looking at matters objectively – for the purpose of being relied on by NRAM. Ms Steel had demonstrated in two previous transactions where NRAM did not have their own solicitor acting for them that she could be trusted. She knew that 'Helen/Neil' were not solicitors and that NRAM did not have a solicitor acting for them in relation to the Unit 1 transaction; indeed, there was, on the Lord Ordinary's findings nothing to afford NRAM justification for thinking she could not be trusted on this occasion. NRAM did in fact rely on her word 'as a solicitor' (see Lord Ordinary's opinion at para 25). The representations made were, on the terms of the email, Ms Steel's representations; they were not, for instance, qualified under reference to what her client had told her. Further, she had no authority for the representations of fact in the email or for the representation that NRAM required to sign and return discharge documents. The email was sent at close of business on 23 March and related to a transaction that was to settle the following day; there was a palpable sense of urgency in its terms.
>
> Further, I consider that there is merit in Mr Clancy's[3] submission that, properly understood, this was not an arms' length transaction. It was in the interests of both NRAM and HCL to ensure that the sale of the unit was completed. Both would benefit financially from the proceeds of sale ... The key aspects of the email were unequivocal: NRAM needed to provide Ms Steel with a letter of non crystallisation and signed discharges in the form attached, as a matter of some urgency, and they needed to do so in circumstances where the whole loan due (for which she had a settlement figure) was being paid off. That was the purpose of the email; its message was clear and unequivocal. It was also, of course, wrong but there was nothing in the body of the email to cause doubt as to the veracity of that message. For reasons which I explain below, resultant harm to NRAM in the form of economic loss was reasonably foreseeable.

1 [2016] CSIH 11, 2016 SC 474, 2016 SLT 285. Lady Smith, and Lady Clark of Calton were in the majority; Lord Brodie dissented. Lady Clark of Carlton gave a brief Opinion concurring with Lady Smith.
2 Paragraphs 45–47. We focus on Lady Smith's Opinion because, of the four Opinions issued (one in the Outer House and three in the Inner House), this was the only substantive Opinion in favour of the pursuer.
3 Ronald Clancy QC represented the pursuer.

In these circumstances, the Lord Ordinary required to ask whether this was one of those cases where the law attributes assumption of responsibility to the solicitor and, in doing so, provides a complete answer to the duty of care question, obviating the need for further inquiry including inquiry as to whether or not NRAM could or should have checked their file. I cannot read his opinion as indicating that he did so. Had that question been asked, I consider it to be inevitable that the conclusion would have been that this was one of those cases. The factors I have referred to – which are all drawn from the Lord Ordinary's findings in fact and are more extensive than those listed by him in para 73 – weigh heavily in favour of the law attributing assumption of responsibility to Ms Steel and thus, without further inquiry, imposing on her a duty of care. It being conceded that if she did owe the duty then it was breached, that would be an end of matters.

Evaluation

To the extensive discussion of the duty of care and its supposed breach by the defenders we have little to add. We do, however, prefer the approach of the Lord Ordinary. Perhaps the shortest entry to the issue is the following sentence in the pursuer's pleadings: 'It was ... necessary for NR to rely exclusively on the borrower's solicitor.'[1] This will surely raise the eyebrows of those familiar with conveyancing practice, or banking practice. Banks are, *of necessity*, at the mercy of the borrower's solicitor? In this case the bank chose not to employ a solicitor, whether in-house or independent. In street language, it chose to freeload.[2]

Freeloading is in itself not wholly incompatible with a duty of care. Imagine – to take a strong case – that, instead of a bank, the lender had been an elderly person of limited education who really *was* relying on the borrower's solicitors. Circumstances alter cases. But here the lender was a professional moneylender. Moreover, whilst the pursuer's witnesses said much about relying on Ms Steel's expertise as a solicitor, this was not, at bottom, a legal issue at all. The issue was not some conveyancing technicality about the type of deed to be granted – something a solicitor would know about and a banker might not. The issue was a banking issue, an issue about the state of the account. The issue was whether in March 2007 (i) all the loan was being repaid or (ii) only a large part of it. About that the professional moneylender knew what the position was, and knew it better than the defenders, who were pigs-in-the-middle between a commercial lender and a commercial borrower.

We do not think that there was a duty of care. Indeed, a cynic might suggest that, if any duty of care existed, it would have been a duty of care running the other way – owed *by* the pursuer. 'Entitled to rely' is the watchword in this area of law.[3] Was the bank entitled to rely on the email? This essential point was explored by Lord Doherty and Lord Brodie (who dissented in the Inner House), whereas

---

1 Quoted at [2014] CSOH 172 para 4.
2 In some well-defined cases it can happen that the same law firm acts for both borrower and lender, but in such cases the law firm has two clients and, obviously, owes duties to both. That was not the case here. The defenders had one client and only one client, the borrower.
3 The expression is widely used, but perhaps the most pertinent reference would be to its use by Lord Bridge in *Caparo Industries plc v Dickman* [1990] 2 AC 605 at 621.

Lady Smith does not, we suggest, give it sufficient weight. In this connection, Lady Smith said, in a passage already quoted in part:[1]

> I consider that there is merit in Mr Clancy's submission that, properly understood, this was not an arms' length transaction. It was in the interests of both NRAM and HCL to ensure that the sale of the unit was completed. Both would benefit financially from the proceeds of sale. In these circumstances, the Lord Ordinary ought not, I agree, to have regarded the case of *Dean v Allin & Watts*[2] as being of no assistance. It involved circumstances which, whilst not identical, were comparable.

We prefer the approach of Lords Doherty and Brodie. The description of the transaction as 'not an arms' length transaction' does not commend itself to us. *Dean* was a case in the English Court of Appeal in which Mr Dean had wished to lend money on mortgage. Messrs Allin & Watts were a law firm that acted for the borrowers. Mr Deans was legally unrepresented. He was granted a mortgage of a type that had once been valid, but was no longer valid.[3] The borrower became insolvent, and Mr Deans sued Messrs Allin & Watts in negligence. He succeeded. The decision is significant. But there are two large differences which make it very different from the facts in *NRAM*. In the first place, the negligence in *Dean* concerned a matter of *legal* knowledge: what type of mortgage was or was not valid at that time in English law. In *NRAM* the pursuer was not relying on the legal knowledge of Messrs Bell & Scott LLP. In the second place, in *NRAM* the lender was a bank. In *Dean* the plaintiff was … a car mechanic.[4]

Beyond the mysterious email

Thus far, a story of muddle: the defenders somehow got into a muddle, and the bank followed, with ovine financial alertness. We have suggested that these facts did not give rise to a valid claim. But the story has more to it than that. The bank not only had standard securities, but also an all-assets floating charge. And the story about that is as strange, or stranger, but largely unexplored in the litigation, for unknown reasons.

The core of the bank's case was that it had thought, relying on the email, that the whole loan was being paid off. That account is consistent with the fact that discharges of all the standard securities were granted. But is it consistent with what happened to the floating charge? The bank granted a certificate of non-crystallisation *but only for unit 1*. Why? How can this overtly limited certificate be reconciled with the idea that immediate full repayment was expected?

Next, what happened to the floating charge after the events of March 2007? The pursuer's account was that it had expected the whole loan to be paid off following on the sale. That did not happen. What happened was that, following

---

1 Paragraph 46.
2 [2001] 2 Lloyd's Rep 249.
3 The mortgage was by simple deposit of the title deeds. This type of mortgage had ceased to be valid as a result of s 2 of the Law of Property (Miscellaneous Provisions) Act 1989.
4 And in this connection consider the remarks of Lord Griffiths in *Smith v Bush* [1990] 1 AC 831 at 859–60.

the sale, only £495,000 was remitted to the bank. How did the bank react to the fact that instead of receiving £1,221,850, which (so it asserted in its pleadings) was the sum that it was expecting, it received only £495,000? Did it protest? Did it ask that the standard securities which it had mistakenly (so it asserted) discharged should promptly be reinstated? There is no suggestion that any such thing happened. Indeed, rather the opposite.

It will be recalled that the debtor company was selling all four units, the last two being sold later in the same year as unit 1: unit 4 in September/October 2007 and unit 2 in December 2007. It will also be recalled that the bank still had security over these properties by way of its all-assets floating charge. It could be reasonably sure of being paid out of the proceeds of these two sales for the simple reason that refusal to grant the necessary certificates of non-crystallisation would prevent the sales from taking place. In other words, notwithstanding the discharge of the standard securities in March, the bank still had the leverage to obtain full repayment. So what happened? It happily granted the certificates for units 2 and 4 without repayment. Hence the simple story told by the bank – namely, 'we were misled by the defenders, in March 2007, into thinking that we would be receiving full payment, and acted accordingly, and thereby incurred loss' – is not easy to understand.

One could also put the matter more technically, and suggest that even if an actionable wrong had been committed by the defenders in March 2007, the chain of causation was thereafter broken, not once, but twice – in September/October 2007, and again in December. The pursuer had, after all, to establish that, had the discharges of the standard securities not been granted in March 2007, it would have made a full recovery of all sums owed to it. It is difficult to discern, on the facts as disclosed in the case, any solid basis for that view. This large aspect of the matter – what happened to the floating charge after March 2007 – is almost undiscussed in the litigation. It is not mentioned in the Inner House, and only briefly in the Outer House.[1] We do not know why it was almost entirely left on one side. And as to what actually happened from March to December 2007 we are more or less in the dark.

Implications

If the decision survives the appeal to the Supreme Court, the implications for practitioners are worrying. One view would be that if the other side to a transaction is not legally represented, then the law firm in question may (depending on the circumstances) have to consider refusing to act. For instance, if Messrs Law & Practice LLP acts for client X and becomes aware that the other side to the transaction, Y, is unrepresented, then Messrs Law & Practice LLP might have to make it clear to client X that it cannot act. We say 'depending on the circumstances' because there will be cases where the risks are too low to cause concern. That would depend in particular on the financial size of the

---

1 [2014] CSOH 172 at paras 50 (second half) and 82.

transaction. As an alternative, would it be enough to advise Y to seek independent legal advice? Possibly, but there is no indication of that in *NRAM*.

Finally, to repeat what has already been said, there are types of case where a law firm does act for both sides, eg in vanilla-flavour residential purchases where the same law firm commonly acts for both the buyer and the buyer's lender. There are, of course, difficult issues about that situation, and we will not here dive into the 'sep rep' debate, because in *NRAM* the bank was *not* the law firm's client. The firm had only one client. The bank had, by its own choice, no legal representative.

An astonishing complaint

Mr and Mrs Price owned a property, 'Ewenburn', in Gwydyr Road, Crieff, Perthshire. Mr Price took the view that the property had, in relation to a part of a neighbouring property ('Ardlarich'), (i) a servitude right of pedestrian and vehicular access and (ii) a servitude of parking. He said that (i) had been constituted by deed, and that (ii) had been constituted by prescription. He (and perhaps Mrs Price, but she seems to make no appearance in the story) asked the neighbouring owner, a school, to grant a deed of servitude in respect of both access and parking.[1] This seems to have been prompted by the fact that the school was about to sell the property.

The school was willing to grant a deed for a servitude of access but not of parking. There was also lack of agreement as to who should pay for any deed to be granted, Mr Price taking the view, it seems, that all expenses should fall on the school. Discussions broke down and in the end no deed of any kind was granted. The sale of the neighbouring property, by the school, went ahead.

Mr Price lodged a complaint with the Scottish Legal Complaints Commission against the school's law firm, Messrs Miller Hendry:[2]

(1) Miller Hendry inappropriately advised their client, Ardvreck School to demand that the owners of ... Ewenburn prepare Deeds of Servitude and be responsible for all the legal costs. Yet Miller Hendry were well aware that Servitude Rights were well established, having advised the owners of Greenways in 2002 and 2004. By their actions, Miller Hendry showed a complete lack of professional judgment, and indeed common sense for the sole objective of satisfying their client's wishes which was to deny the owners of Ewenburn ... the right to park in any part of the access lane.

(2) Miller Hendry failed to ensure that the Ardvreck School management made the purchaser of Ardlarach fully aware of the area effected by the burdens he would inherit as evidence by the letter from the purchaser to our solicitor 24 March 2015 in which the purchaser wrongly stated that we do not have any access rights over either his property or the access lane to the side of his property which remains in the ownership of the school. By their actions, Miller Hendry were in breach of the Law Society of Scotland's Rules of Conduct as set out in section 1.4.1 and 1.4.3.

---

1 If the access servitude had already been granted by deed, it is not clear why he wished it to be granted again.
2 This is taken from [2016] CSIH 53 para 8.

(3) Miller Hendry failed to ensure that Ardvreck School management were fully aware of their own obligations in terms of the law relating to sections 10(1), 10(2) and 76(2) of the Title Conditions (Scotland) Act 2003 which came into effect in 2004.

The Scottish Legal Complaints Commission rejected the complaint. Mr Price appealed to the Inner House, but without success.[1] Giving the Opinion of the court, Lord Brodie noted that:[2]

Once it is understood that it was no part of Miller Hendry's duties to arbitrate on the strengths of the applicant's claims to have rights of access over and parking on the lane, far less to advocate the strength of these claims to their clients and the solicitors acting for the purchaser of Ardlarach; and that, similarly, it was no part of the function of the commission to assess the strength of the claims, the substance of the applicant's proposed appeal falls away. The applicant may be entirely correct in his assessment of the law as it applies to the facts of the case but if that is so the action to be taken in the light of that and in the light of the attitude of the other parties is entirely a matter for him and his own legal advisors. Essentially that is the point made by the commission.

No award of expenses was made against the applicant. We quote again from Lord Brodie:[3]

With some hesitation I make an award of no expenses due to or by. I am aware that in so doing I am throwing quite unnecessarily incurred expense amounting to a sum in four figures on to a public body which insofar as not publically funded is funded by the profession whose conduct its function is to investigate. The usual rule is that in appeals, as is generally the case in this court, expenses follow success, in other words the unsuccessful party pays, unless some circumstance strongly points in another direction. Here I consider that Miss Ross[4] was justified in being sceptical about the applicant's assertion that he had not been aware that he was at financial risk beyond court fees, although even if true that is not a relevant consideration; those who litigate are expected to know the law. That applies to party litigants as well as to counsel. The applicant was articulate and well able to express himself both orally and in writing. He appeared to be intelligent. He referred to his high level business experience. As Miss Ross pointed out he was intent on seeking financial recovery from other parties. He repeatedly stressed the wisdom of avoiding going to court in that this is likely to benefit lawyers rather than their clients. And yet it is clear that in this matter he has directed his energies and resources in an entirely misguided manner and in doing so has involved others in trouble and expense which includes the commission's legal expenses in this appeal. None of this has advanced resolution of what may be a real and difficult problem over parking in the cul-de-sac and it never had any prospect of doing so. The usual course for the court to follow would be to mitigate the commission's expenses by an award in its favour, so requiring the applicant to bear, at least in part, the cost which he has caused so unnecessarily to be

1 *Price v Scottish Legal Complaints Commission* [2016] CSIH 53, 2016 GWD 22-408.
2 Paragraph 19.
3 Paragraph 23.
4 Morag Ross, counsel for the Scottish Legal Complaints Commission.

incurred. However, I have been unwilling to contribute to the applicant's self-inflicted harm and have considered my discretion is wide enough at this preliminary stage in the appeal in relation to a matter originating in a complaint against members of the legal profession to depart from the usual rule.

We are most reluctant to suggest any criticism of this approach, set forth by a distinguished judge. But unless there is some aspect of this case of which we are unaware, it appears to us to have lacked from the outset any possible merit. The distinguished judge speaks of 'the applicant's self-inflicted harm', yet he was a party litigant and thus incurred no legal fees. The harm to the other side – not self-inflicted, but imposed – must have been much greater. We would venture to suggest that an award of expenses should have been made in the interests of justice.

RECTIFICATION OF 1979 ACT TITLES
UNDER THE 2012 ACT

The facts

Highland Ventures Ltd v Keeper of the Registers of Scotland[1] is the first application for rectification under the Land Registration etc (Scotland) Act 2012, and also the first case to make use of the transitional provisions in schedule 4 paras 17–24 of that Act. The application was, in the end, unopposed and proceeded in a straightforward manner. This makes it an especially helpful illustration of the workings of the new procedure.

Highland Ventures Ltd owned the Drummond Hotel in St Fillans, Crieff, Perthsire, on a Sasine title. In 2006 it sold the hotel but retained a certain amount of land for the personal use of one of its directors. The disposition induced first registration in the Land Register. Later, it was discovered – and, after initial disagreement, accepted on all sides – that the boundary as shown on the new title sheet for the hotel was not entirely correct in respect that it incorporated, in three separate places, land which had been withheld by Highland Ventures from the disposition. Meanwhile, ownership of the hotel had passed into the hands of a third party, Marketing Management Services Ltd ('MMSL'), the disposition in its favour being registered on 7 November 2013. As the Land Registration etc (Scotland) Act 2012 did not come into force until 8 December 2014 (the so-called 'designated day'), MMSL's title was registered under the Land Registration (Scotland) Act 1979. That, as we will see, was important.

The transitional provisions

Two questions

Where today, after the designated day, an inaccuracy is alleged to exist in respect of a 1979 Act title, such as MMSL's, the issue falls to be determined by

---

1   2016 GWD 22-403. The Tribunal comprised Lord Minginish and D J Gillespie FRICS.

the transitional provisions contained in paras 17–24 of schedule 4 of the 2012 Act.[1] Essentially, two questions require to be asked and answered. First, was the Register inaccurate immediately before the designated day? And, secondly, if so, was this an inaccuracy which the Keeper would, at that time, have had the power to rectify? Both questions must, of course, be answered on the basis of the 1979 Act and not the 2012 Act. 1979 Act titles, logically enough, are governed by the 1979 Act; and to this extent at least the Act lives on, and will live on for many years to come.

The answer to the first question, in the present case, was not in doubt. The disposition which had induced first registration did not convey the disputed areas. They should not, therefore, have been included in the title sheet which was made up for the hotel. Of course, under the 1979 Act's Midas touch, the effect of registration was to confer ownership on the registered proprietor.[2] But the person who *ought* to be owner – the 'true' owner, in the terminology often used – was Highland Ventures. From this it followed that the Register was (bijurally) inaccurate at the point of first registration in 2006, and that it remained inaccurate on 7 December 2014, the day before the designated day.[3]

The second question was less straightforward. Despite the Register being inaccurate, the inaccuracy could not be rectified, under the law in force on 7 December 2014 (ie the eve of the appointed day), where this would be to the prejudice of a proprietor in possession.[4] MMSL was, of course, the (registered) 'proprietor' of the hotel, including of the disputed areas. Whether the Keeper was empowered to rectify on 7 December 2014 would therefore depend on whether MMSL was in 'possession' on that day.

Proof of historic possession can, of course, be difficult and will become increasingly difficult as the distance lengthens from 7 December 2014. The legislation seeks to assist by presuming that possession on 7 December 2014 was held by whoever was registered as proprietor.[5] Like most presumptions, this can be rebutted by contrary evidence; but in the absence of such evidence, the registered proprietor is taken to have been in possession – and the Keeper is taken *not* to have had power to rectify (at least in the normal case).[6]

The registered proprietor of the disputed areas, on 7 December 2014, was MMSL. Accordingly, MMSL was presumed to have been in possession. But in this case the presumption was overcome by showing from, for example, the position of the fences that the areas had been possessed by Highland Ventures through one of its directors. No doubt this would have been rather less easy if the application had been opposed.

---

1 For a discussion of these provisions, see K G C Reid and G L Gretton, *Land Registration* (2017) paras 11.9–11.11.
2 Land Registration (Scotland) Act 1979 s 3(1)(a).
3 See Reid and Gretton, *Land Registration* paras 2.7–2.9.
4 LR(S)A 1979 s 9(3)(a).
5 Land Registration etc (Scotland) Act 2012 sch 4 para 18.
6 There were, however, a few cases where the Keeper was able to rectify even against a proprietor in possession, such as where the inaccuracy was caused by that proprietor's fraud or carelessness: see LR(S)A 1979 s 9(3)(a).

Yes and yes

The answers to the questions were therefore yes and yes. Yes, the presence of the disputed areas in the hotel's title sheet was an inaccuracy on 7 December 2014. And yes, MMSL not being in possession of the areas on that day, the Keeper could have rectified the inaccuracy. The consequence is spelled out in the transitional provisions. Since the Keeper could have rectified before the designated day had she chosen to do so, the parties were given the same rights, on that day, as if rectification had taken place.[1] There was, in other words, a sort of deemed rectification of the Register. Hence, Highland Ventures, having lost ownership of the disputed areas back in 2006, regained that ownership on 8 December 2014.

A deemed rectification, however, is not the same as an actual rectification. The Register was not *actually* rectified on 8 December 2014; and though Highland Ventures were owners once more, the Register continued to show the owners as being MMSL. The Register was therefore still inaccurate. But this was now an inaccuracy of a different sort. Before the designated day there had been a 1979 Act inaccuracy: the entry on the title sheet had been true in one sense (due to the Midas touch, MMSL really was the owner), but untrue in another (the 'true' owner was Highland Ventures). But on the designated day this 'bijural' inaccuracy had given way to an 'actual' inaccuracy – to a 2012 Act inaccuracy.[2] Now the entry on the title sheet was simply wrong. It showed MMSL as owner when the owner was actually Highland Ventures. It therefore fell to be rectified.

Yes and no

What difference would it have made if the answer to the second question had been no – if it was MMSL and not Highland Ventures who was found to be in possession on 7 December 2014 with the result that rectification could not have taken place? The consequence under the transitional provisions would have been completely different. Where there was no power to rectify, the entry on the title sheet would have ceased, on the designated day, to be inaccurate.[3] And with the inaccuracy thus cured there could have been no question of rectification, whether then or at any time in the future. Highland Venture's remedy would have been compensation from the Keeper and not rectification.[4]

The procedure

Where an entry on the Register is claimed to be inaccurate, the first port of call is to apply to the Keeper for rectification.[5] And if the inaccuracy is obvious – 'manifest' in the words of the 2012 Act – the Keeper will, indeed must, proceed

---

1 LR(S)A 2012 sch 4 para 17.
2 For this terminology, see Reid and Gretton, *Land Registration* para 2.8. The definition of 'inaccuracy' in LR(S)A 2012 s 85(1) begins by saying that a title sheet is inaccurate 'in so far as it misstates what the position is in law or in fact'.
3 LR(S)A 2012 sch 4 para 22.
4 LR(S)A 2012 sch 4 para 23.
5 See generally Reid and Gretton, *Land Registration* paras 11.13 ff.

to rectification.[1] With 1979 Act titles, however, inaccuracies are often not obvious or manifest. This is because the status of the entry, as we have seen, depends on the state of possession immediately before the designated day, and on matters of possession the Keeper will not adjudicate. Of course, sometimes the state of possession will be obvious, or is conceded. But where it is not, the application for rectification will be rejected.

What then? Unless he is simply to give up, the applicant must apply to the Lands Tribunal or the ordinary courts, in practice usually the former. Applications to the Tribunal must now be made under the 2012 Act even if, as in *Highland Ventures*, they are in respect of a 1979 Act title. The 2012 Act offers two different routes. There can either be a direct appeal against the Keeper's decision, under s 103, or the applicant can refer the matter to the Lands Tribunal under the new jurisdiction created by s 82. Section 82 was used in *Highland Ventures*, and the Tribunal suggested that this would be usually be the preferred route:[2]

> It could, arguably, have been raised under sec 103 rather than sec 82 of the 2012 Act, as an appeal against a decision of the Keeper not to rectify the register, but sec 82 is within the part of the Act, Part 8, dealing specifically with 'Rectification of the Register' and refers to questions relating to the accuracy of the Register. It therefore seems to us to be more apt as a vehicle for rectification than sec 103.

We would agree but would give a different reason. Many cases involving rectification are in substance disputes between neighbours rather than disputes with the Keeper. The s 82 procedure, which allows the Tribunal to rule on any question relating to the accuracy of the Register, ensures that the proper parties are in court.[3]

ENFORCING STANDARD SECURITIES

Failure to advertise and its consequences

In *Peters v Belhaven Finance Ltd*,[4] Mr and Mrs Peters had bought the Townhead Hotel in Lockerbie in 2005, borrowing most of the money needed to pay the purchase price (£202,000) from Belhaven Finance Ltd. The loan was secured by standard security. The business did not thrive. In August 2009 the licence lapsed, and in October 2009 the heritable creditor took possession of the hotel as a preliminary to sale.

During the summer of 2009 the Peters had marketed the property at an upset figure of £250,000 but no offers had been received. The heritable creditor advertised the hotel for sale at an upset figure of £135,000, and a sale was effected in February 2010 at that figure. The secured debt was the same

---

1 LR(S)A 2012 s 80.
2 Paragraph 25.
3 Reid and Gretton, *Land Registration* para 3.20.
4 2016 SLT (Sh Ct) 156, 2016 Hous LR 35.

amount, so that the sale cleared the secured debt, but left no surplus payable to the Peters.[1]

The Peters considered the sale price too low. They 'strongly suspected that the defenders were interested only in recouping the sums owed to them and had no interest in recovering any equity which would have been due to the pursuers'.[2] Accordingly they raised the present action seeking damages, the quantum being the difference between (i) the actual sale figure and (ii) what they considered to be the fair market value of the property as it was in the relevant period, ie October 2009 to February 2010. The legal basis for such a claim is well known. A creditor enforcing a security right has not only his own interest to consider, which, after all, is merely the interest of clearing off the secured debt. He must consider also the interest of the owner and, where applicable, the interests of other secured creditors. This duty exists at common law, but, more relevantly for present purposes, is spelt out by the Conveyancing and Feudal Reform (Scotland) Act 1970, s 25 of which provides that 'it shall be the duty of the creditor to advertise the sale and to take all reasonable steps to ensure that the price at which all or any of the subjects are sold is the best that can be reasonably obtained'.

The suspicions of the Peters were understandable. The hotel was being sold for much less than they had paid for it, even though they had, they said, put a significant amount of money into it during their period of ownership. The precise match between the sale figure and the amount of the outstanding debt was odd. Then there was the fact that during the previous summer, when the Peters had been marketing the property themselves, they had had some expressions of interest at figures higher than £135,000. Perhaps the strongest point in their favour was what the lender had done by way of advertising. No sales agent had been appointed. The lender had failed to make contact with the persons who had indicated an interest in buying the hotel when it had been on the market during the summer. There had been no advertising in the trade media. There had been no advertising in the local press. There had been only a 20-word advertisement, placed in *The Scotsman*, an advertisement, moreover, which was hardly what was called for:

> PUBLIC HOUSE, LOCKERBIE. OFFERS OVER £135,000. Unlicensed and in shell condition. For further details please contact the Belhaven Group 01368 862734.

The sheriff[3] came to the conclusion that there had been a serious failure in the duty to advertise the property. He said:[4]

1. The advertisement in *The Scotsman* did not correctly identify the subjects as a hotel, instead describing them only as a 'Public House'. Such a description was liable to

---

1 Paragraph 62. How the expenses of the sale come into the picture is not clear.
2 Paragraph 3.
3 Brian Mohan.
4 Paragraph 52.

mislead any potential purchaser as it suggested that a property costing £135,000 offered only the facilities and potential of a public house rather than the other facilities and opportunities available in a hotel business.

2. The advertisement described the subjects as in 'shell condition' which was inaccurate.

3. There was nothing in the advertisement designed to give any positive message to a potential purchaser. It did not seek to attract interest in the property.

4. The defenders failed to advertise the property elsewhere, and in particular ignored recommended trade publications.

Hence, he concluded, 'the defenders failed in their duty under s 25 of the Conveyancing and Feudal Reform (Scotland) Act 1970 to advertise the sale of the subjects'.[1]

So the Peters won? Not necessarily. An action for damages seeks to recover loss (*damnum*) in respect of a wrongdoing (*injuria*). There can be loss without wrongdoing (*damnum sine injuria*), in which case the pursuer will lose, and, conversely, there can be wrongdoing without loss (*injuria sine damno*). Here there had been wrongdoing – breach of the obligation to advertise – but had that wrongdoing caused loss? That was a question of fact: whether the price of £135,000 had in fact been a reasonable price. On this question evidence was heard, as a result of which the sheriff concluded: 'The defenders did sell the hotel for its market value. Indeed, the sale price achieved was at the higher end of that market value.'[2] Accordingly, '£135,000 was the best price that could be reasonably obtained by the defenders for the sale of the subjects.'[3] So the case was one of wrongdoing without loss.

What decision was made as to expenses is not known. Normally expenses follow success. But here, given the conduct of the lender, there might be a nothing-due-or-by decision.

The case rather suggests that the provision of the 1970 Act may be imperfect, for what is the point of imposing a duty if breach of that duty has no consequences? Indeed, that argument might be applied also to the 'all reasonable steps' provision. Either the creditor obtains a reasonable price or he does not. Advertising etc would always be done by the prudent creditor, for without it there would be a grave risk of not obtaining a reasonable price – with resulting liability. If that argument goes too far, one could argue that at least the specific requirement for advertising is redundant, because the phrase 'all reasonable steps' would automatically include it. After all, s 25 does not impose a specific duty to, for instance, allow potential buyers to look at the property: that is obviously a 'reasonable step'.

The case will not serve as a green light to shoddy marketing by creditors. Any creditor who fails to market properly will be taking a pointless risk.

---

1 Paragraph 1 of the findings in law.
2 Paragraph 59.
3 Paragraph 1 of the findings in fact and in law.

The battle of Harperfield Farm

Introduction

In 2009 Euan Lindsay borrowed £1,335,000 from Outlook Finance Ltd. The loan was repayable in full on 30 September 2011, and in the meantime interest was payable on a monthly basis. To secure the loan Mr Lindsay granted a standard security over Harperfield Farm in Lanarkshire. The property was still in the Register of Sasines, and accordingly, as the law stood at that time, the standard security was recorded in that register. In June 2011 Mr Lindsay died. Until late in 2012 the executor kept up the monthly interest payments, so that the principal sum remained, up to that time, unchanged at £1,335,000. Thereafter the executor stopped paying, and in the autumn of 2014 the lender served a calling-up notice. This did not lead to payment.

Because the farm included 'a residential building' (presumably the farmhouse itself) it was a matter of concession that the security in respect of the *whole* property was subject to the special rules about enforcing securities over residential property.[1] This was no doubt a correct concession on the part of the lender, for the special rules apply if the property is 'used *to any extent* for residential purposes'.[2] Accordingly the lender had (i) to 'comply with the pre-action requirements' required by the special legislative rules[3] and thereafter (ii) to obtain the authority of the court for the enforcement.

The lender served the requisite notices, and thereafter the present action was raised: *Outlook Finance Ltd v Lindsay's Exr.*[4] Thus far, thus ordinary. But now matters began to become interesting. The defender raised two objections, both formidable. One was that the standard security was invalid, and, consequently, the calling-up notice was invalid. The other was that the pre-action notice was invalid.

Invalidity of standard security?

'Just copy out what this deed says on page 2. I've marked the bit in pencil.' That works fine – usually. Here the security was granted 'over ALL and WHOLE the subjects and others described in the schedule annexed and signed as relative hereto ...'. The property was described in the standard security's schedule in the usual way, ie copied and pasted from the existing GRS title. The description was lengthy and no doubt that fact was a disincentive to close study. There are those who would be more alert and engaged when reading, let us say, a sonnet by Shakespeare than when struggling through the stilted and leaden prose of a prolonged and probably unpunctuated Sasine description. Not even the pendicles may suffice to sustain unswerving concentration. We quote the sheriff, Derek O'Carroll:[5]

---

1 See in particular Conveyancing and Feudal Reform (Scotland) Act 1970 ss 24–24E, and the Applications by Creditors (Pre-action Requirements) (Scotland) Order 2010, SSI 2010/317.
2 CFR(S)A 1970 s 24(1A).
3 See in particular CFR(S)A 1970 ss 24(1C) and 24A.
4 [2016] SC LAN 58, 2016 Hous LR 75.
5 Paragraphs 5 and 6.

The description of the subjects in that standard security contained both a description of the subjects by reference to the name of the subjects and by reference to a Sasines title recorded in the Register of Sasines on 24 November 1989[1] (all of which was accurate) as well as a particular description of the subjects contained in a schedule to the standard security. That particular description was taken from the description in the Sasines title and, as might be expected in the title to a sizable farm, is lengthy containing as it does various exceptions and reservations. Unfortunately, the solicitor who prepared that schedule did so incorrectly. Missing from the particular description, in about the middle, are about 8 lines which includes the end of the second (of four) exceptions from title and most of the third exception. Unfortunately, nobody, including the Keeper, noticed this at the time.

In other words, the deed had both (i) a description by reference to the 1989 disposition and (ii) a particular description of the property, this latter being, we take it, a copy-out (or, rather, what was intended to be a copy-out) of the description given in the 1989 disposition.[2] As for the calling-up notice served in the autumn of 2014, it repeated the text of the deed.

After the action was raised the defender's law agents – to their credit – noticed the error and raised it as a defence. The error, they said, was fatal, and was fatal equally to the security and to the calling-up notice. It may be observed that if the standard security was fatally flawed, then a correct description in the calling-up notice would not have helped anyway.

The pursuer's response was a double one: (i) it argued that the error was not fatal and (ii) on an *esto* basis it sought (by way of amendment) rectification of the description in both the security and the notice. We deal with the rectification point elsewhere.[3] Here we deal with the question of whether the error was fatal.

The sheriff held that it was not fatal: the property was sufficiently adequately identified and there had been sufficient compliance with the requirements of the Conveyancing and Feudal Reform (Scotland) Act 1970.[4] *Falsa demonstratio non nocet dummodo constat de corpore*: an inaccurate description does not matter

---

1 Although Lanarkshire became operational for the Land Register on 3 January 1984, the 1989 disposition was gratuitous and therefore, as the law then stood, did not trigger first registration.

2 We are not quite clear from the judgment precisely what appeared in the body of the deed, and what appeared in the schedule, but this issue does not matter.

3 See p 61 above.

4 This case involved one of the rare instances where Westlaw proved inaccurate. We quote the sheriff at para 16. '[S]ection 9(2) of the 1970 Act provides that "a standard security over any land or real right in land [is] to be expressed in conformity with one of the forms prescribed in schedule 2 …". The relevant form is Form B. Note 1 to the form used to provide inter alia that "Note 1. The security subjects shall be described by means of a particular description or by reference to a description thereof as in Schedule D to the Conveyancing (Scotland) Act 1924 …". That was the version of Note 1 lodged in Court by the pursuer and as I understood the submissions made to me, that was thought to be the relevant version of the schedule. Unfortunately, that version of Note 1 is now out of date. Counsel were perhaps misled by the fact that amendments to Note 1 made by schedule 12(23) to the Abolition of Feudal Tenure etc (Scotland) Act 2000 ("the 2000 Act"), with effect from June 2000, have not found their way into the Westlaw version of schedule 2 to the 1970 Act.' The sheriff took the view, however, that the error in the Westlaw version – an error which, to his credit, he discovered from his own research after the conclusion of the debate but before issuing his judgment – was not crucial to the matters in dispute: see para 17.

provided that the thing in question is in fact identifiable,[1] a principle applied in such decisions as *Matheson v Gemmell*[2] and *Murray's Tr v Wood*.[3] The sheriff summed up his approach, which we would endorse as far as GRS titles are concerned:[4]

> [A] description of the subjects in a standard security which is faulty, will be sufficient so long as what is contained within the description is sufficient, if necessary after reasonable search and enquiry, to enable the subjects of the security to be correctly identified with certainty.

It might be added that the omitted eight lines referred to an exception from the subjects. So the schedule did include all the relevant property, even if it may, because of the omission, have purported to grant (invalidly) security over some neighbouring area.

Invalidity of pre-action notice?

Now for the other defence. In terms of s 24A of the 1970 Act a creditor in residential cases must, after the calling-up notice, 'provide the debtor with clear information about' various matters including 'the amount due to the creditor under the standard security, including any arrears and any charges in respect of late payment or redemption'.[5] This is amplified by article 2 of the Applications by Creditors (Pre-action Requirements) (Scotland) Order 2010[6] which says that, in providing clear information for the purposes of s 24A:

(a) information about the terms of the security must include a description of the nature and level of any charges that may be incurred by virtue of the contract to which the security relates if the default is not remedied; and
(b) information about the amount due to the creditor under the security, including any arrears and any charges in respect of late payment must be broken down so as to show –
  (i) the total amount of the arrears; and
  (ii) the total outstanding amount due including any charges already incurred.

The defender argued that this requirement for clear details of the debt had not been complied with. The focus of the defender's case was on a letter sent to the

---

1 The sheriff discusses some versions of this maxim at para 22. A thorough discussion would require a full-scale academic article. As a starter see the entries in John Trayner, *Latin Phrases and Maxims* (various edns) for *'constat'*, *'dummodo'* and *'falsa demonstratio'*, and George Watson (ed), *Bell's Dictionary and Digest of the Law of Scotland* (7th edn 1890, reprinted Edinburgh Legal Education Trust, 2012) under *'falsa demonstratio'* where the form given is *'falsa demontratio non obest nec vitiat cum constat de corpore.'* See further Detlef Liebs, *Lateinische Rechtsregeln und Rechtssprichwörter* (1998).
2 (1903) 5 F 448.
3 (1887) 14R 856.
4 Paragraph 24.
5 Conveyancing and Feudal Reform (Scotland) Act 1970 s 24A(2). Perhaps it would be a good idea if this obligation applied to all cases, not only to residential cases and was applicable to the calling-up notice as well.
6 SSI 2010/317.

defender by the pursuer's agents, dated 23 December 2014, which, one imagines, was delivered, along with Christmas cards, on 24 December. It was on this letter that the pursuer relied to establish that the pre-action requirements had been met. Here is the Yuletide missive:

Dear Sir

Our client: Outlook Finance Ltd
Account: The Harperfield Loan
Account balance: £2,884,539.97
Account Arrears: £2,884,539.97
Your property: [...]

We refer to previous correspondence and in particular to the Calling Up Notice which was served on you.

You should also be aware that you will be liable for all costs and any arrears charges under the terms of your account terms and conditions that result from the default on your account. You will also be liable for any financial loss suffered by our client should your property be taken into possession and subsequently the sale results in a loss.

The details of any charges that may be incurred on your account (excluding legal charges) as a result of the default are detailed in the undernote below and have also already been sent to you by our client. You will also have already received statements detailing the position of your account including any charges to date on your account is [sic] contained in our client's account terms and conditions ...

Undernote
Description of charge

Increased interest rate on default 0.1% per day.

The sheriff remarked:[1]

It is in my view a notable feature of this case that initial borrowing of about £1.3 million in 2009, where interest was fully paid until October 2012, has turned into an alleged liability of over £2.61 million by October 2014 which rose to £2,884,539.97 by 23 December 2014. ... It is quite impossible to tell from the terms of the letter how the figure of £2,884,539.97, which is said to be the account balance, is made up. All the debtor is told is that £2,884,539.97 is the total account balance and, oddly, that the arrears amount to the same sum. ... [T]he obligation is on the creditor to provide the clear information, not for the debtor to attempt ... to infer the way in which the figure has been arrived at. ... Not only has the clear information and breakdown not been provided by the creditor, it cannot even be said that the information which the statute provides must be supplied can be deduced or inferred in some other way. Quite simply, at least so far as the material that has been relied on in this debate is concerned, the defender is faced with a simple bald and very large figure presented to him by the creditor without any attempt to explain how that figure has been arrived at. In my view, that approach does not comply with the requirements under section 24(A)(2) and Article 2. The onus is on the pursuers to demonstrate compliance with the pre-action requirements. They have failed to do so. It follows therefore that this action is incompetent and falls to be dismissed.

---

1 Paragraphs 57 and 58.

This decision is an important one. Everyone is familiar with communications from organisations demanding money in ways that often baffle the recipient: utility companies, telecoms companies, the HMRC and others. Lenders are no exception, and if this case leads to more transparency, so much the better. For lawyers the message is twofold: when acting for a debtor, failure by the creditor to comply with the clarity requirements may provide the client (debtor) with a defence in an enforcement action; when acting for a creditor, before sending out the letter it may be necessary to insist that the client (the creditor) should provide a proper and readable statement of how much is due, how, and why.

'Arrears'

We conclude with a reflection on the question of 'arrears'. In the passage quoted above, the sheriff said: 'All the debtor is told is that £2,884,539.97 is the total account balance and, oddly, that the arrears amount to the same sum.' The word 'oddly' can be explained by the terms of the applicable legislation, which, as indicated above, has 'arrears' as a specific category. Yet there is a puzzle here. Take the case of an on-demand loan. As soon as the creditor makes the demand for repayment, and the debtor fails to comply, the whole sum is 'arrears'. Or suppose the loan is not an on-demand one but there has been an event of default that entitles the lender to demand full repayment, immediately. In that case the position is the same: as soon as the demand is issued but not complied with, the whole loan is 'arrears'. Presumably one or other of these was true here, ie either (i) the loan was an on-demand loan or (ii) it was not, but had been converted ('accelerated', to use the standard term) as a result of an event of default. In either case the 'account balance' and the 'account arrears' would have been the same sum – which is what the letter from the lender said.

The concept of arrears is certainly one that can apply before a calling-up notice is issued. But thereafter – assuming the calling-up notice to be valid – the concept ceases to be applicable, or, put in other words, *everything* is arrears. We venture to suggest that the terms of the legislation need to be reviewed.

The spectre of the party litigant

In this country everyone has the right to represent himself in court – the party litigant, or litigant in person. We tend to assume that the same is true everywhere, but that is not so. For instance, in some countries it is true only in the lowest levels of courts and tribunals; in the higher courts it is necessary to have legal representation (which, of course, can be provided for the indigent through legal aid). Party litigants sometimes do a reasonable job. But often they do not, slowing down the judicial process and often throwing unrecoverable expense on to the other side.[1] And sometimes the positions

---

1 See Rabeea Assy, *Injustice in Person: The Right to Self-Representation* (2015) for a sustained examination of the issues, with particular reference to England, Germany and the USA, and arguing that the right of self-representation should not be absolute.

adopted are beyond the reach of rational understanding. *McLeod v Prestige Finance Ltd*[1] was one such case.

In 2007 Mr McLeod granted a standard security over his house at Stewarton, Kilmarnock, Ayrshire in favour of Morgan Stanley Bank International Ltd. In 2009 the standard security was assigned to Prestige Finance Ltd.[2] That company sought to enforce the security. The company was successful in the sheriff court. Mr McLeod appealed to the sheriff principal. He lost again. He then raised the present action in the Outer House of the Court of Session to reduce the sheriff court decree. He lost. He then reclaimed to the Inner House. He lost again.[3]

Mr McLeod denied that standard securities can be assigned. He denied that the sheriff court could hear the case. Only a 'court of record' could hear the case, he argued, adopting Anglo-American terminology. 'The Sovereign Man bares [*sic*] the right and privilege to be heard in a court of Common Law', he pled. He claimed that he had offered to the creditor a cheque drawn on 'WeRe Bank'[4] and that the creditor had illegally declined to take it in satisfaction of the debt.

And so on. There exists a whole world on the internet in which people make imagined legal assertions, usually based on some fantastical idea of English common law as having worldwide force, plus the invalidity of all legislation.[5] The hook for all this is usually that it is possible 'legally' to refuse to pay debt. *McLeod v Prestige Finance Ltd* suggests that this movement may now have arrived in Scotland.[6]

FRAUD

2016 has not brought with it any reported Scottish cases on conveyancing fraud. But the field remains active, on both sides of the border. Below we say something of three types of fraud: payment-instruction fraud (rare until recently, but which is hitting the headlines), owner-impersonation fraud (a perennial favourite), and security-discharge fraud.

---

1 [2016] CSOH 69, 2016 Hous LR 43 affd [2016] CSIH 87, 2016 GWD 39-690.
2 In recent times the assignation of standard securities seems to have become more common. We would guess that what is happening is that lenders have been selling non-performing loans, no doubt at a steep discount. Whilst that is something that has always happened to some extent, the financial downturn of 2008 probably made the practice more common.
3 'Largely incomprehensible' said the Inner House of Mr McLeod's case at para 9.
4 On which see www.fca.org.uk/news/news-stories/consumer-notice-were-bank. The Lord Ordinary (Lord Tyre) noted (para 11 of the Outer House judgment) that the 'WeReBank' had been called a 'fraud'.
5 Google for 'Freemen on the land'. And see also *Meads v Meads* 2012 ABQB 571 (www.canlii.org/en/ab/abqb/doc/2012/2012abqb571/2012abqb571.html).
6 *Landmark Mortgages Ltd v Stirling* [2016] CSIH 89, 2016 GWD 39-697 is also a case of a party litigant resisting enforcement of a standard security on spurious grounds, but we do not see in it the 'Freemen on the Land' ideology. Some Freeman-ish tendencies can be found in the 'Indycamp' case: *Scottish Parliamentary Corporate Body v The Sovereign Indigenous Peoples of Scotland* [2016] CSIH 81, 2016 SLT 1307 (Case (24) above).

Payment-instruction fraud

The boom area over the past year or so has been payment-instruction fraud. This does not necessarily involve conveyancing transactions: it can involve any situation in which money is moving to or from a law firm, and thus might involve, for instance, executries. But conveyancing is where it thrives most. We quote Nada Jardaneh:[1]

> Almost every day, the team at Marsh is made aware of attempted frauds and scams which firms have detected and successfully thwarted. Currently, most of these adopt the same format – an email purporting to be from a client/colleague/supplier with bank account information for a direct transfer paying over free proceeds of sale, paying out entitlement in an executry estate or paying an invoice.

In Scotland, the main thrust has been where fraudsters impersonate clients, and then instruct the law firm to pay the proceeds of sale to a particular account, whereupon the money vanishes. But such frauds can work the other way round, in other words with fraudsters impersonating the law firm, and instructing the client to pay to a particular account, whereupon the money vanishes. Perhaps the reason that the second seems more common in England than here is that in residential transactions a client typically makes two transfers to the law firm, the first for the deposit (shortly before exchange of contracts) and the second for the balance (shortly before completion), whereas here deposits are, with certain exceptions, not generally used in residential cases. Thus in England there are, so to speak, twice as many salmon in the river for fraudulent anglers to try to catch.

In these scams the fake payment instruction is by email. The fraudsters have somehow hacked into the communications between law firm and client. They have all the information that the email chain can disclose, and they use that to make the crucial fake email as plausible as possible. Everyone is familiar with 'Nigerian' email scams, and how the emails are typically poorly written. By contrast, these payment-instruction fraud emails are typically perfectly written. Usually scrutiny of the email will give no grounds for suspicion. 'There may be no effective way of distinguishing a fraudulent email from the real thing.'[2]

Where the email is to a law firm, giving a new bank account to which payment is to be made, that fact is the signal. The email may contain convincing reasons why the change is being made, but nevertheless verification is necessary, even if that verification causes delay. A phone call *from* the supposed client is not enough.[3]

---

1 'Fraud: a battle of wits' (2016) 61 *Journal of the Law Society of Scotland* Feb/44.
2 'Fraud: a battle of wits'.
3 'Fraud: a battle of wits'. This article is one of a series this year on the subject: the others are: Russell Lang, 'Fraud: raising your game' (2016) 61 *Journal of the Law Society of Scotland* March/44; Alistair Sim, 'Payment frauds: the fight goes on' (2016) 61 *Journal of the Law Society of Scotland* June/44; and Nada Jardaneh, 'Payment fraud: take five' (2016) 61 *Journal of the Law Society of Scotland* Oct/44. For a wider-lens view, see also Alistair Sim, 'Risk review 2015, risk forecast 2016' (2016) 61 *Journal of the Law Society of Scotland* Jan/44.

At least a law firm defrauded in this way can make a claim on the professional insurers. If the scam runs the other way, ie the client is deceived and sends the funds to the fraudster's account, the client may have no protection. We understand that it is becoming common south of the border to signal the danger to clients. For instance, some firms say, at the end of every email to a client in a conveyancing transaction, something like:[1]

> Please be aware of cybercrime…We will never change our bank details during the course of a transaction. We will not take responsibility if you transfer funds to the wrong account. … Email is insecure and may have been intercepted or altered before reaching you. … Criminals are known to target emails to and from solicitors' firms in an attempt to alter bank details and thereby divert funds … Please note that we do not send our bank account details by email.

Owner-impersonation fraud

Purrunsing v A'Court & Co

Owner-impersonation fraud is a familiar problem, on both sides of the border. There have been no reported cases this year in Scotland, but an English case, *Purrunsing v A'Court & Co*,[2] is worth mention. Here a fraudster impersonated the owner of a property at 35 Merton Hall Gardens, Wimbledon. The property was empty and mortgage-free. The fraudster, impersonating the owner, Nicholas Robert Dawson, approached Messrs A'Court & Co. We take up the story as told by the judge, noting that by 'Mr Dawson' the judge means the fraudster impersonating Mr Dawson:[3]

> Mr Dawson's instructions to Mr A'Court were that he was not living at the property; the property was vacant and had been given to him by his father in 2008 and that a speedy exchange and completion would be required because he needed the money. Mr Dawson told Mr A'Court that he was living at Flat 1, 14 Market Street, in Maidenhead. He produced a water bill dated 20 August 2012 addressed to him at that address, an electricity bill dated 28 August 2012, also addressed to him at that address, a bank statement addressed to Mr Dawson and his wife at that address for the period 10 July to 9 August 2012 and what appeared to be a British Passport for Mr Dawson. It is common ground that the passport was a forgery but it is not alleged that Mr A'Court should have been able to detect that such was the case.

Mr Dawson was identified in the English Land Registry by two addresses. One was the address of the property in Wimbledon, and the other was an address in Cambridge. The utility bills that the fraudster produced were for neither. Messrs A'Court & Co did not send any correspondence to the address in Cambridge. Thus the sole link between the fraudster and the property in Wimbledon was the passport in the name of 'Nicholas Robert Dawson'. Though

---

1   This is from Messrs Edward Harte LLP, Brighton, Sussex.
2   [2016] EWHC 789 (Ch), [2016] 4 WLR 81.
3   Pelling QC sitting as a Chancery judge. The quoted passage is from para 5.

there was no specific finding on the point, clearly the passport was a fake. Quality fake passports are readily available.[1]

'Mr Dawson' stressed that he wanted a swift sale. A buyer was found, a Mr Crompton, represented by Messrs Peacock & Co. Remarkably, 'Mr Dawson' said that he wished the transaction to be completed – including not only exchange of contracts (our conclusion of missives) but also completion (our settlement) – within seven days from the initial offer. This did not happen. Messrs Peacock & Co sent to Messrs A'Court & Co an email that included the following: 'Can you please confirm that you have verified your client's identity to meet with money laundering regulations? Further, our client has asked for confirmation of the hospital that your client works at in Abu Dhabi?'[2] Seemingly Mr Crompton or his law firm had smelt something that puzzled them, though we do not know what. The consequence was remarkable. 'Mr Dawson' instantly withdrew from the sale. He emailed his law firm:[3]

> I have just read the e-mail from the buyer's solicitors requesting that their client Mr Crompton wishes me to produce evidence of where I work. Please inform the buyers solicitors I no longer wish to proceed with the sale to Mr Crompton as I now feel that he is trying to prolong the transaction and may not proceed to completion which would leave me in a predicament as I may lose the other possible buyers.

Quickly he found a new buyer, Mr Purrunsing, represented by licensed conveyancers called House Owners Conveyancers ('HOC'). This time the transaction went through. Following completion, Messrs A'Court & Co remitted the money (£470,000) to 'Mr Dawson'. Naturally, neither 'Mr Dawson' nor the money – which was promptly sent to the Middle East – were ever seen again.

Also following completion, HOC applied for registration of what we would call the disposition[4] in favour of their client, Mr Purrunsing. Land Registry, on receiving this application, contacted the Cambridge address.[5] The real Mr Dawson promptly replied saying that this was a fraud, and as a result Land Registry rejected the application. Thus the real Mr Dawson remained registered proprietor, and, apart from a nasty fright, suffered no loss. The loss fell on the unfortunate Mr Purrunsing, who sued both his own conveyancers (HOC) and the law firm that had acted for the fraudster, Messrs A'Court & Co. Against HOC he alleged (i) breach of contract, (ii) negligence, and (iii) breach of trust. Against Messrs A'Court & Co he alleged breach of trust.

---

1 For the prices of fake passports for various states, see www.vocativ.com/241487/fake-passport-prices-black-market/. It is said there that 'a forged or stolen British passport is the fifth most expensive travel document on the dark net with a maximum price of $3,490'. Such a sum is a modest investment when the scale of rewards of conveyancing fraud is considered.
2 Paragraph 16.
3 Paragraph 16.
4 The TR1 form. In England the deed of transfer and the application form are combined in a single document, which, in the ordinary case of a transfer of a fee simple, is the TR1.
5 Why? See below.

The contract/tort case against HOC was based on the claim that they had not taken sufficient care to check that 'Mr Dawson' was the owner. The trust case looks odder to Scottish eyes, but the argument was that when Mr Purrunsing handed over the purchase price to HOC, the latter held the money in trust, and when it was handed over to Messrs A'Court & Co that firm also held it in trust, and that both firms were in breach of trust since the money ended up in the fraudster's pockets. We will not attempt to go further into the deep mysteries of English equity, but merely continue with the story. The core of the case was whether the two firms could obtain equitable relief from their breach of equity, in terms of s 61 of the Trustee Act 1925.[1] The court rejected the application for equitable relief. And for the same reasons that it rejected equitable relief, it also found HOC liable in contract and tort, though that made no practical difference, seeing that they were liable anyway for breach of trust. The result: both HOC and Messrs A'Court & Co were jointly and severally liable to Mr Purrunsing for £470,000.

Both firms, said the court, had been negligent. Not enough had been done to check that the person claiming to own the property was in fact the owner. The sudden breaking-off of the previous deal (with Mr Crompton) was one of the facts that should have alerted Messrs A'Court & Co. They should also have contacted the Cambridge address, and should not have been satisfied with the utility bill, which was unconnected with the property being sold. HOC should have been more inquisitive.

How would an action by a Mr MacPurrunsing have played out in Scotland? Probably Messrs A'Court & Co would not have been liable: see for instance *Cheshire Mortgage Corp Ltd v Grandison*.[2] Whether HOC would have been liable depends on one's assessment of the degree of negligence. The point seems to us unclear. If HOC were not actionably negligent, Mr MacPurrunsing would be without a remedy. Possibly that would be an unsatisfactory result from the standpoint of public policy, and indeed one wonders whether the result in the actual *Purrunsing* case may have been to some extent policy-driven.

In practice, it is unlikely that the Keeper would have contacted Mr MacDawson. The result would have been for Mr MacPurrunsing to be registered as owner. That would not, in itself, have disturbed the ownership of Mr MacDawson, who would have been able to have the Land Register rectified so as to restore his name to the title sheet.[3] Thereafter Mr MacPurrunsing would have been entitled to compensation from the Keeper, under the latter's warranty, unless (see above) HOC were to be regarded as negligent.[4]

---

1 The corresponding provision in Scots law is s 32 of the Trusts (Scotland) Act 1921. But whereas s 32 of the 1921 Act is seldom invoked, s 61 of the 1925 Act is often invoked, because, we think, the woof and weft of English law makes breach of trust easier to happen, or be deemed to happen, than it is here.

2 [2012] CSIH 66, 2013 SC 160. For discussion see *Conveyancing 2011* pp 118–21 and *Conveyancing 2012* pp 150–51.

3 This is because registration does not validate an invalid deed: see Land Registration etc (Scotland) Act 2012 ss 49(4) and 50(2).

4 Negligence by HOC would be attributable to MacPurrunsing, and would in turn undermine the Keeper's warranty: see LR(S)A 2012 s 78.

The English 'property alert service'

As mentioned above, when Land Registry received Mr Purrunsing's application, it contacted the Cambridge address, and that led to the application's rejection. It may be recalled that the same thing happened in the Max Hastings case which we discussed last year.[1] Why did Land Registry so act?

Land Registry offers what it calls a 'property alert service' which is available to 'anyone who feels a registered property could be at risk from fraud'.[2] Mr Dawson's property was a typical at-risk-of-fraud property in that it was (i) above average value, (ii) mortgage-free, and (iii) unoccupied. So he had taken the precaution of subscribing to the 'property alert service'. The same presumably had happened in the Max Hastings case, where the property was (i) above average value, (ii) mortgage-free, and (iii) tenanted. Tenanted properties are at risk because a fraudster can become a tenant and thereby more easily pose as owner, eg showing prospective buyers around. Such a fraudster will have three identities, namely the true identity, the identity as tenant, which will of course be in a false name, and the identity as owner. There will, so to speak, be three different passports in the fraudster's pocket.

The Keeper does not offer such a service. There would be a case for doing so. But it will be noticed that the effect of such a service is to transfer ultimate liability away from Land Registry: by being able to reject certain applications, Land Registry steers clear of indemnity claims. Thus it might be argued that Scotland is better off without such a service. We offer no definite view.

Security-discharge fraud

The third type of conveyancing fraud that we mention here is security-discharge fraud. What happens is that an owner has a loan secured over the property by heritable security, or, south of the border, by mortgage. The owner forges a discharge and has it registered. That does not free the owner of the debt, but it enables the owner to transact with the property on an unencumbered basis. The usual form that this fraud takes is that the owner promptly sells the property and disappears.

In Scotland, and we think in England too, where someone makes a personal application to register a discharge, as opposed to applying through a law firm, the Keeper will usually contact the lender to check that all is in order. That fact makes this fraud hard to pull off.

In *Chief Land Registrar v Caffrey & Co*[3] owners of a property in Warwickshire forged a discharge of the mortgage over it, and their solicitors – the defendants – arranged for the discharge to be registered in the English Land Registry. Because the discharge was lodged for registration by a law firm, Land Registry had no grounds to be suspicious. The owners then borrowed money on mortgage from

---

1 See *Conveyancing 2015* pp 174–76.
2 https://propertyalert.landregistry.gov.uk/.
3 [2016] EWHC 161 (Ch), [2016] PNLR 23.

another lender. When the fraud came to light, the first lender was paid indemnity by Land Registry, and in the present action sought to recover that sum from the law firm that had acted for the fraudulent owners. Although in English law there is no equivalent to s 111 of the Land Registration etc (Scotland) Act 2012, the court held that the law firm was liable. The case is factually unusual in that the owners seem to have been as naïve as they were fraudulent, for they did not sell and vanish, but just waited until the truth inevitably emerged.[1]

SURVIVORSHIP DESTINATIONS

Cases never stop coming before the courts about special destinations. The latest is *Hill v Hill*,[2] in which an attempt was made to challenge one of the leading cases in the area, *Perrett's Trs v Perrett*,[3] and which also raised tricky issues about both the law of prescription and the law of land registration.

Evacuation: an introduction[4]

If there is a survivorship destination, and one party dies intestate, the destination will take effect. So if Jack and Jill are married and co-own a house with a survivorship destination in the title, and Jill dies intestate, Jack inherits her half-share. Of course, that would normally be the case anyway, under the law of intestacy, because a surviving spouse will usually take the predeceasing spouse's share by way of prior rights.[5] But where the value of the property is very high, prior rights may be insufficient, and, moreover, there will be no prior rights at all if Jack and Jill were not married. So even in intestacy a survivorship destination may be important.[6]

What about testate cases? If Jill had died with a will which bequeathed her share in the house to X, either as a specific legacy or as part of a general legacy of all her property, which would prevail: the legacy or the destination in the title? It is a situation that crops up quite often. The answer is: it depends. The first question is whether Jill had the *power* to evacuate the destination and the second is whether, if she did have that power, she validly *exercised* it. Unless the legacy passes both tests, it fails, and Jack takes, not X. In practice it is fairly unusual for both tests to be passed. In other words, in practice most special destinations defeat attempts to evacuate them.

First, the power to evacuate. This can be expressly dealt with in the destination itself, either by a declaration that the destination can be freely evacuated *mortis*

---

1 Cf *Frank Houlgate Investment Co Ltd v Biggart Baillie LLP* 2010 SLT 527, 2012 SLT 256, 2013 SLT 993, 2015 SC 187, on which see eg *Conveyancing 2009* pp 108 ff, *Conveyancing 2011* pp 121 ff, and *Conveyancing 2014* pp 189 ff.
2 [2016] CSOH 10, 2016 GWD 3-66.
3 1909 SC 522.
4 See further G L Gretton and K G C Reid, *Conveyancing* (4th edn, 2011) paras 26-13 ff.
5 Succession (Scotland) Act 1964 s 8.
6 Not to mention the fact that it will carry the half-share without need for confirmation.

causa, or, conversely, that it cannot be so evacuated.[1] The inclusion of such a declaration is, we would suggest, good practice, but unfortunately it is fairly unusual. In the absence of such a declaration, the presumptions of the law have to be applied.[2] And here steps on to the stage *Perrett's Trs v Perrett*, holding that if both Jack and Jill contributed to the price, then, absent agreement to the contrary, neither can evacuate. And of course in most cases where two people buy property together, at least part of the price is contributed by each.

Second, exercise of the power. If the power to evacuate exists (and in most cases it does not), exercising that power requires a special procedure. It is not enough for Jill, in her will, to say that she bequeaths her half share to X. The wording of the legacy has to conform to the requirements of s 30 of the Succession (Scotland) Act 1964.[3] If it does not, the legacy fails.

The whole subject is large, and here we can cover only a fraction of it, but one point that must be mentioned, because reference was made to it in *Hill v Hill*, is that if Jack and Jill are married, and then divorce, the effect of the divorce is to evacuate the destination.[4] This change was introduced by the Family Law (Scotland) Act 2006;[5] now it is governed by the Succession (Scotland) Act 2016.[6]

Hill v Hill

The facts in outline

Mr and Mrs Hill bought a house in Foxbar, Paisley, their title being registered in the Land Register in 1989. There was a standard survivorship destination. The deed stated that it was granted 'in consideration of the sum of £11,812.50 paid to us by George Hill and Agnes Hill'. The relationship soon deteriorated, and in June 1991 Mrs Hill executed a codicil to her will, evacuating, or bearing to evacuate, the destination in relation to her half-share, and leaving the half-share to her son, Mr Hill junior.[7] The legacy conformed to s 30 of the 1964 Act. But did she have the power to evacuate?

Mrs Hill died the following month. There was then a 'nomination' of the half-share in favour of the son.[8] In March 1992 the son registered his title to the half-share in the Land Register. As a result, what the Land Register said

---

1 Or even, though we have not seen this in practice, to say that Jill can evacuate, but that Jack cannot, or conversely.
2 For an excellent, albeit now slightly dated, account of the extensive case law in this area, see M Morton, 'Special destinations as testamentary instructions' 1984 SLT (News) 133.
3 Section 30 prevents a legacy from evacuating a special destination 'unless it contains a specific reference to the destination and a declared intention on the part of the testator to evacuate it'.
4 As opposed to merely conferring the power to evacuate it.
5 Family Law (Scotland) Act 2006 s 19.
6 Succession (Scotland) Act 2016 s 2. Section 19 of the 2006 Act is repealed by para 4 of sch 1 to the 2016 Act.
7 The case actually says only that the codicil purported to evacuate the destination. Nothing else is said. But one can infer that as well as the purported evacuation, the codicil contained a legacy of the share to Mr Hill junior.
8 We take it that the reference here is to a docket under s 15 of the Succession (Scotland) Act 1964.

thereafter was that Mr Hill senior and Mr Hill junior were co-owners of the property. Although the point is not expressly stated, it can be inferred that there was no exclusion of indemnity.

Between 1991, when Mrs Hill passed away, and 1995, both Mr Hill and the son, Mr Hill junior, resided in the property, but in the latter year Mr Hill junior moved out. To what extent Mr Hill senior occupied the house after 1995 is not clear. It seems that the house may have been unoccupied for substantial periods.

Eventually Mr Hill junior raised against his father an action of division and sale in Paisley Sheriff Court. Mr Hill senior responded by raising the present action in the Court of Session.

The pursuer's case

The pursuer sought:[1]

1. Declarator that, on 7 July 1991, he 'acquired a real right to the whole title' of the house, by operation of the survivorship destination in his favour;
2. Declarator that the first defender is not and never has been in possession of the house;
3. Declarator that, as from 4 March 1992, the proprietorship section of the Land Register title to the house was inaccurate 'in respect of the inclusion of the first defender as a half *pro indiviso* proprietor';
4. Production and reduction of the 'pretended confirmation';[2]
5. Production and reduction of the nomination of the first defender to a one-half *pro indiviso* share of the house; and
6. An order ordaining the Keeper of the Registers of Scotland 'to rectify the inaccuracies in the Land Register for the County of Ayr' in respect of the house.

The first conclusion was the key one, and its basis was that Mrs Hill had lacked power to evacuate. Standing the authorities, this was clearly a strong argument.

The defenders were the two executors of Mrs Hill. The first of these was the son (Mr Hill junior) in whose favour the half-share had been, validly or invalidly, transferred. We presume that he was also sued as an individual, though this is not stated in the case.

The defender's case (i): *Perrett's Trs*

The defender's first defence was that *Perrett's Trs* should not be followed. Counsel for the defender:[3]

> submitted … that there is a question as to whether *Perrett's Trs* is still good law. In what I take to be in a reference to section 19 of the Family Law (Scotland) Act 2006 …

---

1 See para 3 of the Opinion of the Lord Ordinary (Lord Jones).
2 This seems to mean the whole confirmation, but if so, that cannot be right. Any reduction would have to be limited to the half-share in dispute. No grounds were advanced for reducing the confirmation in general.
3 Paragraphs 10 and 14.

Mr O'Rourke said that legislation now provides that a special destination in favour of a spouse is not effective after divorce. There remains what counsel described as 'this rather isolated set of circumstances' where parties have separated, but are not divorced. A case of that type would be governed by *Perrett's Trs*. Mr O'Rourke observed that the decision in *Perrett's Trs* is noted in Westlaw UK to have attracted 'mixed or mildly negative judicial treatment'. If one follows through the cases over the years, said counsel, it is clear that there is at least some question as to just how sound the decision is in *Perrett's Trs*.

At the conclusion of his submissions, Mr O'Rourke, somewhat tentatively, invited me to report the case to the Inner House for a ruling on whether or not, in the circumstances of this case, '*Perrett's Trs* continues to be good law.'

After reviewing the authorities, the Lord Ordinary concluded that *Perrett's Trs* was good law and was applicable to the facts of the present case. He declined to report the case to the Inner House. We would add just two thoughts. The first is that *Perrett's Trs*, whether a good or bad decision at the time, is surely too well-embedded now to be got rid of by anything except legislation. The second is something already said above: it seems unwise to leave the question of evacuability to mere implication. We think it advisable to add to the destination an express provision, such as: 'this destination may be evacuated by either party' or 'this destination may be evacuated by neither party, except with consent', or, if so desired, there could be a lopsided provision saying that one party has power to evacuate but not the other.

The defender's case (ii): positive prescription

The second defence was that Mr Hill junior had been in possession of the property for more than ten years and that, accordingly, even if his original title were in any way doubtful, it had now been fortified by prescription under s 1 of the Prescription and Limitation (Scotland) Act 1973. We quote:[1]

Within six months of his return,[2] the pursuer stopped making housekeeping arrangements. He stopped paying utility bills. He stopped purchasing any food. The pursuer would routinely leave the [house] for up to 6 weeks at a time to work on Tiree. The first defender was left to maintain the household and his brother from his own employment income. The first defender's relationship with the pursuer deteriorated thereafter due to the pursuer's chronic neglect of his responsibilities. The first defender continued to live at the [house] until about 1995 when he left due to the pursuer's abusive behaviour. He paid the Council tax bills for a period of four years until 1995. He continued and continues to have access to the [house]. He had keys up until his younger brother paid £8,000 for replacement doors and windows. His younger brother then provided him with a new set of keys. Between 2001 and 2010 there was no communication at all between the pursuer and the first defender. The first defender agreed to meet the pursuer in 2010. The pursuer told the first defender that he had moved out of the [house] and was living with his partner. He told the

---

1 Paragraph 8.
2 The pursuer had been living separately from his wife until shortly before her death, when he moved back in.

pursuer that he occasionally visited the [house] in order to check [it]. The pursuer and the first defender discussed clearing out the [house] and putting [it] up for sale. They agreed to do so and agreed a date to start the process. The pursuer arranged for one week's holiday from work in order to clear out the [house]. On entering the [house], the first defender was astonished to find [it] in an appalling state of neglect and disrepair.

To the argument based on positive prescription the pursuer had two responses. The first was that the defender had not in fact been in possession for ten years and that even his averments did not set forth that he had. 'Access' is not the same as possession. The Lord Ordinary agreed and accordingly this defence failed:[1]

> The first defender avers that he continued to live at the house 'until about 1995'. He avers that he continued and continues to have access to the house, but gives no specification of how, when or in what circumstances such access was ever exercised. He refers to having had keys until his younger brother paid for replacement doors and windows, but he does not say when, or in what circumstances, that was done. The first defender's section 1 [of the 1973 Act] case is bound to fail.

The pursuer also had a legal argument against positive prescription. Mr Hill junior's title had been registered without exclusion of indemnity. Under the Land Registration (Scotland) Act 1979, positive prescription could not run on such titles: it could run only on titles where indemnity had been excluded.[2] Accordingly, argued the pursuer, even if Mr Hill junior had had ten years of possession, it would not have helped him. The rule was changed by the Land Registration etc (Scotland) Act 2012, which amended the 1973 Act so as to allow positive prescription to run on titles in the Land Register whether or not indemnity/warranty is excluded. But in the light of difficult questions, not fully discussed by counsel, as to the retrospective operation of the new rules, the Lord Ordinary did not pronounce on this issue.[3]

The defender's case (iii): negative prescription

The defender also pled that any right held by the pursuer had prescribed negatively under s 8 of the 1973 Prescription Act. But this argument was then abandoned, for reasons that are not given.[4] Perhaps – we merely speculate – the reason lay in sch 3 para (a) to the 1973 Act, which provides that 'any real right of ownership in land' is not subject to negative prescription. This issue is one to which we return below, but at this stage we would add that there is a view that s 7 of the 1973 Act would be applicable here, the argument being that the right to have the Land Register rectified is a personal right. We will not discuss here the strength of that view. It was not put forward by the defence.

---

1 Paragraph 34.
2 For some discussion, see Scottish Law Commission, *Discussion Paper No 125 on Land Registration* (2004) paras 3.4 ff.
3 For this issue see K G C Reid and G L Gretton, *Land Registration* (2017) para 17.11.
4 Paragraph 12.

The defender's case (iv): acquiescence

The defender argued that the pursuer was barred by acquiescence:[1]

> *Esto* Mrs Hill did not have power to evacuate the survivorship destination (which is denied) the pursuer's action for reduction comes many years too late. The pursuer is personally barred from now insisting upon the remedy of reduction. The defender has in any event acted to his cost in the intervening years in respect of the [house]. He has in the knowledge of the pursuer paid bills, including repairs and Council tax. The pursuer has accordingly acquiesced in the defender's ownership. In the intervening period of more than 20 years the pursuer has neither said nor done anything to challenge the first defender's title.

This too was rejected by the Lord Ordinary:[2]

> I am satisfied that the first defender has wholly failed to plead a relevant case of acquiescence in this action. The context in which he attempts to do so is that the pursuer has a real right of ownership of the house, having acquired Mrs Hill's joint *pro indiviso* share immediately on her death. The first defender's title has always been open to challenge, and will remain so unless and until he has continuous possession of it openly peaceably and without judicial interruption for ten years. The first defender avers that the pursuer was aware that he had 'become owner of Mrs Hill's half share' of the house, but that cannot be a foundation for an acquiescence case because, whatever the pursuer may have thought or believed, the first defender did not, in fact, become owner of that half share. Consequently, a 'reasonable time' within which to take action against the first defender did not begin to run until the pursuer had reason to do so. Such reason did not emerge until the first defender raised an action of division and sale in Paisley Sheriff Court. The first defender does not offer to prove that any delay between the raising of that action by him and the raising of this action by the pursuer amounts to the requisite *mora*.

Whilst we do not seek to argue that the acquiescence case was sound, we would with respect note that this passage contains an understandable but nevertheless regrettable error. The statement that 'the first defender did not, in fact, become owner of that half share' is not correct. One of the salient features of the Land Registration (Scotland) Act 1979 was its so-called 'Midas touch'.[3] If the Keeper registered X as owner of property, X became owner of that property.[4] That would be so even if the deed inducing registration was wholly void. Of course, if the deed was void, the result was that the entry in the Land Register constituted an inaccuracy, and inaccuracies were in some types of case rectifiable.[5] But unless and until rectification took place, the person named as owner was owner, however wrongfully. And even as and when rectification happened, it was not

---

1 Paragraph 5.
2 Paragraph 37.
3 Something that has ceased to exist under the Land Registration etc (Scotland) Act 2012.
4 Land Registration (Scotland) Act 1979 s 3(1)(a). For discussion, see Reid and Gretton, *Land Registration* para 2.7.
5 LR(S)A 1979 s 9. That proven inaccuracies in the Land Register were specifically declared unrectifiable is one of the conceptual oddities of the 1979 Act.

retrospective.[1] So the correct description of the position is that on 7 July 1991, when Mrs Hill died, Mr Hill senior became owner of her half-share, but that on 4 March 1992, ownership of that half-share passed to Mr Hill junior, as a result of the acceptance of his application by the Keeper.

The whirligig of title

To what has just been said there is a qualification. The Land Registration etc (Scotland) Act 2012 says that if, on the day on which the Act came into force (8 December 2014), X is the registered owner but the entry is inaccurate, in that Y ought to have been the registered owner, and if, furthermore, the inaccuracy was rectifiable under the old rules,[2] then, as from 8 December 2014, Y became owner and X ceased to be.[3] Assuming, therefore, that Mr Hill senior was always entitled to have the Land Register rectified, the way that ownership of the half-share moved was as follows:

- Until 7 July 1991: Mrs Hill.
- From 7 July 1991 to 4 March 1992: Mr Hill senior.
- From 4 March 1992 to 8 December 2012: Mr Hill junior.
- From 8 December 2012 to date: Mr Hill senior.

After 4 March 1992 the Land Register was inaccurate in showing Mr Hill junior as owner, though in the first of the two periods the inaccuracy was 'bijural' whereas in the second it was 'actual'.[4]

Back to negative prescription

Earlier we speculated that the reason that the defence dropped the argument that the pursuer's right had been extinguished by negative prescription may have been sch 3 para (a) to the 1973 Act, which provides that 'any real right of ownership in land' is not subject to negative prescription. From what has just been said, if this was the reason, it was misconceived, because after 4 March 1992 Mr Hill senior did not have 'any real right of ownership' of the property in question.

Compensation from the Keeper

All the defender's arguments having failed, the Lord Ordinary pronounced decree in favour of the pursuer. As a result, it can be expected that the name of Mr Hill junior will be deleted from the title sheet in the Land Register and that of Mr Hill senior substituted. Mr Hill junior might thereupon be entitled

---

1 See eg *Stevenson-Hamilton's Exrs v McStay* 1999 SLT 1175; *Keeper of the Registers of Scotland v MRS Hamilton Ltd* 2000 SC 271.
2 In other words, under s 9 of the LR(S)A 1979. Section 9 said that in many cases inaccuracies could not be rectified. But here we are dealing with inaccuracies that could be.
3 LR(S)A 2012 sch 4 paras 17–24; for discussion, see Reid and Gretton, *Land Registration* paras 11.9–11.12.
4 For this terminology, see Reid and Gretton, *Land Registration* para 2.8. (The 2012 Act uses the term 'bijural inaccuracy' with reference to 1979 Act titles at para 17 of sch 4.) Under the 2012 Act, unlike the 1979 Act, there is only one type of inaccuracy, an actual inaccuracy.

to compensation from the Keeper,[1] but that would depend on various factors, and especially on what was or was not said to the Keeper at the time of the registration application in 1992. The Keeper is good at keeping things, including application forms. We assume that the 1992 application still exists in the archive record.

PRESCRIPTION AND CIVIL POSSESSION

The facts of *McNaughton v Major*[2] read like the question in the Conveyancing exam which, wisely, you decided not to attempt but which has been giving you nightmares ever since. The last recorded title to (the *dominium utile* of) a cottage near Kilmarnock was in 1868. By a disposition executed on 22 September 1961, John McNaughton, a local coal merchant, acquired the superiority title. A further quarter of a century passed before the disposition was recorded in the Register of Sasines, on 31 March 1987. By that time and for some forty years before, Mr McNaughton's mother had been living in the cottage. The person who was entitled to the *dominium utile* was unknown, and the possession of Mrs McNaughton senior was undisturbed.

After Mrs McNaughton senior died, on 20 May 1991, the cottage lay unused for more than a year. It was in a state of some disrepair. Eventually, towards the end of 1992, an arrangement was entered into with a young couple, Scott and Caroline Major, whereby the Majors were allowed to live in the cottage for a small weekly payment (£15) to Mr McNaughton and on the basis that they would have to meet the cost of repairs. The Majors moved into the cottage and have lived there ever since. Over the years they have spent significant sums of money in carrying out improvements, including putting in two bathroom suites, replacing most of the ceilings, installing new windows, and rewiring the house. Meanwhile, another quarter of a century passed. Finally, in 2006, the Majors stopped making their weekly payments, and arranged for a neighbour to grant them an *a non domino* disposition which they recorded on 22 November 2006. The Majors came close to completing possession for the prescriptive period of ten years. But before they could do so, Alexander McNaughton, as executor nominate of his late father, John, raised an action in the Court of Session in which he sought (i) reduction of the *a non domino* disposition, and (ii) an order ordaining the Majors to vacate the cottage.

Quid juris? – as they used to say in exams. Who was entitled to the cottage? The pursuer (John McNaughton's executor)? The defenders (the Majors)? Some other person who, after years of research, might be able to connect himself back to the last recorded title in 1868? Or, failing such a person, the Crown in the form of the Queen's and Lord Treasurer's Remembrancer?[3] The answer turned on whether prescription had run and, if so, in whose favour.

---

1 In cases of the present type, the applicable rules are to be found in LR(S)A 2012 sch 4 paras 19–21.
2 [2016] CSOH 11, 2016 GWD 3-77.
3 It had been anxiety that the property, if unoccupied, might somehow go to the Crown that had encouraged John McNaughton to enter into the arrangement with the Majors.

The defenders had a title sufficient for prescription but could not, quite, muster the necessary ten years of possession. It was true that they remained in occupation of the cottage, at least for the moment, but as the present action amounted to judicial interruption,[1] the prescriptive clock would have to start again from scratch.

The pursuer's father had also had a title sufficient for prescription. At first sight that might seem surprising, because the disposition which was finally recorded in 1987 in favour of John McNaughton had been in respect of the superiority interest. But, as was typically the case with superiority titles, the disposition took the form of a conveyance of the property and made no reference to the superiority. It was therefore a good title for prescriptive acquisition of the *dominium utile*. Possession, however, was a different matter. As Mrs McNaughton senior's possession had begun long before the recording of the disposition, it might be difficult to attribute her post-1987 possession to a new basis.[2] But in any case she had died in 1991, well short of the ten-year period. So prescription could only have run if the defenders' possession could count as possession of the pursuer's – only if, in other words, John McNaughton could be regarded as having been in civil possession of the cottage through the natural possession of the Majors.

For the purposes of positive prescription, as for many other purposes, civil possession is the equal of natural possession.[3] But, at the margins at least, the scope of civil possession is perhaps not entirely clear. Some textbook definitions were cited to the court.[4] One was:[5]

> Civil possession arises where the person detaining the property does so not, or at any rate not exclusively, for himself, but on behalf of some other person, who is known as the civil possessor. The arrangement is of frequent occurrence. Thus tenants detain on behalf of their landlords, vassals on behalf of their superiors, pledgees on behalf of their debtors, liferenters on behalf of their fiars, and custodiers on behalf of the owners of the goods entrusted to them. ... Invariably detentor and possessor stand in a pre-existing legal relationship, the lawfulness of the former's detention resting on some superior right to possession, most typically ownership, held by the latter.

Another was:[6]

> Natural possession by one person amounts to civil possession in another when it acknowledges or is derived from the right of the civil possessor ... There may be room for argument about who enjoys possession through the natural possessor. It is likely to be the person from whom the natural possessor derives his right or whose claim he acknowledges in some way such as the payment of rent.

Common to both definitions is the idea that the right of the person in natural possession must derive from the right of the person alleged to be in civil

---

1 See Prescription and Limitation (Scotland) Act 1973 s 4.
2 So at least the defenders argued: see para 33.
3 PL(S)A 1973 s 15(1).
4 Paragraph 38.
5 K G C Reid, *The Law of Property in Scotland* (1996) para 121.
6 D Johnston, *Prescription and Limitation* (2nd edn, 2012) para 18.13.

possession. The standard example is landlord and tenant, where the tenant's natural possession derives from his lease with the landlord. Accordingly, in *McNaughton v Major* much of the pursuer's energy was devoted to showing that, for as long as they made weekly payments, the defenders were the tenants of – and therefore possessing for – John McNaughton. But, as the Lord Ordinary (Lord Jones) correctly pointed out, it was not essential to the pursuer's case to establish a lease. Lease might be one example of civil possession but there was no 'definitive list'.[1] All that mattered was that the natural possession acknowledged or was derived from the right of the civil possessor. No doubt there might be a question as to whether the arrangement between Mr McNaughton and the Majors amounted to a lease in the strict sense. Apart from anything else, the weekly payment of £15 was described as being towards the cost of insurance. But while this was far too much to be properly attributable to insurance it was also far too little to qualify as a market rent. Be that as it may, concluded Lord Jones, the defenders' entitlement to possess derived from the pursuer's late father:[2]

> Mr McNaughton allowed the defenders to occupy number 2 [ie the cottage] in return for a weekly payment. If the defenders had not been prepared to make a weekly payment, which, as the McNaughtons knew, far exceeded a *pro rata* contribution to what they paid for insurance, and to agree to carry out any repairs and improvements at their own cost, they would not have been allowed to take possession of number 2. Consequently, it is clear that the defenders occupied number 2 only because they had Mr McNaughton's permission to do so. If he had withdrawn permission, subject to the terms of the agreement between them, they would have had to move out. In the circumstances, the defenders' possession of number 2 was derived from Mr McNaughton's right to possess number 2. There was no other basis for their occupation.

Accordingly, Mr McNaughton became owner of the cottage, at latest, on the tenth anniversary of the day on which the Majors first took up possession and began making weekly payments. And as the pursuer thus had title to the cottage and the defenders did not, decree of reduction of the defenders' *a non domino* disposition would be granted.

Two further points seem worth making. First, as the definitions given above show, a civil possessor is normally taken to be one who has a right to natural possession but who has granted natural possession to someone else. In *McNaughton v Major* it was taken for granted that, following the registration of the disposition in 1987, Mr McNaughton was a person with such a right.[3] That view, however, seems open to question for, until prescription ran in his favour, Mr McNaughton's right to the cottage was one of superiority only, and superiors were not usually entitled to natural possession. This is not to say that the decision in the case is wrong. Rather it is to suggest that the definitions of

---

1 Paragraph 47.
2 Paragraph 55.
3 See eg para 56.

civil possession may be in need of refinement. If Mr McNaughton had chosen to occupy the cottage himself, no one could have doubted that he was in (natural) possession for the purposes of prescription. And where, as in the event occurred, he authorised someone to occupy the cottage on his behalf, this seems equally an example of prescriptive (if civil) possession.

Secondly, it was conceded by the pursuer that he could only succeed if the prescriptive possession was completed before the abolition of the feudal system, and hence of superiorities, on 28 November 2004.[1] The concession need not have been made. The disposition in favour of Mr McNaughton was, on its face, a disposition of the property and not of the superiority interest. It would have remained a good title for prescription even after feudal abolition.

PROPERTY TAXES IN SCOTLAND[2]

Introduction

2016 was an important year in relation to taxation in Scotland generally and that affecting land and buildings in particular. On the broadest front, the tax year 2016–17 was the first in which the Scottish Parliament had to take a significant decision on income tax. Even more significant decisions will now require to be taken each and every year. As for that wholly devolved matter, land and buildings transaction tax ('LBTT'), 2016–17 saw the arrival of additional dwelling supplement ('ADS'). This introduced a new worry for every residential transaction in Scotland. Its introduction, it is fair to say, was much more complicated (as well as lucrative for the Scottish Government) than might have been expected. Apart from those two fundamentals, the subject of property taxes in Scotland continues to demonstrate the difficulties of dealing with a partially devolved system of taxation. That seems likely to be the property lawyer's lot for a good number of years to come.

One of the difficulties facing any Scottish Government is that the timing of the UK Budget process does not give much opportunity to react to changes at the UK level. That may improve in future years. This is because the UK Chancellor has signalled that he will not, other than for exceptional reasons, announce changes to rates and the like in the March Budget. After a Spring Budget in March 2017, intended changes will in future be announced in an Autumn Budget (starting in 2017), leaving much more time for consultation and draft legislation before the start of the tax year in which the changes are to come into effect.

The March Budget will be replaced by a Spring Statement, responding to a Spring forecast from the Office of Budget Responsibility, although the Government reserves the right 'to make changes to fiscal policy at the Spring Statement if the economic circumstances require it'.[3] So, after a final potential

---

1 Paragraph 26.
2 This part is contributed by Alan Barr of the University of Edinburgh and Brodies LLP.
3 HM Treasury, *Autumn Statement 2016* (Cm 9362; www.gov.uk/government/uploads/system/ uploads/attachment_data/file/571559/autumn_statement_2016_web.pdf) para 4.1.

double-dose of major tax changes in 2017, there will be a single dose in future years.

This has a coincidental advantage for the Scottish Government's timetable, in that the Scottish Budget can take account of changes announced for the UK as a whole and the rest of the UK, as appropriate. This is important because, lacking a system similar to Provisional Collection of Tax Resolutions, Scottish tax changes may require primary legislation, for which there is simply not the available time following a March Budget and the imminent commencement of the new tax year. The resulting difficulties were illustrated by the introduction of ADS.

Additional dwelling supplement

Additional dwelling supplement ('ADS') is so pervasive and affects so many conveyancers that it is appropriate to deal with it first and in some detail. It was originally to be called the additional homes supplement and was to some extent a reaction to the announcement of a similar increase in stamp duty land tax rates in the rest of the UK in the 2015 Autumn Statement. But the interaction of the planned introduction of the new charge on 1 April 2016 with the need for primary Scottish legislation meant that the new law had to be rushed through the Scottish Parliament in little more than a month.

A Bill was introduced on 27 January 2016. It passed its Parliamentary stages by 8 March and received Royal Assent on 24 March – a speedy and impressive performance, but perhaps a little too speedy given the technical challenges. However, in what might be said of the basic LBTT legislation, it did its basic job well (the tax is being collected!), with the difficulties being some fuzziness around some of the edges.

The Land and Buildings Transaction Tax (Amendment) (Scotland) Act 2016 came into force for transactions settling on or after 1 April 2016. It inserted a new s 26A and schedule 2A into the Land and Buildings Transaction Tax (Scotland) Act 2013.[1]

When the introduction of ADS was announced, in the Scottish Budget for 2016–17, the estimated receipts were in the very wide range (for relatively small numbers) of £17 to £29 million. By the time the draft legislation was first published, at the end of January 2016, the estimate targeted the exact middle of this range, at £23 million. But the total net revenue from ADS at the end of November was in excess of £60 million; and the anticipated revenue for 2017–18 has been increased to £75 million.[2] These figures demonstrate that ADS may affect rather more transactions than was first thought.

The basics

The basics are really very simple. In lay language, if an individual buys a second dwelling for more than £40,000, whether as a holiday home or as an investment

---

1 Land and Buildings Transaction Tax (Amendment) (Scotland) Act 2016 s 1(2), (3).
2 *Scottish Budget: Draft Budget 2017–18* (15 Dec 2016; www.gov.scot/Resource/0051/00511808.pdf) p 17

to let, then an additional amount of LBTT is chargeable. That additional amount is 3% on top of whatever the 'normal' amount of LBTT would be.[1] The same can apply where certain juristic persons[2] (and occasionally individuals) buy a first dwelling. Thus:

Band	Basic LBTT rates	Additional Dwelling Supplement
Up to £145,000*	0%	3%
£145,001 to £250,000	2%	3%
£250,001 to £325,000	5%	3%
£325,001 to £750,000	10%	3%
£750,001 and above	12%	3%

*Supplement payable only on transactions on or above £40,000.

The Scottish Government and Revenue Scotland did not expect ADS to apply to most transactions. As their Guidance notes say (in the original **bold**):[3]

The vast majority of residential property transactions, such as first time buyers purchasing their first property or homeowners moving from one main residence to another, will not be liable to the ADS.

The scope of the new schedule 2A to the 2013 Act is given by paragraph 2(1):

Transactions relating to second homes etc

This schedule applies to a chargeable transaction if the following conditions are satisfied –

(a) the subject-matter of the transaction consists of or includes the acquisition of ownership of a dwelling,
(b) the relevant consideration for the transaction is £40,000 or more,
(c) at the end of the day that is the effective date of the transaction, the buyer owns more than one dwelling, and
(d) either –
   (i) the buyer is not replacing the buyer's only or main residence, or
  (ii) the buyer is replacing the buyer's only or main residence but the subject-matter of the transaction also includes the acquisition of ownership of one or more other dwellings in addition to the one that the buyer intends to occupy as the buyer's only or main residence.

Schedule 2A applies only to 'chargeable transactions'. A land transaction is a chargeable transaction unless it is (a) an exempt transaction, or (b) otherwise

1 Land and Buildings Transaction Tax (Scotland) Act 2013 sch 2A para 4(2).
2 'Non-individual' buyers, in the terminology of sch 2A para 3.
3 See Revenue Scotland, *Guidance on Additional Dwelling Supplement* (2016; www.revenue.scot/land-buildings-transaction-tax/guidance/lbtt-legislation-guidance/lbtt10001-lbtt-additional-dwelling) para LBTT10011.

exempt from charge.[1] Schedule 1 lists exempt transactions, including (very importantly) those for which there is no chargeable consideration. So, there is no question of gifts becoming liable at 3% where they were not liable before. This is a good illustration of the difference between exempt transactions and those that are chargeable but within the 0% rate band.

Other exempt transactions, which thus do not attract ADS, include residential leases, transactions in connection with divorce and the dissolution of civil partnerships, assents and appropriations by personal representatives and (again importantly) variations of testamentary dispositions (including on intestacy) within two years of death.[2] Security transactions will also generally be exempt, because they are not acquisitions of chargeable interests.[3]

ADS does not apply unless and until dealing with consideration (actual or deemed) above £40,000.[4] This very low starting threshold is perhaps tied to the reporting threshold for LBTT, also set at £40,000. Below this, not only is no tax payable, but Revenue Scotland do not need to know about it. But one questions how often any transaction will fall below the level needed to consider whether ADS applies.

Once the £40,000 threshold has been breached, there is then – at least until the normal rates of LBTT cut in – a return to the 'slab' system of tax. In other words, the 3% is charged on the whole consideration, not just on the amount above £40,000 – and that 3% remains chargeable on all the consideration, however large the transaction. So, a transaction otherwise attracting ADS for a consideration of £40,000 would have no tax; a transaction attracting ADS with the unlikely consideration of £40,100 would attract tax of £1,203.

At the other end of the scale, the marginal rate of tax becomes 15%. The introduction of ADS only emphasises the relatively high rates now chargeable overall and serves as a reminder that all levels of LBTT – including ADS – are chargeable on land and buildings alone. At the top end, every £1,000 that can be legitimately apportioned to moveables starts to look very attractive. This problem – or opportunity – is not as crucial as the cliff-edge which used to apply at the edges of SDLT threshold levels, where the apportionment of some thousands to moveables might bring equally large savings of SDLT. But 15% costs are not to be incurred if at all possible. Reasonable apportionments to moveables are permissible, but they must indeed be reasonable.

It is worth a reminder that consideration might exist other than as a price in a sale. So, in partnership transactions, the consideration will be based on market value; and the same will apply to exchanges. Consideration can also take the form of assets other than money, such as the value of works or, conceivably, services.[5] But perhaps the most hidden type of consideration is in the form of debt. If a transfer of property takes place and that property is subject to debt, which becomes a liability of the transferee, then that debt represents consideration.

---

1 LBTT(S)A 2013 s 15.
2 See LBTT(S)A 2013 sch 1.
3 LBTT(S)A 2013 s 5(1).
4 LBTT(S)A 2013 sch 2A para 2(1)(b).
5 On what constitutes consideration generally, see LBTT(S)A 2013 sch 2.

The subject-matter of the chargeable transaction must consist of or include the acquisition of ownership of a dwelling. So, the acquisition of lesser rights, such as servitudes, is unaffected. But that still leaves open the question of what constitutes a 'dwelling'. This is dealt with by reference to the original LBTT legislation.[1] The definition depends on use or suitability for use as a single dwelling, with land occupied or enjoyed with the dwelling being included. There are lists of various types of building that are automatically included or excluded from being dwellings.[2] One can foresee possible arguments at the beginning and end of a 'dwelling's' life. And some properties (such as a house with a granny flat or a property with a front house and a back cottage) may in fact consist of more than one 'dwelling'.

For properties which include a dwelling along with something else, there is a major difference from other aspects of LBTT. For normal LBTT purposes, and in particular in relation to the rates to be charged, transactions are either residential or non-residential. Residential transactions are those in which the subject-matter of the transaction consists entirely of interests in land which are residential property. Thus mixed transactions are treated as non-residential, with lower rates applying to such transactions thus being chargeable. The rules apply to the whole transaction, on an 'either/or' basis.[3] This principle is not applied in relation to ADS. ADS applies if the transaction consists of *or includes* the acquisition of ownership of a dwelling.[4] So, where there is a mixed transaction, ADS applies to the residential element.

In the majority of cases, the consideration to which ADS will apply is simply the whole consideration for the current transaction. But where one is looking at a mixed transaction, it will be necessary to have a value apportioned to the dwelling element. The apportionment has to be on a 'just and reasonable' basis. That is the totality of guidance on the issue of apportionment; and one can thus anticipate discussion and dispute if the apportionment is considered to be inappropriate in relation to the relevant consideration liable to ADS.

The individual and second homes

ADS applies where, at the end of the day that is the 'effective date' of the transaction, the buyer owns more than one dwelling.[5] The concept of ownership of a dwelling is therefore crucial; and the legislation extends that concept considerably.

Dwellings count whether or not they are situated in Scotland.[6] This may require consideration of foreign concepts of 'ownership' and deciding whether the situation is analogous to ownership in Scotland.[7] In particular, the tenant of a lease for more than 20 years is to be treated as the owner (and thus the landlord

---

1 See LBTT(S)A 2013 sch 2A para 20, applying LBTT(S)A 2013 sch 5 pt 6.
2 LBTT(S)A 2013 s 59(3)–(6), imported by sch 5 para 30.
3 See LBTT(S)A 2013 s 24.
4 LBTT(S)A 2013 sch 2A para 4(3)(b).
5 LBTT(S)A 2013 sch 2A para 2(1)(c).
6 LBTT(S)A 2013 sch 2A para 11(2).
7 LBTT(S)A 2013 sch 2A para 18. This may be of particular relevance to timeshare arrangements.

is not to be so treated).[1] But ownership (anywhere) of an interest worth less than £40,000 is not to be counted.[2] So, one will need a market value for dwellings situated outside (as well as within) Scotland, at least to assess whether that value exceeds £40,000. In most cases that will be obvious, but it is possible that some dwellings will be close to this threshold. If that is the case, for foreign dwellings, currency fluctuations may be relevant. It is not specifically provided for, but it is a reasonable assumption that the conversion should be done at the rate prevailing at the effective date.

It is to be noted that, like the basic charging provision, the £40,000 value for the 'other' property is a cliff-edge provision – there is no sliding scale. If the value of the other property is £39,000, it is ignored entirely. If the value of that other interest is £41,000, then ADS will be charged at 3% on the full value of the new property, however large that new value might be.

Property-investment businesses

There is a somewhat surprising concession to certain taxpayers in paragraph 11(3) of schedule 2A. If one is looking at someone who does not own a main residence, but has already been operating a property-investment business, one might expect that purchase of a main residence would be liable to ADS. But this is not the case if the previous purchases have been subject to ADS. This is counter-intuitive. Note that it is dependent on ADS having been paid on the property-investment business properties (or if it would have been paid on foreign properties). But this is of no assistance if the property-investment business commenced before the introduction of ADS, for then ADS could never have applied; and any dwellings owned by an individual for that business will be counted for these purposes. Revenue Scotland have confirmed that this is the case – there is a difference depending on when the dwellings in the property business were obtained.[3]

Joint and common ownership

One of the widest extensions of the normal concept of ownership takes place in relation to joint and (much more often) common owners. Where two or more persons are jointly entitled to the ownership of a dwelling, each is to be treated as the owner of the dwelling.[4] Any joint or common ownership share, however small, is to be treated as ownership of the whole. Thus if four siblings own together a flat in Spain, valued at £100,000, this will count for each of them as ownership of a dwelling valued at £100,000, rather than the £25,000 ownership interest to which they are economically entitled – and which would, if that was the total value of a dwelling to be considered, be ignored for the purposes of ADS.

---

1 LBTT(S)A 2013 sch 2A para 15.
2 LBTT(S)A 2013 sch 2A para 11(4).
3 See for contrasting positions, examples 9, 13 and 18 in Revenue Scotland, *Guidance on Additional Dwelling Supplement*; the detail in these examples requires to be changed to reflect the differing situations in which operators of property businesses can come to own more than one dwelling.
4 LBTT(S)A 2013 sch 2A para 17.

This deals with the 'other' property. What if the property which is being bought is being acquired jointly? The answer here lies in paragraph 5 of schedule 2A:

Joint buyers

(1) This paragraph applies to a chargeable transaction which satisfies the conditions in paragraph 2(1)(a) and (b) or 3(1)(a) and (b) if there are two or more buyers who are or will be jointly entitled to ownership of the dwelling.
(2) The conditions set out in paragraph 2(1)(c) and (d) or, as the case may be, 3(1)(c) are satisfied if they are satisfied in relation to any one of, or more than one of, the buyers.

Taken together, the provisions on common or joint ownership for both properties mean that if any one of the common owners owns any share of another dwelling, then ADS will apply. This is not a proportionate charge in relation to the purchase price: if the transaction is caught at all for any one of the buyers, it is caught for all of them and for the full purchase price. This may require some careful planning.

However, if one co-owner purchases the share of another, Revenue Scotland accept that this purchase is not liable to ADS, as the purchaser is already treated as owning the whole property.[1]

Deemed ownership: spouses, cohabitants, children

The rules on common ownership do at least involve situations where the buyer, thus widely defined to include co-buyers, has an ownership interest in another dwelling – the marker, even if perceived as an unfair one, of a situation where ADS might be expected to apply. But deemed ownership goes much further than that and brings in the ownership of entirely different individuals.

For the purpose of considering whether the buyer at the end of the effective date owns more than one dwelling:[2]

… a dwelling which is owned by —
(a) the buyer's spouse or civil partner,
(b) the buyer's cohabitant,
(c) a person aged under 16 who is a child of –
   (i) the buyer,
   (ii) the buyer's spouse or civil partner, or
   (iii) the buyer's cohabitant,
is to be treated as being owned by the buyer.

This paragraph only applies for limited purposes. It is not a provision which applies for the purposes of the whole schedule, which might increase the availability of certain reliefs. One gets the downside of deemed ownership but not much by way of upside.

---

1 Revenue Scotland, *LBTT Technical Bulletin 1* (2016; www.revenue.scot/sites/default/files/LBTT%20Technical%20Update%20-%20Oct%2016.pdf) para 7.2.
2 *LBTT Technical Bulletin 1* para 6.

As noted above, a person who is an owner in common with others is to be treated as owning the whole of the dwelling – so the provision just quoted will strike not only if a buyer owns a share in another dwelling, but also if a relative or cohabitant owns a share in another dwelling. The net is very wide.

The inclusion of spouses and civil partners is perhaps only to be expected. But the extension to cohabitants and to the minor children of all of spouses, civil partners and cohabitants might create real practical difficulties, not least the perennial problem of deciding whether a couple is cohabiting. Actual ownership by minors will be unusual in practice, but ownership by trustees for their benefit may be enough. It depends on the type of trust: in essence, a bare or a liferent trust will be treated as ownership by the beneficiary.

The rules expect knowledge of dwellings owned by others of which the buyer may simply have no awareness, nor any legal right to obtain the information. While separation of spouses, civil partners or cohabitants is sufficient to break the connection,[1] the possibility of ADS on future purchases becomes another matter to consider when couples split up.

Two further cases of statutory deemed ownership are worth mentioning here. The tenant's deemed ownership under a long lease has already been referred to. The liferenter in a proper liferent is deemed to be the owner of the property (and the fiar is not).[2]

Start and finish of ownership – the 'effective date'

Ownership is deemed to start (or finish) at the 'effective date' of the relevant transaction, rather than the date of registration.[3] As regards inherited property, Revenue Scotland assert:[4]

> We consider that an inherited dwelling is to be counted as being owned by a beneficiary from the earlier of:
> (a) the date that the period of administration of the estate ends – generally, this is the date the residue of the estate has been ascertained, rather than when the executor has carried out all work in relation to the estate; and
> (b) the date that the dwelling is transferred to the beneficiary – that is the date the executor grants a disposition or a docket transfer in favour of the beneficiary (whether or not registration of title is at a later date).

While the second possibility is certainly true, the first must be open to challenge. The position may also be different for foreign property.

Replacing a main residence

Only an individual (or more than one individual) can replace a main residence in relation to ADS. And if they do so, they will either avoid paying ADS in the

---

1 LBTT(S)A 2013 sch 2A para 6(2), (3).
2 LBTT(S)A 2013 sch 2A para 16.
3 LBTT(S)A 2013 sch 2A para 12. By para 12(4), 'effective date' has the same meaning as in pt 4 of the Finance Act 2003. See in particular s 119 of the latter statute.
4 Revenue Scotland, *LBTT Technical Bulletin 1* para 7.1.

first place, or get it back in due course. This is the main reason why ADS affects only a small minority of property owners. There are two versions of events under which this general principle comes into play – the first where it is truly sequential, in that there is a sale of a main residence which is followed by (or contemporaneous with) the purchase of a new main residence. The second is where the transactions take place in the 'wrong' order – the purchase of the new main residence takes place before the old one is sold (or otherwise disposed of). The latter requires a very specific relief – and more significantly may demand the payment upfront of ADS and its recovery at a later date.

In addition to the basic requirement of owning more than one dwelling and the relevant consideration being £40,000 or more, ADS only applies if either:[1]

(i) the buyer is not replacing the buyer's only or main residence, or
(ii) the buyer is replacing the buyer's only or main residence but the subject-matter of the transaction also includes the acquisition of ownership of one or more other dwellings in addition to the one that the buyer intends to occupy as the buyer's only or main residence.

It is worth drawing attention briefly to sub-paragraph (ii). If the overall transaction involves the purchase of more than one dwelling, it does not matter that the transaction includes the replacement of a main residence. By definition, on the effective date, the buyer will own more than one dwelling; and the fact that one of the newly acquired dwellings will be a replacement main residence cannot save the transaction from being subject to ADS. However, ADS will only be charged on the dwellings that are not replacing the main residence.[2]

In terms of paragraph 2(2) of schedule 2A:

A buyer is replacing the buyer's only or main residence if –
(a) during the period of 18 months ending with the effective date of the transaction, the buyer has disposed of the ownership of a dwelling,
(b) that dwelling was the buyer's only or main residence at any time during the period of 18 months, and
(c) on the effective date of the transaction, the buyer intends to occupy the dwelling that is or forms part of the subject-matter of the transaction as the buyer's only or main residence.

It should be noted that the equivalent period for replacing a main residence in relation to the analogous provisions for a higher rate of SDLT in the rest of the UK is 36 months. This is factor to be borne in mind when advising cross-border clients.

Revenue Scotland have drawn attention the fact that, for example, moving from rented accommodation to purchasing a dwelling for the first time is not 'replacing' a main residence. There has to be ownership (as opposed, for example to a tenancy) of the first residence in order for the new one to be a replacement.[3]

---

1 LBTT(S)A 2013 sch 2A para 2(1)(d).
2 LBTT(S)A 2013 sch 2A para 4(4).
3 See Revenue Scotland, *LBTT Technical Bulletin 1* para 7.3.

For the most part, the application of the rule on replacement will be obvious – the same parties will be selling and then buying (or completing both transactions on the same day). The question of whether a main residence is being replaced only becomes relevant if two properties are owned (or deemed to be owned) at the date of settlement of the purchase in question. If this does need to be considered, there are a range of potential difficulties.

Meaning of 'main residence'

One is whether it is a main residence which is being replaced in the purchase transaction or whether some other property is being bought. 'Residence' and even 'main residence' are words that cause confusion and difficulty – they have a very wide range of different meanings within the tax system. It may or may not be a good thing, but no definition of 'only or main residence' is provided within this legislation. Revenue Scotland, with huge optimism, assert that in most cases where an individual owns more than one dwelling, it will be clear which is the individual's main residence. This does not take us very much further. There is no provision to allow an election to be made – this contrasts with the position for capital gains tax where more than one residence is owned, where as long as each dwelling has actually been used as a residence, the taxpayer can effectively elect which one is to be treated as the main residence and thus qualify for principal private residence exemption.[1]

In relation to that exemption, where no election is made, then the question becomes one of fact. But at this point, Revenue Scotland depart from the position taken by HMRC with regard to capital gains tax, and turn instead to that jointly adopted by themselves and HMRC when considering whether someone is a 'Scottish taxpayer'.[2] If HMRC has already made a determination in this regard and the circumstances have not changed, Revenue Scotland will accept the same position. So, what *is* that position? The test is very much a qualitative one, not a quantitative one. It is perfectly possible to spend less time at one's 'main' residence than any other residence one may have. The test for whether or not one is a Scottish taxpayer is gradually becoming better known – but it is one which depends on the rather nebulous concept of 'home'.[3]

A two-part test

There is a two-part test in relation to replacing a main residence. The first part involves looking at the residence disposed of. It must have been the only or main residence of the buyer in the current transaction at some point in the 18 months prior to the date of settlement in the current transaction. The second part of the test is whether the buyer intends to occupy the new dwelling being bought as his or her only or main residence.

---

1 See Taxation of Chargeable Gains Act 1992 s 222(5).
2 Revenue Scotland, *Guidance on Additional Dwelling Supplement* para LBTT10020.
3 See HMRC, *Scottish Taxpayer Technical Guidance* (updated to 31 Aug 2016; www.gov.uk/hmrc-internal-manuals/scottish-taxpayer-technical-guidance).

The first question is clearly one of fact, but it is quite complex. The residence must have been occupied – but does that occupation have the necessary quality to meet the Revenue Scotland test of being the main residence?

The second question is one of intention. That is necessarily subjective; but there may be objective evidence available, such as that the buyer is continuing to live elsewhere or is taking steps to rent out the new property, which indicates that there is no intention that the new property will be the main residence.

Here there are serious traps. This can be seen in a basic example.

Example

Bob and Brenda are a married couple, buying their first property together. Until now they have been living in a property wholly owned by Brenda. Their new purchase will be in joint names. Brenda's sale and their common purchase are scheduled to settle on the same day. Brenda owns a share in a holiday home. Bob owns no other dwelling.

At first sight, and if one was considering the policy of the legislation, then one would think that this should qualify for the relief for replacing a main residence. As far as Bob is concerned, he has no other dwelling; as far as Brenda is concerned, she is replacing her main residence with a share in her new main residence. Surely ADS should not be payable? But 'should not' is not 'is'. The 'buyer' here is the combination of Bob and Brenda. In terms of paragraph 5(2) of schedule 2A, the condition, for ADS, that the buyer is not replacing the buyer's only or main residence is satisfied if 'satisfied in relation to any one of ... the buyers'. So, one of the buyers here (Bob) is not replacing his main residence, because he has never owned one. ADS therefore applies.

To escape from this unexpected result may require some planning – and a degree of artificiality. Furthermore, such arrangements may cause difficulties with lenders, who may (for example) require both members of a couple to become owners of the new property. It may cause problems in relation to other taxes (such as inheritance tax, for an unmarried couple). It is an added complication in what should be a straightforward situation. The same applies to an even greater extent with couples who have split up and where the ownership of matrimonial property, including dwellings, may be dealt with without considering the 18-month deadlines.

Purchase before sale

Thus far the replacement provisions have been considered on the basis of sale taking place before purchase. If the purchase takes place first, then the starting point is that ADS will apply, simply because the buyer will own another dwelling at the end of the effective date. But if the existing main residence is later sold, then the ADS can be repaid.[1] The same principles apply to this form of the relief as that which is available when purchase follows sale. The dwelling later disposed of must have been the main residence of the person disposing. It should be noted that the relief is not available if what is disposed of is the

---

1 LBTT(S)A 2013 sch 2A para 8.

subject of the transaction originally chargeable to ADS – it must be the original main residence.

What is envisaged here is that a new main residence is purchased at a time when it is not possible to sell an existing main residence, but a sale then takes place shortly after the new main residence is purchased. In such cases, ADS will not be payable (the transaction will become exempt from ADS); and if it has been paid then it can be recovered.

A period of 18 months after the purchase is allowed for the sale or other disposal.[1] If the time limit is approaching, the taxpayer may have to decide what to do about the property; for if the period passes with both main residences still owned, then the ADS will not be recoverable. If original property cannot actually be sold, can it be disposed of so that the recovery can be made? Here, the rules on deemed ownership may come back into play. It will not be sufficient to have a disposal which leads to the property continuing to be deemed to be owned by the taxpayer. So, to take obvious examples, disposals to a spouse, civil partner, minor child or a bare trust for the taxpayer will be insufficient. It will thus have to be a 'real' disposal. This may have other tax consequences, even if it is a gift. Thus (for example) an outright disposal to an adult child will be a potentially exempt transfer for inheritance tax purposes. If the property or the proceeds of its sale are later returned to the original owner, then this will be a PET by the transferee. Any attempt to structure matters so that it never leaves the estate of the original owner for IHT purposes may risk being ineffective for LBTT. It is possible, although unlikely, that an actual transfer may have advantages if some estate planning is contemplated in any event.

The mechanics of the relief, when available, depend on how quickly the original main residence is sold. There are three possibilities.[2]

If the sale transaction completes before the LBTT return for the purchase is submitted, there is no need to pay ADS at all, even though technically the buyer is liable because he does indeed own more than one dwelling at the end of the effective date of his purchase. So, if the delay in selling the old main residence is only a few days, it may be tempting to delay the submission of the LBBT return. There are dangers here, however. If the delay is too long, then this may be in breach of the arrangements under which registration in the Land Register can take place in advance of the tax being paid and the return submitted – the so-called 'arrangements satisfactory'. And if one actually delays registration of the new property, the dangers are as obvious as they always are in relation to such delays.

The second possibility is that settlement of the purchase has taken place and the LBTT return has been made. If the gap between purchase and sale is less than 12 months, then the appropriate course is an amendment of the return.

The third possibility is that more than 12 months have elapsed. In that case a separate repayment claim is permitted.

---

1 In addition, the property now being sold must have been the main residence within the 18 months preceding sale.
2 Revenue Scotland, *Guidance on Additional Dwelling Supplement* para LBTT10050.

Non-individual buyers

Purchases by 'non-individual' buyers are set out in the legislation as a distinct category of transaction to which ADS will apply. In fact, the provision – paragraph 3 of schedule 2A – covers a number of different situations. The basic condition (the acquisition of ownership of a dwelling for more than £40,000) is the same as in the 'ordinary' charging provision.[1] The additional possibilities start with the buyer not being an individual.

In principle, any purchase of a dwelling by a person who is not an individual is caught by ADS. This is obviously aimed at companies. There has of course over recent years been a bit of a tax assault at the UK level on residential property owned by companies – the Annual Tax on Enveloped Dwellings and its gradual extension to less valuable properties (now down to £500,000),[2] increased rates of capital gains tax, and a range of other measures. So, any purchase by a company is caught, at any level of consideration over £40,000. It should be remembered that in most cases any transfer of a property to a company connected with the transferor, whether for actual consideration or not, is treated as if it were a purchase at market value.

The same applies to foreign entities. Paragraph 3 probably also applies to a direct purchase of a dwelling by a partnership, although that is caught in most cases by later provisions. This is intended, among other things, to prevent a fairly basic avoidance strategy in which dwellings other than the first one could be bought through a series of individual, wholly-owned companies.

There are of course other entities which are affected as non-individuals, such as statutory bodies, possibly societies and clubs, and more esoteric entities. Among the entities undoubtedly affected are local authorities, adding to local government expense for the benefit of central government. There is no general relief available for local authorities; even in compulsory purchase, where there is a relief, it is restricted where it takes place for the local authority's own purposes.

As already mentioned, paragraph 3 also applies to certain purchases by individuals. Here there are, or may be, surprises. ADS is to apply if the acquisition is made in the course of a business the sole or main activity of which is investing or dealing in chargeable interests.[3] If the owner of a main residence buys his first property for investment, this will be caught for ADS in any event, by the 'ordinary' charging provision. But what about the position where someone who does not own any other dwelling buys his first property to let out? That would appear to be caught, as the first purchase for a property-investment business. But that seems to depend on whether the business has actually started. The ADS Guidance at least seems to contemplate that this first purchase may not be liable to ADS.[4] So it may be necessary to decide whether in fact there is a business, or whether what may become a business has actually started at the time at which

---

1   Ie in LBTT(S)A 2013 sch 2A para 2, discussed above.
2   See p 229 below. The ATED is still fully applicable even although part of the reason for its introduction was SDLT avoidance.
3   LBTT(S)A 2013 sch 2A para 3(2).
4   Revenue Scotland, *Guidance on Additional Dwelling Supplement* para LBTT10016.

this is relevant. But the uncertainty and vagueness that this view creates are not welcome. It would seem to leave open to any first purchaser to assert that, at the time of purchase, he does not know what he might do with the property. He might live there. He might leave it empty. He might let it out. He would not seem to have a property business at that point.

Trusts

The provisions on trusts in relation to ADS are rather confusing and seem to overlap to some extent. The policy is reasonably clear – to apply ADS to purchases of dwellings by trustees as if they were not individuals – but, in relation to bare trusts and (in effect) interest in possession trusts, the legislation works as if the beneficiary of such trusts were the buyer (or owner of other property). The starting point is that even individual trustees acting as such are, at least to some extent, treated as if they were non-individual buyers.[1] Corporate trustees are presumably simply caught by the very fact of not being individuals.

Liability will not apply to all trusts and may not apply to some trusts at different times. This is because bare trusts and (in effect) liferent trusts are treated as transparent. The position depends not on the trustees but on the beneficiary and on whether that beneficiary owns any other dwellings.[2] For bare trusts, that is much as might be expected; in general terms, they are ignored for LBTT and the position of the beneficiary is looked at instead.[3]

The same applies where a beneficiary has a 'relevant interest'. A beneficiary has a relevant interest in a dwelling if he is entitled to (a) occupy the dwelling for life, or (b) income (whether net or gross) in respect of the dwelling.[4] This must be assessed at the time of the relevant purchase. So, in most cases, if the trust provisions are wide enough, there may be an answer to a possible ADS charge by giving a beneficiary one or both of the rights specified, at the time that the trustees make the purchase. There may of course be other tax effects in this connection, although less so since 2006.

There are other provisions which in effect provide a 'mirror': when looking at the personal position of a beneficiary with a relevant interest, the ownership of other dwellings by the trust will be taken into account.[5]

Reliefs and exemptions

Normal LBTT reliefs apply to ADS as much as to the basic levels of LBTT. There is one new relief introduced for ADS, that being for the purchase of six or more dwellings in a single transaction.[6] There are circumstances where it may be important to argue that there are six separate dwellings involved in a purchase, to take advantage of this. Thus the purchase of an estate as a

---

1 LBTT(S)A 2013 sch 2A para 3(5), (6).
2 LBTT(S)A 2013 sch 2A paras 13, 14 and 20.
3 LBTT(S)(A) 2013 sch 18 paras 5–9.
4 LBTT(S)A 2013 sch 2A para 20.
5 LBTT(S)A 2013 sch 2A para 7.
6 LBTT(S)A 2013 sch 2A para 9.

mixed purchase (with both residential and non-residential elements) and with five cottages would require an apportionment of the value of the five cottages, with ADS being applied to that value. But if there were six cottages then ADS would not apply, and the whole thing would be chargeable only at commercial rates.

In a related area, there is a slight modification to the rules on multiple dwellings relief. This provides relief where more than one dwelling is purchased, so that the taxpayer is not taken into higher bands of tax simply because of the additional dwellings. The relief is much less important under the slice system for LBTT than under a slab system, but it can still be significant. The difference means that once the tax on each dwelling has been calculated, the total tax is calculated by adding them up, rather than by multiplying the average tax by the number of dwellings. It can make a difference. If ADS is payable on only some of the dwellings (because one may be a replacement main residence, for example), then the tax on each dwelling will not be the same; and it is necessary to add up the tax on each one to get to the total tax.[1] The change is complex.

Administration

In many ways, the administration situation for ADS is astonishingly simple. One additional question is added to the online and paper return, and further details are requested only if repayment (because of the replacement of a main residence) is likely to be needed. Otherwise, all that is required is to put the amount liable to ADS. There is an additional box in the calculation section for the amount of ADS. A separate (and simple) repayment claim form is available for when a main residence is disposed of after the purchase of a new one.

This simplicity may conceal a wealth of background detail required in discussion with a purchasing client as to whether ADS in fact applies.

Other LBTT matters

Rates and the future

The 'normal' rates of LBTT for residential property, the rate of ADS and the rate of LBTT for commercial property are all intended to remain unchanged for 2017–18. The same applies to all thresholds. This was announced in the Scottish Budget on 15 December 2016.[2] It remains to be seen whether any changes in the rate or thresholds in SDLT for the rest of the UK will prompt a change from this intention, but this will perhaps be less likely in future years, at least after 2017, for the reasons given above in relation to changes in the UK Budget process.

---

1 See amendments made to LBTT(S)A 2013 sch 5 by the Land and Buildings Transaction Tax (Amendment) (Scotland) Act 2016 s 2(1)(d).

2 *Scottish Budget: Draft Budget 2017–18* (15 Dec 2016; www.gov.scot/Resource/0051/00511808.pdf pp 15–17.

Technical guidance, confirmations and changes of view

Revenue Scotland have published what is presumably the first in a series of Technical Bulletins.[1] This provides a selection-box of new and revised views. A welcome change is that it is now accepted that where a charity is one of a number of purchasers of property in common, charity relief will be available for the charity's share of the purchase.[2] It is made clear that holiday homes and lets are considered to be residential and also to be dwellings for the purpose of ADS.[3] There is a more confusing attempt to define where property moves from being commercial to residential or vice-versa.[4]

It is confirmed that the principles of the *Prudential* case[5] will be applied for LBTT. This means that, depending on the terms of contracts, the consideration given for works to be carried out will not be treated as consideration for the land to be purchased, and thus will not be liable to LBTT.[6]

Less welcome is confirmation of Revenue Scotland's views on *in specie* transfers of pension funds, to the effect that if land and buildings are involved, such transfers give rise to liability to LBTT, on the basis that (a) such a transfer is a land transaction and (b) the assumption of the liability by the receiving pension fund is debt as consideration. This view is in contrast to that taken by HMRC in exactly analogous situations for stamp duty land tax.[7]

In relation to leases, Revenue Scotland have confirmed their view that variations of leases (other than of the rent alone) can be liable to LBTT.[8] More generally, increased rent will be quantified by a comparison of the rent following a variation with that actually payable before the variation (rather than the original rent in the varied lease).[9] On a transitional issue, where substantial performance of a lease took place before 1 April 2015 (and thus before LBTT was introduced), but the lease itself was signed on or after that date, that completion of the lease is an LBTT event, which may have LBTT consequences in its own right but also makes the lease subject to the provisions for three-yearly reviews.[10]

Revenue Scotland have also confirmed the unfortunate if not outright ludicrous effects of s 14(1)(c) of the Act.[11] Where A contracts to sell to B and, before completion, B contracts to sell to C, on conclusion of missives between parties B and C, C becomes 'entitled to call for a conveyance'. This is treated as triggering 'substantial performance' of the A to B transaction and creating a tax point, following which the LBTT on the A to B transaction becomes payable in its entirety. It is simply unbelievable that the undoubted policy intention that there

---

1 Revenue Scotland, *LBTT Technical Bulletin 1* (2016; www.revenue.scot/sites/default/files/LBTT%20Technical%20Update%20-%20Oct%2016.pdf).
2 *LBTT Technical Bulletin 1* para 1.
3 *LBTT Technical Bulletin 1* para 2.1.
4 *LBTT Technical Bulletin 1* para 2.3.
5 *Prudential Assurance Co Ltd v IRC* [1993] 1 WLR 211.
6 *LBTT Technical Bulletin 1* para 3.
7 *LBTT Technical Bulletin 1* para 4.
8 *LBTT Technical Bulletin 1* para 5.1.
9 *LBTT Technical Bulletin 1* para 5.2.
10 *LBTT Technical Bulletin 1* para 5.3.
11 *LBTT Technical Bulletin 1* para 6.1.

would not be a general sub-sale relief for LBTT should also have the consequence of advancing the date of payment of LBTT for the original transaction, but that is the line that is being maintained.

In a further contrast with views taken by HMRC, Revenue Scotland consider that payments of less than 90% of the consideration in a transaction may amount to a substantial amount, thus triggering 'substantial performance' of a contract.[1]

Scottish landfill tax

Rates of Scottish landfill tax for 2016–17 were set by the Scottish Landfill Tax (Standard Rate and Lower Rate) Order 2016[2] at £84.40 per tonne (standard rate) and £2.65 (lower rate). In the Scottish Budget, it was confirmed that the rates here are to be increased to the planned UK rates for 2017–18, which are £86.10 (standard rate) and £2.70 (lower rate). The credit rate for the Scottish Landfill Communities Fund (SLCF) is to be maintained at 5.6%, which exceeds the planned UK credit rate.[3]

Details of material which qualifies for the purposes of the lower rate of Scottish landfill tax have been set out in a statutory instrument.[4] The schedule to that Order lists, in eight groups, the description of the qualifying materials with any conditions given alongside. Notes to the schedule amplify the descriptions.[5]

UK taxes on land

High-value and other residential property

The additional 3% charge which in Scotland came in the form of ADS (discussed above) was also imposed as a supplementary stamp duty land tax charge elsewhere in the UK.[6] The provisions to achieve this are very similar to those imposing ADS, but not exactly the same – indicative of a trend under which Scottish tax law can be expected to diverge to a greater extent from that in the rest of the UK as tax devolution progresses.

In the UK context, the advance of additional taxes on residential property, particularly where this is held other than by an individual, continues; and the meaning of 'high value' in this context continues to diminish. The Annual Tax on Enveloped Dwellings[7] applies now (2016–17) to dwellings with a value above £500,000,[8] which increases considerably the number of properties affected. New reliefs were introduced from ATED for certain equity release schemes (home

---

1 *LBTT Technical Bulletin 1* para 6.2. See LBTT(S)A 2013 s 14(1)(b).
2 SSI 2015/94.
3 See *Scottish Budget: Draft Budget 2017–18* pp 17–18.
4 Scottish Landfill Tax (Qualifying Material) Order 2016, SSI 2016/93.
5 SSI 2016/93 sch.
6 Finance Act 2016 s 128, amending Finance Act 2003, primarily by the insertion of a new schedule 4ZA.
7 Finance Act 2013 pt 3, schs 33–35. See *Conveyancing 2013* pp 206–07 and *Conveyancing 2015* pp 210–11.
8 Finance Act 2014 s 110.

reversion plans),[1] and some properties occupied by employees, as well as for caretaker flats owned by management companies from 1 April 2016.[2] A new provision was introduced to extend the relief from ATED for alternative property finance transactions, making it clear that the relief is available for the rather different arrangements that apply in Scotland as compared to the rest of the UK.[3] The annual amount of ATED charges was increased in line with indexation.[4]

Quite apart from the ATED rules on capital gains tax, which have been in force for a number of years, 2015 brought the introduction of capital gains tax for all non-residents on the disposal of residential property.[5] Slight amendments were made to this regime in 2016, correcting some errors and removing the demand for a return in the case of a no gain/no loss disposal.[6] The incredibly tight 30-day deadline for reporting such disposals should be borne in mind.[7]

Following consultation, the 'wear and tear' allowance previously available to landlords (a deduction of 10% from gross rents) was abolished with effect from April 2016.[8] This was replaced with a relief that enables landlords of residential dwelling houses to deduct the costs they actually incur on replacing domestic items in the property.[9]

Minor amendments have been made to the restriction in the deduction for individual landlords' finance costs, including interest, which will start to come into effect from 2017–18.[10] These changes put beyond doubt that the new, more limited deduction is available to beneficiaries of deceased persons' estates; ensure that the total income restriction to the tax reduction applies where the relevant finance costs are higher than total income; ensure that total income is calculated after other reliefs; and ensure that any carried-forward tax reduction is given in any subsequent years in which property income is received, even where there is no restriction in that subsequent year.[11]

In order to simplify and reduce administration, two new allowances of £1,000 each are to be introduced for trading and property income. Individuals with income below that threshold will no longer need to declare or pay tax on that income.[12]

---

1 Finance Act 2016 s 134, inserting s 144A into Finance Act 2013.
2 Finance Act 2016, s 135, amending ss 145 and 146 and inserting s 147A into Finance Act 2013.
3 Finance Act 2016, s 136, amending s 157 and inserting s 157AA into Finance Act 2013.
4 Annual Tax on Enveloped Dwellings (Indexation of Annual Chargeable Amounts) Order 2016, SI 2016/401.
5 Finance Act 2015 s 37, sch 7.
6 Finance Act 2016 ss 90 and 91.
7 Taxes Management Act 1970 s 12ZB, inserted by Finance Act 2015 sch 7 para 43.
8 Finance Act 2016 s 74, repealing Income Tax (Trading and Other Income) Act 2005 ss 308A–308C and providing transitional provisions.
9 Finance Act 2016 s 73, inserting s 311A into Income Tax (Trading and Other Income) Act 2005, and s 250A into Corporation Tax Act 2009.
10 Finance (No 2) Act 2015 s 24, inserting ss 272A, 272B, 274A and 274B into Income Tax (Trading and Other Income) Act 2005 and making similar changes for property partnerships in Income Tax Act 2007.
11 Finance Act 2016 s 26, inserting the lengthy new ss 274A, 274AA, 274B and 274C into Income Tax (Trading and Other Income) Act 2005.
12 See HM Treasury, *Autumn Statement 2016* (Cm 9362) para 4.14.

In a promised move, further extensive amendments are made to the new[1] additional residence nil-rate band for inheritance tax. The changes continue the relief where the taxpayer downsizes or has otherwise ceased to own the relevant home and other assets are left to descendants. The draft legislation was amended before enactment to clarify the date of disposal and allow the relief to apply where certain disposals by trustees are involved.[2]

In a move in the other direction, further progress has been made in plans to bring into charge to IHT the ownership of UK residential property through sophisticated structures (such as trusts and companies) by non-domiciled persons. Detailed draft legislation indicates that this is an extensive change, and will stretch to the creditor's interest in loans used to finance the purchase of such property. This will in effect be a further extension of the ATED regime, although without the restriction to (relatively) higher-value property.[3]

Offshore avoidance

Detailed legislation has been introduced to ensure that all profits from dealing in or developing UK land are taxed fully in the UK, regardless of whether the business is resident in the UK or whether there is a UK permanent establishment.[4] These new rules will make it all the more important to distinguish between dealing and investment in land.

The Scotland Acts 2012 and 2016

The Scottish rate of income tax came into effect on 6 April 2016. Under changes introduced by the Scotland Act 2012,[5] the basic, higher and additional rates of income tax were reduced by 10 percentage points and the Scottish rate of income tax was then added back to the reduced amount. The resulting rate was then applied to non-savings income. The Scottish rate of income tax was set at 10%, thus maintaining for 2016–17 the overall rate for Scottish taxpayers on all incomes at the same level as in the rest of the UK.[6]

This form of the power to set a Scottish rate of income tax will last for only one year. From 2017–18, it will be replaced by new powers from the Scotland Act 2016. Under these powers, the Scottish Parliament can set by resolution[7] all rates and thresholds of income tax (including additional and zero rates).[8] Amendments are also made to the Income Tax Act 2007 to establish potentially

---

1 From April 2017 in a phased introduction.
2 Finance Act 2016 s 93, sch 15, amending and extending ss 8D–8M of the Inheritance Tax Act 1984 which were inserted by the Finance Act 2015 s 9(4).
3 See *Autumn Statement 2016* para 4.15 and draft legislation published in December 2016.
4 Finance Act 2016 ss 76–82, making extensive amendments (including forestalling provisions) to Corporation Tax Act 2009, Corporation Tax Act 2010 (inserting pt 8ZB), Income Tax (Trading and Other Income) Act 2005, and Income Tax Act 2007 (inserting pt 9A).
5 Scotland Act 2012 ss 25–27, amending Income Tax Act 2007 s 6.
6 See Resolution of the Scottish Parliament, 10 Feb 2016; *Scotland's Spending Plans and Draft Budget 2016–17* (2015; www.gov.scot/Resource/0049/00491140.pdf) ch 2.
7 A Scottish rate resolution.
8 Scotland Act 2016 s 13, amending Scotland Act 1998 s 80C.

differing Scottish rates not necessarily tied to the level of UK basic, higher and additional rates.[1] These Scottish rates will apply only to non-savings income. The responsibility for defining the income tax base, including setting or changing income tax reliefs, continues to rest with the UK Government.

The Scottish Government confirmed its policy in relation to the Scottish rates of income tax in December 2016. They proposed freezing the basic rate of income tax at 20%, as well as the higher and additional rates at 40% and 45% respectively. This is the same as in the rest of the UK. However, they also proposed that the higher rate of income tax threshold would increase by inflation to £43,430 in 2017–18, as compared with the UK Government proposed figure of £45,000. The Scottish threshold was later further reduced, to an unchanged amount of £43,000. The Scottish Government also confirmed that the higher rate of income tax threshold will increase by a maximum of inflation in all future years of this Parliament.[2] This again contrasts with a target of £50,000 for the UK threshold in the same timescale.

In the context of land, it is important to note that income from land is treated as coming from a property business and is thus not categorised as savings income. The Scottish rate will affect the rental profits of Scottish taxpayers wherever their property business is located; but it will not affect the profits from a Scottish property business unless the owner of that business is a Scottish taxpayer.

In taxes exclusively affecting land, any tax on the commercial exploitation of aggregates (currently aggregates levy in the UK) will join LBTT and Scottish landfill tax to become a fully devolved tax.[3] There are still apparently legal issues to be resolved before this aspect of devolved tax is implemented.[4]

---

1 Scotland Act 2016 s 14. Consequential changes to other parts of the Taxes Acts, including the Taxation of Chargeable Gains Act 1992, are made by the Scotland Act 2016 s 15, which also provides for any further necessary changes to be made by statutory instrument.
2 See *Scottish Budget: Draft Budget 2017–18* pp 14–15.
3 Scotland Act 2016 ss 18 (inserting s 80M into the Scotland Act 1998) and 19.
4 See *Scottish Budget: Draft Budget 2017–18* p 18.

❧ PART V ❧
TABLES

TABLES

CUMULATIVE TABLE OF DECISIONS ON VARIATION OR DISCHARGE OF TITLE CONDITIONS

This table lists all opposed applications under the Title Conditions (Scotland) Act 2003 for variation or discharge of title conditions. Decisions on expenses are omitted. Note that the full opinions in Lands Tribunal cases are usually available at http://www.lands-tribunal-scotland.org.uk/records.html.

Restriction on building

Name of case	Burden	Applicant's project in breach of burden	Application granted or refused
Ord v Mashford 2006 SLT (Lands Tr) 15; *Lawrie v Mashford* 21 December 2007	1938. No building.	Erection of single-storey house and garage.	Granted. Claim for compensation refused.
Daly v Bryce 2006 GWD 25-565	1961 feu charter. No further building.	Replace existing house with two houses.	Granted.
J & L Leisure Ltd v Shaw 2007 GWD 28-489	1958 disposition. No new buildings higher than 15 feet 6 inches.	Replace derelict building with 2-storey housing.	Granted subject to compensation of £5,600.
West Coast Property Developments Ltd v Clarke 2007 GWD 29-511	1875 feu contract. Terraced houses. No further building.	Erection of second, two-storey house.	Granted. Claim for compensation refused.
Smith v Prior 2007 GWD 30-523	1934 feu charter. No building.	Erection of modest rear extension.	Granted.
Anderson v McKinnon 2007 GWD 29-513	1993 deed of conditions in modern housing estate.	Erection of rear extension.	Granted.
Smith v Elrick 2007 GWD 29-515	1996 feu disposition. No new house. The feu had been subdivided.	Conversion of barn into a house.	Granted.

Name of case	Burden	Applicant's project in breach of burden	Application granted or refused
Brown v Richardson 2007 GWD 28-490	1888 feu charter. No alterations/new buildings	Erection of rear extension.	Granted. This was an application for renewal, following service of a notice of termination.
Gallacher v Wood 2008 SLT (Lands Tr) 31	1933 feu contract. No alterations/new buildings.	Erection of rear extension, including extension at roof level which went beyond bungalow's footprint	Granted. Claim for compensation refused.
Jarron v Stuart 23 March and 5 May 2011	1992 deed of conditions. No external alteration and additions.	Erection of rear extension.	Granted. Claim for compensation refused
Blackman v Best 2008 GWD 11-214	1934 disposition. No building other than a greenhouse.	Erection of a double garage.	Granted.
McClumpha v Bradie 2009 GWD 31-519	1984 disposition allowing the erection of only one house.	Erection of four further houses.	Granted but restricted to four houses.
McGregor v Collins-Taylor 14 May 2009	1988 disposition prohibiting the erection of dwellinghouses without consent.	Erection of four further houses.	Granted but restricted to four houses.
Faeley v Clark 2006 GWD 28-626	1967 disposition. No further building.	Erection of second house.	Refused.
Cattanach v Vine-Hall	1996 deed of conditions in favour of neighbouring property. No building within 7 metres of that property.	Erection of substantial house within 2 metres.	Refused, subject to the possibility of the applicants bringing a revised proposal.
Hamilton v Robertson, 10 January 2008	1984 deed of conditions affecting five-house development. No further building.	Erection of second house on site, but no firm plans.	Refused, although possibility of later success once plans firmed up was not excluded.
Cocozza v Rutherford 2008 SLT (Lands Tr) 6	1977 deed of conditions. No alterations.	Substantial alterations which would more than double the footprint of the house.	Refused.
Scott v Teasdale 22 December 2009	1962 feu disposition. No building.	New house in garden.	Refused.

Name of case	Burden	Applicant's project in breach of burden	Application granted or refused
Rennie v Cullen House Gardens Ltd 29 June 2012	2005 deed of conditions. No new building or external extension.	Extension of building forming part of historic house.	Refused.
Hollinshead v Gilchrist 7 December 2009	1990 disposition and 1997 feu disposition. No building or alterations.	Internal alterations.	Granted.
Tower Hotel (Troon) Ltd v McCann 4 March 2010	1965 feu disposition. No building. Existing building to be used as a hotel or dwellinghouse.	No firm plan though one possibility was the building of flats.	Granted.
Corstorphine v Fleming 2 July 2010	1965 feu disposition. No alterations, one house only.	A substantial extension plus a new house.	Granted.
Corry v MacLachlan 9 July 2010	1984 disposition of part of garden. Obligation to build a single-storey house.	Addition of an extra storey.	Refused.
Watt v Garden 4 November 2011	1995 disposition. Use as garden only.	Additional 2-bedroom bungalow.	Granted but with compensation.
Fyfe v Benson 26 July 2011	1966 deed of conditions. No building or subdivision.	Additional 3-bedroom house.	Refused.
MacDonald v Murdoch 7 August 2012	1997 disposition. No building in garden.	Erection of 1½-storey house.	Refused.
Trigstone Ltd v Mackenzie 16 February 2012	1949 charter of novodamus. No building in garden.	Erection of 4-storey block of flats.	Refused.
McCulloch v Reid 3 April 2012	2011 disposition. No parking in rear courtyard.	Parking of two cars. Erection of two houses.	Refused.
Trustees of John Raeside & Son v Chalmers 2014 GWD 35-660	1989 disposition. Agricultural purposes only.	Erection of mews house in back garden.	Granted
Sinton v Lloyd 11 June 2014	Instrument of sasine of 1813 prohibiting building.	Erection of new house and extension of existing house.	Granted.
MacKay v McGowan 2015 SLT (Lands Tr) 6	Feu disposition prohibiting building.	Erection of 2-storey extension	Granted in respect of new house (only).
Ferguson v Gunby 2015 SLT (Lands Tr) 195	1972 deed of conditions preventing alterations.		Granted.

Other restrictions on use

Name of case	Burden	Applicant's project in breach of burden	Application granted or refused
Church of Scotland General Trs v McLaren 2006 SLT (Lands Tr) 27	Use as a church.	Possible development for flats.	Granted.
Wilson v McNamee 16 September 2007	Use for religious purposes.	Use for a children's nursery.	Granted
Verrico v Tomlinson 2008 SLT (Lands Tr) 2	1950 disposition. Use as a private residence for the occupation of one family.	Separation of mews cottage from ground floor flat.	Granted.
Whitelaw v Acheson 29 February and 29 September 2012	1883 feu charter. Use as a single dwelling; no further building.	Change of use to therapy and wellbeing centre; erection of extension.	Granted subject to some restrictions.
Matnic Ltd v Armstrong 2010 SLT (Lands Tr) 7	2004 deed of conditions. Use for the sale of alcohol.	Use of units in a largely residential estate for retail purposes.	Granted but restricted to small units and no sale of alcohol after 8 pm.
Clarke v Grantham 2009 GWD 38-645	2004 disposition. No parking on an area of courtyard.	A desire to park (though other areas were available).	Granted.
Hollinshead v Gilchrist 7 December 2009	1990 disposition and 1997 feu disposition. No caravans, commercial or other vehicles to be parked in front of the building line.	Parking of cars.	Granted and claim for compensation refused.
Perth & Kinross Council v Chapman 13 August 2009	1945 disposition. Plot to be used only for outdoor recreational purposes.	Sale for redevelopment.	Granted.
Davenport v Julian Hodge Bank Ltd 23 June 2011	2010 deed of conditions. No external painting without permission.	Paint the external walls sky blue.	Refused.
Duffus v McWhirter 2014 GWD 34-647	2005 disposition prohibiting commercial use.	Commercial equestrian use.	Refused.

Flatted property

Name of case	Burden	Applicant's project in breach of burden	Application granted or refused
Regan v Mullen 2006 GWD 25-564	1989. No subdivision of flat.	Subdivision of flat.	Granted.
Kennedy v Abbey Lane Properties 29 March 2010	2004. Main-door flat liable for a share of maintenance of common passages and stairs.	None.	Refused.
Patterson v Drouet 20 January 2011	Liability for maintenance in accordance with gross annual value.	None, but, since the freezing of valuations in 1989, ground floor flats had reverted to residential use.	Variation of liability of ground floor flats granted in principle subject to issues of competency.
Melville v Crabbe 19 January 2009	1880 feu disposition. No additional flat.	Creation of a flat in the basement.	Refused.

Sheltered and retirement housing

Name of case	Burden	Applicant's project in breach of burden	Application granted or refused
At.Home Nationwide Ltd v Morris 2007 GWD 31-535	1993 deed of conditions. On sale, must satisfy superior that flat will continue to be used for the elderly.	No project: just removal of an inconvenient restriction.	Burden held to be void. Otherwise application would have been refused.

Miscellaneous

Name of case	Burden	Applicant's project in breach of burden	Application granted or refused
McPherson v Mackie 2006 GWD 27-606 rev [2007] CSIH 7, 2007 SCLR 351	1990. Housing estate: maintenance of house.	Demolition of house to allow the building of a road for access to proposed new development.	Discharged by agreement on 25 April 2007.

Applications for renewal of real burdens following service of a notice of termination

Name of case	Burden	Respondent's project in breach of burden	Application granted or refused
Brown v Richardson 2007 GWD 28-490	1888 feu charter. No buildings.	Substantial rear extension.	Refused.

Name of case	Burden	Applicant's project in breach of burden	Application granted or refused
Council for Music in Hospitals v Trustees for Richard Gerald Associates 2008 SLT (Lands Tr) 17	1838 instrument of sasine. No building in garden.	None.	Refused.
Gibson v Anderson 3 May 2012	1898 disposition. No building other than 1-storey outbuildings.	2-storey house.	Refused; burden varied to allow limited building.
Macneil v Bradonwood Ltd 2013 SLT (Lands Tr) 41	Mid-Victorian feus limited building at foot of garden to 1 storey.	1.5-storey houses.	Refused; burden varied to allow the proposed houses.
Cook v Cadman 20 December 2013	1876 feu prevented building.	Four additional houses.	Refused; burden varied to allow the proposed houses.

Applications for preservation of community burdens following deeds of variation or discharge under s 33 or s 35

Name of case	Burden	Respondent's project in breach of burden	Application granted or refused
Fleeman v Lyon 2009 GWD 32-539	1982 deed of conditions. No building, trade, livestock etc.	Erection of a second house.	Granted.

Applications for variation of community burdens (s 91)

Name of case	Burden	Applicant's project in breach of burden	Application granted or refused
Fenwick v National Trust for Scotland 2009 GWD 32-538	1989 deed of conditions.	None. The application was for the complete discharge of the deed with the idea that a new deed would eventually be drawn up.	Refused.
Patterson v Drouet 2013 GWD 3-99	1948 deed of conditions apportioned liability for maintenance in a tenement on the basis of annual value.	Substitution of floor area for annual value.	Granted; compensation refused.

Name of case	Burden	Applicant's project in breach of burden	Application granted or refused
Gilfin Property Holdings Ltd v Beech 2013 SLT (Lands Tr) 17	1986 deed of conditions apportioned liability for maintenance in a tenement on a percentage basis rooted in rateable value.	Substitution of a more equitable apportionment.	Granted.
Stewart v Sherwood 7 June 2013	1986 deed of conditions.	Addition of a prohibition on letting.	Refused.
Scott v Applin 16 May 2013	2005 deed of conditions.	Removal of requirement that the full-time manager should be resident.	Granted.
McCabe v Killcross 2013 SLT (Lands Tr) 48	Feu dispositions from 1976.	Altering apportionment of liability for maintenance following division of one of the flats.	Granted except in one respect.

Personal real burdens

Name of case	Burden	Applicant's project in breach of burden	Application granted or refused
Grant v National Trust for Scotland 8 August 2014	Conservation agreement from 1962 prohibited non-agricultural use.	Building of houses.	Granted in part.

Servitudes

Name of case	Servitude	Applicant's project in breach of burden	Application granted or refused
George Wimpey East Scotland Ltd v Fleming 2006 SLT (Lands Tr) 2 and 59	1988 disposition. Right of way.	Diversion of right of way to allow major development for residential houses.	Granted (opposed). Claim for compensation for temporary disturbance refused.
Ventureline Ltd 2 August 2006	1972 disposition. 'Right to use' certain ground.	Possible redevelopment.	Granted (unopposed).
Graham v Parker 2007 GWD 30-524	1990 feu disposition. Right of way from mid-terraced house over garden of end-terraced house to the street.	Small re-routing of right of way, away from the burdened owner's rear wall, so as to allow an extension to be built.	Granted (opposed).

Name of case	Burden	Applicant's project in breach of burden	Application granted or refused
MacNab v McDowall 24 October 2007	1994 feu disposition reserved a servitude of way from the back garden to the front street in favour of two neighbouring house.	Small re-rerouting, on to the land of one of the neighbours, to allow a rear extension to be built.	Granted (opposed).
Jensen v Tyler 2008 SLT (Lands Tr) 39	1985 feu disposition granted a servitude of way.	Re-routing of part of the road in order to allow (unspecified) development of steading.	Granted (opposed).
Gibb v Kerr 2009 GWD 38-646	1981 feu disposition granted a servitude of way.	Re-routing to homologate what had already taken place as a result of the building of a conservatory.	Granted (opposed)
Parkin v Kennedy 23 March 2010	1934 feu charter. Right of way from mid-terraced house over garden of end-terraced house.	Re-routing to allow extension to be built, which would require a restriction to pedestrian access.	Refused (opposed).
Adams v Trs for the Linton Village Hall 24 October 2011	Dispositions of 1968 and 1970 reserved a servitude of access.	Re-routing to a route more convenient for the applicant.	Granted (opposed).
Brown v Kitchen 28 October 2011	1976 feu disposition reserved a servitude of pedestrian access.	Re-routing to the edge of the garden.	Granted in principle (opposed) subject to agreement as to the widening of the substitute route.
Hossack v Robertson 29 June 2012	1944 disposition reserved a servitude of pedestrian access.	Re-routing to end of garden to allow building of conservatory.	Granted (opposed).
Cope v X 2013 SLT (Lands Tr) 20	Servitude of access.	Substitute road.	Granted (opposed).
ATD Developments Ltd v Weir 14 September 2010	2002 disposition granted a servitude right of way.	Narrowing the servitude so as to allow gardens for proposed new houses.	Granted (unopposed).
Stirling v Thorley 12 October 2012	1994 and 1995 dispositions granted a servitude of vehicular access.	Building a house on half of an area set aside for turning vehicles.	Refused (opposed).

Name of case	Burden	Applicant's project in breach of burden	Application granted or refused
Colecliffe v Thompson 2010 SLT (Lands Tr) 15	1997 disposition granted a servitude of way.	None. But the owners of the benefited property had since acquired a more convenient access, secured by a new servitude.	Granted (opposed).
G v A 26 November 2009	1974 disposition granted a servitude of way.	None. But the owners of the benefited property had since acquired a more convenient access (although not to his garage).	Granted (opposed) but on the basis that the respondent should apply for compensation.
Graham v Lee 18 June 2009	2001 disposition granted (a) a servitude of way and (b) of drainage.	None.	(a) was granted provided the applicants discharged a reciprocal servitude of their own, and compensation was considered. (b) was refused.
McNab v Smith 15 June 2012	1981 disposition granted a servitude of vehicular access for agricultural purposes.	None. But the owner of the benefited property could access the property in a different way.	Granted (opposed) but, because works would be needed to improve the alternative access, on the basis of payment of compensation.
Stephenson v Thomas 21 November 2012	1990 disposition granted a servitude of vehicular access.	None. But the owner of the benefited property could access the property in a different way.	Refused (opposed) on the basis that there were safety concerns about the alternative route and the benefited proprietors were proposing to revert to the original route.
McKenzie v Scott 19 May 2009	Dispositions from 1944 and 1957 granted a servitude of bleaching and drying clothes.	None. But the servitude had not in practice been exercised for many years.	Granted (opposed).

Name of case	Burden	Applicant's project in breach of burden	Application granted or refused
Chisholm v Crawford 17 June 2010	A driveway divided two properties. A 1996 feu disposition of one of the properties granted a servitude of access over the driveway.	None. But the applicant was aggrieved that no matching servitude appeared in the neighbour's title.	Refused.
Branziet Investments v Anderson 2013 GWD 31-629	1968 disposition granted a servitude of vehicular access.	Narrowing the servitude to 5 metres so as to allow rear gardens for new houses.	Granted (opposed) except that at either end the width was to be larger.
Mackay v Bain 2013 SLT (Lands Tr) 37	Servitude of pedestrian access over the front garden of applicant's property (1989).	None.	Refused (opposed). The servitude was the only means of access to the respondents' front door.
Pollacchi v Campbell 2014 SLT (Lands Tr) 55	Servitude of vehicular access.	Re-routing to allow creation of garden	Refused.
Yule v Tobert 2015 GWD 39-620	Servitude of vehicular access over yard (1984).	None, but dominant proprietor wished to use access to allow teachers at his nursery to park.	Refused application to restrict servitude to residential purposes.
United Investment Co Ltd v Charlie Reid Ltd 2016 GWD 1-13	Servitude of vehicular access (1963).	Major redevelopment of site.	Granted (opposed) but subject to the possibility of compensation if loss in value to the benefited property could be shown.

CUMULATIVE TABLE OF APPEALS

A table at the end of *Conveyancing 2008* listed all cases digested in *Conveyancing 1999* and subsequent annual volumes in respect of which an appeal was subsequently heard, and gave the result of the appeal. This table is a continuation of the earlier table, beginning with appeals heard during 2009.

Aberdeen City Council v Stewart Milne Group Ltd
[2009] CSOH 80, 2009 GWD 26-417, 2009 Case (6) *affd* [2010] CSIH 81, 2010 GWD 37-755, 2010 Case (9) *affd* [2011] UKSC 56, 2011 Case (13)

Alexander v West Bromwich Mortgage Co Ltd
[2015] EWHC 135 (Comm), [2015] 2 All ER (Comm) 224, 2015 Case (71) *rev* [2016] EWCA Civ 496, 2016 Case (60)

AMA (New Town) Ltd v Finlay
2010 GWD 32-658, Sh Ct, 2010 Case (8) *rev* 2011 SLT (Sh Ct) 73, 2011 Case (1)

Blemain Finance Ltd v Balfour & Manson LLP
[2011] CSOH 157, 2012 SLT 672, 2011 Case (69) *affd* [2012] CSIH 66, [2013] PNLR 3, 2012 GWD 30-609, 2012 Case (70)

Brown v Stonegale Ltd
[2013] CSOH 189, 2014 GWD 2-27, 2013 Case (71) *affd* [2015] CSIH 12, 2015 SCLR 619, 2015 Case (85) *affd* [2016] UKSC 30, 2016 GWD 20-359, 2016 Case (73)

Chalmers v Chalmers
[2014] CSOH 161, 2015 SCLR 299, 2014 Case (22) *rev* [2015] CSIH 75, 2015 SLT 793, 2015 Hous LR 82, 2016 SC 158, 2015 Case (27)

Cheshire Mortgage Corporation Ltd v Grandison; Blemain Finance Ltd v Balfour & Manson LLP
[2011] CSOH 157, 2012 SLT 672, 2011 Case (69) *affd* [2012] CSIH 66, [2013] PNLR 3, 2012 GWD 30-609, 2012 Case (69)

Christie Owen & Davies plc v Campbell
2007 GWD 24-397, Sh Ct, 2007 Case (53) *affd* 18 Dec 2007, Glasgow Sheriff Court, 2007 Case (53) *rev* [2009] CSIH 26, 2009 SLT 518, 2009 Case (82)

Collins v Sweeney
2013 GWD 11-230, Sh Ct, 2013 Case (3) *affd* 2014 GWD 12-214, Sh Ct, 2014 Case (4)

Compugraphics International Ltd v Nikolic
[2009] CSOH 54, 2009 GWD 19-311, 2009 Cases (22) and (90) *rev* [2011] CSIH 34, 2011 SLT 955, 2011 Cases (21) and (74)

Co-operative Group Ltd v Propinvest Paisley LP
17 September 2010, Lands Tribunal, 2010 Case (36) *rev* [2011] CSIH 41, 2012 SC 51, 2011 SLT 987, 2011 Hous LR 32, 2011 Case (38)

Cramaso LLP v Viscount Reidhaven's Trs
[2010] CSOH 62, 2010 GWD 20-403, 2010 Case (58) *affd* [2011] CSIH 81, 2011 Case (57) *rev* [2014] UKSC 9, 2014 SC (UKSC) 121, 2014 SLT 521, 2014 SCLR 484, 2014 Case (31)

EDI Central Ltd v National Car Parks Ltd
[2010] CSOH 141, 2011 SLT 75, 2010 Case (5) *affd* [2012] CSIH 6, 2012 SLT 421, 2012 Case (4)

ELB Securities Ltd v Love
2014 GWD 28-562, 2014 Case (38) *affd* [2015] CSIH 67, 2015 SLT 721, 2015 Hous LR 88, 2015 Case (66)

Euring David Ayre of Kilmarnock, Baron of Kilmarnock Ptr
[2008] CSOH 35, 2008 Case (82) *rev* [2009] CSIH 61, 2009 SLT 759, 2009 Case (93)

Fortune's Tr v Medwin Investments Ltd
[2015] CSOH 139, 2015 GWD 34-552, 2015 Case (87) *affd* [2016] CSIH 49, 2016 SLT 923, 2016 Case (75)

Frank Houlgate Investment Co Ltd v Biggart Baillie LLP
[2013] CSOH 80, 2013 SLT 993, 2013 Case (61) *affd* [2014] CSIH 79, 2014 SLT 1001, 2015 SC 187, 2014 Case (65)

Martin Stephen James Goldstraw of Whitecairns Ptr
[2008] CSOH 34, 2008 Case (81) *rev* [2009] CSIH 61, 2009 SLT 759, 2009 Case (93)

Gordon v Campbell Riddle Breeze Paterson LLP
[2015] CSOH 31, 2015 GWD 12-216, 2015 Case (74) *affd* [2016] CSIH 16, 2016 SC 548, 2016 SLT 580, 2016 Case (63)

Gyle Shopping Centre General Partners Ltd v Marks and Spencer plc
[2015] CSOH 14, 2015 GWD 6-127, 2015 Case (56) *rev* [2016] CSIH 19, 2016 GWD 10-205, 2016 Case (38)

Hamilton v Dumfries & Galloway Council
[2008] CSOH 65, 2008 SLT 531, 2008 Case (37) *rev* [2009] CSIH 13, 2009 SC 277, 2009 SLT 337, 2009 SCLR 392, 2009 Case (50)

Hamilton v Nairn
[2009] CSOH 163, 2010 SLT 399, 2009 Case (51) *affd* [2010] CSIH 77, 2010 SLT 1155, 2010 Case (44)

Hill of Rubislaw (Q Seven) Ltd v Rubislaw Quarry Aberdeen Ltd
[2013] CSOH 131, 2013 GWD 27-545, 2014 Case (11) *affd* [2014] CSIH 105, 2015 SC
339, 2014 Case (10)

Hoblyn v Barclays Bank plc
[2013] CSOH 104, 2013 GWD 26-533, 10313 Case (51) *affd* [2014] CSIH 52, 2014 GWD
30-376, 2014 HousLR 26, 2015 SCLR 85, 2014 Case (60)

Holms v Ashford Estates Ltd
2006 SLT (Sh Ct) 70, 2006 Case (40) *affd* 2006 SLT (Sh Ct) 161, 2006 Case (40) *rev*
[2009] CSIH 28, 2009 SLT 389, 2009 SCLR 428, 2009 Cases (19) and (52)

Hunter v Tindale
2011 SLT (Sh Ct) 11, 2010 Case (16) *rev* 2011 GWD 25-570, Sh Ct, 2011 Case (19)

Jack v Jack
[2015] CSOH 91, 2015 Fam LR 95, 2015 Case (94) *affd* [2016] CSIH 75, 2016 Fam LR
177, 2016 Case (77)

K2 Restaurants Ltd v Glasgow City Council
[2011] CSOH 171, 2011 Hous LR 171, 2011 Case (20) *affd* [2013] CSIH 49, 2013 GWD
21-420, 2013 Case (5)

Kennedy v Dickie & More Holdings Ltd
[2015] CSOH 103, 2015 GWD 25-436, 2015 Case (3) *rev* [2016] CSIH 37, 2016 GWD
18-325, 2016 Case (4)

Kenwright v Stuart Milne Group Ltd
[2015] CSOH 86, 2015 GWD 22-389, 2015 Case (11) *rev* [2016] CSIH 45, 2016 GWD
20-351, 2016 Case (5)

Kerr of Ardgowan, Ptr
[2008] CSOH 36, 2008 SLT 251, 2008 Case (80) *rev* [2009] CSIH 61, 2009 SLT 759,
2009 Case (93)

Khosrowpour v Mackay
[2014] CSOH 175, 2015 GWD 1-8, 2014 Case (17) *rev* [2016] CSIH 50, 2016 Case (17)

L Batley Pet Products Ltd v North Lanarkshire Council
[2011] CSOH 209, 2012 GWD 4-73, 2011 Case (62) *rev* [2012] CSIH 83, 2012 GWD
37-745, 2012 Case (43) *rev* [2014] UKSC 27, 2014 SC (UKSC) 174, 2014 SLT 593, 2014
Case (39)

Liquidator of Letham Grange Development Co Ltd v Foxworth Investments Ltd
[2011] CSOH 66, 2011 SLT 1152, 2011 Case (64) *rev* [2013] CSIH 13, 2013 SLT 445,
2013 Case (47) *rev* [2014] UKSC 41, 2014 SC (UKSC) 203, 2014 SLT 775, 2014 Case (70)

Livingstone of Bachuil v Paine
[2012] CSOH 161, 2012 GWD 35-707, 2012 Case (12) *rev* [2013] CSIH 110, 2013 Case (9)

Luminar Lava Ignite Ltd v Mama Group plc
[2009] CSOH 68, 2009 GWD 19-305, 2009 Case (91) *rev* [2010] CSIH 1, 2010 SC 310, 2010 SLT 147, 2010 Case (77)

McGraddie v McGraddie
[2009] CSOH 142, 2009 GWD 38-633, 2009 Case (60), [2010] CSOH 60, 2010 GWD 21-404, 2000 Case (48) *rev* [2012] CSIH 23, 2012 GWD 15-310, 2012 Case (38) *rev* [2013] UKSC 58, 2013 SLT 1212, 2013 Case (32)

MacQueen v MacPherson
3 October 2014, Oban Sheriff Court, 2014 Case (2) *rev* [2015] CSIH 60, 2015 GWD 26-449, 2015 Case (4)

McSorley v Drennan
May 2011, Ayr Sheriff Court, 2011 Case (14) *rev* [2012] CSIH 59, 2012 GWD 25-506, 2012 Case (6)

Mehrabadi v Haugh
June 2009, Aberdeen Sheriff Court, 2009 Case (17) *affd* 11 January 2010 Aberdeen Sheriff Court, 2010 Case (15)

Mirza v Salim
[2013] CSOH 73, 2013 GWD 17-348, 2013 Case (65) *rev* [2014] CSIH 51, 2015 SC 31, 2014 SLT 875, 2014 SCLR 764, 2014 Case (67)

Moderator of the General Assembly of the Free Church of Scotland v Interim Moderator of the Congregation of Strath Free Church of Scotland (Continuing)
[2009] CSOH 113, 2009 SLT 973, 2009 Case (96) *affd* [2011] CSIH 52, 2011 SLT 1213, 2012 SC 79, 2011 Case (77)

Morris v Rae
[2011] CSIH 30, 2011 SC 654, 2011 SLT 701, 2011 SCLR 428, 2011 Case (39) *rev* [2012] UKSC 50, 2013 SC (UKSC) 106, 2013 SLT 88, 2013 SCLR 80, 2012 Case (41)

Multi-link Leisure Developments Ltd v North Lanarkshire Council
[2009] CSOH 114, 2009 SLT 1170, 2009 Case (70) *rev* [2009] CSIH 96, 2010 SC 302, 2010 SLT 57, 2010 SCLR 306, 2009 Case (70) *affd* [2010] UKSC 47, [2011] 1 All ER 175, 2010 Case (52)

NRAM plc v Steel
[2014] CSOH 172, 2015 GWD 1-34, 2014 Case (63) *rev* [2016] CSIH 11, 2016 SC 474, 2016 SLT 285, 2016 Case (62)

Orkney Housing Association Ltd v Atkinson
15 October 2010, Kirkwall Sheriff Court, 2010 Case (21) *rev* 2011 GWD 30-652, 2011 Cases (22) and (41)

Pocock's Tr v Skene Investments (Aberdeen) Ltd
[2011] CSOH 144, 2011 GWD 30-654, 2011 Case (40) *rev* [2012] CSIH 61, 2012 GWD 27-562, 2012 Case (36)

R M Prow (Motors) Ltd Directors Pension Fund Trustees v Argyll and Bute Council
[2012] CSOH 77, 2012 GWD 21-438, 2012 Case (44) *affd* [2013] CSIH 23, 2013 GWD 12-260, 2013 Case (44)

R & D Construction Group Ltd v Hallam Land Management Ltd
[2009] CSOH 128, 2009 Case (8) *affd* [2010] CSIH 96, 2010 Case (4)

Regus (Maxim) Ltd v Bank of Scotland plc
[2011] CSOH 129, 2011 GWD 27-600, 2011 Case (52) *affd* [2013] CSIH 12, 2013 SC 331, 2013 SLT 477, 2013 Case (43)

Rivendale v Keeper of the Registers of Scotland
30 October 2013, Lands Tribunal, 2013 Case (35) *affd* [2015] CSIH 27, 2015 SC 558, 2015 Case (29) and (84)

Royal Bank of Scotland plc v Carlyle
[2010] CSOH 3, 2010 GWD 13-235, 2010 Case (67) *rev* [2013] CSIH 75, 2014 SC 188, 2014 SCLR 167, 2013 Case (75) *rev* [2015] UKSC 13, 2015 SC (UKSC) 93, 2015 SLT 206, 2015 Case (91)

Royal Bank of Scotland v O'Donnell
[2013] CSOH 78, 2013 GWD 19-388, 2013 Case (59) *affd* [2014] CSIH 84, 2014 GWD 33-641, 2014 Case (54)

Royal Bank of Scotland plc v Wilson
2008 GWD 2-35, Sh Ct, 2008 Case (61) *rev* 2009 CSIH 36, 2009 SLT 729, 2009 Case (75) *rev* [2010] UKSC 50, 2011 SC (UKSC) 66, 2010 SLT 1227, 2010 Hous LR 88, 2010 Case (66)

Salvesen v Riddell
[2012] CSIH 26, 2012 SLT 633, 2012 SCLR 403, 2012 HousLR 30, 2012 Case (51) *rev* [2013] UKSC 22, 2013 SC (UKSC) 236, 2013 SLT 863, 2013 Case (50)

Scottish Coal Company Ltd v Danish Forestry Co Ltd
[2009] CSOH 171, 2009 GWD 5-79, 2009 Case (9) *affd* [2010] CSIH 56, 2010 GWD 27-529, 2010 Case (3)

Sheltered Housing Management Ltd v Bon Accord Bonding Co Ltd
2007 GWD 32-533, 2006 Cases (24) and (35), 11 October 2007, Lands Tribunal, 2007
Case (21) *rev* [2010] CSIH 42, 2010 SC 516, 2010 SLT 662, 2010 Case (25)

@Sipp (Pension Trustees) Ltd v Insight Travel Services Ltd
[2014] CSOH 137, 2014 Hous LR 54, 2014 Case (42) *rev* [2015] CSIH 91, 2016 SLT
131, 2016 Hous LR 20, 2015 Case (51)

Smith v Stuart
2009 GWD 8-140, Sh Ct, 2009 Case (2) *affd* [2010] CSIH 29, 2010 SC 490, 2010 SLT
1249, 2010 Case (10)

STV Central Ltd v Semple Fraser LLP
[2014] CSOH 82, 2014 GWD 16-299, 2014 Case (61) *affd* [2015] CSIH 35, 2015 SLT
313, 2015 Case (59)

Tenzin v Russell
2014 Hous LR 17, Sh Ct, 2014 Case (51) *affd* [2015] CSIH 8A, 2015 Hous LR 11, 2015
Case (43)

Thomson v Mooney
[2012] CSOH 177, 2012 GWD 39-769, 2012 Case (63) *rev* [2013] CSIH 115, 2014 GWD
14-263, 2013 Case (74)

Tuley v Highland Council
2007 SLT (Sh Ct) 97, 2007 Case (24) *rev* [2009] CSIH 31A, 2009 SC 456, 2009 SLT
616, 2009 Case (48)

Van Lynden v Gilchrist
[2015] CSOH 147, 2015 SLT 864, 2015 Case (65) *rev* [2016] CSIH 72, 2016 Case (47)

Wright v Shoreline Management Ltd
Oct 2008, Arbroath Sheriff Court, 2008 Case (60) *rev* 2009 SLT (Sh Ct) 83, 2009
Case (74)

TABLE OF CASES DIGESTED IN EARLIER VOLUMES BUT
REPORTED IN 2016

Chalmers v Chalmers
[2015] CSIH 75, 2015 SLT 793, 2015 Hous LR 82, 2016 SC 158

Homebase Ltd v Grantchester Developments (Falkirk) Ltd
[2015] CSOH 49, 2015 Hous LR 38, 2016 SCLR 45

Marks and Spencer plc v BNP Paribas Securities Services Trust Company (Jersey) Ltd
[2015] UKSC 72, [2015] 3 WLR 1843, [2016] AC 742

PIP 3 Ltd v Glasgow City Council
[2015] CSOH 119, 2016 SCLR 361

Ramsden v Santon Highlands Ltd
[2015] CSOH 65, 2016 SCLR 89

Rivendale v Clark
[2015] CSIH 27, 2015 SC 558, 2016 SCLR 1

@Sipp (Pension Trustees) Ltd v Insight Travel Services Ltd
[2015] CSIH 91, 2016 SLT 131, 2016 Hous LR 20

Swift Advances plc v Martin
[2015] CSIH 65, 2015 Hous LR 50, 2016 SCLR 385

West Dunbartonshire Council v William Thomson & Son (Dumbarton) Ltd
[2015] CSIH 93, 2016 SLT 125, 2016 Hous LR 8